The Colorado General Assembly

The Colorado General Assembly

SECOND EDITION

John A. Straayer

UNIVERSITY PRESS OF COLORADO

Copyright © 2000 by the University Press of Colorado
International Standard Book Number 0-87081-542-3

Published by the University Press of Colorado
5589 Arapahoe Avenue, Suite 206C
Boulder, Colorado 80303

The University Press of Colorado is a cooperative publishing enterprise supported, in part,
by Adams State College, Colorado State University, Fort Lewis College, Mesa State College, Metropolitan State College of Denver, University of Colorado, University of Northern
Colorado, University of Southern Colorado, and Western State College of Colorado.

The paper used in this publication meets the minimum requirements of the American National Standard for Information Sciences—Permanence of Paper for Printed Library Materials. ANSI Z39.48-1984

Library of Congress Cataloging-in-Publication Data

Straayer, John A., 1939–
    The Colorado General Assembly / John A. Straayer. — 2nd ed.
        p. cm.
    Includes bibliographical references and index.
    ISBN 0-87081-542-3 (alk. paper)
      1. Colorado. General Assembly. I. Title.

  JK7871 .S77 2000
  328.788'072—dc21

                                            00-056804

Design by Daniel Pratt

09 08 07 06 05 04 03 02 01 00   10 9 8 7 6 5 4 3 2 1

This book is dedicated to the dream of a safe, beautiful,
historic, fully restored State Capitol Building,
a fitting monument to a civil society.

Contents

Preface to the Second Edition

The first edition of this book was published in 1990. The stimuli for the project were my legislative politics students at Colorado State University. Some of them served as interns in the General Assembly but many did not. For the prospective interns and for the others, I devoted a good portion of my legislative politics course to state legislatures, Colorado's especially. But there was precious little published material on our General Assembly, therefore little for them to read. So I wrote the book.

Since 1990 the General Assembly as an institution has changed in a few important ways, as with the TABOR amendment and term limits. The issues have changed some too, as with the Bronco bill and education reform, and the players have changed considerably. As a result I felt a growing need to revise and update the text. This edition contains new names, a good number of new illustrations, new statistics where applicable, and treatment of TABOR, term limits, and campaign finance reforms. And in the final chapter, I have taken the liberty of generously lacing my reflections on the General Assembly with my opinions. As the readers will see, I think highly of our legislature and believe that the broadly popular negative view of the institution is misguided. At the same time I'm convinced that both the General Assembly and the State of Colorado would be better off with fewer ideologues as members, and with more displays of foresight and political courage by moderates of both parties.

In many instances my sources are recorded in the chapter endnotes, but not always. The *Denver Post* and *Denver Rocky Mountain News*, along with the student-produced *Capitol Reporter* (now defunct), *Colorado Statesman*, *Westword*, and some smaller daily papers, were valuable sources. So too were materials produced by the office of the Secretary of State and the General Assembly's own staff offices. Staffers in Legislative Council, the Office of Legislative Legal Services, and the Joint Budget Committee produce a flood of useful materials on both the institution and the issues. The legislature's small capitol basement library contains literally piles of useful data. These and other sources are discussed more fully in Chapter 11, "The Legislative Enterprise."

Besides the printed materials, my sources were hundreds of conversations with legislators, lobbyists, and staff members and countless hours "soaking and poking," to use Professor Fenno's words, in committees, the lobby, the gallery, the elevator, the cafeteria, the restaurants, and on the Chamber floors.

Much of what I've come to know about the General Assembly I've learned by being there and watching, and much has come from conversations that were not billed as "interviews" for attribution. If I did not specifically ask to quote someone from conversation or when asking my countless questions, I have not done so.

As best I can remember who they were I'd like to thank them, though, so here goes. Thanks to current or former Senators Peggy Reeves, Ed Perlmutter, Don Ament, Bill Thiebaut, Tilman Bishop, Tom Norton, Mike Feeley, Stan Matsunaka, Bill Owens, Bob Schaffer, Dorothy Rupert, and Jana Mendez; Representatives Brad Young, Vickie Agler, Norma Anderson, Chuck Berry, Russell George, Gary McPherson, Shirleen Tucker, Mark Udall, Steve Johnson, Bill Kaufman, Ron May, Dave Owen, Bob Bacon, Steve Tool, Marcy Morrison, Maryanne Keller, Joyce Lawrence, Carl Miller, Michelle Lawrence, Gayle Berry, Gloria Leyba, Mary Ellen Epps, Bob Eisenach, and Peggy Kerns; lobbyists Danny Tomlinson, Peg Ackerman, Amy Mueller, Bob Ferm, Micki Hackenberger, Bob Kirscht, Steve Smithers, Travis Berry, JoAnn Groff, Betty Neale, Leonard Dinegar, Lynn Young, Taylor Stephens, Peter Minahan, Dianne Rees, Bob McLavey, Mark Radtke, and Sam Mamet. Thanks, too, to staffers Dianne Radovich, Dana Waller, Scott Nachtrieb, David Hite, Dan Chapman, Kathy Holland, Donna Acerno, Ken Conahan, Chief Clerk of the House J. R. Rodrigue, Legislative Legal Services Director Doug Brown, and Charlie Brown, Director of Legislative Council. Odds are high, unlike winning Lotto, that this listing is incomplete—my apologies.

The 1990 edition contained a listing of persons who served as legislative sponsors of my student interns, or who provided information for the book back then, or both. Their earlier help was useful for this edition as well.

For many years a special pleasure was spending time in the capitol conversing with Chuck Henning. Chuck enjoyed a career as a journalist, a lobbyist, a legislator, a staff member in House communications, and a wonderful storyteller. Sadly, Chuck Henning has passed away. Hundreds upon hundreds of people remember Chuck, and I want to remember him here. I also want to remember David Rice. If anyone believes that "lobbyist" is a dirty word, they've never had the pleasure of Mr. Rice's company.

In addition to my wife Judy, my kids Jeff, David, and Kathy, and Stanley my dog, three people have helped in this endeavor with both support and infinite patience. They are my Colorado State University department chairman Wayne Peak; Earlene Bell, who runs our department office and much of our working lives; and my friend of nearly thirty years, Fort Collins councilwoman, Representative, and Senator Peggy Reeves. Thanks, friends.

Preface to the First Edition

I was stimulated to produce this manuscript by student interns. As a professor of political science at Colorado State University, I have supervised our legislative internship program for well over a decade. Before each session has begun, I have tried to give the students a short course on Colorado's legislature, and I've run stacks of old bills, journals, and calendars through their hands, as well. The interns are told to follow events throughout the spring session in either the *Rocky Mountain News* or the *Denver Post* to supplement what they observe in person. At the start of each session, legislative staff members have also arranged orientations for the students.

In spite of all this, the papers that the interns have submitted at the end of each semester say, over and over again, "It wasn't like I thought it would be." The experience makes some of the young students feel better about democracy in America; others, regrettably, feel worse. But almost all encountered something other than what they anticipated when they buried themselves in the personalities, the routines, and the politics under the gold dome of Colorado's capitol.

I've cast about to find more materials for the students to read to better prepare them for their Denver experience—materials that convey the politics and the flavor of the institution in addition to the structural and procedural features. But I struck out repeatedly, and it was in response to this that I resolved to write something that will, I hope, give them a head start on the adventure and enrich their learning experience.

Maybe this manuscript will add to the learning of others as well. As a student of politics I should, perhaps, know better, but I continue to be amazed at how little the citizens of the state know about the activities that go on in their capitol and how little they understand the consequences of these activities.

In some ways, this manuscript will be good for the decades; in others, it will be dated before the ink is dry. I am writing in 1988 and 1989, and by the mid-1990s, most of the personalities and some of the issues will be beyond us, and different names and issues will fill the news. Senate President Strickland and Appropriations Committee Chairs Elwood Gillis and Mike Bird may well be long gone from the Assembly. Indeed, two of the more colorful figures of the 1980s, Steve Durham and Ralph Cole, are gone already, and ten-year Speaker Carl "Bev" Bledsoe announced his retirement effective after the 1990 session. Others will replace them, and the structures, processes, and political strategies and stakes will remain. The fights over budgets, the debates on the propriety of killing the bills of minority party lawmakers in election years, the rivalry between parties and branches of government, and the preoccupation of legislators with the next election will remain constant. They'll be around long after Bev Bledsoe, Ted Strickland, Governor Roy Romer, and even this manuscript are replaced.

The information on which this manuscript rests was derived from a variety of sources. Most of it came from more than a decade of personal observation of committee hearings, caucus meetings, floor debates, and decisions. Some came from personal interviews with legislators, lobbyists, and staff members and chats over coffee and cocktails. Certain documents were invaluable. These included Peg Ackerman's *Legislative Almanac;* the yearly legislative directories (pink books) and the Colorado Press Association directories; the *Colorado Legislator's Handbook,* lists of registered lobbyists; abstracts of votes cast; daily calendars, journals, and status sheets; bills themselves; and an assortment of other materials produced by the Legislative Council and the secretary of state's office.

Over the years, I've had occasion to talk with scores of legislators, lobbyists, and staff people in connection with CSU's internship program, the politics of the legislature, or both, and I can't say enough about the unending help they've given to me and to our program. Their names are listed at the end of this preface.

In 1988 and 1989, I revisited some of them with specific questions. These included Representatives JoAnn Groff, Joan Green, Peggy Reeves, Matt Jones, Elwood Gillis, Ruth Wright, Paul Schauer, John Ulvang, Bev Bledsoe, and Ted Strickland; Senator Ray Peterson; former Representatives—now lobbyists—Bill Artist and Bob Kirscht; former Joint Budget Committee Staff Director Bob Moore and current Director Kenneth Conahan; former Senator and JBC Chairman Jim Beatty; lobbyists Dick Kingman, Danny Tomlinson, and Peg Ackerman; Legislative

Council Director Charles Brown, past Director Lyle Kyle, and staff member Scott Nachtrieb; Legislative Legal Services Office Director Doug Brown; Governor Romer's former Chief of Legislative Relations Larry Kallenberger; Office of State Planning and Budgeting's Eugene Petrone; and the National Conference of State Legislatures Director Bill Pound.

Representative Peggy Reeves, past Republican Majority Leader and House Speaker Ron Strahle, former Senator and current lobbyist Bob Comer, lobbyist Peg Ackerman, and journalists Walter Bradley and Carl Hilliard all read the manuscript and offered helpful comments. Kathy Everett typed the manuscript, much of it more than once, and her knowledge of politics in Colorado made the process smooth and enjoyable. Jody Berman and Luther Wilson of the University Press made my role in the production of this book a real pleasure. To these people I give special thanks.

None of these folks asked me to keep their comments confidential. But as they, like the others with whom I've visited over the years, have been so friendly, open, and cooperative, I've chosen to take no risks of misquotation or warped context. I have, therefore, employed direct attribution only when someone's remarks had been previously reported publicly—in the newspapers, for example. As a result, endnotes are few, and readers looking for "who said what about whom" will be disappointed. Finally, the reporting of both the *Denver Post* and the *Rocky Mountain News* has been invaluable. In my estimation, the reporters for these two major dailies, along with Carl Hilliard of the Associated Press, provide an excellent daily account of Colorado's legislative politics. A free and open press is essential to the maintenance and preservation of a democracy, and thus I wish I felt as good about the use to which my fellow citizens put this outstanding professional journalism as I do about the quality of the capitol coverage itself.

Legislators, lobbyists, and staff personnel who have provided information for this manuscript or have supported CSU's internship program—or both:

SENATORS

Wayne Allard	Martha Ezzard
Polly Baca	Dennis Gallagher
James Beatty	Tom Glass
John Beno	Regis Groff
Tilman Bishop	Martin Hatcher
Jim Brandon	Joel Hefley
Ralph Cole	Sally Hopper
Robert DeNier	Don MacManus
John Donley	Robert Martinez

Brian McCauley
Al Meiklejohn
Jana Mendez
Tom Norton
Bill Owens
Robert Pastore
Ray Peterson
Paul Powers
Ray Powers

Jim Rizzuto
Robert Schaffer
Bill Schroeder
Richard Soash
Ron Stewart
Mary Anne Tebedo
Claire Traylor
Larry Trujillo

REPRESENTATIVES

Don Ament
Norma Anderson
Vickie Armstrong
David Bath
Leo Berger
Chuck Berry
Mike Bird
Richard Bond
Robert Bowen
James Brown
Cliff Bryan
Ron Burkhart
Ben Campbell
Mary Dambman
Annabelle Dunning
Lewis Entz
Steve Erickson
Jeanne Faatz
Eunice Fine
Marleen Fish
Faye Fleming
Judy Ford
Elwood Gillis
Joan Green
JoAnn Groff
Martin Hatcher
Charles Heim
Phil Hernandez
Tony Hernandez
John Herzog
Bud Hover

Stan Johnson
Matt Jones
Wayne Knox
Molly Markert
Margaret Masson
Scott McInnis
Don Mielke
Richard Mutzebaugh
Betty Neale
Betty Orten
Chris Paulson
Federico Peña
Barbara Philips
Ruth Prendergast
Jeannie Reeser
Jim Reeves
Peggy Reeves
James Robb
Dorothy Rupert
Paul Schauer
David Skaggs
Ronald Strahle
Gloria Tanner
Carol Taylor-Little
Shirleen Tucker
John Ulvang
Glenn Underwood
Wilam Webb
Dan Williams
Kathi Williams
Walt Youngblood

STAFF MEMBERS

Charlie Brown
Doug Brown
Kenneth Conahan
Lyle Kyle

Bob Moore
Scott Nachtrieb
Sharon Powers

FORMER LEGISLATORS, LATER LOBBYISTS

Fred Anderson
Kathy Arnold
Bill Artist
Bill Comer
Frank DeFilippo

Candace Dyer
Don Eberle
Bob Kirscht
Jean Marks
Peter Minahan

LOBBYISTS

Peg Ackerman
James Bensberg
Ken Bueche
Briggs Gamblin
Maria Garcia
Kay Johnson
Dick Kingman

Sam Mamet
Flo Mendez
Diane Rees
David Rice
Rosalie Schiff
Danny Tomlinson
Dorothy Witherspoon

The Colorado General Assembly

1

The Legislative Show
and the Legislature in Law

There is no shortage of legislatures in the United States. We have policymaking bodies in well over 20,000 cities, more than 30,000 special districts, and some 14,000 school districts. When we think of legislatures, it is usually the U.S. Congress that comes to mind or perhaps the legislative branch of one of the fifty states. But, clearly, there are many more, and they vary considerably in size, structure, and mode of operation.

This volume is designed to provide an interesting analysis of the Colorado legislature for students and other interested citizens. Many people have only vague images of how legislatures work and how bills become law; these mental pictures are often derived from dry textbook descriptions or stick-figure sketches of Mr. Bill walking his way through the legislative process, moving from house to house and landing on the governor's desk. Sketches of this sort are routinely given to visitors who tour state capitol buildings. But few people have any idea what really happens in institutions like the Colorado General Assembly, and they are surprised at what they observe under the gold leaf big top on Denver's Capitol Hill. Even newly elected legislators, who have heightened political interest and information to start with, often express surprise at what they discover. What is going on, of course, is a complex series of interrelated sideshows, complete with ringmasters, comedians, and clowns.

One of many objectives of this book is to help readers understand, appreciate, and enjoy the show to the maximum. It is an effort to supplement the reader's knowledge of government with a healthy dose of politics. Government is much like an engine. The structure and parts may all be in place, but they are useless without some oil. If the oil is clean, the engine works well. If it is not, the parts will wear, with unfortunate results. Politics is the oil of government.

THE SHOW

The Capitol is a curious and fascinating place when the General Assembly is in session. Among the first features that visitors notice, particularly on a formal tour, are the gold dome itself (an enormous rotunda that rises 272 feet above the ground and is accessible only by an exhausting series of stairs), the mile-high marker on the west side of the building, the grand marble staircase at the center of the rotunda, beautiful stained glass windows and bronze work, and the murals throughout the Capitol that vividly depict historical events. A recent addition is an unsightly painted wooden ramp leading up to the lobby of the House chambers. For those who ascend the stairs to the top of the rotunda, the view of downtown Denver and the Rocky Mountains to the west is breathtaking.

People who stay around for a while may see both the House and Senate, the old Supreme Court chambers, and the governor's office complex. The House and Senate are located on the second floor. So are the old Supreme Court chambers, which now serve as an oversized committee hearing room or a place for citizen groups to meet with legislators. All three rooms are ornate, replete with fine old wood and marble, and striking stained glass windows depicting some aspect of the state's history. The governor, state treasurer, and lieutenant governor are housed on the first floor, along with a handful of minor executive branch offices.

A longer visit reveals lobbyists milling around and perhaps committees in session, with legislators and lobbyists running in and out for coffee or exchanges with colleagues or staff members. When legislators are on the floor there will be throngs of lobbyists just outside the House and Senate doors—in the "lobby." When the chambers recess for the day and members go into committees, the lobby crowd moves with them, to the third-floor Senate committee room area, and to that of the House in the basement—the "garden level."

Visitors might also stumble onto the basement coffee shop. Just out the north doors are public restrooms, frequented by humanity of all sorts coming in off East Colfax Avenue. The cafeteria serves up a limited menu of everyday sandwiches. Tables will be full of lobbyists—swapping stories, exchanging notes, watching time pass. Many used to smoke endlessly, but some of the women in the legislature moved them to a small designated area.

On any given day, there is a lot going on under the gold dome. On the west steps of the Capitol, there may be demonstrations by senior citizens expressing their support of tax breaks for older folks; industrial bank depositors who lost money in bank failures and are seeking legislative remedy, or students advocating greater funding for higher education. The Senate floor may be vacant, save for a few interns and staff members and perhaps one or two sergeants at arms. The members of the body may be scattered all over the building—some in committees, some having coffee, some excused for the day. The House may be in session with a full agenda, complete with third readings on many bills. That agenda may include the receipt of conference committee reports where House and Senate conferees have attempted to iron out differences between the two chambers on specific bills and come to agreement on single versions. Or the House may be considering Senate amendments to bills it passed earlier. Visitors may witness the body acting as a Committee of the Whole, considering bills that have been reported out of committee for second reading on the floor.

A trip back to the front steps of the Capitol may reveal the industrial bank victims preparing to march around the Capitol just as a group of eight-year-olds exits a school bus. Some walk and some run into the Capitol, weaving their way through the older demonstrators. One observer who walked out of the building to watch the industrial bank depositors demonstrate was asked, "Are you a legislator?" "No," he answered, as another person commented, "he certainly can't be. He looks honest." The depositors were waiting for members of the House or Senate to join them. They had a long wait.

The inside of the Capitol can also be a place where members of the public express their concerns. Once, for example, a sizeable group from small business descended on the House Finance Committee to vent their anger over a proposal by the newly created Transit Construction Authority that would impose a tax to build a rapid transit system between downtown Denver and the Denver Technical Center. The bills before the Finance Committee that day had nothing whatsoever to do with the Transit Construction Authority. In fact, the law authorizing the TCA had been enacted during the previous session, when virtually no one came to testify or complain. Nevertheless, when the citizens showed up, the Finance Committee felt compelled to move the hearings from a rather small House committee room to the old Supreme Court chambers that could hold several hundred people. Some members of the Finance Committee left. Others stayed, explaining all the while that the legislation before them that day had nothing to do with the concerns of the protestors. But the lawmakers listened politely. In the end, the complainants had some success, as the media provided coverage of the event, and later in the session a bill was introduced to restrict the taxing power of the Transit Construction Authority. More recently credit union partisans showed up in similarly large numbers to kill a banking bill that they opposed.

On occasion, it is hard to tell who is in the Capitol to observe whom. When cookie entrepreneur Wally "Famous Amos" came to Denver to announce a store opening and visited the Capitol, legislators lined up to get their pictures taken with him. Similarly, when Melanie Palenick, an Olympic skier from Littleton, Colorado, visited the Capitol, she quickly became the center of lawmaker attention. So did former Oakland Raider quarterback Ken Stabler, and former Colorado Rockies manager Don Baylor. Even Yogi, the Colorado bloodhound of the Aurora Police Department, was able to command center stage on the House floor.

The combination of sideshows running simultaneously in the Capitol sometimes seems incongruous. Forty-five cleanly scrubbed seven- and eight-year-old girls in red shirts and cowboy hats stood under the golden dome on the first floor one day, singing, "God Bless America," a musical version of the preamble to the U.S. Constitution, and "America the Beautiful." The Heritage High School choir, orchestra, and band all filled the rotunda with some much needed joy and warmth over the noon hour one March legislative day when lawmakers were in party caucuses discussing the state's major budget bill.

At the same time, the House of Representatives was debating a bill to create new designer license plates (or "yuppie plates," as one legislator described them) to raise a little extra money for the state coffers. And hearings were going forward on legislation related to rape, sexual contact between psychiatrists and patients, the sexual exploitation of children, and tax favors for farmers and businesses. An altogether curious combination of events occur at the same time, all within a distance of 300 feet.

Sometimes the Capitol takes on the characteristics of a comedy club. Senator Dave Wattenberg used April Fools Day once to dress up as an old woman named Mildred and ask at the Senate microphone why colleague Don Ament was selling his old Mercury, "after all those good times we had in that car?" Although he didn't think it was funny at the time, veteran Senator Tilie Bishop received a box in the mail containing a human skull and bones, apparently from someone unhappy with Bishop's proposal to protect historical artifacts.

One Republican House member suggested that Denver's trouble-plagued airport be named after Roy Romer, a Democratic governor. A lobbyist explained, as he exited the Capitol, that he had to return to his office to get out of "the cave of the winds." Another likened the legislature to a rabbit: "you put in one handful of food, and two come out the other end."

Occasionally, Capitol activities are not amusing at all. Workers who were busy regilding the Capitol's gold dome reported hearing rifle bullets ricocheting off the structure. One weekend the Capitol was closed to fight a chemical war on an aggressive cockroach population. Outside consultants have warned of fire dangers in the aging structure. A Martin Luther King Jr. portrait on display was defaced, and new brass on the elevators was scratched by vandals. Purse snatchings and assaults have occurred in the Capitol neighborhood.

The people who populate the halls of the Capitol are a varied and interesting lot. Some are somber, others can't seem to get serious. Many are warm, friendly, and easy to talk with, but a few are downright nasty. Some of them worry deeply about the plight of the downtrodden in our society, others are preoccupied with protecting their own luck and privilege. A goodly number are mature, experienced, and thoughtful. There seems always to be a number who are driven by ideology, undiluted by either experience or contemplation. Many see the legislature as an instrument for pushing their religious preferences into the laws of the state. More and more of them are women, both in the ranks of elected lawmakers and among the lobbyists. All of them eventually come to live in an ever-smaller world bounded by Colfax, Grant, 14th, and Lincoln. And when they venture out, it is often to gatherings that are sponsored by political parties or clients; there, they spend still more time with men and women they see all day at the Capitol.

Casual visitors and constituents who only drop in to see their representatives from time to time are likely to miss much of the show. Some might not find it attractive in any case, unless they stay long enough to become participants. In highly politicized environments like state capitols, games and sideshows multiply, and the participants sometimes seem to play the games just because they are there to be played.

In years past, visitors and constituents were quite likely to learn something about the gallery patrol. Both the House and Senate galleries were guarded by a small cadre of watchpersons who are half visitor information agents and half all-seeing shock troops. Visitors, fidgety schoolkids especially, learned quickly that even citizens may not lean over the railing, stand up to watch, or put fingerprints on the brass. Even legendary House Speaker Bev Bledsoe, operating in his post-legislative life as a lobbyist, was once subjected to a gallery behavior lesson by a patrol woman in the Senate. The reaction of one six-year-old visitor who had been set straight in the gallery was, reportedly, the posting of a handwritten note to the patrol: "Dear mean lady, I don't think Jesus loves you." The gallery environment has changed in recent years, though. The visitor guides remain vigilant, but they wear smiles; the place is now properly inviting.

Lawmakers and lobbyists choose up sides and fight to pass or defeat hundreds of bills and thousands of amendments, to pick leaders,
and to affect the budget. They fight because some are Democrats and
others Republicans. They go at it because some are senators and some
representatives. They oppose each other on one measure and team up
on another. They trade insults in committee and on the floor, then buy
each other lunch. Games beget games, and it never stops.

THE STAKES

Amidst all the sightseeing, touring, demonstrating, hustling, vote-
seeking, and deal-making, serious business is being conducted. Critical
and far-reaching decisions are being made: Who gets how much of what
pie? When? And who has to pick up the check afterwards? All legislatures, the Colorado General Assembly included, make authoritative
public policy. They establish public programs and restrain or regulate
some people but not others. They decide who will be taxed and at what
rate. They define some behavior as unacceptable and arrange for fines
and incarceration for violators. Public policy is serious stuff, and the
stakes are high. Why else do clients pay $50,000 to $200,000 in fees to
lobbyists who represent their interests? And why else would political
action committees pour hundreds of thousands of dollars into House
and Senate elections every two years?

The range of subjects that the legislature confronts in any given year
is broad indeed. In one recent session alone, the Colorado General Assembly looked at bills addressing these and other subjects: permitting
parents to keep their children out of public or licensed private schools
and teach them at home; barring automatic withdrawals from bank
accounts; setting heavy penalties for assault on police officers; limiting
jury awards for medical malpractice judgments; making it a crime to
interfere with a hunter; enacting a statewide smoking ordinance; lowering the blood alcohol level at which a driver's license is suspended;
allowing the courts to order automatic child support payments; permitting out-of-state banking in Colorado; restricting the way in which
automobile windows can be tinted; putting Colorado on year-round
daylight saving time; creating diesel emission standards for trucks and
cars; reorganizing the juvenile parole system; shortening the sentences
for certain nonviolent crimes to alleviate a serious problem in prison
overcrowding; creating a system of lotto gambling in Colorado to raise
money for new prisons; requiring the owners of sailboards to register
with the State Division of Parks and Outdoor Recreation; eliminating
marriage as a defense against rape; requiring drug dealers to obtain a
license and pay tax on their drug sale profits; letting bars stay open
during elections; clamping down on child pornography; authorizing

the state Health Department to gear up to test women for breast cancer; reducing the severance tax on coal; expanding the types of tire chains that are permissible in blizzard conditions on Colorado highways; and restructuring the way the state funds elementary and secondary education.

This list could go on and on for there are literally hundreds of bills introduced in each session, ranging from sweeping and serious changes in policy to minor technical corrections in the law. There are also some downright silly and frivolous measures. But through it all, vital decisions are made. Taxes are imposed, roads are scheduled to be built, the professions are licensed, and prison terms are altered. It is not surprising, then, that the legislature is constantly swarming with lobbyists who represent literally hundreds of diverse interests across the state.

One might think of the legislature as an arena in which a score of basketball games are progressing, all at once, on the same floor, with games at different stages, with participants playing on several teams at once, switching at will, opposing each other in some instances and acting as teammates in others. Colorado's General Assembly has 100 elected members. There are 500 or more registered lobbyists and scores of staffers, and they're all playing with over 600 bills each session. Different and shifting coalitions develop to support and oppose each bill, and the contests proceed simultaneously through the 120-day session. Indeed, well in advance of each session, bills are proposed, teams are formed, and strategies planned—a sort of "spring training."

It is also tempting to see the legislature as a casino. In a casino there are lots of tables, lots of games. The stakes can be high. Cards are held tight. Self-interest prevails. There are winners and losers, but the outcome is never final, for there is always a new day and a new game just around the corner.

The players in the Capitol are fully aware of the stakes in the multitude of games in progress, but few members of the public are. This is attributable partly to the nature of media coverage. Bills proposing gun controls or mandating the use of motorcycle helmets, for example, gain extensive TV, radio, and newspaper coverage—much like Yogi, the dog, or a KKK Capitol steps rally. But the high-stakes politics of tax advantages, tort liability, and banking often garner brief mention and inside page coverage at best. Sadly, most citizens know very little about what goes on in their state capitol.

THE STATE OF COLORADO

Colorado, which joined the Union in 1876, is the eighth largest state geographically and the twenty-sixth most populous. It is bordered by Wyoming to the north, Nebraska and Kansas to the east, New Mexico to the south, and Utah to the west. The land is diverse in many ways. In the east, where a good deal of farming occurs, the land is flat. The Rocky Mountains cut through the middle of the state from north to south, and there are many high mountain valleys. The terrain in the west is mixed. Colorado is an arid state, with the Platte, Arkansas, Rio Grande, and Colorado Rivers draining its watershed.

The population of the state of Colorado is concentrated along the Front Range on the eastern edge of the Rockies; nearly three-quarters of the people live in a nine-county area that stretches from Fort Collins and Larimer County on the north, down through the Denver metropolitan area, and into Colorado Springs and Pueblo (El Paso and Pueblo Counties) to the south. Although metropolitan Denver is crowded, many areas of the state are sparsely populated. Denver County has a population of approximately 500,000, and its suburbs have well over a million more. But Hinsdale County, high in the mountains, has a total of only 467 residents, according to the 1990 census. Indeed, many Colorado counties have actually lost population in recent years, while the state as a whole, and the nine-county Front Range area in particular, have grown.

Throughout the 1990s, the state population grew rather rapidly. Between 1990 and mid-1997, the numbers grew by 600,000, to a total of roughly 3,900,000. In the late 1990s, Colorado was the fifth fastest growing state in the nation. The State Demographer's 2000 statewide population estimate stood at 4,227,389. The causes of this growth, according to the state demographer, include a California "bounce-back," the attractiveness of the area to retirees and others, and the growth in the globalization of the economy and technology. The most rapid growth was occurring in the mountains, and on the Western Slope.

Economically, both summer and winter tourism is big business for Colorado, with skiing ranked as one of the state's predominant industries. Colorado is the home of a number of government facilities and defense contracting operations. The Denver Mint and Region Eight Federal Offices are located in the state, as are NORAD, the Air Force Academy, Fort Carson, and huge defense contractor Lockheed-Martin. Agriculture and the livestock business continue to be significant elements in the state's economy. New high-tech industry is also important, and it is growing.

Economic, geographic, and demographic factors help define Colorado's political agenda and the configuration of its politics. Water is scarce yet vital to agriculture, to both urban and suburban development, and to the tourist industry. As the legislative agenda in any year or the Two Forks Dam controversy will attest, major political battles rage constantly over water use, water rights, and questions of transmountain and regional diversion. The state is united in its will to keep as much Platte, Arkansas, and Colorado river water as possible within its boundaries. However, it is anything *but* united on such matters as the movement of water from the Western Slope to metropolitan Denver or the construction of more dams and reservoirs.

Colorado's legislative alignments demonstrate the state's diversity. Rural legislators are outnumbered by their metro Denver and Front Range colleagues, and they guard what power base they have jealously. For years, they have dominated the agriculture committees of both houses, and for the entire decade of the 1980s, they had one of their own in the position of House Speaker. Lawmakers from the city of Denver often find themselves at odds with suburban representatives on such matters as funding for core city programs. Indeed, the Denver-suburban political suspicion and split enhance the strategic position of the rural folks. And so it goes. Sometimes the "cowboys" pull together and Western Slope representatives unite against their colleagues. At other times, those from the Western Slope and eastern plains join forces on water issues.

Political division can follow geographical patterns, as well. The sparsely populated areas on the Western Slope and the eastern plains both tend to be Republican, as do many of the Denver suburbs in Arapahoe and Jefferson Counties and the cities to the east, south, and southwest. Colorado Springs and El Paso County, to the south of Denver, are very Republican, with partisans who are generally more conservative than their colleagues in and around Denver.

For some years, there were signs that a coalition might be built around gender. By the later part of the 1980s, and on into the 1990s, nearly one-third of the Assembly's members were women, with the largest contingent and most of the recent growth in the majority Republican party. By and large, the women were politically moderate and, with time and the development of some group identity, they might have constituted a powerful force within the General Assembly. But by the twenty-first century, the political orientation of the women reflected that of the men; some are liberal, some moderate, and a good number are extremely conservative.

Denver itself, some of its northern suburbs in Adams County, parts of Boulder, and areas south in Pueblo historically have been bases of Democratic strength. Larimer and Weld Counties, roughly fifty miles north of Denver, tend, like the Denver suburbs, to be Republican, although Democrats there enjoy some electoral successes. Areas with heavy concentrations of military and ex-military personnel are among the most conservative and staunchly Republican, favoring generous federal spending for military materials and personnel in their own districts, but little on state programs. Pockets of Hispanic and African-American populations lean most heavily in the Democratic direction.

AMERICAN LEGISLATURES

Like the other states and the nation as a whole, Colorado has a government organized according to the separation of powers doctrine. And like the national government and forty-nine of the fifty states (but unlike virtually all cities, counties, school districts, and special districts in the United States, as well as the state of Nebraska), Colorado's legislative branch is bicameral—it has two houses. Given their colonial experience, our forefathers were skeptical of man's nature and viewed us all as potential dictators. As a result, they preferred weak governments with divided and widely distributed powers. The separation of powers initially splits into executive, legislative, and judicial branches. Bicameralism splits legislative authority once again. Presumably, a power-divided system is difficult for would-be tyrants to manipulate in an abusive fashion. Similarly, our political history shows that the American people have a fear of a strong executive and a preference for legislative dominance.

In many western states, the late nineteenth-century experience with political corruption and the resultant populism encouraged people to weaken the powers of governments even further. The fifty American states vary in the relative power of their legislative and executive branches, but in Colorado, the relationship is clear: Ours is a system of legislative dominance. This is evident in the budgetary process, where the legislature and its six-member Joint Budget Committee control the budget. Although the governor is constitutionally required to prepare a state budget, he plays a limited role in determining the state's financial priorities and policies. Legislative dominance is also evident in the constitutional provision of the initiative and referendum processes through which citizens can play direct roles in lawmaking.

The nature of executive-legislative relations, with legislative dominance as the hallmark, has been all the more visible in recent years because of a pattern of divided party control. The Republican party has controlled the legislature, but the governors have been Democrats. Two Democratic governors in succession, Richard Lamm and Roy Romer, were able to dominate the state's political spotlight. The Republican legislature's response was to make it clear who controls the lawmaking process and whose fingers are on the purse strings. Not surprisingly, a good deal of tension and friction has resulted. In 1998 this changed, of course, with the election of Republican Governor Bill Owens, but he then sometimes faced opposition from his own party.

Legislatures in the American states vary considerably in size. There are over 7,400 legislators in the ninety-nine state legislative chambers. The largest house of representatives is New Hampshire's with 400 members, followed by Pennsylvania with 203, and Georgia with 180. The smallest one is Alaska's with 40, followed by Delaware with 41. The largest senates are those of Minnesota with 67, New York with 61, and Illinois with 59. The smallest are Alaska with 20, Delaware and Nevada with 21 each, and New Hampshire with 24. The Colorado legislature has 35 members in its Senate and 65 in its House.

State legislatures also vary greatly in what is often called their level of "professionalization" (more recently referred to as their level of "congressionalization"). That is, they differ in terms of pay, staff and office support, and length of legislative sessions. Some states, including California, Illinois, Massachusetts, Michigan, New Jersey, New York, Ohio, Pennsylvania, and Wisconsin, have come to resemble the U.S. Congress in certain respects, as their legislatures are now virtually full-time bodies, offering high pay, extensive staff support, and private offices for members. Others look more like the state legislatures of the 1940s, meeting for just 85-, 60- or 40-day sessions every other year and, in a few cases, receiving minimal salaries of $4,000 to $10,000 or no regular annual salary at all. In all states, legislators receive some expense money, but that, too, varies widely.

There are differences of opinion on the matter of how modernized, or professionalized, state legislatures should be. Before the modernization period of the late 1960s and 1970s, critics panned state legislatures as outdated and ineffective, and called for such reforms as better pay, more staff, expanded quarters, and long annual sessions. The model, then, was the U.S. Congress. The reforms, which took hold in varying degrees in the states, made legislative service attractive to more people. Now, lawmakers are lampooned for being political "careerists," and a new breed of reforms is calling for term limits, shorter sessions, spending limits, and staffing reductions—for a return to the "citizen legislature."

Colorado leans slightly toward the uncongressionalized side. Salaries are set at $30,000 per year, and when coupled with expense allowances, lawmakers pocket around $42,000 per year. Staff support is minimal, members share office space, and session length is limited. Indeed, in November 1988, voters passed a legislatively initiated amendment to the constitution to impose a 120-day limit on legislative sessions. The idea of the "citizen legislature" is alive and well in Colorado.

Turnover among the members is fairly high, as it has been historically in most states. It is not unusual to see thirty or forty new faces among the hundred members of the General Assembly after each biennial election, most of them in the sixty-five-member House of Representatives. Indeed, with the imposition of eight-year term limits in 1990, steady turnover is now guaranteed.

There has also been a steady movement of House members into the Senate. This should not be surprising since Colorado senators serve four-year terms (rather than the two-year terms of House members) and there-fore face the costly and time-consuming task of running for reelection just half as often as do their House colleagues. Here again, term limits are prompting even more House members to seek a place in the Senate.

There are other ways in which the Colorado General Assembly re-sembles other American legislatures. There is a large, experienced, and ever-present lobby corps composed of everything from long-term, pro-fessional contract lobbyists (many of whom are ex-legislators) to direct-hire employees of corporations. There are volunteer citizen advo-cates representing religious and nonprofit groups, such as Common Cause and the League of Women Voters. Big businesses, small businesses, doz-ens of professions, cities, counties, special districts, teachers, school superintendents, brewers, unions, car dealers, retirees, builders, renters, candy makers, Christians, and lawyers—they can all be found in the Capitol lobby and coffee shop. And so can their money. Elections have become increasingly expensive, and interest group money has played a larger and larger role.

The Colorado legislature is a very partisan body. The Republicans control both houses and have done so for the past two decades. But the Democrats held the governor's position from 1974 to 1999. Republi-cans criticized the governor, killed the bills of Democratic legislators, and gave them all a rough time in general. In turn, Democratic gover-nors blamed the Republicans for state problems and vetoed some of their legislation. Sometimes—though not when an election is close at hand—they talk about working together. But even when one party con-trols both branches, tension can occur. Some years back, for example, the House Republican caucus spurned a request by Republican Gover-nor John Love to attend a caucus meeting and lobby the members on an education bill.

Like all political bodies in a democracy, American state legislatures display a combination of formal rules and procedures, informal norms, and pockets of concentrated power. The Colorado General Assembly is no exception. Parliamentary procedure governs the business of the As-sembly. All members may introduce bills, and they all have one vote in committees and on the floor. Procedures are in place to check abuses of power by committees or by the leadership.

Informally, a few members are powerful, and many have relatively little influence. The leaders of the majority party, savvy veterans, and those with a quick wit and a knack for negotiation wield power. New-comers, those not willing to be team players, and lawmakers who do not or cannot do their homework well are political lightweights. But this is no different from other deliberative bodies nor, indeed, from any other forms of human organization.

THE LEGISLATURE IN LAW

The Colorado Constitution creates the General Assembly, gives it its charge and authority, and also places some restrictions on it. Article III divides the powers of government three ways:

Article III

Distribution of Powers

The powers of the government of this state are divided into three distinct departments—the legislative, executive and judicial; and no person or collection of persons charged with the exercise of powers properly belonging to one of these departments shall exercise any power properly belonging to either of the others, except as in this constitution expressly directed or permitted.

Article V, Section One of the constitution begins with these words: "The legislative power of the state shall be vested in the general assembly consisting of a Senate and House of Representatives, both to be elected by the people. . . ." It goes on to state that the people reserve to themselves the authority to initiate laws and amendments through the initiative process and also reserve the right of referendum:

The people reserve to themselves the power to propose laws and amendments to the constitution and to enact and reject the same at the polls independent of the general assembly, and also reserve power at their own option to approve or reject at the polls any act, items, section or part of any act of the general assembly.

Article XXV, Section Four sums up nicely the responsibility of the General Assembly: "The general assembly shall pass all laws necessary to carry into effect the provisions of this constitution."

In Article V, entitled "Legislative Department," there are a number of provisions that give some structure and direction to the General Assembly. For example, this section specifies the manner in which vacancies are filled; instructs the General Assembly when it shall convene; provides for the selection of leadership in the form of a President of the Senate and a Speaker of the House; empowers each chamber to establish and enforce its own rules, subject, of course, to other constitutional provisions relating to open meetings and procedures; calls for the development of a journal of proceedings and for open sessions; makes members privileged from arrest during their attendance in the legislature; specifies when bills are to take effect; makes it clear that each bill is to have a tight title and address just one subject; and prohibits special legislation. The constitution, again in Article V, stipulates that revenue bills must originate in the House of Representatives and that there shall be no trading of votes, for that would be considered bribery and punishable by law. Members are to be elected from single-member districts, and periodic reapportionment is to be done by a bipartisan reapportionment commission.

Article X, Section 20, which was adopted by the voters in 1992, places significant restrictions on the legislature with respect to state finances. Under this provision, no new tax or tax rate increase may occur without voter approval. Further revenues, and thus spending, may not increase more than those of the prior year plus inflation and population growth. Budgets are really policy priorities expressed in numbers. With this constitutional provision, the voters severely limited the power of the General Assembly and effectively made themselves a "legislature at large" on some major budget matters.

The legislature, along with the other divisions of the state government, are subject to restrictions in the Colorado constitution's bill of rights. These restrictions apply to search and seizure, religious freedom, freedom of speech and press, the right to bear arms, the right of defendants in court, the prohibition of ex post facto laws, the right to trial by jury, the right to due process of law, and more.

In addition to the Colorado constitution, there are many statutes enacted by the legislature itself that guide the General Assembly and the legislative process. Among these are statutory provisions that require candidates and political committees to report campaign receipts and expenditures; provide compensation for legislators; mandate publication of the Senate and House journals; give details on the reapportionment system; establish legislative audit committees and the state auditor post; establish a Joint Budget Committee and a joint Capital Development Committee within the legislature; provide for the Legislative Council and create a Committee on Legal Services; call for legislative oversight, including oversight of administrative agency rulemaking activities; and require the registration of lobbyists.

Finally, the Colorado General Assembly is very much like other American state legislatures with respect to its processes. In a formal sense, the process is really quite simple. Ideas for bills may originate with private citizens or organizations, administrative agency personnel, the governor, or legislators themselves. However, only legislators may introduce them. The General Assembly's Office of Legislative Legal Services phrases these ideas in proper legal language, and each bill has at least one legislative sponsor in each house.

Bills may be introduced in either house. The President of the Senate or the Speaker of the House then assigns each bill to one or more of a dozen or so committees that are specialized by subject matter. In due time, the committees hold hearings, where citizens or organizations and their lobbyists may speak for or against the bills. After these hearings, bills may be "reported out" (acted upon) favorably, unfavorably, or with recommendations for amendment; they may be killed; or they may be referred to yet another committee. If a bill is reported out, it is considered twice in the full House or Senate—once on a second reading and again on a third reading. If the bill survives, it repeats the process in the second chamber. Any resultant differences in the versions of the bill are resolved in conference committees or, more often, one house will accept the other's amendments. The bills then go to the governor for his signature or veto. Most bills that make it this far are signed and become law.

No seated legislature can legally bind a future legislature. Each is free to change state statutes as it pleases; thus, although laws that take the form of constitutional provisions constrict a legislature, statutes enacted in the past are always subject to change by later legislative bodies. This is the way it happens in the U.S. Congress and in other states. It looks and sounds simple, but the process is much more complicated than this brief sketch suggests. It is also much more interesting.

2

Elections and the General Assembly

There are 100 members of the Colorado General Assembly, sixty-five in the House of Representatives and thirty-five in the Senate. House members serve two-year terms; their senatorial colleagues serve four years at a stretch. Although there is no prohibition against self-succession, most members serve for relatively short periods, typically four to eight years. In the past some have remained lawmakers for sixteen, eighteen, or even more than twenty years, sometimes in the same chamber. This is changing now, of course, with term limits of eight consecutive years now in effect in both chambers. In any given election year, all sixty-five House seats are up for reelection, as are either seventeen or eighteen of the thirty-five Senate seats. All 100 members are, by constitutional provision, elected from single-member districts.

DIVERSITY OF DISTRICTS

House districts in 1990 contained roughly 55,000 people on average, and the population in senatorial districts averaged approximately 100,000. These numbers were up from 1982, when they were closer to 44,500 for the House and 82,500 for the Senate. With Colorado's population growth, they'll be considerably higher following the 2000 census.

The districts vary enormously in terms of size and economic, demographic, geographic, and political character. House Districts 1 through 10, for example, are located within the most populous section of the city of Denver and are very small geographically. Others, such as Districts 60, 61, and 63, cover enormous expanses of territory. District 63 covers the entire east-central section of the state and includes all of Elbert, Lincoln, Kit Carson, Yuma, Cheyenne, and Kiowa Counties, and part of Arapahoe County, as well. District 60, in the extreme south-central part of Colorado, covers all of seven counties and part of another. District 61, in the high meadows of South Park, includes all or parts of seven counties. Beyond these, two districts encompass all or sections of six counties, two more cover all or parts of five counties, and five take in all or portions of four counties. Senate districts, of course, are even larger. Colorado is, at once, both a very urban state and one with vast expanses of sparse populations.

The populations of House Districts 7 and 8 in Denver are nearly one-half African-American. Others, such as District 2, 4, and 5 in Denver; 46 in Pueblo; and 60 in the south-central section of Colorado, are heavily Hispanic. Thirty-one districts have a black population below 1 percent; many of these are rural or in the Denver suburbs. Twelve Colorado House districts are over 20 percent Hispanic, and five of these are over 44 percent. In 1997–1998, seven of these twelve were represented by Democrats, and five by Republicans. Of the eleven House districts with Hispanic populations under 5 percent, seven were represented by Republican lawmakers. Senate districts show the same variations. Some districts are politically competitive, but most are not. In 1996, eighty-four seats were up, and twenty-three candidates ran unopposed. Only seventeen were within the 55–45 percent range, or close enough to be considered competitive.

APPORTIONMENT

Colorado's House and Senate district lines are redrawn every ten years when new U.S. census numbers become available. The current House and Senate district lines are shown in Figures 2.1 and 2.2. Prior to 1974, redistricting (or reapportionment, as it is called) was done by the Colorado legislature itself. Needless to say, it is a tough and very political proposition to have a representative body reapportion itself. The outcome of a new districting plan can well determine the balance of power between the parties for a full decade. As a result, battles fought within a legislature over district lines may create divisions and hard feelings that spill over into the session and affect the normal legislative agenda.

In 1974, Colorado voters approved a constitutional amendment that established a bipartisan commission outside the General Assembly to handle reapportionment. This commission is an eleven-member body. Four members are appointed by the Colorado Supreme Court chief justice, three by the governor; the other four are leaders of the General Assembly or persons designated by them. The commission must have both geographic and political diversity by congressional district and can have no more than six members from one political party. Furthermore, no more than four of the members may be legislators. When new census data become available, the commission has ninety days to study

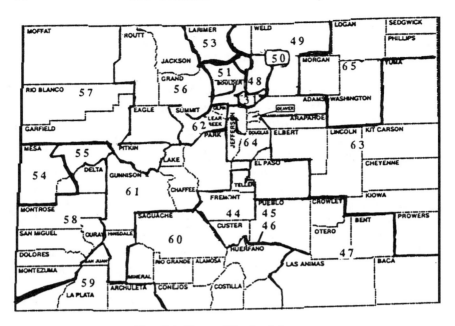

Fig. 2.1 House District Map

the numbers, hold public hearings on the matter, and develop a plan. The final plan must, of course, comply with the court's one-man, one-vote criteria, as well as those related to minority representation, district compactness, and maintenance of communities of interest. It must also be reviewed and approved by the full Colorado Supreme Court.

The assignment of reapportionment responsibilities to the commission does not, however, remove political considerations from the procedure. District lines can be drawn in a variety of ways to help or hurt individual incumbents or the parties themselves. Leaders in the House and Senate placed four members on the commission for the 1992 reapportionment, and the Democratic governor placed three. The remaining four were named by the chief justice of the state Supreme Court.

All sorts of people, besides the parties, have a vital interest in the outcomes of redistricting. Incumbents want to see their seats kept safe, or made even safer by the inclusion of a large majority of registrants from their party. Of course, this runs counter to the needs of the parties themselves to maximize the number of winnable seats. Ethnic minorities want lines drawn in such a way as to ensure the election of candidates of their own ethnic background. Cities and counties oppose district

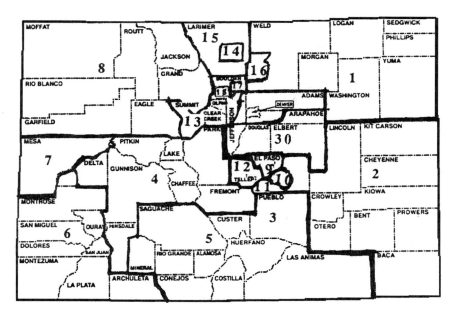

Fig. 2.2 Senate District Map

lines which cut through their jurisdictional boundaries. And communities of interest, such as recreational or farming regions, resist being divided or combined with some other sort of area, such as a suburb. This makes the redistricting process highly political and an interesting challenge for the makers of the new maps.

Redistricting following the 1990 census was fraught with controversy and legal wrangling nationwide and Colorado did not escape the fight. In state after state there were lawsuits challenging new district maps on the grounds that they either failed to include enough African Americans or Hispanics to make seats winnable for minority candidates or, conversely, that by gerrymandering so as to create "majority-minority" districts, race had unconstitutionally become the driving criterion.

The 1965 Voting Rights Act was amended by Congress in 1982 to mandate efforts by the states to maximize the chances of minority voters to elect minority candidates. That enactment, along with court and U.S. Department of Justice interpretations of the law, led to the creation of majority-minority districts, districts in which half or more of the voters were ethnic minority. This required the creation of some oddly shaped districts. The "racial gerrymandering" needed to get the job done led eventually to court actions voiding some majority-minority districting schemes and backing away some from the heavy focus on race and ethnicity in the design of district maps.

Like so many other states, Colorado's 1990 districting plan was challenged in court. Three Hispanic plaintiffs residing in the San Luis Valley in the south-central part of the state sued the state, arguing that the boundaries of House District 60 should be altered to include a majority of voters of Hispanic origin. As it stood, roughly 42 percent were Hispanic. The district was represented by Anglo Lewis Entz, a potato farmer who had represented the district for well over a decade. The suit was first filed in 1992 and after failing in state courts and federal district court, the plaintiffs prevailed in the federal court of appeals. The state was thus faced with a court order to redraw the District 60 lines.

Colorado's 1990 reapportionment commission had long since disbanded, so the legislature chose to establish an interim committee to draw a new plan. During 1997 the committee did just that, and in early 1998 the legislature adopted the revised map.

The process was not without controversy. Heated criticism was leveled at the court for requiring a new map so close to the 2000 census, when redistricting would begin all over again. Within the San Luis Valley itself, the Hispanic community was divided. The movement of more Hispanic voters into District 60 meant the movement of those voters out of adjacent House districts. Indeed, two districts that stood to lose Hispanic voters were at the time represented by Hispanics, Democrat Gil Romero and Republican Mike Salaz. A late minor adjustment kept Romero's district from such a loss, but given the unavoidable impact on many other districts, criticism and opposition did not abate. Just prior to the last-minute adjustment, Senator Bob Martinez, a Denver Democrat, commented, "As a Mexican-American legislator, I can't help but notice we are now weakening two House districts represented by Mexican-Americans."[1]

District 60's court-ordered reconfiguration was also caught up in the state's never-ending high-stakes political controversy over water. Many San Luis Valley citizens and organizations feared that any districting scheme that split the valley would weaken its political ability to protect its underground water supplies from thirsty Front Range cities.

One attorney, himself a Hispanic and opposed to the redistricting, alleged that one of the plaintiffs had been associated with Canadian interests that had an eye on the valley's water. The *Rocky Mountain News* reported that "more than 60 organizations, including town councils, school boards, county commissions, water conservancy districts and civic and business organizations had joined to fight the redistricting."[2]

However, the state legislature was left with no choice but to comply with the court's decision. It did so, with a new map that went into effect for the 1998 and 2000 legislative elections. After that, a new

Table 2.1—Party Control in Colorado Legislative, U.S. Congressional, and Statewide Offices, 1969–2000

	Governor	Secretary of State	Attorney General	Treasurer	House R-D	Senate R-D	U.S. Senate R-D	U.S. House R-D
1999–2000	R	R	D	R	40-25	20-15	2-0	4-2
1997–98	D	R	R	R	41-24	20-15	2-0	4-2
1995–96	D	R	R	R	41-24	19-16	2-0	4-2
1993–94	D	R	R	D	34-31	19-16	1-1	4-2
1991–92	D	R	R	D	38-27	23-12	1-1	3-3
1989–90	D	R	D	D	39-26	24-11	1-1	3-3
1987–88	D	R	R-D	D	41-24	25-10	1-1	3-3
1985–86	D	R	R	D	47-18	24-11	1-1	4-2
1983–84	D	R	R	D	41-24	21-14	1-1	3-3
1981–82	D	R	D	D	40-25	22-13	1-1	2-3
1979–80	D	R	D	D	38-27	22-13	1-1	2-3
1977–78	D	R	D	D	35-30	18-17	0-2	2-3
1975–76	D	R	D	D	26-39	19-16	0-2	2-3
1973–74	R	R	D	R	37-28	22-13	1-1	3-2
1971–72	R	R		R	38-27	21-14	2-0	2-2
1969–70	R				38-27	23-12	2-0	1-3

Source: Assembled from *State of Colorado, Secretary of State, Abstract of Votes Cast*, various years. U.S. Senate and House seats are Colorado representatives only.

census, a new apportionment commission, and more recent U.S. Supreme Court decisions will be in place and yet another set of district maps will be produced. And once again, interests ranging from incumbents, hopeful challengers, cities, counties, the state parties, and ethnic groups will be seeking to affect the outcome. In 1997 House Speaker Chuck Berry said it as well as anyone could: "You can't take partisan politics out of reapportionment. It is an inherently political process."[3] Somewhat ironically, the 1998 election cycle produced no District 60 Hispanic candidate in either party.

PARTY CONTROL

The Republican party has dominated the Colorado General Assembly for over two decades. Interestingly, though, Republicans have not dominated other elected posts in Colorado. In fact, the Democratic party has held the governorship from 1974 to 1998—twelve years with Richard D. Lamm, whose popularity grew with each election, followed by Roy Romer, who won handily in 1986, 1990, and again in 1994. The two parties have shared Colorado's U.S. congressional delegation. Democrats Floyd Haskill, Gary Hart, and Tim Wirth, and Republicans Peter Dominick, Bill Armstrong, Hank Brown, and Wayne Allard were sent to the U.S. Senate; Democrats David Skaggs, Pat Schroeder, Ray Kogovsek, Ben Campbell, Tim Wirth, Mark Udall, and Diana DeGette, and Republicans Hank Brown, Dan Schaefer, Ken Kramer, Mike Strang, Tom Tancredo, Wayne Allard, Joel Hefley, Scott McInnis, and Bob Schaffer have been elected to the U.S. House of Representatives. Ben Campbell switched from the Democratic to the Republican party after his election to the U.S. Senate.

As noted before, the Republican party has been dominant in the General Assembly for almost all of the past two decades. Indeed, except for 1975 and 1976, the Republicans have held the majority in both chambers since 1969, and they enjoyed the two-thirds edge needed to override gubernatorial vetoes in both houses in 1985 and 1986. Table 2.1 displays the pattern of party control in the Colorado House and Senate and in statewide offices, together with the party split in the U.S. congressional delegation since 1969.

There are several theories about why the Republican grip has been so much tighter on the legislature than on other elective offices. Some Republicans have suggested that their dominance in the General Assembly is an accurate reflection of citizen preferences and the political configuration of the state. They suggest that the party has simply dropped the ball in its candidate selection and campaign strategies for statewide office—had it not, they say, the party would have been dominant there as well. In addition, the residue from heated primaries may have left some Republicans bitter and unsupportive of the party's candidate in the November general election. Others (mostly Democrats) have argued that the Republican dominance is the result of gerrymandering, with large numbers of Democratic voters clustered in a few districts, primarily in Denver. The excessively heavy Democratic majorities in these districts drain away Democratic strength that is needed elsewhere.

Without question, the apportionment schemes of the 1980s and 1990s have helped the Republicans. Indeed, since the districting of the 1990s included the formation of predominantly minority districts, as seemingly required by interpretations of the Voting Rights Act of 1965 and its 1982 amendments, the concentration of Democratic voters into predominantly minority districts weakened Democratic candidacies in others. But some individual Democratic candidates were helped as well. Although the concentration of Democratic voters in Denver and in minority districts may have given Republicans more seats than their statewide numbers might justify, the arrangement has also made a number of Denver-area Democrats very secure electorally.

Yet another explanation focuses on the differences in campaign styles in statewide and legislative races. Statewide races are very expensive and make heavy use of the mass media. Messages are packed in fifteen- to thirty-second ads where personality, appearance, and style are the focus and it is the persona of the candidate, rather than party identity or stance on issues, that predominates in the voters' consciousness. Legislative races, on the other hand, do not lend themselves to campaigns with intense use of mass media because the territory covered by television and the major Denver papers does not at all match the boundaries of the much smaller legislative districts. It is simply not cost-effective for a candidate to pay for television ads that reach a statewide audience when running in a district with just one sixty-fifth (House) or one thirty-fifth (Senate) of the population. As a result, voters see the candidates less frequently, or not at all, and thus retreat to their party inclinations, however strong or weak these may be. And although statewide voter registration had for years been split fairly evenly between Democrats, Republicans, and the unaffiliated, the overall tilt, when not influenced by television spots and candidate personalities, is in the Republican direction.

The Republican advantage is reinforced and extended by patterns of interest group campaign-giving and incumbency. Incumbents always have an advantage, in extensive name recognition and other ways, and interest groups give much more frequently and generously to incumbents. In the 1992 election, incumbents received six times as much money from PACs as did challengers.[4] Thus, the pattern of Republican dominance is perpetuated.

Heading into the 1994 election, Democrats had high hopes of controlling one or both chambers. They had been gaining on the Republicans slowly, and in 1993 and 1994 were just three seats back in each house. As it turned out, though, the sweeping Republican gains made in the U.S. Congress were replicated in Colorado and the Democrats slipped, once again, into a heavily minority status in the House while making no gain in the Senate. For 1997–1998 the numbers were virtually the same; Republicans gained one Senate seat in November 1996 and there was no change in the House. The Democrats may have owned the governor's office, but the General Assembly has belonged to the GOP.

The 1998 election changed the picture significantly, however. The party balance in the Senate remained the same, at twenty Republicans and fifteen Democrats. In the House the Democrats gained one seat but still trailed by the count of forty to twenty-five. But for the first time in twenty-four years, a Republican legislature did not face the policy preferences and the veto possibilities of a Democratic governor. Bill Owens, a conservative former Republican House and Senate member and incumbent state treasurer, was elected governor.

The 1998 elections also produced some controversy, the likes of which had not been seen for several decades. In two House districts with very close races, the apparent losers disputed the outcome, alleging irregularities. Republican Pam Rhodes lost to incumbent Democrat Paul Zimmerman by 109 votes. On election day one Boulder County precinct had received the wrong ballots. Said Rhodes, in requesting a special election, "Our concern is that 270 people did not get to vote for the right candidate. We're asking for a special election for the entire district."[5]

In the second race, House district loser Kathi Williams, a Republican House member some years before, asked that the House itself exercise its authority to determine whom to seat. Williams lost to Democrat Lois Tochtrop by just eighty-four votes in the contest in which 459 ballots proved to be missing, and observed that the election featured "significant voting irregularities and potential fraud."[6] Newly elected House Speaker Russell George consented to establishment of a credentials committee to examine the facts, but also observed that "it's worrisome, none of us are wanting this."[7] The Speaker was clearly worried about the prospect of having a Republican body examine even the possibility of rejecting an apparent Democratic winner.[8] Later, Speaker George and Majority Floor Leader Douglas Dean indicated that legislation providing for special elections might well be introduced early in the 1999 session. In the end both Rhodes and Williams dropped their challenges, thus avoiding what had promised to be an unpleasant partisan fight.

RUNNING FOR OFFICE

It is no simple task to win a seat in the Colorado General Assembly, and most people don't have the inclination to try. It is relatively easy to meet the constitutionally set qualifications. Candidates must be U.S. citizens, at least twenty-five years old, and residents in the district for at least a year. Individuals who meet these criteria must then secure the nomination of one of the two major political parties. This involves getting on the election-year primary ballot in August by winning at least 30 percent of the delegate vote in the relevant House or Senate district assembly, and then, of course, winning the primary election. It is possible to gain a spot on the primary ballot by way of a petition, but it is difficult. A would-be candidate needs the signatures of 1,000 registered voters, or a total equal to 30 percent of votes cast in the last primary. Moderate Republican incumbents Marcy Morrison and Tambor Williams, squeezed in the low-attendance assemblies by the religious right, went the petition route in 1998. Primary winners square off in the November general election, and the victor is rewarded with a seat and desk in the House or Senate come the following January.

But it's a little tougher than it sounds. First, if the district and the party are at all competitive, the would-be candidate will have to make the rounds of party activists to drum up support at the precinct caucuses and district nominating assemblies in April. The candidate will have to find someone to make the nomination at the assembly and hope to garner a minimum of 30 percent of the delegate vote. If there is only one candidate, the nomination for the November election is locked up at that point. If two or more candidates receive 30 percent of the delegate vote at the assembly, they face each other again in August, with the top ballot line going to the person with the most delegate votes. If there are candidates nominated by petition, they are listed after those nominated in assembly.

A candidate who makes the primary ballot has a lot of work ahead. A campaign committee must be formed if it hasn't been already. The candidate will have to raise money, walk dozens of miles ringing doorbells, and solicit the support of fellow party members by phone until the ear falls off. And that's just for the primary.

Most people who make a run at a legislative seat are already experienced in politics. Many have held public office or party positions before. Some of them are long-term local party leaders, such as county chairs, precinct committee members, party fund-raisers, or central figures in the campaigns of other officeholders. Many have experience as elected county officials or city council members. Most have served on one or more boards or commissions at the state and local levels.

The political past of Senator Gigi Dennis, a Republican from Pueblo, provides a good example. Before her election, Senator Dennis was the Rio Grande County Republican party secretary for eight years, and House District 60 chairperson as well. Another legislator, Representative Debbie Allen, had served as secretary and vice chairperson of the Arapahoe County Republican party and president of the Aurora Republican Forum. House members Bill Swenson (Longmont), Peggy Kerns (Aurora), Vi June (Westminster), Moe Keller (Wheat Ridge), Peggy Reeves (Fort Collins), Joyce Lawrence (Pueblo), Ron May (Colorado Springs), and Carol Snyder (Northglenn) all served as city council members. So did Senator Elsie Lacy. Vi June was Westminster's mayor.

The nature of the chase for legislative office can vary significantly, depending on the competitiveness of the district and whether an incumbent is seeking reelection. Incumbents have faced challengers in district assemblies and primaries, but more often than not, they don't. In a 1988 nominating assembly in Arapahoe County, veteran state Senator Jack Fenlon was, in the words of the *Rocky Mountain News*, "blind sided by challenger Mounier at the district assembly." Fenlon, previously an Aurora city councilman and a state representative, was seeking his second term in the Senate. He was taken by surprise by the unusual district assembly challenge and barely garnered the 30 percent delegate vote needed to make the August primary ballot. Fenlon's critics attributed the challenge to the fact that he had lost touch with the district and said that he was a bit too liberal for his conservative Arapahoe County constituency. In the end, however, Fenlon won both the August primary and the November general election.

In the Colorado Springs area, Marcy Morrison faced several primary challenges from Ken Gray and his supporters who believed that as a moderate Republican she was too liberal. In 1992 her religious right opponent came within twenty-seven votes of defeating Morrison. In 1994 he tried again, but fell short by 923 votes. In both years, Marcy Morrison won handily in the November general election in her heavily Republican district. In 1996 Morrison was unopposed in both the primary and general election, but in 1998 the religious right appeared again. This time Morrison chose to bypass the district assembly nominating stage and petition her way onto the August primary ballot.

Morrison's moderate Republican House colleague Tambor Williams of Greeley similarly ran into her party's right wing and was shut off the 1998 primary ballot in district assembly voting. Williams, too, petitioned onto the primary ballot. In Williams's Weld County, the party chose to establish a candidate review board that would interview potential Republican candidates to determine if they were "morally and ethically qualified for public office." At this, subtle humorist and Representative Steve Johnson wondered, "since just a third of my district is in Weld County do I have to be moral and ethical just one-third of the time?" Weld County Republicans went on to pass a resolution stipulating that Republican candidates must exercise "moral uprightness, integrity and marital fidelity" and another requiring candidates to support a ban on partial-birth abortions.[9]

But a successful challenge to an incumbent is atypical. Indeed, in 1994, when eighteen Senate seats were up for election, eleven incumbents ran; two faced primary opposition, and both won. In the House of Representatives, three members faced primary challenges and they, too, all won. In 1996 four House members and four Senate incumbents faced primary opposition, and all eight survived the challenge. Six of these were on the Republican side, and represented challenges of moderates by Republicans on the right-wing fringe of their party. And in 1998 just two Republican House incumbents faced primary challengers; both incumbents prevailed.

Assembly and primary challenges are most likely to occur in non-competitive districts where a primary win is tantamount to victory in the November general election. Both House members who lost in the 1988 primaries were succeeded by members of their own party who won easily in November, by margins of 73 and 74 percent. This happened also in all three House districts and two Senate districts in 1994. The districts of Senator Dennis Gallagher and House member Rob Hernandez were both in heavily Democratic Denver. The House seats of Marcy Morrison of Colorado Springs and Bill Kaufman of Loveland, along with the Senate seat of Jim Roberts, were overwhelmingly Republican. As it turned out, Roberts prevailed in his primary in Loveland but lost the general election to Democrat Stan Matsunaka in a very close race in which Matsunaka spent nearly $100,000. Incumbent Roberts was handicapped by his image as an extremist who saw all sorts of odd federal conspiracies afoot, including the presence of black helicopter spy planes overhead.

The pattern was similar in 1996. Democratic House member Gloria Leyba defeated her primary challenger, and was then unopposed in the November general election. The same was true of Republican Representative Jeanne Adkins and Republican Senator Ray Powers.

As noted earlier, districts vary greatly as to the degree of interparty competitiveness. Of the nineteen contests for seats in the Colorado Senate in 1996, just five were settled with margins closer than 55–45 percent. Six candidates, all of whom were incumbents, were unopposed. In the House of Representatives, just twelve of the sixty-five races were within the 55–45 percent range, and seventeen candidates, four Democrats and thirteen Republicans, ran unopposed. In 1998, the first

Table 2.2—Competitive Status of Colorado House and Senate Seats: 1996, 1998

| | 1996 | | 1998 | |
	House	*Senate*	*House*	*Senate*
Seats up	65	19	65	17
Only one candidate	17	6	9	3
Contested seats	48	13	56	14
Outcome closer than 55–45%	12	5	14	9

Source: Abstract of Votes Cast, Secretary of State, 1996, 1998.

Note: In 1998, three contests in each chamber were exactly 55–45 percent.

election following the impact of term limits, competition was just a little stiffer. Of the eighty-two seats up, twelve went uncontested and twenty-three were settled by margins within the 55–45 percent range. See Table 2.2.

This variation has consequences. In districts that overwhelmingly favor one party, it is difficult for the minority party to recruit candidates who are willing to put loads of time, opportunity costs, and psychic involvement, not to mention money, into the role of sacrificial lamb. On the other hand, noncompetitive districts will sometimes spawn competition within the ranks of the majority party because success in the nominating assembly and primary means victory in November.

Another consequence of low interparty competition within a district is that the decision about who will end up in the General Assembly is effectively made in low-participation precinct caucuses, district assemblies, and August party primaries. As participation drops, the clout of the most intense and often politically extreme factions within the party rises. In recent years, the religious right within the Republican party has exercised its muscle at these early stages of the electoral process.

In every election, there are some districts with no incumbents in the race because turnover in the Colorado General Assembly is rather high. This was the case even before term limits. The pay is only moderate, the workload is heavy, staff help is in short supply, and elections are very draining. In addition, the legislators' personal, family, and professional lives take a beating. Consequently, the burnout rate is high; indeed, the rate of voluntary withdrawal from the legislature is much higher than the rate of defeat of incumbents at the polls. With the impact of term limits, the pattern of turnover resulting from factors other than electoral defeat is sure to continue. When seats are open, entry into the fray is obviously more attractive to newcomers since the chances of success are increased in the absence of an incumbent opponent. In open seat districts, the parties find it easier to attract candidates.

Every so often an incumbent, even one with an opponent, gets lucky. In 1996 Republican Senator David Wattenberg, a Walden rancher who had served previously in the House, faced a Democratic opponent named Laurie Bower. In the course of the campaign Bower discovered that her policy views and those of Wattenberg were much the same. So she endorsed him. Said Bower, "I have withdrawn my opposition to Dave Wattenberg who has worked hard for our community and state and deserves respect." The news was too good to be true for Wattenberg, who responded, "It's a new ploy. I'm not convinced whether she is in or out." Actually Bower, who still said she'd serve if elected, meant what she said, even if it was an unusual action. She noted, "I think it is more important to put the needs of the community over any personal ambition or party goals."[10] Unsaid by Bower, and perhaps not understood, is the cold truth that the "needs of the community" are defined differently by Republicans and Democrats, and the party that is in the majority in the Capitol gets its way.

Both sitting legislators and their challengers tell the world of their political intentions in a variety of ways. Candidates often schedule press conferences in the Capitol pressroom, in the hope of gaining media attention and receiving some free publicity. Publicity and public recognition are problems for all candidates, especially for nonincumbents who lack the most basic element for success, namely, recognition with the voters. In some cases, candidates announce well in advance, hoping to preempt the field and discourage potential rivals. In early 1996, for example, sitting House members Ken Chlouber, Jim Congrove, and Peggy Reeves all announced their intention to seek Senate seats in the coming November election. Chlouber's aim was to unseat Democratic Senator Linda Powers; Reeves aimed for the seat of Bob Schaffer who, in turn, was after the Republican nomination for the seat of U.S. House member Wayne Allard, who sought the Republican nomination for the U.S. Senate seat of retiring Hank Brown. Jim Congrove's aim was to take the position of Al Meiklejohn who was leaving the state Senate after twenty-four years of service. All three House members won their Senate seats.

Not infrequently, candidates have their legislative careers launched for them and become incumbents even before running for election. For example, eleven of the thirty-five senators sitting in that chamber in 1996 first came to the Senate by way of appointment to fill a vacancy. This is often a purposeful ploy; a legislator who plans to retire from office will often resign before the end of the full term so that a fellow party member may be appointed. Then, in the next election, the appointed legislator can run as an incumbent, with all the advantages that entails.

It is not unusual for Senate candidates to have served previously in the House of Representatives. This seldom works in the other direction, though, as legislators would much rather face the arduous tasks of running for election and reelection once every four years than every two. In the 1999–2000 sessions, twenty-two of the thirty-five sitting members of the Colorado Senate had previously served in the House, but no House member had served in the Senate. With term limits setting in, however, senators who aren't ready to call it quits and go home may well decide that a stint, or another stint, in the House is worthwhile. Indeed, Don Ament, who served two terms in the House before his two terms in the Senate, was reelected to the House for the 1999–2000 sessions. He resigned, though, to accept a position in newly elected Governor Owens's cabinet.

One interesting twist on the movement of members from one chamber to the other is that displayed by Mary Ellen Epps. She literally moved from one house to another so as to be able to move from the House to the Senate, which she did successfully. Epps was first elected to the House of Representatives in 1986 from a Colorado Springs district. After twelve years in the House, and forced out by term limits in 1998, she decided to run for the Senate. Her problem was that her Colorado Springs residence of thirty-one years was in the Senate district of Democrat Jim Rizzuto. Rizzuto was also forced out of his seat by term limits, and his seat was open. But the district, Senate District 2, was highly competitive politically. Besides, the district was large and rural, encompassing nine counties and just a portion of Epps's home environs of El Paso County. After representing a slice of easy Republican El Paso County for a dozen years, the sprawling rural territory housing lots of Democrats was not Epps's type of place.

On the other hand, Senate District 11 was open since Senate Republican Floor Leader Jeff Wells had also reached his term limit, and his district was, unlike District 2, overwhelmingly Republican, fully within El Paso County, and reasonably compact and urban.

So Mary Ellen Epps moved, she said, into District 11. But her move became a "she said, they said" controversy. According to Representative Epps, she moved from her Senate District 2 home of thirty-one years to a rented room in the house of an elderly couple a mile away, within Senate District 11. A neighbor lady said, to the contrary, "Of course [she] hasn't moved, she's there right now; her white Cadillac's parked in the driveway. She comes and goes all the time." Epps stayed with her relocation claim, commenting that "I don't think it's anybody's business where I spend the night. I pay rent and its nobody's business how often I'm there."

Her new landlords were of no help solving the puzzle. Said the owner of Epps's new domicile, "It's none of your business, and we have nothing to say." One Republican El Paso County Republican party veteran was more conclusive. She said, "This is a cover up for her to run for office so she can stay in politics."[11]

Mary Ellen Epps was not alone in the 1998 play of musical homes for musical legislative houses. Her Colorado House colleague Barry Arrington decided that he'd prefer the U.S. House to Colorado's House. Second District Congressman Dan Schaefer was not running for reelection and Arrington wanted the seat. He didn't live in District 2, so he moved six blocks away. Unlike Epps, Arrington was unsuccessful.

Is It Worth the Effort?

Making the run for a legislative seat in a November general election is a costly enterprise, especially in a competitive district. In a noncompetitive one, the uphill climb may be in the primary instead, and it may be no climb at all for the incumbent. The race in competitive contests can be very costly in terms of money, time, and energy. Therefore, among the first things a potential candidate must do is take a hard look at the numbers of both voters and dollars.

Anyone anticipating state legislative candidacy will want to look long and hard at voting statistics, too. How many voters are registered as Republicans? How many as Democrats? And how many are unaffiliated? What have the trends been of late? And how do these people actually vote? Do the unaffiliated, possibly the largest block of registered voters, lean Democratic or Republican? It is important to look at actual voter behavior in past elections, as well as registration figures.

Past voting behavior in U.S. House and Senate races, in contests for the governor's office and in other statewide posts, and in prior state House and Senate contests can provide clues about what to expect the next time. Voter registration numbers may suggest a rather even party split, but voter behavior may indicate a pattern of regular support of one party or the other in state legislative elections. The district may contain a block of precincts with heavy unaffiliated registration and voters who switch frequently, supporting both Democrats and Republicans on the same election day. This would suggest that many voters can be swayed and that certain campaign strategies may work well for the candidate.

It obviously makes a big difference to the candidate whether an incumbent is running or if the seat is open. Incumbents find it relatively easy to raise money, but challengers must struggle. Incumbents already have a network of contacts and a legislative record, but challengers are usually novices. Furthermore, a majority of the voters have supported the incumbent before, and the successful challenger must break that voting habit. Since the record clearly shows that incumbents almost always win, is it worth it, then, to even make the run? Potential candidates must carefully analyze the numbers and the past behavior of the voters and decide if there is a realistic chance of winning.

MONEY

Candidates will also want to put pencil to paper to determine whether the race is financially feasible. It is not unusual to spend $40,000, $50,000, or even more to mount a credible race for a state Senate seat and $20,000 or more for a House seat. In 1992, the average expenditure for a Colorado Senate seat was over $25,000; in the House, it was roughly $20,000.[12] One 1996 Senate race set the record for spending. Several weeks before the election, incumbent Linda Powers had raised over $147,000, including $2,500 from Don Henley of the musical group the Eagles. Her opponent had raised nearly $60,000.[13] Clearly, less is spent in noncompetitive races, and a good deal more in the contested ones.

Where will all the money go? The candidates must plan on heavy design and printing costs for one or more brochures, with perhaps thousands of copies of multicolored pieces. There may be lawn signs, bumper stickers, buttons, pens, and pencils. Design and rental payments for billboards may be needed. Newspaper ads and radio spots will have to be developed, and space and time purchased. There will be copy costs for voter lists, labels, envelopes, postage stamps, and mass mailings, probably several of them. It may prove necessary to pay something, if only a token amount, to a campaign manager or consultant. And fund-raisers not only make money, they cost money, too, for if people pay to attend a cocktail party or cookout, they expect something to eat and drink. Altogether, then, it doesn't take long at all to spend $20,000 to $50,000.

PERSONAL COSTS

But money isn't the most precious resource the candidate must consider. Personal time and energy are. An incumbent must begin preparing for the November election as soon as the General Assembly adjourns, which is in early May. Challengers must begin much earlier. And once the campaign really starts to move, the demands make it all but impossible to do anything else, unless the candidate is unopposed or is an incumbent in a lopsided district and without a primary challenge. In the early stages of the campaign, the candidate must worry about assembling a staff, developing a campaign plan, and raising money—lots of money. Someone will have to obtain and study voter registration lists, precinct by precinct, targeting those in need of the most attention and forming a plan for mailings, for literature drops, for phone calling, for the placement of signs, for door-to-door canvassing by the candidate, and more. How many mailings will be sent? To whom? What exactly will they be and when will they be sent? Citizens can now vote before election day, and that complicates decisions on when to send out campaign mail. How much will it cost? Which precincts should the candidate walk? And should some be walked more than once? Who will help? What kinds of signs are needed? How many? These are just a few of the myriad questions that must be answered as all the phases of the campaign are put on the calendar, counting backward from election day.

Meanwhile, questionnaires pour in. They come from "right-to-lifers," the pro-gun lobby, educators, medical and business groups, and others, all asking the candidate to check off answers or write opinion essays on a litany of issues. More questions arise. How specific should the candidate be? Should all the questionnaires be filled out? What are the political consequences of ignoring them? Decisions must be made and time invested in every response. Then there are newspaper and radio interviews that require the candidate to spend long hours studying the tough issues that inevitably will be raised.

On and on it goes, and all the while, the candidate must run from a 7:00 A.M. breakfast talk to a midday panel to an afternoon reception and a 7:00 P.M. dinner. As the election approaches, one eighteen-hour day will disappear into another, as audiences of senior citizens are replaced by realtors, then teachers, then students. The exhausting merry-go-round doesn't stop until the Wednesday morning after the election, when the candidate wakes and realizes that hundreds of thank-you notes must be written, legislative leadership selection is on the horizon, and bills must soon be filed.

FUND-RAISING

Needless to say, the candidate needs help, mostly unpaid, and that is not always easy to come by. So the development of a core of reliable supporters, even a small one, is absolutely necessary. One of their primary tasks will be to raise money. Generally, the sources are likely to be the same in most House and Senate contests, namely, family, friends, local party members, and interest groups; a small portion will likely come from the state party. There will probably be a handful of cocktail parties or cookouts, with guests asked to pay $10 to $50 to attend. Many of the same folks will be solicited again and again. Some of the food and drinks will be donated, perhaps by a local business or a statewide wine and liquor group. And with some luck, the governor, attorney general, secretary of state, or a congressional officeholder will show up to swell the crowd and attract the local media; news stories provide good visibility and are cost-free. Maybe, too, a string of statehouse lobbyists will be invited but fail to show up, sending their $50 or $100 checks nonetheless.

Local funds derived from $5, $25, and $50 gifts from friends and party members can amount to thousands of dollars, but rarely enough to win. Money must also come from interest groups and their political action committees. Many candidates will solicit the money; they simply ask for it. Some, primarily incumbents (especially those who are in positions of leadership or are chairs of House and Senate committees), will receive it unsolicited, even if their opposition is weak or nonexistent. For example, in a 1994 contest in House District 21, Republican veteran and House Speaker Chuck Berry ran unopposed. Berry received $19,534 in campaign contributions, most of it from political action committees. Senate President Tom Norton was also unopposed in both the primary and the general election. He received over $30,000 in contributions, mostly from PACs, and spent just over $11,000, running against nobody.[14]

In 1992, 58 percent of all candidate contributions for House seats came from political action committees; in the Senate, it was 65 percent. This contrasts with just 29 percent from PACs in the 1986 governor's contest and 25 percent in the other 1986 statewide contests. The PAC role in the state races is almost twice what it is in congressional races.

Incumbents are the chief beneficiaries. In 1992, 73 percent of incumbents' funding came from PACs, and challengers garnered just 40 percent of their receipts from such interest groups. Most interest groups give to both parties, sometimes in the same legislative district. In 1986, Mountain Bell, for example, gave contributions ranging from $50 to $800 to virtually every member of the General Assembly, sometimes in more than one installment. They clearly like to go with the odds and cover all the bets.[15]

From the candidates' perspective, it is difficult to mount much of a campaign without PAC money, and although there are literally hundreds of interest groups that contribute to legislative campaigns, a few large ones dominate the giving. The Common Cause campaign reform measure (Amendment 15) adopted by the voters in 1996 changed that for the 1998 election. But in 1992, the most generous PAC donors were, in order, the Colorado Trial Lawyers Association, the Colorado Association of Realtors, the Colorado Education Association, the AFL-CIO, Colorado Concerns, and the Colorado Medical Society. The gifts from these groups show up on the candidates' contribution lists in most legislative districts in the state.

Interestingly, candidates have often received campaign funding from one another, due, in part, to the fact that candidates may not personally retain excess campaign money. In 1994, open-seat House candidate Bill Swenson received campaign donations from the campaign coffers of incumbents Norma Anderson, Russell George, Pat Sullivan, Steve Acquafresca, Vickie Agler, Jeanne Adkins, Tim Foster, Phil Pankey, and Tom Blickensderfer. He also received a donation from the reelection fund of U.S. House member Scott McInnis. Indeed, the McInnis campaign shared its donations with state legislative candidates Ken Chlouber, Tim Foster, Joyce Lawrence, Marilyn Musgrave, and Gigi Dennis.[16] In a 1995 local school board election in Larimer County, state Senator Bob Schaffer donated to a slate of candidates out of both his state Senate campaign fund and his fund from a failed 1994 lieutenant governor's chase.

It's been a dizzying cycle for campaign money, and donors can never be sure whose political fortunes their cash will be advancing. While citizens contribute their own money, and PACs pass out either corporate profits or bundled employee donations, officeholders generally transfer somebody else's gifts rather than their own cash.

Before 1997 when campaign finance laws changed, candidates often concluded a campaign with a substantial sum left over. This obviously positioned them well for the next round of elections, and it also served to discourage quality opposition. Incumbents have all sorts of advantages as it is, ranging from an established campaign organization, electoral experience, and connections with PACs to name identification with the voters and attention from the media. When they could head into an election with a bundle of cash already in the bank, they were all the more formidable to potential opponents.

Here are a few examples from the 1994 election. Veteran Western Slope Senator Tilie Bishop ran unopposed in both the primary and general election, yet he took in $49,615 in contributions, mostly from political action committees. Bishop spent $23,785, and was thus left with $25,630 in the bank. Senate President Tom Norton was also unopposed in both the primary and general elections, and he spent just $11,325 of the $30,312 given to his campaign. Senator Ed Perlmutter received a whopping $90,808, spent $77,293, and thus left $13,515 in the bank for use later. Perlmutter did face opposition in the November general election. Senator Stan Matsunaka, who successfully challenged incumbent Jim Roberts, took in more than Perlmutter, $95,289.95, but spent every penny in a very tight contest.[17]

The same pattern prevails in the House. Following the 1994 election, for example, Debbie Allen ended with a positive balance of more than $10,000, Jeanne Faatz ended with over $7,500 to the good, and Bill

Jerke was in excess of $7,000 in the black. Doug Friednash collected over $100,000 and concluded the campaign with a surplus of around $15,000, which is more than many candidates spend for an entire race.[18]

For a few candidates, the numbers run in the opposite direction. In 1992 incumbent Senator Bob Schaffer found himself in an unexpectedly tight contest and spent $3,000 more than he took in. Senator Al Meikeljohn went over $10,000 beyond his collections, and their Senate colleague Pat Pascoe exceeded her contributions by over $15,000. In many such instances the excess of spending over contributions is covered by the positive balances from prior election years. In others, it constitutes campaign debt that may well be retired by donations received after the election.

The state Republican and Democratic parties can usually be counted on to provide some help to candidates. But it is not much and is often in the form of services rather than money. For example, the state parties usually try to recruit candidates for all 100 House and Senate districts. They will provide prospective candidates with statistical data on registration and voting patterns within the district. During a campaign, they will often help with printing and mailings, providing labels, mailing lists, and door-to-door walking lists. They will help write copy and sometimes design literature that can be tailored for individual candidates and districts. In the November 1988 election, for example, the Colorado Republican party assisted several candidates with last-minute mailings of negative leaflets that blasted Democratic opponents and carried the return address of the state party headquarters in Denver. Similarly, the Democratic governor hosted a breakfast and strategy session for his party's legislative candidates, complete with photo sessions and endorsement language ideally suited for campaign literature. For the 1994 election the national Democratic party put some money into the state to seek to narrow the party's numerical disadvantage in the General Assembly.

The state parties also help candidates plan and structure campaigns and will usually target a dozen or so districts that promise to feature close contests that appear winnable. They will put extra resources behind the candidates in these targeted districts.

Actual cash help from the state parties is usually minimal. Lately, the legislative caucuses themselves have moved more directly into the business of raising funds to support legislative candidates. In this regard, Colorado is following practices in the U.S. Congress and many other states. In the fall of 1987, Republicans in the Colorado Senate held a shindig at the Denver Radisson Hotel, charging $100 per ticket and marketing them through lobbyists. The Republican House leadership planned a similar effort soon after and reportedly raised around

$100,000. In 1994 and 1995 their fund-raisers included a "Fiesta" with a taco bar for $75 admission, a chili cook-off for another $75, and a dessert auction. Democrats held similar fun-for-all events.[19] When the legislative session begins, party fund-raisers must, by law, stop. So just before the 1997 session kicked off, both parties in both houses scheduled events, all four on the same day.[20]

Fund-raising isn't easy. In an election year, each party's candidates for a host of offices and the county and state party organizations themselves are all competing for money. Candidates for county offices, state House and Senate districts, the U.S. House and Senate, and perhaps even the presidency all hit up the same people, and both asking and giving can get old in a hurry.

Candidates, like PAC contributors and lobbyists, must, by law, report their receipts and expenditures periodically to the secretary of state's office. The contributions report of House District 47 candidate Jim Brown, an incumbent who was defeated in 1986, illustrates a typical pattern. Early in the campaign, Representative Brown's committee held an outdoor barbecue to raise money. Dozens of donors came up with $50 to $100 to help consume $1,000 worth of lamb chops. Some of these were locals from the Fort Collins and Larimer County area. Some were from local businesses, such as Markley Motors, John Clarke Photography, and Anheuser-Busch. Others were from political action committees, like the Colorado Beer Distributors PAC, the Wine and Spirit Wholesalers, and the Mountain Bell PAC. Still others were contract lobbyists—Frank DeFilippo, Wally Stealey, Diane Rees, and the firm of Hays, Hays & Wilson. Candidates in other races gave, too, including state Senators Jim Beatty and Dave Wattenberg and Representatives Paul Schauer, Lewis Entz, Pat Grant, and Chris Paulson. In all, Brown raised nearly $8,000 serving those lamb chops.

Other political action committees, lobbyists, businesses, legislators, and citizens gave later, and the campaign ultimately collected $28,758. Among the later donors were House Speaker Bledsoe, the state Republican party, an organ of the national Republican party, and out-of-state groups like Phillips Petroleum, Chevron Corporation, Conoco, the Tobacco Institute, Philip Morris, Inc., the Santa Fe and Union Pacific Railroads, and the National Rifle Association. The Colorado Association of Realtors, Adolph Coors Company, and the Northern Colorado Home Builders each came up with $1,000, and Colorado Concern gave $2,000. Of course, candidate Brown was not the only one to receive contributions from large interest groups. His opponent, former Representative Peggy Reeves, whom he defeated in 1984 only to lose to her in 1986, raised $18,613, $10,050 of which came from political action committees, including $5,000 from the Colorado Education

Association.

Brown's report also detailed the costs associated with a competitive campaign. He spent roughly $5,000 on brochures and printing, $7,000 on radio advertising, $3,000 for newspaper ads, and over $6,200 for labels and mailing. There were also bills for invitations to that lamb chop dinner and for the chops themselves, for photography and paint and a string of miscellaneous items. Together, Brown and Reeves raised over $47,000 in their pursuit of what then was a $17,500-per-year job. But of course, the salary and accompanying expense allowances aren't the real prize. Nor was the $47,000 their own money.[21]

MONEY AND THE LAW

Colorado law requires PACs to report their political gifts. Until recently, corporations that gave from their general fund were not required to report, but a Colorado Supreme Court decision and subsequent legislation have changed that. Until 1997 there were no contribution or spending limits, and this became a political issue in Colorado, in other states, and in national elections.

In the 1996 session, the General Assembly adopted a campaign reform policy that limited contributions from individuals, PACs, parties, corporations, and labor unions. Adoption of such a policy proved politically impossible for years, but finally, as Colorado Common Cause was working to adopt one through the initiative process, the legislature acted. The new law limited contributions to $1,000 for House candidates and $2,500 for candidates for the state Senate.

But the Common Cause initiative, Statutory Proposal 15, passed anyway in November 1996 and imposed even lower limits. Contributions from individuals and PACs were limited to $200 per election cycle in both House and Senate races. There were also limits on contributions from the political parties of $10,000 for the House and $15,000 for the Senate. Contributions from other candidates, unions, and corporations were prohibited altogether. In addition, money carried over from a prior campaign was counted as PAC contributions, and candidates were limited in the total amount of PAC money they may receive to $15,000 in the Senate and $10,000 in the House.

The new initiated campaign reform measure, supported by two-thirds of the voters in 1996, underwent a lengthy court challenge. Two dozen plaintiffs, ranging from the Republican party and Colorado Right to Life to the Colorado Education Association and Democratic State Senator Bill Thiebaut of Pueblo, challenged the act as an unconstitutional limitation on expression—on free speech. Common Cause and the state's attorney general defended the measure.

The plaintiffs' beef with the law was clear, as were their motives.

They claimed that money is needed to get one's message out during an election, and excessively low contribution limits hamper the ability to get the word out; they restrict expression, or speech, in constitutional terms. The defendants, on the other hand, argued that the past pattern of giving and spending in elections has had a corrupting influence on the state's politics.

In 1997 testimony at the trial, the defendants received a boost when it was revealed that campaign contributions traveled a strange path that hid the identity of the donors. In 1996 tobacco interests gave money to the Colorado Senate Republican Election Committee. That committee, in turn, shipped money to former Republican state Senator, now lobbyist, Steve Durham's consulting firm, Colorado Winning Edge. Durham sent funds to the Colorado Republicans for Choice PAC, which then contributed to the senatorial campaign fund of Republican candidate Fran Raudenbush.

The shipment of political money was not just a Republican party enterprise. State Senator Bill Thiebaut, a Democrat, said that he received $1,000 from R. J. Reynolds with the request that he send it on to Democratic state Senate candidate Rocky Germano of Arvada. Thiebaut, like many others, defended this sort of activity and his opposition to the newly initiated limitations by noting that "you can't elect people without money."[22]

The new limits altered the way candidates and interest groups alike approached elective politics in 1998. A variety of groups, including several of the big donors of the past, organized so-called independent campaign operations in attempts to shape the General Assembly's membership to their liking. Reports following the 1998 election revealed the pattern. Also, candidates themselves had to look to an expanded base of contributors, as each one was limited to donations of $200 per election cycle. The positive aspect of this was clearly the probability that more citizens participated in the process. The downside was the increased fund-raising time costs for the candidates themselves, and the proliferation of "independent expenditures" by advocates who operated independently of the candidates and who were thus beyond the control of the candidates.

Indeed, the 1998 elections, the very first ones following the adoption of the campaign reform measure, saw an explosion in independent expenditure activity. Longtime Republican activists set up three such committees, all claiming to collect money and operate only to "educate" the public. "Colorado Wins" was established by two former Republican legislators, named Cliff Dodge and Steve Durham. Dodge spent the 1998 legislative session as advisor to Senate President Ray Powers, and Durham continued as a lobbyist. They sought large and unreported contributions by way of a solicitation letter from Senate President–to–be Ray Powers in which the importance of maintaining Republican party control of the Senate was emphasized.

"Colorado Votes" was set up by past Republican party chairman Don Bain and Chris Paulson, former Republican House floor leader. "Centennial Spirit" was the child of Republican Congressman Scott McInnis, past Republican Secretary of State Natalie Meyer, and, again, Don Bain, among others.

Obviously none of these groups, like their Democratic party counterparts, were truly nonpartisan. But under the law, and with opportunities to pour money into candidate campaigns now severely limited, so-called educational organizations could, and did, proliferate and pour hundreds of thousands of dollars into the state elections.

The political establishment's distaste for the Amendment 15 election reforms was very evident in the 1999 legislative session when legislation was introduced to modify the law. Amendment 15 was statutory, not constitutional, so it was subject to change by the legislature.

Legislators objected that the contribution limits were unrealistically low and that this led to spending by independent groups whose political messages were beyond the control of candidates. The attempt to change the law was a highly contentious issue, and it finally died as the two chambers could not agree on precisely what to change. Some legislators wanted to allow higher individual contributions, some favored an enriched role for the political parties, others pushed to let corporate and union funds back in, and still others argued whether the matter should be put to a popular vote.

The 1999 bill died, but the issue remained very much alive, and in the 2000 session the legislature did rewrite the campaign finance law. The bill was sponsored by Republican House Speaker Russell George. Republicans supported it, Democrats did not. Basically, the new law allows much higher individual contributions to candidates and political parties, and allows union and corporate donations as well. Individual contributions to Senate candidates are limited to $1,500 and for House candidates, the limit is $1,250. Contributions to the political parties may go as high as $25,000. Common Cause was understandably unhappy with the liberalization of the money flow and promised another initiated measure for the November 2000 election.

CAMPAIGNING

Through all the problems of organizing, developing literature, enlisting volunteers, handling questionnaires, dealing with the media, studying the issues, and trying to raise money, the candidate must spend an increasing amount of time on the street as the election draws near.

Signs, media advertisements, and mailings are important, but there is no substitute for door-to-door visits by the candidate. Not every doorbell must be rung, and such canvassing is certainly more important in some contests than in others. But personal introduction is the surest route to success. Door after door, block after block, week after week, one pair of shoes after another—that is what it takes. And if the candidate is seeking a seat in one of the spacious rural districts, the campaign may require literally thousands of miles of driving, as well. It is no wonder, then, that after elections candidates are exhausted, their cars are littered with campaign paper, and all the dishes in their kitchens are dirty.

It is no wonder, too, that legislators learn to hate campaigning. Indeed, that is the reason given by one long-term veteran, Betty Neale, for retiring. Neale retired from the House after eighteen years, noting that while she had not tired of the legislature, she was sick of the campaigns. "It has become a chore to me," she explained.[23] The dislike for the tiring campaigns can be seen in the increase in legislative retirements following each redistricting. For many members new district lines mean new territory for them and often the veterans of multiple campaigns just aren't up to plowing new ground. So they make redistricting the opportunity to call it quits.

Candidates know the importance of door-to-door campaigning and personal contact with voters. Most don't like it, but they do it anyway, especially in tight races. A good example of this is provided by the response of Republican Colorado Senator Jack Fenlon when he faced a challenger in the primary race. He immediately set about walking his district and knocking on doors, even while the legislature was still in session. Another is Peggy Reeves. A veteran of seven House campaigns, she ran for an open Senate seat in 1996. Half of her Senate district was new territory. She responded with a vigorous door-to-door walking program and covered nearly the entire new part and much of what had been her House territory. She won easily.

Walking a district is tiring, and, since much of it is done around the dinner hour and on weekends when people are busy with family or personal matters, candidates can expect a few unpleasant receptions tossed in among the many pleasant, if brief, chats with constituents. They can also expect surprises. Just weeks before a recent election, incumbent House member Peggy Reeves ended up in the hospital emergency room with a dog bite. Frank DeFilippo was told by a voter that her dog never bites, just as the dog was munching on his leg. Former Senator Ray Peterson let a German Shepherd bite holes in his clipboard to escape holes in his body. Former Senate President Ted Strickland had a voter answer her door dressed in absolutely nothing.[24]

Throughout a campaign, candidates must make decisions about how to present themselves to the voting public. They often feel an urge to communicate with voters in some detail about the issues and the problems of the state. Sooner or later, though, most discover that such an approach is extremely time-consuming and has a limited political payoff. Name identification, impressions, and image become the name of the game; thus, campaign strategies emphasize the visual and the short and sweet.

In one of his state Senate campaigns, for example, Bob Schaffer ran a half-page community newspaper ad sporting the names of dozens of persons who allegedly supported him. Included were the names of lobbyists and state party personnel from outside the district, and the names of children. The relevance of the names to voters in the district was beside the point. What mattered was that the list of "endorsements" would have a visual impact and imply extensive support.

The major difficulty facing candidates who challenge incumbents is the lack of name identification. Most voters know very little about legislatures and legislative candidates at all, but if they know anything, it will be the incumbent's name. And name identification alone often provides the only cue the citizen has in the voting booth in November. Challengers normally lack even that rudimentary advantage. To overcome this, they need money—and lots of it—to put their names before the public on signs, mailings, and media ads. But this effort is often thwarted by another issue—the propensity of the big contributors to put their money on incumbents.

As a result, it is even more critical for the challenger to invest heavily in shoe leather. Some begin planning their campaigns six months to a year in advance, although others may not get going until just before the April nominating assemblies, especially in noncompetitive districts where the minority party has a difficult time recruiting candidates. For many sitting lawmakers, especially those who know well in advance that they plan to run for reelection, the campaign will begin exactly one day after their last election. Thus, reelection is a constant preoccupation in the Capitol. Certainly the focus on an upcoming election becomes more overt later in the session in election years, but the preoccupation is always there. Indeed, the parties run what are called "incumbency programs," which are planned strategies to keep the sitting legislators safe for the next election by keeping them continuously visible in the home district via news releases, personal visits, questionnaires, and newsletters.

CAMPAIGN ORGANIZATION

Candidates' campaign styles and organizations differ, just as their districts, their personalities, and their backgrounds vary. Republican Representative Joan Green served in the House for two terms, from 1984 through 1988. Twenty-seven years old when first elected, Representative Green had a political science degree from Colorado State University, where she had been a member of the college Young Republicans. As a student, she had worked on the campaigns of former Larimer County Representative Ron Strahle, former U.S. Representative Jim Johnson, Larimer County Sheriff Jim Black, and Republican U.S. Senator Bill Armstrong. She had also worked for one year in the Chicago office of Ronald Reagan's presidential campaign. When Republican Representative Jack Fenlon ran for the Colorado Senate in the Aurora area, his House seat opened up, and Joan Green decided to run for it. Although she faced opposition in both the primary and the general election in November, she said there was never a doubt in her mind that she would win. She had thought of running for a long time and knew the district well.

In preparation for the nomination stage, Green talked to all the assembly delegates. For the general election, she walked two-thirds of the precincts door-to-door, concentrating on the Republican and swing areas. Her election staff was small. Her father managed the campaign, and she, her family, and a few friends constituted the core of the campaign. She stated that when pursuing a goal like this, "You've got to have the fire in your guts."

Former Senate Minority Leader Ray Peterson was first elected to the Senate in 1982 at the age of forty-four. He, too, was a Colorado State University graduate. Peterson had been active in a number of Denver Democratic party activities and had served as Denver County vice chairman, a member of the Denver County Democratic Party Election Committee, the Colorado Democratic State Central Committee and Executive Committee, and more. But like Joan Green, Ray Peterson had never held an elective political office.

Peterson's campaign staff was more structured than Green's. He set the general parameters, but left it to a campaign manager to run the campaign. In addition, his staff included a volunteer coordinator, a finance director, a person in charge of literature, a treasurer, and others. His candidacy was announced officially on April 1, 1982, but work had already begun the previous February, six months before the campaign was in full swing. In fact, the entire campaign was planned well in advance. So, too, was the cash flow. Precincts were categorized as Democratic, swing, Republican, and so forth. Certain ones were targeted for special attention.

Like Green's, Senator Peterson's campaign core was relatively small, consisting of a dozen or so people who met weekly. However, he had a much larger group of volunteers. Campaign finance was not a problem for Senator Peterson in either his 1982 campaign or in his 1986 reelection effort. In 1982, after it appeared that he might well be the winner, some political action committees jumped on the bandwagon with late contributions. And in 1986, when he ran as an incumbent, PAC funds came in unsolicited, sometimes even twice from the same source.

Senator Ed Perlmutter is a Colorado native who never left home and in 1994 ran a state Senate campaign with organization and funding of massive proportions. His district, Senate District 20, encompassed the west Denver suburbs of Wheat Ridge and Golden and part of Arvada.

Perlmutter was supported by a campaign contingent that had a steering committee of twenty-five persons. He received contributions from 450 people, taking in over $90,000. He faced and defeated Barry Arrington in a decidedly nasty contest. Two years later Arrington won a House seat and after a single term chose to run for Congress.

Ed Perlmutter represented the area in which he grew up. His family was in the construction business, and was well known in the community. Perlmutter graduated from high school in Jefferson County and received both a bachelor's and a law degree from the University of Colorado. He practices law in the Denver area and is a vice president in his law firm. For years Perlmutter was active in Democratic party politics and in a wide variety of community activities.

Ed Perlmutter decided to run for the state Senate, he said, because his experiences as a kid had given him an itch for politics, and because he'd come to believe that he owed public service to a community and state that for a long time had been good to him and to his family. The community and state were good places and, Perlmutter said, he wanted to help keep them that way. He saw himself as a political moderate, someone with both a quality-of-life and a business perspective.

Perlmutter's campaign organization was extensive by state legislative standards. He had a twenty-five-member steering committee and a much larger army of volunteers. Two people served as campaign co-chairs and beyond that, steering committee members divided the labor for such chores as fund-raising, volunteer coordination, scheduling, yard signs, and more. Some on the campaign were experienced and provided perspective and stability to the enterprise; others were novices who brought enthusiasm.

Members of this extensive campaign organization, an enterprise that Perlmutter said was large enough to run a congressional campaign, "did it all." That allowed candidate Perlmutter to walk the district, participate in such activities as parades and other such civic events, and deal with the candidate debates and other public appearances. The organization left him free of the worry of financing the campaign and the inevitable blizzard of details.

Money, it turned out, was no problem. First of all, others handled most of the fund-raising chores, especially once the campaign pace accelerated. Perlmutter did work on fund-raising from February to May but thereafter he did none of it, except to speak at fund-raising events. His initial effort was in the form of a kickoff event attended by 300 family members and friends in Wheat Ridge. After that the money "just came in."

Ed Perlmutter spent a lot of time on the streets. He walked fifty of the sixty-two precincts in the Senate district, stopping, he estimated, at some 20,000 homes. Generally he walked with two or three other people.

The door-to-door efforts began in June and continued up to election time. Perlmutter started in what he called "easy precincts," those with heavy and thus "friendly" Democratic party majorities. From there he went on to so-called swing precincts that contained a large proportion of unaffiliated voters. He walked a number of heavily Republican areas as well. He was generally well received because, in his words, "I've lived there all my life and my family is well known and knows a lot of the people." Near to November the attention was shifted back to Democratic party territory to help get out the vote.

Perlmutter's 1994 opponent was Barry Arrington, a combative social-agenda right-wing Republican who in 1996 was elected to the Colorado House of Representatives. Arrington raised $50,000 to oppose Perlmutter, with significant contributions from the National Rifle Association; the NRA also assisted Arrington with a computerized phone-call system. In his own estimation Perlmutter was the more visible of the two in parades and with yard signs.

Debates between the two candidates were combative and the campaign featured one ugly and widely publicized episode. During a parade some Arrington partisans confronted Perlmutter's children and characterized the candidate as a murderer—"Perlmurder"—for his stand on reproductive choice. In another instance Arrington contended in a candidate debate that the Perlmutter campaign was organized and financed by the "radical homosexual community."

The campaign organization sent out four mailings, two of them prior to the "early voting" deadline. Some of the mailings were specially tailored and targeted to certain groups—seniors, for instance. Besides his door-to-door visits, Perlmutter spent time in front of grocery stores passing out literature including maps of the district. The campaign did no polling, although it did receive some data from interest groups that did so. Perlmutter won with 54 percent of the vote.

Since winning in November 1994, Senator Perlmutter has spent some time trying to maintain contact with the constituency and staying visible. He did some walking in the district, distributing legislative newsletters, and spent more time at weekend and evening "town meetings."

Like other legislators, Perlmutter says it is hard to find sufficient time for his law practice, his family, direct legislative work, and outreach within the district.

In anticipation of his 1998 reelection bid, Senator Perlmutter started in late 1997 to host fund-raisers. The new Campaign Practices Reform Act adopted by voters in 1996 restricts donations to state legislative candidates to $100 each for the primary and general election. Perlmutter's objective was to hold the fall events plus four or five "announcement" fund-raisers soliciting contributions up to the $100 limit, and have $50,000 "in the bank" by June. After that, he figured, sufficient additional money to support the campaign would flow in from PACs and individuals. In addition, with the bulk of the money in the bank, he could concentrate on voter contact, as he did in 1994.

In his initial 1998 spring fund-raisers, Perlmutter met with some frustration at the hands of mother nature as two of his first few events were snowed out. They were rescheduled and while the crowds were good and the attendees willing to contribute, the new election laws kept the cash flow somewhat low. Perlmutter's fund-raising invitations stated that he would accept contributions up to $100, the legal limit. Twenty-five- and fifty-dollar checks were the norm. Whereas Perlmutter was able to raise over $90,000 in 1996 from 450 donors, he estimated that for 1998 it would take 1,000 contributions to reach his 1998 target of $75,000. While the new law is clearly making political fund-raising more difficult for candidates, it is also, in Perlmutter's estimation, broadening the base of citizen participation in campaign financing.

Ed Perlmutter won reelection in 1998, again with 54 percent of the vote, but he did not get a free ride. A former liberal Democrat-turned-Republican challenged him with a high-profile campaign. Perlmutter said the challenger was recruited by two members of the legislature's Republican right wing, Senator Jim Congrove and House member Mark Paschall.

As happens with all elected officeholders, Perlmutter found that some elements of his initial 1994 political organization had melted away. Some folks moved. Others assumed responsibilities that robbed them of time to support the reelection bid. And of course many of the campaign novices who infused the 1994 effort with rookie enthusiasm were no long rookies.

Gayle Berry is a Republican. She was elected to the House of Representatives in 1996, filling a seat held previously by Democrat Dan Prinster who, in a desire to spend more time with his young family, chose not to run for reelection. Had he decided to seek reelection, Berry would have been his opponent. They were acquaintances; indeed she characterized Prinster as a friend, but a friend she planned to oppose politically, and she told him so.

Berry represents a district on Colorado's Western Slope. Her district, House District 55, is in Mesa County and contains a small portion of the city of Grand Junction plus some rural territory and several small towns. Representative Berry was born in nearby Fruita and grew up in the area, attending Fruita High School and Mesa State College. Her district was her native territory.

Gayle Berry's interest and participation in electoral politics were the consequences of working for and with politicians, and hanging around with them. Before becoming a candidate herself, she helped others on campaigns, including those of former Representative and House Majority Leader Tim Foster, state Senator Tilman Bishop, a county commissioner, and the Mesa County district attorney.

Occupationally and politically, Berry was closely associated with the Foster family. She had worked a spell for Bill Foster, the father of Tim, the former representative. Bill Foster was a lawyer, was active in Mesa County politics, and once served as that county's Republican party chairman. So Gayle Berry spent much of her time in the company of Republican political activists.

In 1993 Gayle Berry was running her own business, a secretarial support service. Representative Tim Foster came by and presented her with a form for enrollment in the Republican Party Leadership Program. He told her she should be thinking about running for office someday, and the experience would help. Indeed, the program functions as a farm team for Republican candidates. Her 1993–1994 Leadership class had forty participants, including Doug Dean, Joyce Lawrence, and Larry Schwarz, who all ended up as members of the Colorado House. Following the Republican Leadership experience, Berry attended a 1995 campaign management program.

Berry began her run at the District 55 seat in September 1995, a full fourteen months prior to the election. By state legislative standards, her campaign organization was typical. The team included herself and her husband at the time, along with two co-managers, both of whom were longtime friends and paralegals she had known in Bill Foster's law firm.

In addition, Peggy Foster, the wife of the senior Foster and the mother of Representative Tim, was a core adviser. Besides Berry, her husband, and the Foster crowd, her organization included a volunteer coordinator, a parade coordinator, a special events coordinator, and a person who handled scheduling. The group met regularly in Berry's business office to review the agenda, make plans, and go over a range of specific items. Candidate Berry enjoyed a good flow of offers of help. As they came, she recorded them on a form and passed them on to her volunteer coordinator.

Unlike Senator Ed Perlmutter, whose organization largely freed him of the onerous task of hustling money, Gayle Berry did her own fund-raising. Overall she raised $34,000, $15,000 of that from individual contributions with the remaining $19,000 coming from political action committees and businesses. Tim Foster served as her honorary chairman and both helped her and pressured her to raise the money. She pulled in $3,000 during the first three months of the campaign, but then to avoid political problems and excessive attention, she relaxed her efforts during the 1996 January to May legislative session.

Berry herself made phone calls soliciting campaign contributions. She also held some fund-raisers, such as a May 1996 tea at which she raised $2,000. Attendees were Republicans mostly, with the invitation list drawn from the volunteer list and her assemblage of personal friends. She picked twenty people from the volunteer list and asked each of them to invite ten others. Besides, the contributors received door prizes. The turnout, like the money, was good. As a native of the area, someone who was well known in Republican circles, and with a solid campaign organization in place, Berry faced no primary opposition. Only martyrs and persons with little else to do run uphill against tough political odds.

Berry's campaign featured what most campaigns feature—door-to-door voter contact, direct mailings, yard signs and billboards, exposure at public events, and occasional media advertising. Door-to-door walking by the candidate is enormously exhausting and time-consuming, but it is generally recognized as the single most effective campaign technique. Gayle Berry started her walking in July, roughly five months prior to the election. Sometimes she used "walking lists" showing the names of actual registered voters. But sometimes, in small towns like De Beque for example, she just hit every door. The technique is to greet the resident, leave some literature, and move on quickly. Berry figured that she covered half of the district, including part of Grand Junction and all of several small towns.

Like all candidates, she logged some interesting experiences. One De Beque gentleman asked her immediately if she was a Democrat or Republican. When the answer was Republican he picked up his coffee cup, turned, and told her that they needn't talk anymore. To that Berry assured him that "when I'm elected I'll work just as hard for you as for anyone else."

The campaign, Gayle Berry said, "literally littered the district with yard signs, some 500 in all." Her yard sign coordinator was a property manager, so placements were plentiful. She also advertised on three commercial billboards.

Berry's organization issued several different types of direct mail. Some were "newsletters" reporting the progress of the campaign, announcing upcoming parades or other events, and asking recipients if they'd like to volunteer. Each mailing included some commentary on public issues as well. Among the prime targets of the mailings were newly registered voters.

Like all campaigns that are any fun, Berry's featured some gimmicks. She had printed raspberry-colored T-shirts and gave them to volunteers. Who knows how many voters connected the color with the candidate. Thirty of her berry-colored T-shirters marched en masse in a county parade. She also ordered boxes of handheld fans resembling stop signs. This turned out to be fortuitous, as they were available for distribution at a July Fourth parade where the temperature ran over 90 degrees.

Gayle Berry received a number of helpful endorsements. The Mesa Valley Educational Association supported her, in a somewhat unusual move; most often teachers' groups back Democrats. In addition the Home Builders backed her, as did U.S. Congressman Scott McInnis, state Senator Tilman Bishop, and former Colorado House members Tim Foster, Jim Robb, and Ed Carpenter.

Berry's opponent, Joseph Marie, worked hard and was visible during the campaign but proved to be no match at all, even though Democrat Prinster had held the seat previously. Berry won by a count of 17,060 to 6,614. Actually, the Mesa County Democratic party had experienced some difficulty in fielding what they considered a strong candidate. Everyone knew that Berry had deep roots in the area, was well organized, and had money. Under such circumstances political parties often struggle to find someone knowingly willing to be a sacrificial lamb, and that's what Marie was.

In spite of her preparation, organization, and money, Gayle Berry worried throughout the campaign that she might lose the election. She had seen campaigns in the past where the underdog had seemingly risen from the dead, and so, she said, she would wake up nights with the thought that she could be the victim of such a turn of events. Of course this problem is not unique to Berry; virtually all candidates with opposition report some measure of sleep disorder, a malady that seems to grow as November draws nearer.

Elected officials never stop thinking about the next election, Gayle Berry included. Her belief, she said, was that by doing the representation job well and being very responsible to constituents, matters would take care of themselves. In the summer of 1997 she supplemented that approach with a constituent newsletter that reported a summary of the session and, in 1998, before the coming election, she did it again.

Representative Berry reported just minor surprise at what she found when she assumed her role in the Capitol. The fast pace of legislative life was something of a surprise, as was the fact that about 40 percent of the bills were heard in the last week leading up to deadlines. But prior to her election she had served as chairperson of the local Chamber of Commerce governmental affairs committee, and that experience, plus the extensive pre-session orientation provided for newly elected members, led her to expect what was coming in her first session.

In 1998 incumbent Gayle Berry was unopposed in both the primary and general election. She was a supporter of Russell George as the new House Speaker and was rewarded with a seat on the powerful six-member Joint Budget Committee.

After the Election

Immediately after an election, the winners must worry about completing thank-you calls and notes to the dozens, even hundreds, who have helped ensure the victory. But for many candidates, exhaustion sets in just about then, making this a tough job. In addition, the winners must now face the biennial intraparty scramble for leadership positions. This can quickly consume a good deal of time and mental energy. Furthermore, the winners must concern themselves with the substance of the upcoming January session and lay plans for the bills they will introduce. There will be requests from lobbyists to carry certain bills. The legislators will also want to be responsive to any legislation sought by interests within their own district. And they will be ever-conscious of the implications of their decisions and their records in light of the next reelection effort.

The Campaign Never Ends

Once in Denver, legislators begin immediately to prepare for the next election. Ultimately, everything they do serves other, generally more primary, purposes, but reelection is always high on the list of motivations.

Consequently, questionnaires are sent out. The state party may coordinate this effort for Republican lawmakers, but Democrats do it, too. The alleged purpose is to identify citizens' views on a variety of issues, and the responses do impact legislative behavior from time to time. Colorado Springs Republican Senator Ray Powers voted for a year-round daylight saving time bill based upon constituent responses to his questionnaire; he would not otherwise have supported the bill. But everyone knows (and lawmakers acknowledge privately) that the real reason for mailing questionnaires is to campaign—to get the incumbent's name into the homes of voters through the pretext of statesman-like solicitation of citizen opinion.

Even the design of questionnaires serves political purposes. A questionnaire paid for by the state Republican party, for example, phrased a question this way: "Which of [Democratic] Governor Romer's tax increase proposals would you support to improve Colorado's highways?" The point, of course, was to paint the governor as a tax advocate.

Legislators are sensitive to mail and phone calls, but are quick to note which ones are from their own district and which are not. A few legislators have routinely piled mail and phone messages on their desks, only to unceremoniously dump them in the trash later on. Persons who have witnessed this approach to representation have been amazed. And many lawmakers are exceedingly slow to respond to any contact from persons outside their district, if they respond at all. But most are sensitive in the extreme to any and all contact from citizens within their own district, and they are quick to respond as best they can. "The constituent, the almighty constituent," one observer mused in noting the trigger-quick sensitivity of many legislators to contacts from home.

Sometimes the messages from home express constituent views on a bill or an issue generally. Sometimes they are direct questions. And sometimes they are requests for help. For years, "constituent service" has been a big part of the job for representatives and senators and their army of staffers in the U.S. Congress, providing opportunities, never passed by, to do favors for voters and thus solidify reelection bases.

Although constituent service has not loomed as large in the Colorado legislature, it does seem to be increasing. Legislators are asked whom constituents can contact in the state bureaucracy to resolve specific problems. They are asked to expedite the processing of state agency paperwork (for unemployment compensation, for example). They are asked for data that can be provided by the Legislative Council or the Office of State Planning and Budgeting. Sometimes they are asked for help on a federal matter, so they simply steer citizens to the proper agency of the vast federal bureaucratic establishment or to their congressperson. In 1997, the Legislative Council, the General Assembly's research unit, geared up to help members respond to constituent questions and requests.

Legislators are sensitive to activities in the district. They almost always subscribe to local newspapers and pay close attention to the political reporting. When reporters in the district call, legislators call them back. They may or may not want to talk with them, and they may or may not trust the reporters or appreciate their coverage. But if a message is from the home district and if it can create newsprint, legislators respond.

The lawmakers' sensitivity to the folks back home is constantly evident in their approach to legislation. After the legislature looked at proposals to significantly overhaul the mechanisms of state funding of local school districts, rural Republican Don Ament observed that every legislator was examining the new formula to see how it would affect schools in the home district.

Like members of Congress, legislators take the initiative in many ways to generate visibility for themselves. Some comb local newspapers for events that offer excuses to drop congratulatory notes to constituents. Mailings of congratulatory notes to graduating high school seniors is common. Some hold periodic breakfasts and lunches around the district to give the voters opportunities to discuss matters of public concern. No matter that very few people show up at these events— the scheduling of the events appears in the newspaper, and that's what matters.

Like members of Congress, state legislators look for ways to let the public know all the good things they are trying to do for their constituents. For example, former state Senator Bob Schaffer from Fort Collins announced that Larimer County would receive two state grants totaling $88,000 for programs for the homeless. Schaffer had been appointed to fill out the remaining year of state Senator Jim Beatty's term after the seven-year veteran resigned. On the announcement date, Schaffer had been in office less than two weeks, but that didn't matter. What did matter was the media coverage that placed his name before the public in a positive way.

As one would expect, the style of campaigns, the cost, the level of energy and organization candidates put into an election, as well as the extent of incumbents' preoccupation with reelection during legislative sessions all vary significantly. Some lawmakers have little ambition for a long-term legislative career and don't worry too much about the next election. Those from noncompetitive districts, and this includes a very large number of legislators, need not worry much, save for an unlikely but always possible primary challenge. Nonetheless, most representatives in some of the rather noncompetitive districts seem to be extremely sensitive to their constituents.

The presence of an election on the horizon has a very profound impact on behavior under the gold dome, especially if control of the legislative and executive branches is divided between the two parties. In legislative sessions preceding November elections, the majority party will make it difficult for minority party members to have their bills passed, trying to deprive them of a record of legislative successes to cite in the upcoming election. In 1994, for example, 63 percent of the bills sponsored by majority House Republicans passed, while just 42 percent of the Democrat's measures made it. Indeed, some Democrats from marginal districts were allegedly "targeted" for the next election, and only 39 percent of their bills passed into law.[25] In 1998 the pattern and the strategy were repeated.

When the governor is a member of the other party, efforts will be made to stop legislation that the chief executive supports, thereby denying the governor highly publicized policy successes. The governor, in turn, will seek to place blame for serious state problems on the shoulders of the legislature, citing its inability to address the needs of the state. And certainly no one wants to be associated with a tax increase just before an election.

The 1998 political donnybrook following the legislature's inability to enact a method to refund excess tax revenues provided a vivid example. A group of right-wing House Republicans refused to move refund legislation, arguing that they'd already compromised with the Democratic governor, and would no more. Romer termed them extremists and said he'd call a special session to get the job done. To that some Republicans said they'd meet, do nothing, and adjourn to await the 1999 session when they thought they'd have a Republican governor. As so often happens, name-calling and political hardball polluted the legislature's agenda.

The interplay between the Republican-controlled General Assembly, Senate President Ted Strickland, and House Speaker Carl "Bev" Bledsoe on the one hand and Democratic Governor Roy Romer on the other also illustrates this phenomenon nicely. Romer won the governorship in 1984, trouncing Republican candidate Ted Strickland in the process. He continued the highly aggressive stance that he assumed during the campaign and pressed for state efforts to revitalize the economy and invest in a new airport, highways, and more. Romer and the Republican-dominated General Assembly struggled to develop and maintain a cooperative posture, something that had been lacking during much of the twelve-year tenure of the former governor, Democrat Dick Lamm. Romer was popular on election day; going into the spring 1988 legislative session, he was more popular than ever. Republicans didn't miss this. State Republican party spokeswoman Lauren Lehman commented: "When somebody is riding that great wave of popularity, we're going to watch him very carefully."

In late March of that year, Romer made it clear that he planned to campaign for Democratic House and Senate candidates in selected districts where his party had opportunities to pick up some seats and where incumbents had supported his highway plans and other policy initiatives. In April, Democratic House member JoAnn Groff introduced the governor's highway legislation, a bill that would have raised $720 million for highway repairs and improvements through higher gasoline taxes, automobile registration fees, and a slight income tax hike. The House Transportation Committee quickly cut it in half by substituting for the Groff-Romer version a tax package drawn up by Republican Transportation Committee Chairman Bud Hover. That, too, died later in a party-line vote in the House Appropriations Committee.

Some weeks later, several House and Senate Republicans attempted to place Romer's original $720 million tax package on the ballot for the November election. They claimed that this would offer a chance to test the Democratic governor's claims that the voters were willing to pay for better roads. But the governor and other Democrats contended that the Republicans were shirking their duty to make a decision and were irresponsibly tossing a complex issue to voters who lacked the information and background to make such a decision. They claimed the Republicans were actually trying to embarrass the governor.

Without question, there are many hardworking legislators whose prime motivation is to serve the people well and solve the state's problems. Nevertheless, neither party is anxious to give the other a chance to enter into an election taking credit for much of anything and certainly not for making great strides in solving the state's problems. This distinctly affects the substance of legislation in an election year and drives the political tactics and rhetoric in the Capitol.

TERM LIMITS

Term limits came to Colorado in the 1990s, just as they did to many other states. Adopted by the voters in 1990, term limits impose an eight consecutive–year limit on members of both chambers. Members can serve more than eight years by laying out four years or more, and then returning, and they may serve in the other chamber after eight consecutive years in the first one. Since the eight-year clock began to run on seated members in 1990, the entire legislative membership was transfused by 1998.

What difference is this making? With respect to the average length of service, not much. In the decade prior to the adoption of these limits the average length of service for House members was four and a half years, and for senators it was six years. Clearly, these numbers are well below the eight-year limit. The impact is in the ascension of inexperienced lawmakers into leadership positions, and the absence of those few long-term veterans with lengthy institutional memories.

One study of the likely impact of the limits hypothesized their imposition one decade earlier and then examined the impact during the 1980s. The results showed that there would be little impact in terms of the identity of committee chairpersons, but that virtually the entire leadership structure would have been wiped out. Specifically, Senate President Strickland and Majority Leader Jeff Wells, along with House Speaker Bledsoe and Majority Leader Strahle, would have been booted out by the limits. So too would such longtime veterans as Senators Meiklejohn and Cole and Representatives Kopel and Knox.[26]

When the term limits hit in 1998, they did impact committees and the leadership, as well as the overall experience level in the House. The House Speaker, Senate President, and both majority party floor leaders were ejected by the limits. So too were eight of the ten chairpersons of House committees of reference, and three of the ten in the Senate. In addition, four of the six members of the powerful Joint Budget Committee were term limited. The influx of twenty-five new House members reduced the aggregate level of House experience, but in the Senate the level stayed much same, because seven of the ten Senate vacancies were filled by former representatives. The longer-term impact of term limits is sure to be greater on the House than on the Senate, because the Senate will continue to be the destination of experienced, and term-limited, House members.

Do term limits, and their impact on members' tenure, make any difference? The answer is clearly "yes." Legislative rules and procedures are complex, and it takes years to master them. Much of the proposed legislation is complicated and can embody a wide range of less-than-obvious, and unintended, consequences. This can be troublesome in such critical areas as tax policy. The volume of work is heavy, with over 600 bills coming into the process annually.

Now with term limits the scramble for leadership positions is virtually continuous, leaders will be less experienced, and the veterans who have mastered both the process and substance of policy areas will be gone. Will novice leaders be able to build coalitions or hold their party members together on critical issues? Who will be there to provide voting cues to freshman members on complex and high-stakes issues?

The answers, of course, are the staff and the lobby corps. Staff members tend to be politically impartial, but they are elected by no one. And lobbyists, by definition, are not there to pursue a public interest but are there to secure special advantages for special groups.

There is some danger, though, in overestimating the consequences of term limits. Colorado's General Assembly has always had membership turnover in the range of 25 to 30 percent and that is not likely to change much. Furthermore, the movement of representatives to the Senate will mute the aggregate loss of legislative experience.

The public attraction to term limits seems to have emerged from a broad national disaffection with careerist politics that was manifest most clearly in the Congress. Ironically, though, when this discontent attached itself to the term-limits movement, the states, which had relatively high turnover anyway, became the targets. This was possible, of course, because in some of the states, but not at the national level, citizens could employ the initiative process to statutorily or constitutionally limit terms.

This irony may turn out to be cruel indeed. Colorado's voters may have used the right bullet to hit the wrong target. Term limits are likely to have little impact on the average length of service of state lawmakers. But they may well roughen the procedural edges of the legislative process itself, especially in the House, by foisting upon it novice leaders, and heightening the advantage of special interests by making lobbyists, not seasoned veteran elected legislators, the founts of historical and policy wisdom. Breweries, utility companies, the insurance industry, banks, and lawyers may replace pools of Republican and Democratic voters and seasoned legislative veterans as the information and cue sources for those who make our laws.

NOTES

1. "Quote of the Day," *Denver Post*, January 28, 1998.
2. Dick Foster, "New District 60 map disputed," *Rocky Mountain News*, February 3, 1998.
3. House Floor, April 29, 1997.
4. *Study of Contributions to 1992 Colorado Legislative Candidates*, Denver, Colorado Common Cause, 1993.
5. Dan Luzadder, "Another House race disputed," *Rocky Mountain News*, December 4, 1998.
6. Fred Brown, "Losing candidate appeals to House for ruling on vote," *Denver Post*, December 4, 1998.
7. Ibid.
8. Ibid.
9. Jason Blevins, "Weld GOP seeks straight, narrow line on character," *Denver Post*, April 20, 1998. See also Burt Hubbard, "Open season on Republican moderates," *Rocky Mountain News*, May 11, 1998.
10. Mike Patty, "Candidate endorses foe," *Rocky Mountain News*, November 4, 1996.
11. Cara DeGette, "Residency dispute threatens lawmaker's Senate hopes," *Denver Post*, March 6, 1998.
12. Ibid.
13. *Rocky Mountain News*, October 26, 1996.
14. See Margaret E. Ackerman and Kenton D. Kuhn, *1996 Colorado Legislative Almanac*, Denver, Colorado Capitol Connection and Ackerman Information Corporation, 1996.
15. Colorado Common Cause, *Contributions*.
16. Ackerman and Kuhn, *Almanac*.
17. Ibid.
18. Ibid.
19. Peter Blake, *Rocky Mountain News*, January 10, 1994.
20. *Rocky Mountain News*, January 1, 1997.
21. Secretary of State reports.
22. See "Spin Cycles," *Westword*, April 16–22, 1998, p. 17.
23. *Rocky Mountain News*, March 21, 1992.
24. *Rocky Mountain News*, April 11, 1992.
25. *Capitol Reporter*, May 18, 1994.
26. John A. Straayer, "Possible Consequences of Legislative Term Limits," *Comparative State Politics*, June 1992, pp. 1–15.

3

Members of the General Assembly

Following each November election, the legislature fills with many new faces and a lot of old ones. The 1997–1998 session began with seventeen freshman legislators in the sixty-five-member House (26 percent). The Senate had five new faces (14 percent), three of whom had served previously in the House. Back in 1988 the freshman class in the House constituted 26 percent of the total; in the Senate, it was 34 percent by the time the vacancies were filled. Legislative turnover of this magnitude is not unusual in state legislatures, but it is clearly higher than in our U.S. Congress, where the incumbent return rate often exceeds 90 percent.

TURNOVER

The turnover rate has a cumulative impact, leaving long-term and highly experienced lawmakers in a distinct minority. At the start of the 1994–1995 session, only twenty-two House members had been there more than four years, only sixteen had served at least six years, and just ten had eight or more years of experience in the General Assembly. In the Senate, only eleven of the thirty-five had served two or more full, four-year terms. Indeed, of all the lawmakers serving in the General Assembly during the 1984–1985 term, just nine representatives and eight senators remained to begin the 1994–1995 term.

In 1998 term limits hit the General Assembly with a vengeance, pushing twenty-seven members out. The House Speaker, Senate President, both majority leaders, and a majority of Joint Budget Committee members and committee chairpersons were among the casualties. In substantial measure, it is an institution of rookies and novices, especially in the House of Representatives.

BACKGROUND

Many of these people may be new to the Colorado legislature, but they are generally not new to government, to politics, and to community activities. A glance at their backgrounds reveals an extensive array of past involvement. Many have worked with local chambers of commerce, state and local boards and commissions, councils of government, hospital and other special district boards, and the two major political parties. They have experience in city and county elective offices and with groups like the Elks, Shriners, Masons, American Legion, VFW, Women's Forum, Farm Bureau, Colorado Cattlemen's Association, American Association of University Women, National Organization for Women, League of Women Voters, Colorado Black Women for Political Action, YMCA, and a seemingly endless string of others.

Lawmakers have diverse and interesting backgrounds apart from politics and also a variety of interests. Chris Paulson's military experiences included the crash landing of an Air Force jet, and Dan Williams is a talented musician. Ted Strickland once played minor league professional baseball; Bob Schaffer paints detailed and intricate Ukrainian eggs.[1] Ken Chlouber is an ultra-marathon runner and pack burro racer, Bill Kaufman dabbles in model railroads, and Peggy Lamm is a target shooter. Barry Arrington holds a black belt in Tae Kwon Do and Gayle Berry sews and lifts weights. Mary Ellen Epps swims, Jeanne Faatz walks, Ken Gordon hikes, Mark Hillman collects baseball cards, Shawn Mitchell climbs rocks, Ron Teck cooks, Lauri Clapp cans jellies, Mark Larson rides motorcycles and so does Lois Trochtrop, Don Lee reads the Bible, Brad Young reads science fiction, Todd Saliman travels, Bill Swenson shoots, Penn Tate fishes, Paul Zimmerman does woodworking, and Gigi Dennis walks her dog. Given their multiple political involvements, their duties as elected representatives of the people, and their outside interests, they seem to have plenty to do.

AGE

Most of these folks have been around on planet Earth for a while, too. At the start of the 1995 session, only three Colorado senators were under thirty-five years of age. Twenty-two were over fifty, with ten of these over sixty. Just ten were between thirty-five and fifty years of age. Seven House members were under thirty-five and thirteen over sixty, with the bulk in the middle range; twenty-seven were thirty-five to fifty and eighteen were fifty to sixty years old. By 1999 not much had changed. There was just one senator less than thirty-five years of age, and four House members were. On the high end, eight senators and sixteen Republicans were over sixty years old. Most of them, almost two-thirds, fell into the forty-one to sixty age range. Colorado's is not a "kiddie" legislature.

As the American states go, Colorado is a relatively new one, and most members of the state legislature were, at some time other than birth, new to Colorado, as well. This is especially true in the House, where just twenty (31 percent) of the members in the 1995 session were natives. In the 1995 Senate, fifteen (43 percent) were Colorado-born. As of 1998, these numbers had not changed.

OCCUPATION

There is a long-standing notion that legislatures, including the General Assembly, are packed with lawyers. One sometimes hears the comment, "That's why our laws are written in such a legalistic way, and, with all those graduates of the University of Colorado Law School, CU gets favored treatment." However, the truth is that, in 1995, just twenty-one of the 100 members were attorneys, with only two of these holding University of Colorado degrees. The others graduated from Denver University (five) or institutions in other states. By 1999–2000 the lawyer count had dropped to seventeen.

Occupationally, the members of the General Assembly are a varied lot indeed. In the pre-reapportionment decades long past, state legislatures were full of farmers and ranchers. One finds very few of them today. In 1999 only five in the entire General Assembly had a tie to agriculture.

A dozen or so call themselves legislators when asked their profession. A growing number claim the label of "consultant." A handful are employees of large businesses, and a small number are in real estate. There are a half dozen or so teachers or retired teachers and two retired medical doctors. A large number seem to hold two or more roles at once, such as retired, practicing politician, community or party activist, and dabbler in some form of small business. Representative Zimmerman is a truck driver, Senator Chlouber an auctioneer, Senator Pascoe is a writer, and Senator Mary Anne Tebedo says she is a "consulting parliamentarian." It is surely not the case that any one occupational class is dominant. But it is also true that neither the blue-collar worker nor the unemployed are well represented unless, of course, one wishes to characterize dabblers in politics as among the unemployed. With several consultants and seventeen lawyers in the General Assembly there is no shortage of advice. Wisdom, of course, is another matter.

GENDER

One of the more interesting changes in the Colorado legislature in recent years has been the significant increase in the number of women lawmakers, especially Republican women. In 1968, there were just four women in the General Assembly—one in the Senate and three in the House of Representatives. Two were Republicans and two were Democrats. By 1978, there were two female senators and twelve women representatives. Eight of these were Democrats and six Republicans. In 1989 there were seven women senators and twenty-two female House members, and eighteen of these twenty-nine were Republicans. As of 1998 twenty-seven House members and ten senators were women. That was 37 percent of the membership and ranks Colorado among the top few states for female membership. Twenty-one were Republicans and sixteen Democrats. As of the 1999 session, the number of women had shrunk to thirty-three, with twelve women senators and twenty-one female representatives. But over the years, there clearly has been a significant increase in female membership in the legislature, with most of the growth being on the Republican side.

Women have done well in holding positions of leadership and influence. Senator Elsie Lacy serves as chair of the Joint Budget Committee. Senators Dottie Wham, Sally Hopper, Mary Anne Tebedo, and Gigi Dennis chair Senate committees of reference. In 1995 the House minority leader, whip and caucus chair were all female. So too were the chairpersons of five House committees. In 1997, Norma Anderson became the first female House majority floor leader in Colorado history.

One might well ask if the growth in female membership makes any difference. As it turns out, it does, in Colorado as in state legislatures generally. Students of state legislatures have shown that the policy preferences of women lawmakers differ some from those of their male counterparts. Women tend, for example, to focus more on issues dealing with women, children, families, and health. In addition, their legislative style tends to be more consultative and less confrontational.

These findings are reflected, generally, in Colorado's General Assembly. It is not unusual to see cross-party and cross-chamber coalitions of women on issues such as those noted above. At the same time, one shouldn't go too far in emphasizing gender differences. House members Vickie Agler, Nancy Spence, Lynn Hefley, Lola Spradley, Debbie Allen, and Lauri Clapp have been as conservative as any of the men, and so have Mary Anne Tebedo and Marilyn Musgrave in the Senate. And members such as Senate Appropriations Committee Chair Elsie Lacy and House Floor Leader Norma Anderson have been as hard-nosed and combative as any of their male counterparts. Indeed, colleagues affectionately and jokingly referred to Anderson as the "dragon lady."

ETHNICITY

The significant growth in the number of female legislators is not matched by increases in the number of ethnic minorities. In 1978, Colorado had one African-American and two Hispanic senators and one African-American and five Hispanic House members. By 1989, the number of African Americans in the Senate remained the same, and the number of Hispanic senators had only grown from two to three. In the House, the number of Hispanics was up slightly from 1978 at seven, and the number of African Americans had grown from one to just three. In 1998 and 1999 the numbers were about the same. There were two African-American representatives and one African-American senator, and two Hispanic senators and six Hispanics in the House. Clearly, these numbers do not match the percentage of the minority populations in Colorado. The only Native American to serve in the General Assembly in recent years was former House member Ben Campbell, who has since gone on to the U.S. House of Representatives from Colorado's Third Congressional District, and then to the U.S. Senate.

Despite their small numbers, ethnic minorities have done rather well in holding positions of leadership, although, since they have almost all been Democrats, the only leadership posts available for most of the past twenty years have been in the minority party. For the two years in the 1970s when the Democratic party controlled the House of Representatives, Hispanic Ruben Valdez served as Speaker. By and large, however, positions in the leadership of the majority party and the chairmanships and vice chairmanships of committees have been available to Republicans only, and there are no African-American Republicans and just one Hispanic Republican recently in the Colorado legislature.

AFTER THE LEGISLATURE

Many members of the Colorado Senate have served previously in the House. In 1996, former House members included Senators Ament, Bishop, Blickensderfer, Coffman, Duke, Hernandez, Linkhart, Martinez, Mutzebaugh, Norton, Ray Powers, Rupert, Tanner, Tebedo, Thiebaut, Wattenberg, and Wham, a full seventeen of the thirty-five total. For 1997–1998 two more former representatives, Peggy Reeves and Ken Chlouber, joined the Senate ranks, and in 1998 Doug Lamborn moved from the House to the Senate to fill the slot vacated by Charles Duke. The start of the 1999–2000 session saw Norma Anderson, Jim Dyer, Mary Ellen Epps, Tony Grampsas, Marilyn Musgrave, Alice Nichol, and Dave Owen all move to the Senate from the House and when Grampsas passed away, House member Bryan Sullivant replaced him.

Similarly, many legislators from both the House and Senate go on to other roles in politics in elective or appointive positions. When U.S.

Senator Bill Armstrong announced in the spring of 1989 that he would not seek another term, he set off a mad scramble among many members of the General Assembly. Colorado District 3 Congressman Ben Campbell, then a Democrat, expressed an interest in the seat, and District 4 Republican Hank Brown announced his intention to run for the seat in 1990. The names of a number of state legislators quickly surfaced as possible candidates for the congressional vacancies that were expected. Democrats Larry Trujillo, Bob Pastore, Dick Bond, Jim Rizzuto, and Peggy Reeves and Republicans Wayne Allard, Jim Brandon, Scott McInnis, and Elwood Gillis were all said to be eyeing the congressional seats. State Senator Terry Considine considered challenging Brown for the nomination for the U.S. Senate slot, and Representative Chris Paulson was said to have thought along the same lines.

U.S. Senator Hank Brown vacated his seat in 1996. When U.S. Representative Wayne Allard declared an interest in the position, Colorado Republican Senators Ament and Schaffer immediately took an interest in Allard's seat, as did Representative Pat Sullivan. Democrats behaved similarly. The U.S. House seat vacated by Pat Schroeder became a target for Colorado House members Doug Friednash and Diana DeGette.

It happened again in 1998 when Republican Congressman Dan Schaefer announced his intended retirement from District 6 and triggered a parade of congressional wannabes, including state Senators Tom Blickensderfer and Bill Schroeder and House members Barry Arrington and Martha Kreutz. Representative Paul Schauer considered a run at it too. District 2 Congressman David Skaggs likewise chose to quit, prompting first-term Colorado House member Mark Udall to jump into the race.

Like a pebble tossed into calm waters, a high-level political vacancy creates ripples throughout the system. Before a routine roll call in the 1989 legislative session, Senate President Ted Strickland jokingly said, "The clerk will call the names of those who are candidates for the U.S. Senate."

A wag in California once noted that no officeholder wants to be where he or she is. State House members want to be in the Senate. State senators want to be in the U.S. House. U.S. representatives aspire to the U.S. Senate, and they all want to be either President or a high-level judge. The ambitious chase the ambitious. It's no different here; Colorado's legislature of 100 politicians constitutes a bottomless reservoir of candidates for political office. Table 3.1 lists some of the legislators who have sought or filled elective or appointive positions following their legislative careers.

Table 3.1—Postlegislative Activities of Selected General Assembly Members

Legislator	Initial Position in General Assembly	Subsequent Political Activity
Jeanne Adkins	Representative	Treasurer Candidate, Assistant Director, CCHE
Vickie Agler	Representative	County Commission Candidate, Republican Party Finance Chair
Ben Alexander	Senator	Lieutenant Governor Candidate
Don Ament	Representative	U.S. House Candidate; State Representative; Director, Department of Agriculture
Norma Anderson	Representative	Senator
Kathy Arnold	Representative	Senator, Lieutenant Governor Candidate
	Senator	Candidate, CU Regent
Barry Arrington	Representative	U.S. House Candidate
David Bath	Representative	U.S. House Candidate
Chuck Berry	Representative	Governor Candidate
Mike Bird	Representative	Senator, Governor Candidate
Tom Blickensderfer	Senator	U.S. House Candidate
Dick Bond	Representative	U.S. House Candidate
Mike Callihan	Senator	Lieutenant Governor
Ben Campbell	Representative	U.S. House Member, U.S. Senator
Ken Chlouber	Representative	U.S. House Candidate, State Senator
Mike Coffman	Senator	Treasurer
Diana DeGette	Representative	U.S. House Member
Nancy Dick	Representative	Lieutenant Governor, U.S. Senate Candidate
Charlie Duke	Representative	Senate, U.S. Senate Candidate
Jim Dyer	Representative	Senator
Mary Ellen Epps	Representative	Senator
Martha Ezzard	Senator	U.S. House Candidate
Jeanne Faatz	Senator	Senate Candidate
Tom Farley	Representative	Governor Candidate, Agricultural Board Member
Mike Feeley	Senator	Governor Candidate
Doug Friednash	Representative	U.S. House Candidate
John Fuhr	Representative (Speaker)	Governor Candidate
Dennis Gallagher	Senator	Denver City Council
Tony Grampsas	Representative	Senator

continued on next page

Table 3.1—*continued*

Legislator	Initial Position in General Assembly	Subsequent Political Activity
Daphne Greenwood	Representative	Colorado Treasurer Candidate, State Senate Candidate
Joel Hefley	Senator	U.S. House Member
Steve Hogan	Representative	U.S. House Candidate
Miller Hudson	Representative	Denver Mayor Candidate
William Hughes	Senator	Colorado Treasurer Candidate
Joan Johnson	Senator	Secretary of State Candidate
Bob Kirscht	Representative	Governor Candidate
Ray Kogovsek	Representative	U.S. House Member
Ken Kramer	Representative	U.S. House Member
Martha Kreutz	Representative	U.S. House Candidate
Dick Lamm	Representative	Governor, U.S. Senate Candidate
Jim Lloyd	Representative	County Commissioner
Don Mares	Senator	Denver City Auditor
Jack McCroskey	Representative	Regional Transportation District Board Member
Jana Mendez	Senator	County Commissioner
Don Mielke	Representative	County Attorney
Marylin Musgrave	Representative	Senator
Dick Mutzebaugh	Senator	Attorney General Candidate
Tom Norton	Senator	Governor Candidate; Director, Colorado Department of Transportation
Dave Owen	Representative	Senator
Bill Owens	Representative	Senator, Colorado Treasurer, Governor
Federico Peña	Representative	Denver Mayor, U.S. Cabinet Member
Linda Powers	Senator	U.S. House Candidate
Tom Redder	Representative	U.S. House Candidate
Roy Romer	Representative	Treasurer, Governor
Gill Romero	Representative	U.S. House Candidate
Mike Salaz	Representative	Lieutenant Governor Candidate
Dan Schaefer	Senator	U.S. House Member
Bob Schaffer	Senator	Lieutenant Governor and U.S. House Member
Bill Schroeder	Senator	U.S. House Candidate
David Skaggs	Representative	U.S. House Member
Carol Snyder	Representative	County Clerk and Recorder
Ted Strickland	Senator (president)	Governor Candidate (twice)
Pat Sullivan	Representative	U.S. House Candidate

continued on next page

Table 3.1—*continued*

Legislator	Initial Position in General Assembly	Subsequent Political Activity
Paul Swalm	Representative	Denver City Councilman
Shirleen Tucker	Representative	Colorado Department of Health and Environment
Mark Udall	Representative	U.S. House Candidate
Paul Weissmann	Senator	U.S. Senate Candidate, U.S. House Candidate
Jeff Wells	Senator	Attorney General Candidate; Assistant Director, Department of Labor
Duane Woodard	Senator	Attorney General

The political trail of some of these lawmakers is long and interesting. For example, Bob Kirscht was first elected to the House of Representatives from Pueblo as a Democrat. He served as a Democratic House minority leader, then switched to the Republican party, where he once again assumed a position of leadership, serving on and chairing the Joint Budget Committee. In 1986, Kirscht became a candidate for the Republican nomination for governor, but lost in a three-way race with Steve Shuck and Ted Strickland. Shortly thereafter, he maneuvered the Republican candidate in his old House district off the ballot and assumed the nomination himself, only to be defeated. Kirscht then became one of the better-paid and better-liked statehouse lobbyists, representing such interests as the American Heart Association, Lucent Technologies, Colorado Community Colleges, and the Public Employee Retirement Association.

Ken Kramer is another politician with an intriguing history. He moved from the Colorado House to the U.S. House, representing the district centered in and around Colorado Springs. In 1986, he made a run for the U.S. Senate, losing narrowly to Tim Wirth. His U.S. House seat was then taken by Colorado state Senator Joel Hefley. Shortly thereafter, Kramer announced an intention to win back his House seat from Hefley, creating a storm of controversy and protest within the Republican party and glee in the Democratic ranks. Kramer eventually retreated.

Bill Owens was elected state treasurer for a four-year term ending in 1998. Before that he served a term and a half in the state Senate, and prior to the Senate, Owens was in the House for three terms. He made it clear that he had ambitions for state higher office and, indeed, was elected governor in 1998.

Still another is Bob Schaffer. Schaffer moved to Colorado in 1985 after graduating from college and serving as a legislative aide in Ohio. He took a job as an aide in the Colorado Senate and in 1987, when Senator Jim Beatty resigned, a party vacancy committee gave Schaffer the job. He won the seat on his own a year later, at age twenty-six, and in 1992 he took an unsuccessful shot at the position of Colorado lieutenant governor. In 1996 he was elected to the U.S. House of Representatives. One is reminded again of the comment of the California wag.

We often associate insatiable political ambition and careerism with those in the U.S. Congress, the Senate especially, where there is always a goodly supply of solons who see themselves as excellent presidential timber. But as we've already seen, Colorado's legislature has its own supply of lifetime politicians. This became more evident than ever in 1998 when members first felt the impact of term limits. Here is a rundown of the plans of some of the 100 members, as the 1998 election season approached.

In the thirty-five-member Senate, President Tom Norton and Minority Party Leader Mike Feeley were gubernatorial candidates. Majority Leader Jeff Wells was running for state attorney general, as was Republican colleague Dick Mutzebaugh. Ben Alexander, Republican, wanted to be lieutenant governor. Republican Mike Coffman had declared his candidacy for state treasurer. Democrat Joan Johnson tried to petition her way onto the ballot for secretary of state. Both Tom Blickensderfer and Bill Schroeder were Republican primary congressional candidates. Don Ament was planning to run for the Colorado House of Representatives where he had once served before. In all, ten of the thirty-five senators were seeking other public offices.

It was the same in the House. Speaker Chuck Berry was a gubernatorial candidate for a while, but then dropped out. Tony Grampsas, Alice Nichol, Jeanne Faatz, Jim Dyer, Mary Ellen Epps, and Marilyn Musgrave, along with Majority Floor Leader Norma Anderson, all were seeking state Senate seats. Jeanne Adkins wanted to be state treasurer, Mike Salaz saw himself as lieutenant governor, Gil Romero, Mark Udall, and Martha Kreutz were chasing congressional seats and both Vickie Agler and Carol Snyder ran for commissioner and clerk recorder in their respective counties.

That total of seventeen in the House, plus ten in the Senate, means that more than a quarter of all state legislators were running or laying plans to run for some other office, while also serving the public during the 1998 session. And these numbers do not include the dozens of others who were positioning themselves for the leadership and committee slots that would become available with the departure of their term-limited colleagues.

It was no different going into the 2000 election season. Every one of the Senate seats that was opening up was targeted by House members seeking to move.

There are many more such stories. The point is simply that members of the Colorado General Assembly are rarely apolitical citizens who just come to Denver to do a good-hearted and brief public service stint for the benefit of their fellow citizens. Instead, they come from political backgrounds and stay active after leaving the Capitol. Many, like Bob Kirscht, never leave the Capitol at all, and others, like Bob Schaffer, find life as a careerist politician addictive at a very early age.

THE PAPER BLIZZARD

The life of a candidate is fast-paced during a campaign, and it doesn't slow down when the election is over. The weeks following an election are consumed with jockeying for leadership positions and committee assignments and arranging bills to introduce and carry. Once the session begins, legislators are on the run again and buried under a blizzard of paper. Phone calls come in a steady stream, some from constituents and others from interest groups. The mail, too, is endless. Bills and reports pile up quickly. Legislators watch the newspapers daily. Status sheets, journals, calendars, new bills, amendments, and new versions of old measures soon cover their desks.

Legislators have relatively little staff help to deal with the paperwork. Bills are filed for the legislators in their desks on the House and Senate floors, and secretarial pools are available to receive phone messages and type correspondence. The Legislative Council performs some research tasks for legislators, and state agencies will often provide data upon request. The Joint Budget Committee has its own staff, the Office of Legislative Legal Services handles the formal drafting of bills, and legislators in leadership positions have some secretarial help of their own. Members can always get information from lobbyists, and many have student interns. Beginning in 1997 members were authorized to spend $1,000 for hired help, but that's the extent of it. By and large, legislators are on their own to deal with the calls, the mail, and the paper swamp.

Some of the letters that legislators receive are carefully and thoughtfully constructed expressions of constituent opinion. Some of the correspondence is garbled, much is uninformed, and almost all is self-centered. Most legislators try to respond to the incoming communication if it is from someone in their district, although these responses are, of necessity, frequently late, as the pressure of committee and floor work doesn't always permit quick turnaround. A few legislators are extremely cavalier about their calls and mail, in some cases simply trashing their messages and letters. But that is not common; for the most part, legislators are very sensitive to communications from the voters, especially if constituent questions or opinions are individualized, brief, and well presented.

INDIGESTION

Each year, legislators are invited to literally scores of breakfasts, lunches, dinners, and cocktail parties. Most are free, but some are not. Virtually every morning, one interest group or another provides legislators and others in the Capitol building with free coffee, juice, and rolls. Some of it is healthy, as with fruit and whole grain bread. Other times it is simply fattening. Lobbyists look for legislative company at lunchtime. Legislative staffers keep a master social calendar, and by early in the session virtually every morning period, noontime, cocktail hour, and dinnertime has been reserved by one or more groups. Indeed, on any given evening, a lawmaker may have as many as four or five cocktail or dinner invitations. Table 3.2, constructed from invitations to then-Representative Peggy Reeves in just one session, illustrates this phenomenon.

CUE SOURCES

In any given session, legislators must vote on hundreds of bills and even more amendments. They vote in the several committees on which they serve and on second and third readings of bills presented on the floor. They decide whether to support or reject amendments added by the other house to bills passed out of their own chamber. But no human being can be on top of that many issues. Where, then, do they turn for voting cues?

Fortunately, there are many sources for guidance. In the first place, all legislators have their own philosophies, which will often provide a general predisposition. Furthermore, much of the legislation has been proposed in previous years; so, members are already familiar with many bills, except for some new wrinkles here and there, and have previously thought through their positions.

Legislators do listen to constituents, and that can definitely make a difference. Heavy communication from back home on a measure, or even just a little from thoughtful sources, can have a real impact. Communications from persons within their districts who hold other elective positions also carry weight.

Good committee testimony by proponents of a bill can make a difference too, although in most instances it appears that prehearing communications among members themselves and the ubiquitous lobby corps have predetermined the outcome. Still, even if evidence and perspectives given in hearings do not determine the votes on bills, they often result in amendments that make bills more palatable to constitu-

Table 3.2—Invitations Given to House Members to Events Sponsored by Interest Groups, 1983

	Frequency	*Percent*
Event		
Cocktail parties	48	27.6
Lunches	44	25.3
Breakfasts	40	23.0
Dinners	19	11.0
Others	23	13.2
Total	174	100.1
Hosts		
Business and industry groups[1]	57	32.7
Public institutions[2]	38	21.8
Social issue groups[3]	28	16.1
Professional groups[4]	16	9.2
Private groups supporting public institutions[5]	14	8.0
Political bodies[6]	11	6.3
Environmental groups	3	1.7
Labor	2	1.1
Other	5	2.9
Total	174	99.8[7]

1. Includes corporations such as Coors, Mountain Bell, Colorado Cattlemen's Association, etc.
2. Includes colleges, universities, local governments, etc.
3. Includes NOW, Right to Life, Planned Parenthood, Common Cause, churches, veterans, retired citizens, etc.
4. Includes groups such as ophthalmologists, dentists, nurses, planners, etc.
5. Includes alumni groups.
6. Includes party and legislative gatherings.
7. Totals do not equal 100 percent due to rounding.

ents. One legislator commented that she had seen the outcome of a bill turned around because of the views of one citizen and that votes can and do change with testimony as the probable consequences of a bill become clearer and clearer.

On most bills, though, legislators hear little or nothing from constituents. One legislator noted that sometimes they hear a lot from constituents, but often it is little or nothing. "Ninety percent don't know what's going on or what's at issue." But constituent communication tends to be high on such well-publicized issues as abortion, concealed weapons, or public employee residency requirements.

This same legislator went on to suggest that, although good law-makers know they must be in tune with constituents, they must also realize that they are elected to make decisions. Legislators have detailed information and are on the spot when decisions must be made; the average citizen is not. Therefore, a balance must be struck; views from the district must count, but they cannot substitute for a representative's own judgments and decisions.

Legislators often get valuable guidance and information from col-leagues and lobbyists, especially when they are relatively new to the General Assembly. Bill sponsors, committee chairs, and veterans are often expected to provide information and voting advice. New legislators learn quickly whose views generally match their own, and that helps. Over time, lawmakers come to specialize in one type of legislation or an-other—the criminal code or taxes, for example. Colleagues then tend to gravitate to them for help in making their own decisions. "You get to know whose judgment you can trust," one legislator observed.

Although lobbyists usually have good information, they also have a position to sell. Lawmakers know that. The good lobbyists, legisla-tors say, are those whose information and word are trustworthy, who will provide the full story on a bill (including a rundown of existing and potential opposition), and who understand the consequences of the measure. Good ones do not lean hard on legislators for promises or votes. "All you have is your word down here," said one House member, and that applies to legislators and lobbyists alike. Again, the legislators come to know quickly which members of the lobby corps they can trust.

The political parties provide some voting direction, too, but not a great deal on most bills. On some of the more important ones, and on what are considered to be critical votes, pressure will build within the caucuses of both parties to stick together. It can become especially in-tense if an attempt to override a gubernatorial veto is at issue.

One lawmaker noted some danger in interactions with colleagues and lobbyists. "You need to be careful about making commitments on bills too far in advance, as the context can change. Your word is all you've got down here, and you've got to keep your word. So you need to keep your options open." A quite different posture was assumed by House Republican Floor Leader Doug Dean in a 1999 fight on gun legislation, when he scheduled floor debate at a time when National Rifle Association lobbyists, with whom he had close association, would be available to the House members.

For most legislators, there is a continuous preoccupation with the next election, which heightens their sensitivity to constituent calls and letters. It is also a major reason for the periodic mailing of newsletters and questionnaires and the frequent visits to all sorts of functions within the district, all adding to the stack of paper and ceaseless tasks that must be faced.

All legislators are, of course, guided by their own political values, but to varying degrees. Some are pragmatists, usually willing to compromise and always interested in accomplishing the possible. But some have quite extensive and confining value systems, and are therefore more rigid. A deep attachment to a notion like free enterprise, for example, leads some lawmakers to seek to privatize much of what government now does and generates hostility to existing government programs and agencies. Others harbor deep-seated suspicions of some parts of the business community, and this colors their views, too.

Colorado voters amended the state's constitution in 1990, limiting lawmakers to eight consecutive years in office. Over time, this is certain to alter the cue-giving patterns in the legislature. There will be fewer and fewer longtime seasoned legislative veterans, and more new, or relatively new, members. Much of the institutional memory held by veterans will be lost. The overall impact may be to open members more to stories and perspectives from both the lobby corps and staff members.

BURNOUT AND TURNOVER

Members can become overwhelmed by the pace of life in and around the Capitol. They work together all day and sometimes far into the night. They eat together and drink together. Many move to apartments in the Capitol Hill area during the session, and some live together. One observer quipped, "It seems like some of these people are away at a summer camp for adults that lasts 120 days."

Life in the legislature is not only energizing and appealing, it can also be costly and stressful. It is commonly said that legislative life does precious little to help marriages. It clearly doesn't do much for other aspects of the members' personal and professional lives either. The pay has been fairly low—just $17,500 per year (although with expense payments it totals $22,900 for Denver-area lawmakers and $29,380 for those who live elsewhere in Colorado). In 1999 the annual pay jumped to $30,000 plus expenses, and that will help. Staff help and office accommodations are modest. And, inevitably, reelections keep rolling around. The level of activity year-round makes it very difficult for members to pay much attention to their jobs, professions, or businesses back home.

These conditions contribute to high turnover and also help explain the midterm resignations that occur from time to time. Several Colorado senators resigned just before the 1988 session, and others announced during the session their intention not to seek reelection. The reasons they gave are instructive.

Senator Jim Beatty, an attorney from Fort Collins, was in his second four-year term and had chaired the Joint Budget Committee during the spring 1987 session. He resigned in October and commented, "What happens in the Joint Budget Committee is . . . you get to the Capitol at 7:30 A.M. and you quit at 6:30 P.M. You're lucky if you get 15 minutes in the morning and 15 minutes in the afternoon to talk with anybody about anything other than the budget. That started to reflect itself on my practice."[2]

Beatty's colleague, Senator John Donley from Greeley, resigned shortly thereafter. Donley said, "If I could be there from January 1 to April 1 the employer would say 'good, we've got nine months of your time, we'll subsidize you.' "[3] But, as Donley went on to note, legislature lasts six months or more now, and employers aren't that generous.

Republican Senators Paul Powers and Jim Lee finished their terms in 1988, but both declined to run for reelection. So did House member Vickie Armstrong, who eventually found the pace exhausting. Powers said, "It's been eight years and time for me to focus on the business and the ranch and maybe have more of a personal life."[4] Lee expressed dissatisfaction with the ability of the legislature to move through its business quickly and commented, "I don't want to wait for the pace to pick up while I earn $17,000 a year."[5]

Sometimes employers who are affected by the time demands of their employee-legislators beat the lawmaker to the punch. In 1995 two House Republicans, Larry Schwarz and Bryan Sullivant, lost their jobs because of their absences while serving the public in Denver. So did their fellow representatives Doug Dean and Mark Paschall.[6]

Ironically, although legislators routinely grumble about the mismatch between the demands of the job and the compensation, they are terribly skittish about increasing the pay. Indeed, in the 1988 session, a bill to increase the salary of legislators to $21,000 per year floundered. Instead, legislators eventually took action to shorten the sessions. In 1989, the Senate passed a measure to raise the pay to $25,000, but the House killed it, preferring instead to raise the daily expense allowance. And in 1996 yet another such bill was introduced, this one proposing to raise the pay and reduce the expense payments. It too died. Finally, in 1997 the members got up the gumption to raise the pay, beginning in 1999.

Many citizens would undoubtedly have a heightened appreciation for their elected representatives if they knew more about the pace and workload. But in a few cases, there may be another side to that coin. As one citizen commented after attending a committee hearing, "Some of those clowns are downright rude. They're mean to people who testify.

Their constituents back in the district should see them." However, the vast majority of constituents do not see them, and it isn't clear if most visitors have any real sense of what goes on in the Capitol. Even college students who have made a study of politics and served as aides for a session remark that, prior to their experience at the Capitol, they had no idea what went on under the dome.

The issues of pay, staffing, and session length pop up from time to time, especially when there is a rash of resignations at least partially attributed to finances. For much of the past several decades, state legislatures have been criticized for being antiquated and nonprofessional, and, in fact, many other states have lengthened sessions and upgraded pay and staff support. But the Cadillac model for professionalizing the legislature is the U.S. Congress. Ironically, there is a widespread disenchantment with that institution. Some argue that too much money and too many staffers transform a legislature into a home for lifelong incumbents whose political choices are directed by a desire to survive and whose staff members do the research, write the speeches, deal with constituents, and use publicly paid time to guarantee their bosses' reelection.

Recent sentiment in the Colorado General Assembly, complaints about pay from resigning legislators aside, is to maintain and even strengthen the "citizen" nature of the body.

THE CHARACTERS

The 100 members of any given General Assembly vary in many respects. They differ in terms of party, gender, ethnicity, age, and occupation, as well as in devotion to the legislative job and simple competence. Two of the more unusual and interesting lawmakers retired from the legislature after the 1988 session. One, seventy-three-year-old Ralph Cole, left his Senate seat after twenty-four years in the legislature. Cole was first elected to the House of Representatives in 1964 and moved to the Senate in 1972. He was an attorney by profession and tended to focus his legislative attention on matters of prisons and the criminal code. Senator Cole became well known for his colorful ways. He conducted a running battle with Democratic Governor Dick Lamm and later with Republican-turned-Democrat Attorney General Duane Woodard. Cole was famous for his tenacity and his willingness to pursue issues to the end. He was described in newspapers as "contemptuous, arrogant, stubborn, irascible, cynical, petulant, obstinate, narrow-minded, pig-headed, intractable, self-important and obdurate" but as having "stern conservative principle, high intelligence, unquestionable honesty and deep legislative experience."[7] As House Speaker Bledsoe described him, Cole "isn't afraid of the devil himself."[8]

For anyone who finds sport in observing deliberative bodies at work, Senator Cole was a treat to watch, at least for a spell. With his full mane of white hair, he appeared quite statesman-like. His comments and frequent jokes were issued in measured fashion, and he took all the time he wanted to lay them out in the order and tone with which he felt comfortable. It is said that Senator Cole never accepted campaign contributions in all his twenty-four years of legislative life, preferring to preserve his autonomy by funding his races from his own pocket.

Few people interrupted Senator Cole. Some would roll their eyes in reaction to having to listen to all he wanted to say, but they stopped short of interrupting him. For his part, Ralph Cole did little to hide his true feelings on matters, contending that "it's really hard to legislate against the stupidity of the legislators."[9]

Another unusual character was Republican Senator Steve Durham who, like Cole, served in the House before going to the Senate. Durham was first elected to the House of Representatives in 1974 at the age of twenty-seven, part of a very conservative group newly elected to the House and self-dubbed as the "House Crazies." Durham served three House terms before being elected to the Senate. He resigned to serve a short and rocky stint as an appointee of Anne Burford in the Environmental Protection Agency, then was again elected to the Senate in 1984. While in the House, Durham served on the Joint Budget Committee, where he was tough, quick, and caustic.

Not everyone loved Steve Durham, but few failed to take him seriously. He was extremely conservative and sarcastically suspicious of public agencies and their programs, especially those in the education field. When Durham served as an EPA administrator, he "reduced the staff of Region 8 by about 20%," he said, adding, "Not nearly enough, but it was a good start."[10]

Durham did his homework and was bright enough to do it well. (This is in stark contrast to one of his Senate colleagues who was heard to ask during a roll call whether a yes or no vote was needed, noting that he had no idea what bill was at issue.) At the same time, Durham had a propensity to support issues that many of his conservative fellows wouldn't touch. For example, he fought against giving police the right to stop and check a driver's sobriety without probable cause, quipping that a driver who has been drinking "might as well be in the Soviet Union . . . I suppose he'd probably get a fair hearing over there."[11]

Durham would never be described as sneaky; frontal attack was his preferred style. Friend and former Senate colleague Cliff Dodge said of him, "If Durham is out to get you . . . he'll look you in the baby blues. He's not going to stab you in the back like some people around here."[12] Former Senator Regis Groff, a Democrat, referred to Durham as an "equal opportunity bully," for he was, Groff said, as willing to confront Republicans as Democrats. "I've grown to respect his intellect, although I think his politics smell to high heaven," Groff added, noting that "he'd let folks go down for the third time in defense of their liberties, and their right to drown."[13]

A more recent legislative character who has received more than the usual amount of attention, and about whom attitudes are rarely neutral, was Senator Charles Duke. Duke's politics may be described as to the right of right-wingers, and his style was often direct and acerbic.

A former House member, Duke won his seat by beating House colleague Tom Ratterree with tactics that caused the House majority leader to comment that Duke "has let it be known that he will win the election at any cost," and, "he's a take-no-prisoners kind of guy."[14] Duke displayed his antipathy toward the federal government with a steady stream of bills designed to have the state ignore or confront Washington. In 1995 he helped orchestrate opposition to a national gathering of state lawmakers designed to reassert state rights. Duke and his soul mates feared that it would become a runaway gathering, perhaps seeking to write a new U.S. Constitution. Understandably, Duke became the hero of an assortment of antigovernment groups. He proved more successful at building fan clubs outside the legislature than within it.

In 1996 Duke sought the Republican nomination for the U.S. Senate. Then, in the midst of the 1998 legislative session, Duke resigned and shortly thereafter disappeared from the Colorado scene. God spoke to him, said Duke. God, he said, told him to quit the legislature and to suspend relations with his current lady friend, with instructions about the future to be communicated later. Duke followed instructions.

Lawmakers vary considerably with respect to their styles and competence. Some are mild and pleasant; others are hot-tempered and occasionally rude. Some take their work seriously, do it well, and are respected as experts in one policy area or another; others have difficulty explaining their own bills. In direct interaction, lawmakers, lobbyists, and staff members all tend to treat each other with some degree of respect. Privately, however, they are a bit more forthcoming. Explaining why a bill went to one committee rather than another, one legislator remarked that it was "because the Neanderthals on the other committee would have killed it." And a lobbyist described a House member as "too thick to even know how stupid he looks to his own leadership."

Two legislators who are charged with high voltage have been the Senate's Ken Chlouber and Barry Arrington in the House. In 1997 Arrington sponsored a bill to outlaw partial-birth abortions. The bill made it out of the very conservative State Affairs Committee and to the House floor, but then a coalition of moderate Republicans and Democrats voted to recommit the bill, to send it to the more moderate Judiciary Committee. Judiciary members listened politely to some additional testimony and then promptly killed the bill on a 10–3 vote with five of Arrington's fellow Republicans voting with the majority.

Arrington stormed out of the hearing room, exclaiming, "I think democracy has been misused here. I am not going to participate in this charade. I protest!" Outside in the hallway Arrington went on, "I knew that was what the vote was going to be. I had better things to do than participate in those liberal Republicans' dog and pony show."[15]

Senator Chlouber's expressive style went on display not in a disagreement with fellow party members, but in a rage against the national government's Environmental Protection Agency. At a meeting in Fort Collins, an EPA employee reported that when he went to shake hands with the state senator, Chlouber said to him, "You scum-sucking low-life. You're one of the lowest life forms on the planet." Chlouber disputed this version of the remarks. Said the senator, "I did say EPA is a scum-sucking low-life and one of the lowest life forms on the planet, because that is the truth. But I did not say the person was a scum-sucking low-life. I said the EPA was. Maybe he took it personally."

But the story didn't end. EPA Regional Director Bill Yellowtail wrote to Chlouber expressing his displeasure with the senator. And Chlouber in turn responded, "In the simplest terms, Mr. Yellowtail, I am unlikely to accept admonishments concerning my conduct from an individual who has admitted beating his wife, was convicted of stealing merchandise and of felony burglary and of failing to pay child support." Chlouber's remarks were in relation to reports of Yellowtail's past, reports that emerged in the context of Yellowtail's 1996 failed congressional candidacy in Montana.[16]

An extreme contrast in style is seen in House member Maryanne "Moe" Keller. Keller is a special education teacher of deaf children. She represents a west suburban Denver district and previously served on the Wheat Ridge City Council. Her style is decidedly low-key and non-confrontational. Keller's legislative stock in trade is conversation, information, homework, the facts, persistence, and quiet persuasion. As a minority party Democrat, the partisan cards are stacked against her. Still, she enjoys significant legislative success, as in 1998 she managed to steer an expensive adoption bill through a committee of reference and the notoriously stingy House Appropriations Committee, then garnered a unanimous vote on the floor. All of this was done in an environment where the noose of the TABOR spending limit had turned the Appropriations Committee in both chambers into killing fields for bills with costs attached.

Then there was Representative Bud Mollenberg. The representative had been elected to the House in 1990, 1992, and 1994. Before that he served several terms as a Yuma County commissioner. Mollenberg was a farmer and a rancher. He was a big man, tall, quiet, and soft-spoken. Mollenberg passed away in January 1996.

When Bud Mollenberg died, his legislative colleagues and friends had a short service for him on the Capitol grounds and planted a tree in his memory. House colleague Gary McPherson said, "I laid a rose on his desk this morning." And fellow House member Doug Dean, who like McPherson was a generation younger than Mollenberg, honored him with this tribute on the House floor: "The whole time I was here, I never heard him say a bad word about anyone on either side of the aisle. I hope I can learn to be more like Bud Mollenberg."[17]

Life changes for lawmakers when they leave office. While serving, they are sought after by citizens, lobbyists, and other legislators. They hold the spotlight and are given deference. But much of that is gone the moment they are replaced, and a new person becomes the center of attention. One former senator put it this way: "When I was in the Senate I was bright, good-looking and in top shape. The minute I left office I became ordinary, ugly and fat."

Just as members differ, so, too, do the two chambers. In the 1980s, one of the chief differences between the Colorado Senate and House was in the nature of party cohesion. In the House, the Republicans, with their nearly two-to-one margin, often went their own ways on uncontroversial matters but held together as a party on major issues. House Speaker Bev Bledsoe would keep members in line when he felt the need to do so. But in the Senate, the Republican party also enjoyed a two-to-one margin, but was persistently and deeply divided between a moderately conservative group and an extremely conservative group. In no small measure, the division related to the friction between Steve Durham and Senate President Ted Strickland. Strickland, a conservative lawmaker himself, was clearly the more moderate of the two. These men had no use or respect for each other and made the fact known widely. Durham once called Strickland "a complete idiot" and openly questioned the Senate President's integrity. In Strickland's opinion, Durham was "a disruptive force ever since he became a member of the General Assembly."[18]

Again in the 1990s, the House and Senate differed some in character. This time the Senate was more cohesive, as the 1994 election of a group of young social-agenda conservatives in the House loosened up the Republican caucus. Dubbed by some as the "new House crazies," these newcomers pushed liberalized concealed weapons measures, bills requiring parental notification of abortion, and more. Most of their agenda died in the Senate, at the hands of more experienced and moderate Republicans. In the meantime, though, they caused some indigestion for House leaders.

In many ways the members of the General Assembly resemble almost any collection of 100 adult Coloradans. They vary in age, gender, ethnicity, energy, intelligence, and ethics. Some are retired, some are young ideologues, some are friendly, and a few are just nasty. They have rebellious kids, spouses, affairs and divorces, occupational anxieties, and future plans. They are just like us.

But the lawmakers are different too. They have a deep interest in public policies, histories of political involvement, and, most often, continuing political ambitions. Most of us do not.

NOTES

1. John Sanko, "Lawmakers are more than they seem," *Rocky Mountain News*, Sunday Magazine, March 5, 1989.
2   *Fort Collins Coloradoan*, October 15, 1987.
3   Peter Blake, "State Sen. Donley to resign, cites increasingly long sessions," *Rocky Mountain News*, November 4, 1987.
4   John Sanko, "Denver's Powers will leave Senate seat," *Rocky Mountain News*, date unknown.
5. Peter Blake, "Lee declares he won't run for third term," *Rocky Mountain News*, January 28, 1988.
6. *Denver Post*, February 9, 1997.
7. John Sanko, "Cole decides 24 years enough, won't run again," *Rocky Mountain News*, March 24, 1988.
8. Ibid.
9. Quote of the day, *Denver Post*, February 26, 1988.
10. Peter Blake, "Durham did it his way," *Rocky Mountain News*, April 17, 1988.
11. Ibid.
12. Ibid.
13. Ibid.
14. *Capitol Reporter*, March 9, 1994.
15. Dan Luzadder, "Arrington storms out of House," *Rocky Mountain News*, February 26, 1997.
16. Mark Obmascik, "Chlouber talks toxic," *Denver Post*, November 2, 1997.
17. Dan Luzadder and John Sanko, "Legislator to be buried today," and "Quote of the Day," *Rocky Mountain News*, January 30, 1996.
18. Peter Blake, *Rocky Mountain News*, April 17, 1988.

4

Legislative Leadership

Little happens in groups of thirty-five or sixty-five people without some sort of purposeful organization and leadership. Imagine trying to deal with hundreds of proposals for public laws on a wide variety of complicated subjects in less than four months without ceding to a few members the responsibility and authority to make things move.

In addition to the simple need to get the work done, there is another reason to have leadership in American legislative bodies, and that is to provide focal points for organizing the opinions and policy preferences of the two major political parties. In a body of sixty-five, like the Colorado House, there may well be sixty-five opinions on certain matters. But the diversity of views must somehow be distilled into just a few positions that can eventually be made manifest through majority votes and the expression of minority opinion. Leadership helps accomplish this. Sometimes leadership is strong and majorities are built to push into law coherent public policy packages. But other times leadership is weak or divided, so the legislators squabble and the legislature flounders. In the recent past Colorado has experienced both scenarios.

Leadership systems vary considerably among American state legislatures, and many states differ from the U.S. Congress as well. In some instances, party caucuses select House Speakers and Senate Presidents who, in turn, appoint others to leadership positions. More commonly, the caucuses select all leaders by majority vote. This is how it is done in Colorado and in the U.S. Congress.

In some states the rules empower Senate Presidents and House Speakers to appoint committee members and chairs, assign bills to committee, waive the rules, and control staffing and other resources. In other states, these powers are shared with other leaders or party committees.

In Colorado, the House Speaker makes most of these decisions, while in the Senate the Senate President shares these decisions with other leaders.

There are some states wherein the party leadership calls the shots on policy matters and the membership falls into line. In others, leadership is weak, and members feel no particular urgency to follow the party line. Colorado falls between these two extremes, as leaders exert some measure of influence on the voting behavior of members of their party, but are by no means in complete control. Further, the strength and influence of leadership vary some with the personalities of the leaders and the willingness of their members to follow.

LEADERSHIP SLOTS

Although there is some variety in the numbers, titles, and roles of persons in leadership slots across the American states, there is considerable similarity, as well, and Colorado fits into the general patterns. In the House of Representatives, the main leader is the Speaker. This is a powerful position, one that is actively pursued and always occupied by a member of the majority party, which, for more than two decades, has been Republican. The caucus of the majority party selects the Speaker, and he or she is formally "elected" to the position by the full House in early January as the session begins. In addition, the majority party caucus selects the majority floor leader, assistant majority floor leader, whip, and chair of the party caucus, which meets frequently on legislative matters throughout the session. The caucus also selects a Speaker Pro Tem.

The House minority party, which has been the Democrats for more than two decades, will also hold a caucus and select leadership, consisting of a minority floor leader, an assistant minority floor leader, a whip, and a caucus chair. The Democrats also elect their Joint Budget Committee member, and they may nominate their minority floor leader for the Speaker's position as a symbolic gesture. Leaders hold their positions for two years, until the next regular November election.

The pattern is similar in the Senate, where the majority party—again, the Republicans for the past two decades—selects a Senate President, the presiding officer. That selection is made formal by Senate vote when the General Assembly convenes in January. The Senate majority party selects a majority floor leader, an assistant majority leader, and a caucus chair. It also picks a Senate President Pro Tem.

As in the House, the Senate minority party elects a minority floor leader, assistant minority leader, and caucus chair. See Table 4.1.

The six slots on the Joint Budget Committee and the chairs of the committees of reference in each house are considered by some to be positions of leadership, as well.

Table 4.1—Legislative Leadership

House—Speaker (majority party)

Majority Party	*Minority Party*
Majority Floor Leader	Minority Floor Leader
Assistant Leader	Assistant Minority Leader
Whip	Whip
Caucus Chair	Caucus Chair
Speaker Pro Tem	President Pro Tem

Senate—President (majority party)

Majority Party	*Minority Party*
Majority Floor Leader	Minority Floor Leader
Assistant Leader	Assistant Minority Leader
Whip	Whip
Caucus Chair	Caucus Chair

LEADERSHIP SELECTION

As we noted earlier, all party leaders in the Colorado legislature are selected by ballot in the House and Senate party caucuses. There are some states where only the House Speaker and Senate President are elected by party colleagues, with others in leadership positions then appointed by the Speaker and President. Clearly, the latter system makes for more cohesive and powerful leadership systems. With the positions all elective, as in Colorado, the possibility exists for divisions among leaders, and intense political maneuvering in the chase for leadership slots. In 1998 that is precisely what happened. On several major issues House and Senate leaders were divided. The House Speaker was at odds with his floor leader, committee chairs torpedoed leaders' policy preferences, and vote counting and jockeying for 1999–2000 leadership slots started during the session, a full six to nine months before the 1998 November elections. The pattern continued throughout the 1999 and 2000 legislative sessions.

Sometimes the selection of leaders is a mad scramble and sometimes it is not. If a past leader has been reasonably popular—or feared—and wants another term, there may well be no opposition at all. But when leadership positions come open or if someone in a leadership slot has had problems, it is an altogether different story. Speaker Berry, first selected in 1991, was reelected in 1993, 1995, and 1997 with never a whisper of opposition. Past Senate President Ted Strickland and former

Speaker Ron Strahle, on the other hand, faced opposition from within their own party even as incumbent leaders.

Jockeying for positions of leadership may begin many months before an election, and the scramble for support within each party becomes most intense just before and after the November election. Many considerations and calculations are involved. Within the majority party, for example, there will be members seeking the Speaker's slot, others who would like to serve as majority floor leader, and still others who want to take a shot at caucus chair. Some may have an eye on a seat on the powerful Joint Budget Committee. Some veteran members will want to chair a certain committee. Freshly elected members will have some ideas about the committees that interest them. Who will get what? Who will support whom? Like a baseball card swap, no one gets a Stan Musial or Ted Williams for free. Trading, mutual support, cutting deals, picking the right side—call it what you will, nobody gets something for nothing; and like a game of craps, one can lose something of value if a chip is played in the wrong place.

Term limits combined with an ideological split among House Republicans to create a leadership contest sideshow during the 1998 legislative session. The Speaker, majority floor leader, assistant leader, House Joint Budget Committee members, and eight of ten standing committee chairpersons were term-limited at the end of the year, so there was no shortage of leadership slots available for continuing ambitious members. At the same time Republican moderates were in a minor war with a combination of extreme fiscal conservatives and religious right supporters. So the lines were drawn and the candidates were made known. For Speaker it was moderate Russell George versus Andy McElhany and the floor leader contestants were Gary McPherson against sometimes religious-righter Douglas Dean. George and Dean prevailed in leadership struggles, which included the lobbying of newcomers elected to open seats right down to the night before the caucus met to vote. George's victory over McElhany was linked in part to the concern of some members to avoid having the leadership dominated by the El Paso County delegation.

Not all members of the majority party are realistic candidates for leadership positions. Candidates for Speaker will, in all likelihood, be veteran lawmakers, who have held other positions of leadership before. They may have served as caucus chair or majority floor leader or chaired one or more of the major committees in the past. This is changing, however, because as veterans are pushed out by term limits the pool of leadership candidates is increasingly composed of short-timers. Speaker candidate George, for example, was first elected to the House in 1992 and McElhany came in 1994, as did both Dean and McPherson.

Four men who served as either House Speaker or Senate President in recent years offer useful, albeit different, illustrations of leadership before the onset of term limits. In 1990, Carl "Bev" Bledsoe completed eighteen years in the House of Representatives, ten of them as House Speaker. When first chosen as Speaker, Representative Bledsoe was already an eight-year veteran of the House and had served on eight House committees: Business Affairs and Labor, Legislative Audit, Finance, Education, Appropriations, State Affairs, Rules, and Legislative Council.

Representative Ron Strahle had been Speaker some years earlier. He served just two years in this post, losing to Bob Burford in 1979 as a result of the swelling ranks of the extreme conservative wing of the Republican party in the House after the 1978 election. But before becoming Speaker, Representative Strahle served as the Republican minority leader (1975–1976) and assistant majority leader (1969–1970), and upon his selection as Speaker in 1977, he was a ten-year veteran of the House. Interestingly, Strahle served as his party's floor leader again, this time as the House majority leader, from 1981 until his retirement from the legislature in 1986.

Tom Norton was elected as Senate President in 1993 in a race against Senator Dottie Wham. Norton was first elected to the legislature as a House member in 1986. In 1988 he was appointed to the Senate to fill the vacancy left by the resignation of John Donley, and was then elected to full four-year terms in 1990 and 1994. Prior to his election as Senate President, Norton had served on the Agriculture, Business Affairs, State Affairs, and Local Government Committees, and had chaired the joint House-Senate Committee on Capital Development. Norton's opponent Dottie Wham was similarly a veteran lawmaker, having served in the House, then having been appointed to fill a Senate vacancy in 1987, and twice elected to full Senate terms.

From 1975 to 1982, Fred Anderson was the President of the Senate. Indeed, he was the first Senate President, following a 1974 constitutional amendment that removed the lieutenant governor as that chamber's presiding officer. Before becoming Senate President, Anderson was assistant majority leader.

Candidates for majority floor leader, assistant majority leader, and caucus chair have also been legislators who were around a few years, and even chairs of the committees of reference were usually not newly elected representatives. To a lesser extent this has been true in the minority party where, although members do not chair either chamber or the committees of reference, the party leaders are apt to be legislative veterans. Fellow Senate Democrats selected Larry Trujillo as minority leader for the 1989–1990 sessions just two years after his election to the Senate. But prior to that, Trujillo had served two terms in the House, where he had functioned as minority caucus chair. Trujillo resigned near the end of the 1994 session and his term was completed by Sam Cassidy. For 1994–1995, Senate Democrats then chose as their minority floor leader Mike Feeley, who had first been elected to the Senate in 1992. They elected him again for 1997–1998 and 1999–2000. House Minority Leader Ruth Wright was elected to the General Assembly just four years before gaining her leadership post. It is worth noting that, given the high turnover in the state legislature, pre-leadership tenure in the General Assembly is not nearly as lengthy as it is in the U.S. Congress, where members often served for twenty years or more and, as a result, waited a long time for leadership slots to open.

Legislators make their interest in leadership positions known well in advance. Both before and following elections, they will seek support from their colleagues, be they returning members or freshmen. Indeed, legislators may help each other financially or otherwise during a campaign in the hope of building support for a later leadership bid. Everyone knows that those providing political support expect something in return, so even the freshman legislators must make some calculations, choosing where to place their support in light of their own goals and the expected returns. It was no accident that after Russell George was selected Speaker in 1999, supporters Bill Kaufman, Steve Tool, and Gayle Berry received prized appointments. And although no newly elected representatives or senators may expect to become presiding officers or majority leaders immediately, they are likely to seek assignment to certain committees and may well decide whom to support with that in mind.

Both parties in both houses meet in November or December following the general elections to choose leaders for the session that begins in January. Their discussions and reciprocal lobbying at that time have a significant impact on the outcome. But so, too, do the letters and the phone calls they make to each other, and the one-on-one breakfasts and lunches during the weeks that precede these party caucuses.

The transition in House Speakers from ten-year veteran Bledsoe to the much younger Chuck Berry illustrates the dynamics of leadership races. Near the end of the 1990 legislative session, Majority Leader Chris Paulson announced his decision not to seek reelection. Berry, then, became interested in the position and visited with Speaker Bledsoe about his interest. In the course of conversation Bledsoe commented, "let's see what happens," a line that caused Berry to wonder if Bledsoe too might be contemplating retirement from the legislature.

It turned out that Bledsoe did retire, and Chuck Berry's interest then turned to the Speakership. After consultation with his wife, Maria, a seasoned veteran lobbyist, and Tony Grampsas, a fellow legislator, close friend, and confidant, Berry made the run.

Berry's rival was Paul Schauer, a longtime veteran of the House and Republican moderate. Berry won the race, a contest in which Schauer was noticeably the less aggressive of the two. Berry's strategy, with the active help of Grampsas, was to ask members of the Republican caucus for their support, starting with those most likely to give him their backing. Those who agreed received a note of thanks from Berry, confirming the commitment.

Representative Berry also fished for votes during the November election. He contributed to the campaigns of other Republican candidates and visited districts to walk door-to-door with them. Berry refrained from asking for their vote as Speaker but, of course, his interest in their support was implicit.

Before the House Republicans met to select their leaders for 1991 and 1992, Representative Schauer withdrew and Berry was then unopposed for Speaker. This speaks pointedly to the ability of candidates to count votes. Following Berry's selection as Speaker, Representative Grampsas was appointed by Speaker Berry as chairman of the House Appropriations Committee and vice chairman of the Joint Budget Committee, a position that would make him JBC chairman every other year.[1]

Just as it pays to back a winner, as seen in the Grampsas case, it is not profitable to back losing candidates or to challenge a winner. Stories abound in the legislature about the consequences for Republicans who challenged or supported the challenges to Speaker Bledsoe in the House of Representatives and to President Strickland in the Senate. Their bills and committee assignments are said to have suffered too dramatically to be the products of mere chance. In 1998 it paid to back Speaker George, as the moderates who did so were favored for appointments to committee chairmanships and to the Joint Budget Committee.

What kinds of leaders will we have in the new term-limit era, and what will the leadership chase look like? The contests will likely look the same, with aspirants currying favors, seeking commitments, and counting votes early. Indeed, the hustle for support to be the Speaker for 2001–2002 began almost immediately after Speaker George was selected for 1999–2000. George was to be term-limited after the 2000 session. In the House, the leaders will be less experienced than previously. The change may well be less pronounced in the Senate, however, as most members in that chamber are veterans of some years in the House.

THE SPEAKER OF THE HOUSE

The presiding officers clearly hold the positions with the greatest formal authority in the General Assembly, with the Speaker of the House potentially the more powerful of the two. The list of the Speaker's duties is lengthy and includes both activities carrying considerable political clout and functions of a pro forma nature. The formal rules charge the Speaker with convening the House; maintaining order; deciding questions of procedure; accrediting members of the press and assigning them seats; signing bills, resolutions, warrants, and subpoenas; administering oaths; and more.

Responsibilities that arm the Speaker with considerable political power include deciding the size of committees of reference and the number of members from each party who will sit on those committees, assigning majority party members to those committees and to the Joint Budget Committee, assigning bills to committees of reference, selecting committee chairs and vice chairs, and appointing the House members of conference committees. In addition, the Speaker can generally give late-bill status to bills after the passage of legislative deadlines and waive the need for fiscal notes on bills. Further, the Speaker is a very influential member of the majority party, a precondition to selection for that post in the first place. Until 1989, when the House Rules Committee was abolished, the Speaker was also a member of that committee, which controlled the flow of legislation to and on the floor.

These are formidable powers. Although politically no Speaker can take extreme liberties with the numbers, the House leader can tilt the balance between the two parties on committees and make it very difficult for the minority party to ever have its way. With a narrow interparty difference—of, say, six to five on an eleven-member committee—the minority party can realize some victories by moving just one majority party vote. But a seven-to-five split on a committee of twelve members will make it all the more difficult. For the 2000 session, House committees of reference varied in size from eleven to thirteen members, with the typical party breakdown of seven to four or eight to five in favor of the majority party Republicans. With the power to decide who in the majority party will serve on which committees, the Speaker can both amass IOUs from members and determine the political and stylistic character of these committees.

All members have committee assignment preferences, and the Speaker can either grant them or deny them. Committee chairmanships carry considerable political clout, and the Speaker can dole these out, too. Thus, the Speaker has numerous opportunities to reward supporters and punish foes, as well as encourage support from members who always have the next round of assignments in mind.

Sometimes in past years, the Speaker has capitalized on the power to assign majority members to committees by waiting to make assignments until the minority leader made the minority recommendations for committee. This knowledge gave the Speaker important information for structuring the personality and political composition of each committee. Consequently, individuals can be matched and balanced by knowledge and skill and by political party. House minority leaders can counter that power to some extent by refusing to make the first move. Past Democratic leader Ruth Wright did just that in 1989.

This power to make committee assignments and designate committee chairs, coupled with the knowledge of the political predisposition of members, allows the Speaker to construct committees that will behave according to the Speaker's preferences and tastes. The House State Affairs Committee, for example, has long been viewed as the "killer committee" or the "graveyard" for bills opposed by leadership. State Affairs can also serve as a place of predictable support for certain types of bills. More recently, the House Appropriations Committee has become a bill graveyard. By carefully placing certain representatives on such committees, a Speaker can find convenient places to send bills for a very predictable fate, either positive or negative.

The Speaker has considerable latitude in deciding what bills go to which committees. A bill related to schools, for example, might logically go to the Education Committee, Local Government Committee, Finance Committee, or State Affairs Committee or even to two or more of these. And, knowing which committees are most likely to be for or against any given measure, the Speaker can do much to either kill or boost its chances of survival.

Thus, past Speaker Bledsoe assigned bills on daylight saving time, year-round kindergartens, and smoking bans in the Capitol to committees that made sure they were "dead on arrival." Bledsoe, himself a rancher and opposed to year-round daylight saving, sent that bill to the Agriculture Committee, which heavily represents farmer/rancher interests. The kindergarten bill, sponsored by Democrat Wilma Webb, went to the Education Committee, which killed it; it was also assigned to Agriculture, where it would have died had it made it out of Education. Bledsoe, a chain-smoker, sent the Democrat-sponsored smoking bill to State Affairs. As a veteran Republican committee chair commented during the committee hearing on this bill, "It'll die. See those guys on the left? They're all from safe districts. They'll kill it." The Speaker can also save bills that would otherwise be dead. A comment to a member, to the chair of a committee of reference, or to someone on a conference committee can sometimes get a stalled bill moving again.

Prior to the 1989 session, the House Rules Committee also provided the Speaker with an opportunity to exercise power. As a part of that eleven-member group and the person who named the other majority party members, the Speaker had yet another chance to determine the fate of bills. The Rules Committee had several options. It could let bills go on to the House calendar in roughly the same order in which they flowed from committees. It could place a bill on the House calendar out of order. It could bury a bill by referring it back either to the same committee or to another. Or it could simply refuse to let it go on the calendar at all. The Speaker did not, of course, have the only vote on the Rules Committee, but his views mattered a great deal, and he could make them known and apply pressure as he pleased. A constitutional amendment approved by the voters in November 1988, known as the GAVEL amendment, now requires floor action on all bills reported out of committee. This amendment led to the abolition of the Rules Committee.

The Speaker is one of three representatives on a committee that, by joint House and Senate rules, may give late-bill status to a measure. The legislature has one set of deadlines for reporting bills both out of committees and from the floor of the house in which they originated and another set of deadlines for reporting bills from committees and from the floor of the second house. The bills pile up in committees as deadlines appear, and many receive only cursory review and are killed due to legislative volume, political design, or both.

The bottleneck becomes especially heavy in the Appropriations Committees because all bills with fiscal impacts must be reviewed there, as well as by the substantive committees of reference to which they were first assigned. So, as a deadline comes and goes, up to fifty or sixty bills can be killed in the Appropriations Committee of each house and in other committees, as well. In 1996 the two Appropriations Committees killed roughly two dozen bills during the final week of the session and several dozen more in the month leading up to the session's end. In 1998 nearly three dozen measures were killed in Appropriations in the two weeks leading up to adjournment.

But bills may be given new life and new bills can even be introduced beyond the deadline dates if the Speaker so chooses. With the Speaker and the majority leader constituting two-thirds of the late-bill committee, the Speaker can make some members and their casts of supportive lobbyists happy by giving them permission to introduce bills after the deadline. Near the end of the 2000 session the House leadership had given permission to introduce roughly eighty bills after the deadline, all but six of them to majority party Republicans. The fact that all bills that may have a fiscal impact of some sort (by costing or saving money or by impacting state or local taxes and revenues) must go to Appropriations often diminishes the chances of passage. Sometimes even bills with no fiscal impact are sent there to die. This gives the Speaker yet another political lever—sending a bill to Appropriations or waiving the fiscal impact designation and thereby facilitating its movement.

It is important to note that the ultimate influence of a House Speaker, or any House or Senate leader for that matter, is a function of personality and style as well as formal authority. Speaker Berry, for example, was often very "hands-off," purposefully refraining from pushing his party colleagues on policy matters. Speaker George wasn't "hands-off," but he simply viewed it as improper to employ the rules to minimize the voice and influence of other members. At the same time, George sometimes would lean on members to support or oppose certain decisions as he did, for example, during House deliberations on the 2001 state budget.

THE SENATE PRESIDENT

The roles and powers of the President of the Senate are like those of the Speaker in some ways, but not all. Like the House counterpart, the President assigns bills to committee and can, as a result, largely determine if a bill will have an easy ride through committee or a bumpy or even fatal one. And like the Speaker, the President is familiar with the personalities and politics of colleagues and can steer a measure into calm or stormy seas. Indeed, a House concurrent resolution that was sponsored by the House Speaker recently passed the House. The Senate President did not like it; when it arrived in the Senate, he assigned it to three separate committees, ensuring its demise.

In 1997 Senate President Norton doomed a bill sponsored by Representative Vickie Agler, a bill designed to scrap affirmative action in state institutions. Agler's bill had made it easily through the House, but when it reached the Senate, President Tom Norton put the bill in the hands of the Judiciary Committee, a moderate panel chaired by Senator Dottie Wham. That was the end of the line for Agler's bill, and she knew it. "It wasn't to be," she commented. Her preference was the Senate's State Affairs Committee, which, like its House counterpart, is a much more conservative panel than is Judiciary.[2]

Norton also employed his control over bill referral to turn labor lobbyist Bob Greene's glee to chagrin. A 1997 "right-to-work" bill had passed the House, and Senate President Norton shipped it to his Business Affairs and Labor Committee. Organized labor opposed the bill and Business Affairs and Labor was likely to kill the measure since two Republicans, Dave Wattenberg and Ken Chlouber, supported labor on right-to-work issues. But then Norton realized what he had done and, "I said, whoa"; he then asked Business Affairs and Labor to ship the bill to State Affairs, and they did. Democrats on Business Affairs and Labor opposed the transfer, but lost on a party-line vote. State Affairs passed the bill, as Norton knew it would. This lineup always occurs on procedural matters that are viewed as support for the majority party and its leadership. Like everyone else in the Capitol, Greene knows that committees are not all the same, and that committee selection is often driven by leadership desire to save or kill bills.[3]

The Senate President, as a member of the three-person late-bill committee, has some influence over bills, their sponsors, and the interest groups that chase them, especially if the President also has influence with the majority leader, another member of that committee.

But there are important differences between the House Speaker and Senate President. In the Colorado Senate, the President shares with the majority leader the power to set the interparty numerical balance on committees, appoint majority members to committees, and designate committee chairs. The Senate rules state that the majority leader "shall determine the number of members, shall designate the number from each political party, and shall appoint the majority members to the committee of reference."[4]

The formal assignment of these powers to the majority leader rather than the Senate President dates back to the days when Colorado's lieutenant governor served as the presiding officer of the Senate. Back then it was clearly possible for the lieutenant governor to be a member of one political party with the Senate majority to be controlled by the other. Indeed, this was often the case. Since no majority party would tolerate having committee appointments controlled by a member of the other party, the Senate rules placed these powers in the hands of its majority leader. The senatorial role of the lieutenant governor has since been eliminated, but the rule has not changed.

It is common practice in the Senate for majority party leaders to consult with each other on matters of committee size and assignment. A leadership "committee," including the Senate President, participates with the majority leader. Clearly, the President retains some influence in this area. Having won the nod of majority party colleagues as presiding officer, he has considerable influence on committee memberships, chairmanships, and the granting of late-bill status. But the power in these vital areas is shared with the majority leader, assistant majority leader, caucus chair, and the President Pro Tem.

The Senate has never had a counterpart to the House Rules Committee. Rather, bills are initially calendared in the order in which they emerge from the committees of reference and scheduled for floor action by the majority leader.

Yet another way in which leaders can exert influence is by playing the role of mediator and facilitator in contentious situations. In 1998, for example, a bill by Democratic Senator Joan Johnson designed to regulate waste and odor from hog farms ran into opposition from the owners of some large feed lots. A good number of eastern Colorado farmers and ranchers wanted the legislation to protect groundwater sup-plies, and free their air from the stench. Large corporate hog producers resisted, as did their employees. Johnson's bill passed successfully out of the Senate Agriculture Committee, but stalled on a tie vote in the Sen-ate Appropriations Committee. Senate President Tom Norton had been instrumental in stopping Johnson's bill and although his work proved unfruitful in the end, Norton did seek to develop a compromise among the competing interests.

To be most effective, members must avoid crossing the leaders who are in a position to send their bills to favorable or hostile committees or breathe new life into them with late-bill status. And in the House, mem-bers don't go far if they get on the wrong side of a Speaker who can assign them to committees they don't favor or deprive them of chair-manship or vice-chairmanship posts.

Consequently, most members go along, especially in supporting the Speaker or the Senate President. Sometimes, they also support the leader's policy preferences and the majority party position and, certainly, they must keep their distance from any move to install new leadership. High turnover further complicates any attempt at a challenge to leadership, for it takes time to build a countercoalition. That is hard to do with a constantly changing membership, particularly when the incumbent chief holds all the keys to power.

The House and Senate differ somewhat due to the character of the two bodies and dissimilarities in the presiding officers' formal author-ity. Senators serve four- rather than two-year terms; as a result, they may feel a more relaxed sense of permanence and self-confidence. Most members come to the Senate with prior legislative experience in the House. So the smaller group—thirty-five as opposed to the House's sixty-five—tends to know the legislative ropes well and displays more assur-ance and independence. Not surprisingly, then, most often it has been more difficult for leadership to keep the troops in line in the Senate.

Majority Floor Leaders

After the presiding officer, the next most important position is that of floor leader in the majority party. For the past two decades, that post has been held by a Republican in each chamber. The majority leaders often work closely and continuously with the Speaker in the House and the President in the Senate. It is the majority floor leader's task to keep things moving on the floor—hence the title. The order of business for each day is set forth in the daily calendars, although it is often changed. But as legislative business progresses on the floor, the majority leader will make motions for occasional calls of the House or Senate to summon all members to the floor, to recess for lunch or for committee hearings, or after second readings to have the Committee of the Whole rise and report its actions to the chamber. It is the floor leader's job to orchestrate the movement of the day's business, at the same time guarding the interests of the party. The leadership generally knows what it wants passed or amended, and those issues are often addressed by the floor leader. Together with the assistant majority leader and whip, the floor leader may work to see that the votes are lined up and on the floor when needed. Obviously, the majority does not have party positions on every measure, but when it does, its floor leader will do everything possible to ensure success.

Sometimes majority leaders play the role of "junkyard dog," especially when it comes to dealing with the other party. Past House Majority Leaders Chris Paulson and Scott McInnis regularly took opportunities to criticize the Democratic governor, and McInnis, especially, was quick on the rhetorical counterattack whenever he disliked the comments or tone of voice of Democratic members at the chamber podium.

During the 1993 session Majority Leader Tim Foster angrily but effectively rallied his Republican party troops when, on the floor, Democrat Bill Thiebaut was perceived as challenging the Speakership of Chuck Berry. A party disagreement on a bill and Foster's postponement of a vote led to a procedural ruling by the Speaker, which was then challenged. Tradition has it that such a challenge to a procedural ruling is tantamount to a challenge of the Speaker himself. "It's kind of like leveling charges against him," said Foster.[5] Foster and his party quickly caucused and reasserted the power of the majority and its Speaker. Retribution in the form of death to some minority party bills followed.

The role of the majority floor leader varies between the House and Senate. As noted earlier, in the Senate, committee assignments and the designation of committee chairs are done by a "committee on committees" composed of the majority party leadership, with the majority leader as the central figure. To some extent, then, the Senate majority leader shares some of the power that in the House is held fully by the Speaker.

Depending upon the personalities of those in leadership, majority floor leaders can be as influential as their Speakers or Senate Presidents. Indeed that has often been the case in recent years. Both Senate Majority Floor Leader Jeff Wells and his House counterpart Tim Foster have been extraordinarily influential through their control of the calendar and scheduling of floor action. In 1997 and 1998 Floor Leader Norma Anderson was similarly in control of floor action, although the lack of unity within the Republican party made it impossible for anyone in leadership to control the outcome of policy decisions.

Despite the 1998 fracture in the House Republican party, Floor Leader Anderson was widely praised for her style and her work in running the House's processes. In the midst of a contentious committee hearing fellow Republican Penn Pfiffner sought to acquire testimony from a staff member. It was Anderson's bill that was on the table and she informed Pfiffner that it was out of line to haul the legislature's nonpartisan staffers before committee. Veteran legislator, now lobbyist, Bob Kirscht praised Anderson: "She's a fighter, Norma is. That's the way it ought to be done. She doesn't take any crap."

Majority Leader Anderson was often called the "Dragon Lady," mostly in affectionate terms. At the conclusion of the 1997 session, Anderson received a standing ovation from both sides of the aisle for the manner in which she had run the chamber's floor business. Her Republican colleague Larry Schwarz observed at the podium that Anderson "exemplifies [the] best of everything . . . about teachers and mentors . . . and I want her to know I will remember her along with my favorite teachers and mentors for the rest of my life."

From the Democratic side praise came as well. Minority Leader Carol Snyder said, "She's organized, she's a good vote counter, and she's got guts. She's tough. But I think she's been pretty fair in how she's handled things.[6]

Norma Anderson was term-limited following the 1998 session and proceeded to run successfully for the Senate. She was followed in the majority leader position by Douglas Dean whose style was more akin to that of Tim Foster. That style featured frequent deviation from the published daily calendar through use of "special orders" wherein the floor leaders' preferences, announced on the spot, dictated the order of business.

Dean also used his leadership slot in the Republican caucus to seek to influence budget results. Once in 1999 he persuaded his colleagues to support the severing into two items of a $1.18 million bill appropriation for public health and family planning, one funding public facilities and the other supporting private clinics. Dean said it was to facilitate the tracking of the money.

But as it turned out, the maneuver set up the private clinic support, $430,000, for a governor's veto. The funds were to pay for cancer screenings, mostly for poor women. But one of the several dozen health clinics in question also performed abortions, albeit not with public money. Still, anti-abortionists, Dean included, had an interest in killing the funding, believing that clinic budget items are easily interchangeable.

The episode triggered vocal opposition from many, including Republican women who met with and wrote to the governor defending the appropriation. Said Joint Budget Committee member Gayle Berry, "It's less expensive to have pap smears than to be treated for uterine cancer." An angry Budget Committee chairperson, Senator Elsie Lacy, said of the action, "I believe they understand very clearly what they were doing and they misled the body." Dean responded, "I didn't intentionally mislead her." The governor, in the end, let the appropriation stand.[7]

In two other instances Representative Dean's actions stood in contrast to the style that won Norma Anderson such acclaim. He used the floor leaders' prerogatives to deny one Democratic colleague's request for a scheduling delay, and he threatened to kill all the legislation of another member unless Dean's policy preferences were met. Democrat Gloria Leyba was House sponsor of a controversial measure on discrimination based upon sexual orientation. On the day the bill was scheduled for floor action, Leyba requested a delay so that an absent but supportive colleague and members of her family could be present. Such requests are commonly granted as a matter of collegial courtesy. But this one was not; debate, often heated and emotional, followed, and Leyba's bill died on a largely party-line vote.

In the second case, Dean had attached an anti–photo radar amendment to Democrat Bob Bacon's bill that dealt with driver's license information privacy. Bacon had not yet secured a Senate sponsor for the measure, and indicated that in light of the alteration of his bill's contents, he might just forgo a Senate sponsor, and thus let the bill die. To that, Dean allowed as how he'd retaliate by using his scheduling powers to ensure the death of all of Bacon's bills, including one designed to authorize a large wildlife preserve purchase in Bacon's home county. Bacon did proceed to secure a Senate sponsor, moderate Republican Dottie Wham, who then killed the bill.

In the life of the legislature, it is not unusual for one member to seek to hijack another's bill and use it as a vehicle to carry the hijacker's policy preferences. But it is also customary to allow members to terminate the life of their own bills without open threats of political retaliation.

Scheduling and timing can drive political results. There are times when the votes are in place to pass a bill, and there are instances when delays will serve to doom a measure or to give proponents needed additional time to lobby. There are times when the body is in the mood for lengthy debate, and there are times when it is necessary to move through an extended calendar in short order. Sometimes on close votes members may be outside the chambers, or absent. Delay, then, can make or break a bill.

At the start of each legislative day a printed calendar announces the schedule. But that schedule is rarely followed exactly as printed. Rather, bills are laid over or rearranged, or the entire calendar is put off to another time or another day.

It is the majority floor leaders who control the floors. They are the first to be recognized. They make the motions to adjust the calendar, to break for lunch or for the day, or to have the body consider what the floor leader wants considered, "special orders" as they are called. A smart and aggressive floor leader, working with a compliant Speaker or President, can be enormously powerful and appear to members and lobbyists alike as the engineer who drives the train on a daily basis. Students in a Colorado State University legislative politics course once asked Floor Leader Anderson when she planned to bring to the floor a tax measure that she was sponsoring and that had made it out of committee. "When I've got the votes and not until then," was her response.

MINORITY PARTY LEADERS

The task of the minority party leader is, in some ways, the flip side of the majority leader's job. Although it is not up to the minority leader to control the schedule or make the proper motions and keep the body moving through the day's calendar, the minority leader is charged with the prime responsibility to voice the viewpoints of the minority party. The minority leader also follows the procedure closely and often makes motions for strategic purposes. For example, votes on third readings are recorded in the Colorado General Assembly, although second reading votes taken in the Committee of the Whole are not. But the minority party may want a record of the second reading votes for political purposes. To achieve this, after the Committee of the Whole formally reports second reading actions to itself, sitting as the House, the minority party can move to show that a given bill that passed on a voice or standing vote "did not pass." Votes on such a motion are then recorded, and members supporting the bill must cast a recorded "no" vote to defeat the "did not pass" motion, thereby putting themselves on record.

The position of minority party leader can be a frustrating one, especially if the party remains sentenced to minority status for long periods of time. There are no committee chairmanships to distribute and the minority party leader doesn't control the scheduling or floor action. The other party's leaders assign bills to committees, the minority party is on the losing side of most critical votes, and minority party colleagues' bills are killed with frequency.

It is no wonder, then, that there tends to be more rotation in minority party leadership than in the majority. While House Republicans have had just two Speakers from 1981 through 1998, Bledsoe and Berry, House Democratic minority leaders during that same period have been Federico Peña, David Skaggs, Ruth Wright, Peggy Kerns, and Carol Snyder.

The pattern is similar in the Senate where, as in the House, Democrats have been in the minority for over two decades. From 1975 to 1998 only Republicans Fred Anderson, Ted Strickland, and Tom Norton have been Senate Presidents. But minority leaders have included Regis Groff, Ron Stewart, Ray Peterson, Larry Trujillo, Sam Cassidy, and Mike Feeley. It took term limits to conclude the leadership careers of Speaker Berry and President Norton. Minority leader Democrats have understandably found other reasons to abandon their posts.

OTHER LEADERS

The assistant majority leader, the majority whip, and the assistant minority leader, as their titles suggest, basically help the majority or minority leader. They "sit in" if their leaders are off the floor, in conversation with others on the floor, or absent. They will often tally probable votes or work to persuade members prior to a vote. And their leaders are always in need of help in assessing the distribution of political sentiment on specific bills.

Each party in both houses also selects a caucus chair whose task is to chair the group when it meets to discuss issues and legislation. Sometimes, the parties will caucus several times a week; other times, they won't meet at all for a spell. They may meet in hearing rooms in the Capitol or over lunch in a Denver restaurant. Restaurant meetings tend to be social occasions; caucus meetings in the Capitol are strictly business. The parties have always caucused on the budget, and those meetings go on for several days. Often, they will also meet on bills or issues of particular importance. The majority party's purpose when it caucuses is usually to find the support of enough party members to constitute an absolute majority in the House or Senate. This guarantees the party victory on the floor vote, with no need whatsoever to obtain support from minority party members.

The job of the caucus chair hasn't always been easy. On the Republican side in the House, the recent election of extreme conservatives with a social agenda has created tension. On one occasion the "new crazies," as they've been called, invited an announced primary challenger to a moderate Republican colleague to speak at a caucus luncheon—an action viewed as an offensive personal affront by others. In 1998 Republican Caucus Chairman Gary McPherson had his hands full, as his caucus split badly in late session meetings over tax legislation. To make matters worse, Speaker Berry was on one side of the issue and was joined by Finance Committee Chairperson Vickie Agler and Doug Dean, McPherson's 1998–1999 opponent-to-be for the floor leader slot, while Majority Floor Leader Norma Anderson along with the leading 1998–1999 Speaker candidate Russell George were on the other. McPherson's struggles continued through the 1999 and 2000 sessions as he then chaired the House Finance Committee, which dealt with the contentious tax issues. Other challenges facing caucus chairs are less spectacular but equally taxing, such as coaxing members to show up for meetings, speaking in order and paying attention during budget deliberations, and paying up for the minor caucus expenses.

LEADERSHIP STYLES AND STRATEGIES

Leadership styles and the extent to which leaders seek to hold a tight rein on members can vary by party, chamber, and the personalities of the leaders. The tightest control in recent years was exercised by the Republican majority in the House of Representatives. As of 1990, Bev Bledsoe had served as House Speaker for ten years and was, as a result, the longest-sitting Speaker in Colorado history. He was also one of the three most senior members of the House.

Bledsoe was said to be very careful with his choices for committees and chairmanships. He had trusted some of his chairs more than others; if he knew them well and trusted their political positions, little or no day-to-day communication was needed to produce decisions to his liking. As one former legislative leader noted, "There is direct communication between committee chairs and leadership, but since leadership is careful to pick chairs whose philosophy is compatible with its own, it is not necessary to communicate directly on all issues." Another House observer commented, "Bledsoe has a tight rein on committee chairs, some more than others, some are trusted more and have more discretion. He meets with the chairs more at the end of a session and will let them know if he does not like what is happening."

At times, Bledsoe moved members from committees at the start of a new session or even moved them from the chairmanship of one committee to another. Some of these moves may have been at the member's request, but some came as a complete surprise. Freshman Republicans occasionally were made vice chairs of committees, which, it has been said, was designed to foster loyalty early. One legislator observed, "Bledsoe puts people who do what he wants in key positions, such as committee chairs and on the JBC. Length of service and experience seem unrelated."

Bledsoe's successor, House Speaker Chuck Berry, displayed a more open and relaxed style, although he too exercised power through committee appointments. Berry sought to give each majority party member at least one committee appointment of their choice and tried to ensure that there were geographic balance and experienced members on each committee. Berry would begin his appointment process with committee chairpersons and vice chairpersons; freshmen got what was left. At the same time, Berry sought to assemble predictable committees, ones unlikely to produce surprise results as they considered bills he sent their way. The Appropriations Committee, Berry himself noted, was populated with fiscal conservatives.

Speaker Berry's assignment of bills to the various committees, he said, was driven in substantial measure by the preferences of the sponsoring members and by an effort to keep the workload balanced. On perhaps half of all bills, no one had intense preferences with respect to committee assignment.

Leaders in both the House and Senate make it a practice to meet regularly with the chairs of their committees of reference. These meetings allow the participants to assess the remaining workload in relation to upcoming deadlines, and discuss specific bills and party policy preferences was well.

While Chuck Berry's style over his eight years as Speaker was always quite relaxed, he seemed to observers to take a particularly "hands-off" posture as his tenure came to an end. He mounted a campaign for governor in 1997 only to withdraw from the race during the spring 1998 legislative session. At the end of that session, Berry was forced out, as were many others, by term limits. At one point, Berry left the session for a brief time to vacation with his family. The 1998 session also featured divisions within the Republican caucus and between members of leadership. All in all, it added up to a "hands-off" style that contrasted with that of predecessor Bledsoe.

The style of Russell George, who assumed the Speaker's position in 1999, was different from that of either Bledsoe or Berry. Unlike Bledsoe, George was gregarious and communicative. And unlike Berry, Speaker George took a more "hands-on" approach to legislation and the operation of the House floor. George's personality was well suited to the situation existing when he became Speaker, because the Republican caucus was fractured into coalitions of moderates, extreme fiscal conservatives, and members of the party's religious right. But like both Bledsoe and Berry, Speaker George used his committee appointment authority to structure predictable committees. His Judiciary Committee was moderate, while State Affairs was very conservative. George could send bills to them for predictable outcomes.

House and Senate leadership also get together from time to time. Sometimes meetings are informal discussions of ways to handle major issues and sometimes they are in the formal context of the Legislative Council's Executive Committee. The Legislative Council is a joint legislative committee whose role is to oversee the General Assembly's major research staff and to help guide the legislative agenda. The committee has an Executive Committee composed of the Senate President and House Speaker, and the majority and minority leaders from each party in each chamber.

Party leadership cannot realistically enforce party positions on all issues. Indeed, with hundreds of bills flowing through the legislature each session, that would be all but impossible—the time costs of hammering out hundreds of caucus positions would be prohibitive. But on those issues that are deemed "major," the leadership *has* taken stands and sought to hold the troops together tightly. One observer described House leadership this way:

> They know what bills they want passed, which ones not, which committee is likely to do what. They get bills to the committees they want, they talk with the chairs. Most of the time leadership does not care which way you go, or at least does not press members. You can't use your power all the time. You can't take positions on everything.

Still, there are many ways in which leadership can affect policy outcomes. One way is to carefully structure committee memberships and strategically direct bills to certain committees. For example, a bill to permit parents to keep their children out of public schools and teach them at home was referred to the House Education Committee, where it died. The following year, the Speaker sent it to the State Affairs Committee, and it died there, too. But on a third try, it again went to the House State Affairs Committee; this time, it passed comfortably.

Leadership can also use the budget process effectively. Four of the six members of the Joint Budget Committee are from the majority party. Since the budget bill is revised relatively little after emerging from that committee, majority party leadership can influence the content of the budget in its formative stage.

As long as it doesn't try to make every matter a major issue and demand too much from members, leadership can work its will in various ways. Veteran lawmakers, it is said, have been denied reappointment to committees on which they had served because they pursued excessively independent courses of action or a political philosophy too divergent from that of the leadership.

At the same time, there are instances when the apparent will of the majority leadership is foiled. In the 1996 session an economic development bill carried by Senate President Tom Norton and House Speaker Chuck Berry lost. Another 1996 measure, an enterprise zone bill sponsored by a Democrat but opposed vigorously on the floor by House Speaker Tim Foster, passed in spite of Foster's leadership role and the sponsor's minority party status. Senate President Norton, Speaker Berry, and House Floor Leader Anderson all failed to get what they wanted on taxation issues during the 1998 session, and when one major tax measure sponsored by Norton and Anderson did pass, it did so only with the help of a united Democratic caucus.

In still another instance, former Republican House Majority Leader Chris Paulson found himself at odds with almost all of his colleagues in both parties. He vigorously opposed a highly consequential bill sponsored by fellow Republican and Joint Budget Committee member Vickie Armstrong that fundamentally restructured state funding of elementary and secondary education. The legislation passed the House overwhelmingly, passed the Senate, and became law.

The grip that Democratic leaders in the House have over their members is loose, to say the least. Like their Republican counterparts, Democrats caucus and discuss issues and bills at length. The minority leader seeks to persuade fellow Democrats, and they will come to certain understandings among themselves. But they rarely adopt official party positions to which all members are expected to adhere.

The general philosophy of the Democrats, the makeup of the group, and its long-term minority status all work against development of a tightly organized unit. The Democrats pride themselves on their diversity and individuality, and party members believe they represent a broad spectrum of views. Historically they have had internal battles over the best posture to assume in the House of Representatives. Should they be a militant and vocal minority, constantly flailing the majority Republicans? Or should they be accommodating and seek to make progress on certain issues? Such disagreements spill over into contests for positions of leadership.

By gender, ethnicity, and constituency, the Democrats in recent years have been a mixed lot, indeed. In 1998, all except one ethnic minority member in the House of Representatives were Democratic—five Hispanics and two African Americans. Ten of the twenty-four Democrats were women. Several Democrats represented core-city Denver districts with heavy minority populations. Others came from "out-state" cities.

The Democrats share many core values and thus stick together when these values are at stake. Examples include sponsorship of bills supporting labor, public schools, and the environment. Additionally, the House Democrats usually have stuck together and supported Democratic governors when the Republicans attempted to override vetoes. Such overrides require votes of two-thirds of the full House membership, and as long as the Democrats stayed united, the Republicans fell short of that number. But on simple majority votes, the Republicans have more than the thirty-three needed to pass bills; therefore, the motivation of a numerical minority to stick together is often lacking. After all, what good would it do for a minority of twenty-four to unite against a majority of forty-one?

Should the Democrats come to hold a simple majority of thirty-three or more House seats someday, or eighteen in the Senate, the incentive structure would change radically. With enough votes to provide majorities on the floor and in committees, the Democratic leadership would have good reason to call for party discipline and unity. And the members would have good reason to follow for, by sticking together, they would call all the shots.

It was noted earlier that the formal powers of the presiding officers of the two chambers differ in several important ways, with the Speaker's power being the greater of the two. It is often the case, too, that the grip Republican leadership has on members in the Senate is looser than that in the House, the late 1990s divisions in the House Republican caucus notwithstanding. In substantial measure, the greater dispersion of formal authority explains the difference. Unlike the Speaker, the Senate President does not unilaterally appoint committee members and chairs.

Additionally, senators tend to have more lawmaking experience than their House colleagues, since most of them have previously served in the House. Senators face reelection just once every four years, rather than every two, as do House members. With thirty-five members, the Senate is a relatively small chamber. It is much more informal in its operations, and the role of each member looms larger than that of a representative in the sixty-five-member House. For this and other reasons, senators appear to be more independent. In fact, former House Majority Floor Leader Chris Paulson is said to have commented that the senators "don't have a herd mentality like we do."

Of course, personalities make a major difference too. Some years back the Senate had what were essentially three parties—the extremely conservative Republicans, the so-called moderate Republicans, and the Democrats. In 1987 and 1988, the Republicans held a twenty-five-to-ten numerical majority, but roughly ten of the twenty-five, the extreme conservatives, were at odds with Senate President Strickland, who had served in that slot since 1984. This made it impossible for leadership to hold the group together in a fashion that resembled the Republican unity in the House. Senate President Strickland was not always able to whip the troops into line. They lined up when they pleased, and often only for the price they asked.

More recent Senates have seen divisions within majority Republican ranks, too, but none to match those of the 1980s. In the 1990s, staunch conservatives such as Bob Schaffer, Mike Coffman, Mary Anne Tebedo, and Jim Congrove were on the other side of policy disputes with more moderate Republicans such as Dottie Wham and Sally Hopper, and even Senate President Tom Norton and Floor Leader Jeffrey Wells. But in large measure the moderate perspective prevailed and a sharp and personalized caucus fracture did not reemerge.

In the House, long-term Speaker Bledsoe was known to be calculating and careful about what he said; he played his cards close to the vest. Former Senate President Strickland, by contrast, was more expressive and accessible. Both were highly sensitive to criticism. Bledsoe, for example, irritated by criticism he had received, paid for space in rural newspapers after the 1988 election to denounce Democrats. He periodically hammered his critics from the House podium, too, and used the platform to critique the U.S. Supreme Court, socialism, and other political phenomena he found distasteful. Bledsoe is said to have chastised lobbyists for orchestrating pressure on him from home district citizens and allegedly took offense at those who provided electoral support for Democratic candidates. Similarly, following a close leadership struggle, Strickland attacked lobbyists he believed had worked against him.

LEADERSHIP TURNOVER

As one might expect in a legislature where turnover among members is high, changes in leadership are fairly frequent as well, and this will increase with the impact of term limits. With its regular rotation of leaders, Colorado reflects the national trend toward steady decline in the number of longtimers. According to Lucinda Simon, "Leadership changes seem to be occurring with increasing frequency, and the long-term leader is becoming a breed of the past."

Bev Bledsoe served as House Speaker from 1981 to 1990. Chuck Berry succeeded him and held that post from 1991 to 1998. The House majority leader position changed hands more often, with Ron Strahle, Chris Paulson, Scott McInnis, Tim Foster, Norma Anderson, and Doug Dean all occupying that slot since 1980. For House Democrats, their floor leaders have been Bob Kirscht, Federico Peña, David Skaggs, Ruth Wright, Peggy Kerns, Carol Snyder, and Ken Gordon.

In the Senate just four persons have held the Presidency of that chamber since 1980—Fred Anderson, Ted Strickland, Tom Norton, and Ray Powers, and Jeff Wells ran the floor from 1986 to 1998. He was followed by Tom Blickensderfer in 1999. Minority leaders have included Regis Groff, Ron Stewart, Ray Peterson, Sam Cassidy, Larry Trujillo, and Mike Feeley. Turnover in other leadership positions, such as the assistant floor leaders, whips, and caucus chairs, has similarly been high, in the minority party especially.

If the past couple of decades have witnessed rather high rates of turnover among Colorado's legislative leaders, the coming decades will show even faster rates. The term-limit constitutional amendment, effective as of 1990, limits members to eight consecutive years in a seat. Thus those who were serving in 1990 were ousted in 1998. Prior to the 1996 election, House Majority Leader Foster and House Minority Leader Peggy Kerns chose not to seek reelection. As of 1998, Speaker Berry and Speaker Pro Tem Tony Grampsas, along with Senate President Tom Norton, Senate President Pro Tem Tilman Bishop, and Senate Majority

Leader Jeff Wells, were similarly forced out by term limits. Further, House Assistant Minority Leader Diana DeGette was elected to the U.S. House of Representatives in 1996 and House Caucus Chair Peggy Reeves won a seat in the Colorado Senate. Term limits, in short, have accelerated an already speedy system of leadership turnover. In the process, term limits are pushing into positions of power those with limited experience and short institutional memories.

This result was made crystal clear in the selection of leadership for the 1999–2000 General Assembly, in the House especially. Russell George, the new Speaker, came to the post with six years of House experience and faced term limits after just two years as Speaker. Floor Leader Doug Dean had just four years under his belt. The average length of House service for new committee chairpersons was four and a half years and for committee vice chairpersons it was almost two and a half.

The impact of term limits on Senate leadership was somewhat different but it nonetheless left that chamber with leaders mostly inexperienced in their new roles. Senate President Ray Powers, while new to that position, was a twenty-year legislative veteran, due to be term-limited in 2000. New Floor Leader Tom Blickensderfer had just six years in the legislature. The average Senate experience of new committee chairpersons was not quite four and a half years, but when one added the House experience of the senators, that number jumped to ten years. Eight of the ten chairpersons of Senate committees of reference had prior service in the House, and four of them were just elected to the Senate in 1998. At the same time, three Senate committee vice chairs had absolutely no legislative experience.

Besides sapping the experience and institutional memory of the legislature generally, limiting terms is expanding differences between the House and the Senate. With the eight-year limit applying to consecutive service in a single chamber, the House is becoming the home of the inexperienced while the Senate serves as the next stop for experienced former House members.

Women Leaders

Just as women have increased their numbers in the House, so, too, have they realized additional successes in occupying positions of leadership. Such change has been slower in coming to the Senate, however. In the 1981 House of Representatives, there were ten Republican women; none of them were formal leaders, but five did serve as chairs or vice chairs of committees of reference. In 1988, the number was seventeen; one, Kathi Williams, held the post of whip, and nine others were chairs or vice chairs of committees of reference. For the new session that began in 1989, thirteen of the thirty-nine Republicans were women, with one serving as caucus chair, two as committee chairs, and six as committee vice chairs. On the Democratic side, one of the three leaders in 1980 was a woman, and two of the three leaders in both 1988 and 1989 were women.

During the 1996 session, women in the House were well represented in both the membership generally and in leadership. Twenty-three of the sixty-five representatives were women—one-half of the twenty-four Democrats and eleven of the forty-one Republicans. Four of the nine committees of reference were chaired by women, and all four leadership slots for minority party Democrats were women. On the Republican side, the assistant majority leader and whip were both women.

The 1996 Senate was much different. While ten of the thirty-five senators were women, and four of the nine committee of reference chairs were held by women, there were no women in leadership positions in either party. But at the same time, Elsie Lacy chaired the Senate Appropriations Committee and thus chaired the Joint Budget Committee in alternate years, and Dottie Wham, Sally Hopper, Gigi Dennis, and Mary Anne Tebedo chaired standing Senate committees.

For 1997–1998, the House Republicans made history by selecting Norma Anderson as the first woman majority leader. On the Democratic side, women continued to occupy positions of influence as Carol Snyder was elected minority floor leader and Gloria Leyba was chosen assistant minority leader. The proportion of women in the full Senate and House memberships remained high as well. The 1998 session ended with ten women senators and twenty-seven women representatives. This 37 percent was an all-time high for Colorado's General Assembly.

The 1999–2000 legislature saw a slight decline in both the number of women members and of women in leadership positions. The numbers fell to twelve in the Senate and twenty-two in the House. The caucus chairpersons for both parties in the Senate were women, as were both whips in the House, two Joint Budget Committee members, and six committee chairpersons in the Senate and two in the House. But the top leadership slots, the presiding officers and floor leaders of both parties in both chambers, went to men.

In a March 1988 editorial, lobbyist Roger Walton defended former House Speaker Bledsoe against criticism for alleged misuse of power. Walton's words provide a nice reference point on which to close a discussion of leadership. Walton described the formal process correctly, noting that:

1. All representatives are elected by voters,
2. All have an equal vote in the General Assembly,
3. Leaders are elected and removed by their peers,

4. All members vote on rules,

5. The rules permit bills stalled in committee to be blasted out by majority vote, and

6. A speaker may be overruled by a vote of the members.

But Walton omitted politics from his equation and, as a result, came to a faulty conclusion. As anyone who has watched statehouse politics objectively knows, members are significantly constrained in their free use of the almighty vote, and, in point of political fact, not all members are equal. The authority to assign members to committees and select committee chairs, the power to determine which committees hear which bills, the ability to provide late-bill status—these and other formal prerogatives can and often do translate into enormous political power. Members have not just blasted bills at will or challenged Speakers—at least not without enormous risk to their own political fortunes.

Still, there *are* limits to power—not the formal constraints that Walton lists, but political ones. To stay in power, leaders must maintain their bases of political support. And to do that, they must give something to their followers. So, they give them preferred committee assignments. They dish out late-bill status. They help move bills through the process. They shy away from tasteless and highly visible retribution against dissidents. And of course when severe ideological fissures appear, they may simply not be able to keep the party's troops in line.

Perhaps all 100 members of the Colorado General Assembly are created equal on election day. But they don't stay that way for long. Deliberative bodies cannot function without direction, and direction requires leadership. Ultimately, leadership spells power.

NOTES

1. Author's conversations with Speaker Berry.
2. John Sanko, "Bill doomed by GOP moderates," *Rocky Mountain News*, March 19, 1997.
3. *Denver Post*, March 4, 1997.
4. Senate Rule 21a.
5. *Denver Post*, February 27, 1993.
6. Michelle Daly Johnston, "Majority leader receives bipartisan ovation," *Denver Post*, May 8, 1997.
7. Michelle Daly Johnston, "Veto threat puts budget in limbo," *Denver Post*, April 17, 1998. See also John Sanko, "Abortion politics delays budget bill," *Rocky Mountain News*, April 17, 1999, and Peter Blake, "Abortion funding in budget bill puts Owens on spot," April 18, 1999.

5

The Committee System

It is not possible for a deliberative body to function effectively without a committee system, just as it could not operate without leadership. Bills are introduced by the hundreds, and the subject matter varies enormously in terms of the problems addressed and the complexity and scope of the issues involved. In Colorado, as in other legislatures, the membership is divided into groups that can specialize and give intense scrutiny to proposed laws before they hit the full chambers of thirty-five or sixty-five members. Committees perform this function; they specialize and so divide the labor.

THE COMMITTEES

The Colorado House and Senate both have nine committees that deal regularly with substantive legislation. In addition, each has an Appropriations Committee, and there are House and Senate Services Committees that attend to the staffing and equipping of the General Assembly. There are also five joint committees, and, until 1989, the House of Representatives had a Rules Committee. In the opinion of some, the Rules Committee functioned simply as a body to schedule legislative business for House floor action. For others, it was a tool the majority party leadership used to kill bills it didn't like. However, the 1988 GAVEL amendment to the constitution now requires that all bills reported out of committee be heard on the floor, and the Rules Committee was therefore abolished. The Senate had no parallel committee.

The nine substantive committees, called "committees of reference," are established in the rules of the House and Senate. These are the committees to which bills are "referred" for study by the House Speaker and Senate President. The rules do not define the subject matter of bills that go to each of these committees, but an information document produced by the Legislative Council, the research arm of the General Assembly, does. The formal rules do specify the executive branch departments over which each committee has oversight responsibilities, and that provides a further clue to each committee's jurisdiction. These committees of reference and the subject matter of each are listed in Table 5.1.

The Appropriations Committees in both chambers hear bills that have fiscal impacts—that is, those that affect the program or personnel costs of the state, its agencies, or local governments. Bills with no fiscal impact will go to just one committee of reference, and occasionally to a second one. If a bill makes it through those committees, it progresses to the floor for debate. Bills with fiscal impacts or probable fiscal impacts go to Appropriations after receiving attention in the committee of reference and before advancing to the full House or Senate. And just as bills may fail to be reported favorably out of a committee of reference, they may also die in Appropriations. In addition, bills with no fiscal impact will sometimes be sent to Appropriations as a political move to kill them.

Each of the five joint committees is specialized, too. The best known of the five, perhaps the best known of all legislative committees, is the Joint Budget Committee. The JBC's six members, three from each chamber, also sit on the House or Senate Appropriations Committees. The task of the Joint Budget Committee is to assemble the state's budget each year, a formidable task that brings with it enormous political power.

In addition to the Joint Budget Committee, there is a joint, six-member Capital Development Committee that examines the capital needs of the state and advises the Joint Budget Committee and legislature accordingly; an eight-member Legislative Audit Committee that, among other things, oversees the work of the state auditor; a ten-member Committee on Legal Services that supervises the office responsible for drafting and revising statutes; and a committee called the Legislative Council. The Legislative Council, with six representatives, six senators, plus six members of House and Senate leadership who are ex officio members, oversees the work of the General Assembly's research unit, which is called the Legislative Council. This committee, made up as it is largely of those in leadership, also helps to steer the legislature's agenda, especially during the interim.

COMMITTEE RULES

Both the House and Senate have formal rules to structure the operations of their committees. In the House, the Speaker appoints committee members for the majority party and designates a chair and vice chair for each at the start of the session. The appointments run for two

Table 5.1—House and Senate Committees

SENATE COMMITTEES

1. *Agriculture, Natural Resources, and Energy*—agriculture, water, natural resources, wildlife, parks and recreation
2. *Business Affairs and Labor*—financial institutions, insurance, regulated activities, labor
3. *Education*—elementary and secondary education, higher education
4. *Finance*—taxation, property tax relief, school finance
5. *Health, Environment, Welfare, and Institutions*—health, welfare, social services
6. *Judiciary*—criminal code, juvenile code, courts, consumer credit, corrections
7. *Local Government*—counties, municipalities, special districts, environment and land use
8. *State Affairs*—elections, organization and operation of state government, land transfers, resolutions and amendments of state constitution
9. *Transportation*—highways, motor vehicles, environmental quality

HOUSE COMMITTEES

1. *Agriculture, Livestock, and Natural Resources*—agriculture, water, natural resources, wildlife, parks and recreation
2. *Business Affairs and Labor*—financial institutions, insurance, regulated activities, labor
3. *Education*—state financial assistance to public schools, elementary and secondary education, higher education
4. *Finance*—taxation, property tax relief
5. *Health, Environment, Welfare, and Institutions*—health, welfare, social services
6. *Judiciary*—criminal code, juvenile code, courts, consumer credit, corrections
7. *Local Government*—counties, municipalities, special districts
8. *State Affairs*—elections, organization and operation of state government, land transfers, resolutions and proposed amendments to the state constitution
9. *Transportation and Energy*—highways, motor vehicles, energy conservation and development, environmental quality

Source: Legislative Council 2000.

years, until the legislature convenes again after the next November election. In the Senate, majority party committee appointments are made formally by resolution, but only after the designations are set by the majority floor leader, generally in consultation with the Senate President and others in majority party leadership. In both houses, minority party members are placed on committees as specified by the minority leader.

House rules stipulate that each committee will have ten to nineteen members. In fact, all committees of reference have eleven or thirteen members, with the number from each party roughly reflecting the proportions in the full House. Senate rules do not specify committee size, but they do call for party proportionality on committees to reflect that of the chamber itself. Recently, each Senate committee of reference had seven or nine members; the Appropriations Committee had ten. Consequently, senators usually have two or three committee assignments each, and representatives typically have two. Of course, the majority party leaders determine both committee size and proportionality, and a shift by just one member in either direction can have a meaningful impact on party influence and the fate of legislation.

The committees are categorized, and no member is allowed to serve on more than one committee in each category. This categorization is then used to schedule meeting times. Table 5.2 provides examples from each chamber. Committee chairs are allowed to set meetings at special times, provided these are announced on the floor in advance; meetings may also be canceled with advance notice on the chamber floor. Both the House and Senate rules specify that committees shall not meet while the chamber is in session, to avoid conflicts in meeting times of the committees and so everyone will know when and where committees are meeting.

In both houses, the rules give chairpersons considerable authority in the conduct of committee business, as well as a vote on all matters. Until 1989, committee chairs could also decide what bills to hear and when to hear them. The committees generally took some type of action on all bills sent to them, but the chair's power to delay and schedule at their whims was in no way constricted. However, the 1988 GAVEL amendment outlawed what some called a form of "pocket veto" whereby committee chairs simply refused to schedule hearings and action on bills they disliked. All bills now have a hearing of some sort, and some formal action is always taken.

Or so the state constitution seems to say. There are occasions when it doesn't work that way. In the final days of the 1998 session, with the legislature struggling with the problem of rebating to taxpayers some of the excess tax receipts, House Finance Committee Chair Vickie Agler pulled two tax measures off the table and rescheduled them, but too

Figure 5.2—Senate and House Committee Schedules

Morning Senate Committee Schedule *

Senate Committee Room	Monday 10:00 – 12:00	Tuesday (Category 1) 9:00 – 12:00	Wednesday (Category 2) 9:00 – 12:00	Thursday (Category 3) 9:00 – 12:00	Friday
354		Bus Affairs & Labor Chr: Norma Anderson Staff: Susan Liddle	Education Chr: Ken Arnold Staff: Julie George	Finance Chr: Ron Teck Staff: Ron Kirk	
353		St, Vet, & Mil Aff Chr: MaryAnne Tebedo Staff: Geoff Johnson	Ag, NatRes,&Energy Chr: Dave Wattenberg Staff: David Beaujon	Local Government Chr: Jim Congrove Staff: L. Johnson	
352		Judiciary Chr: Dottie Wham Staff: Colette Peters	HEWI Chr: Mary Ellen Epps Staff: Jim Hill	Transportation Chr: Marilyn Musgrave Staff: Geoff Johnson	

Afternoon Senate Committee Schedule

Senate Committee Room	Mon & Wed (Category 1) 1:30 – 6:00	Tuesday (Category 3) 1:30 – 6:00	Thursday (Category 2) 1:30 – 6:00	Friday* (Category 1) 1:00 – 2:30	(Category 2) 2:30 – 4:00	(Category 3) 4:00 – 5:30
354	Bus Aff & Labor Chr: Norma Anderson Staff: Susan Liddle	Finance Chr: Ron Teck Staff: Ron Kirk	Education Chr: Ken Arnold Staff: JulieGeorge	Bus Aff & Labor Chr: Norma Anderson Staff: Susan Liddle	HEWI Chr: Mary Ellen Epps Staff: Jim Hill	Transportation Chr: Marilyn Musgrave Staff: Geoff Johnson
353	St, Vet,&Mil Aff Chr: MaryAnne Tebedo Staff: Geoff Johnson	Local Govt Chr: Jim Congrove Staff: L. Johnson	Ag,NatRes, &En Chr: Dave Wattenberg Staff: David Beaujon	St, Vet, &MilAff Chr: MaryAnne Tebedo Staff: Geoff Johnson	Education Chr: Ken Arnold Staff: Julie George	Finance Chr: Ron Teck Staff: Ron Kirk
352	Judiciary Chr: Dottie Wham Staff: Colette Peters	Transportation Chr: Marilyn Musgrave Staff: Geoff Johnson	HEWI Chr: Mary Ellen Epps Staff: Jim Hill	Judiciary Chr: Dottie Wham Staff: Colette Peters	Ag, NatRes,&En Chr Dave Wattenberg Staff: David Beaujon	Local Govt Chr: Jim Congrove Staff: Lori Johnson

Morning House Committee Schedule *

House Committee Room	Monday 10:00 – 12:00	Tuesday (Category 1) 9:00 – 12:00	Wednesday (Category 2) 9:00 – 12:00	Thursday (Category 3) 9:00 – 12:00	Friday (Category 1) 7:30 – 9:00
0107		**St, Vet, & Mil Aff** Chr: Andy McElhany Staff: Jeanette Chapman	**Education** Chr: Debbie Allen Staff: Cathy Eslinger	**Finance** Chr: Gary McPherson Staff: Steve Schroeder	**St, Vet, & Mil Aff** Chr: Andy McElhany Staff: Jeanette Chapman
0109		**Bus Affairs & Labor** Chr: Jack Taylor Staff: Larry Thompson	**Local Government** Chr: Matt Smith Staff: Scott Grosscup	**Trans and Energy** Chr: Bill Swenson Staff: Brad Denning	**Bus Affairs & Labor** Chr: Jack Taylor Staff: Larry Thompson
0112		**Judiciary** Chr: Bill Kaufman Staff: Carl Jarrett	**HEWI** Chr: Marcy Morrison Staff: Whitney Gustin	**Ag, Lvstk, & NatRes** Chr: Brad Young Staff: Allison Pasternak	**Judiciary** Chr: Bill Kaufman Staff: Carl Jarrett

Afternoon House Committee Schedule

House Committee Room	Monday (Category 2) 1:30 – 6:00	Tuesday (Category 1) 1:30 – 6:00	Wednesday (Category 3) 1:30 – 6:00	Thursday (Category 1) 1:30 – 6:00	Friday* (Category 2) 1:30 – 3:00	Friday* (Category 3) 3:00 – 4:30
0107	**Education** Chr: Debbie Allen Staff: Cathy Eslinger	**St, Vet, & Mil Aff** Chr: Andy McElhany Staff: Jeanette Chapman	**Finance** Chr: Gary McPherson Staff: Steve Schroeder	**St, Vet, & Mil Aff** Chr: Andy McElhany Staff: Jeanette Chapman	**Education** Chr: Debbie Allen Staff: Cathy Eslinger	**Finance** Chr: Gary McPherson Staff: Steve Schroeder
0109	**Local Govt** Chr: Matt Smith Staff: Scott Grosscup	**Bus Aff & Labor** Chr: Jack Taylor Staff: Larry Thompson	**Trans & Energy** Chr: Bill Swenson Staff: Brad Denning	**Bus Aff & Labor** Chr: Jack Taylor Staff: Larry Thompson	**Local Govt** Chr: Matt Smith Staff: Scott Grosscup	**Trans & Energy** Chr: Bill Swenson Staff: Brad Denning
0112	**HEWI** Chr: Marcy Morrison Staff: Whitney Gustin	**Judiciary** Chr: Bill Kaufman Staff: Carl Jarrett	**Ag, Lvstk, & NtRs** Chr: Brad Young Staff: Allison Pasternak	**Judiciary** Chr: Bill Kaufman Staff: Carl Jarrett	**HEWI** Chr: Marcy Morrison Staff: Whitney Gustin	**Ag, Lvstk, & NtRs** Chr: Brad Young Staff: Allison Pasternak

JBC meets 3rd floor Leg Svcs Bldg 9:30 - 11:30 Tue - Thu. Mon/Fri mornings = floor action.

Committees meet infrequently on Fridays.

late to complete the full legislative process. Some said she violated GAVEL. Agler said she thought Republicans had already compromised enough with the Democratic governor on tax legislation. She added that she acted alone, without consultation with either the Speaker or majority floor leader. She did, however, apparently have the backing of the conservative wing of the House Republican caucus, which wanted no compromise with the governor. Floor Leader Norma Anderson commented that she would have acted differently: "I wanted at least one of the two alternative bills to come out of committee."[1] GAVEL thus may have limited the prerogative of committee chairs, but their power was by no means eliminated.

Committees must have a quorum of a majority of the members to conduct business, and all committee actions are made via roll call vote, recorded, and open to public inspection. Committee hearings are open to the public.

When committees vote to amend bills, the amendments are not immediately made part of the bill, but are forwarded to the full House or Senate in the committee report as recommendations along with the bill itself, assuming that the bill is not voted down in committee. Committees can, if they wish, refer bills to other committees. When committees conclude work on bills, they report their actions to the parent chamber within three days (in the House) or five days (in the Senate), with the chair signing committee reports. In both houses, Legislative Council provides one staff person to sit with the committee during the hearings and handle the paperwork. This includes maintaining a file on each bill with records of committee votes on amendments and motions to pass or kill bills, lists of those who testify, copies of materials that witnesses or others may have given to committee members, and the report of the committee action that is sent to the full chamber. Other rules prohibit proxy votes by absent members and forbid more than three consecutive days of absence.

Appointments to Committees

The House and Senate rules formally specify how committee appointments are made, but, as with most things in life, there is a great deal of informality and custom involved along the way. Appointments to certain committees are actively sought by members; other committees are less popular. This does, of course, vary with the individual member. For example, lawyers may want Judiciary; educators often seek appointment to the Education Committees; and ranchers like the Agriculture Committees. Still, there are patterns of general preference.

The committees that deal with money tend to be the most popular— the Joint Budget Committee, the Capital Development Committee, and

Appropriations are coveted spots. So, too, is Judiciary. State Affairs, on the other hand, is not generally a prized catch, as it is often viewed as a bill "graveyard" or "the Speaker's committee." In the words of one former member of leadership, State Affairs often "gets populated with a lot of insensitive people." A lobbyist commented that to serve on State Affairs "you don't have to do a lot of thinking." A Capitol reporter described State Affairs as "a killing field for enterprising Democratic proposals" and as "fertile ground" for Republican measures.[2] Another observer quipped, "When they remodel the Capitol they should put in sawdust floors and folding chairs for the State Affairs Committees."

In 1997 and 1998 State Affairs was populated by members of the religious right and the Speaker sent to it contentious bills dealing with abortion and guns. In a hearing on an abortion bill, 1998 House State Affairs Chairman Mike Salaz quipped to a testifying medical doctor, "We may not be qualified but we are authorized." Representative Jeanne Faatz served as the only woman on the 1998 committee, to which one person commented, "She must think she's in some sort of testosterone purgatory."

For some members, Health, Environment, Welfare, and Institutions (HEWI) has been an unpopular committee. The health and social services bills it handles are "tough issues generally, ones which offer no easy answers, but lots of frustrations," in the words of a party leader.

The stakes in securing desired committee assignments may be higher for members of the majority party. Majority party members are always the ones chosen to chair committees and to serve as vice chair. In addition majority party members are more likely to move their bills successfully through committee than are members of the minority.

At the start of each new General Assembly, leaders of each party in each chamber ask members to identify their preferred committee assignments. Some members go beyond a listing of preferences, and lobby directly for an appointment to, or chairmanship of, a desired committee. Obviously, it is not possible to grant everyone's wishes.

Those who make the assignments, the Speaker and minority leader in the House, and the majority party leadership group and minority leader in the Senate, must balance a variety of criteria as they make their choices. To some extent, members are thought to have a right to return to their previous committees following an election, but unlike the custom in Congress, this "right" is not absolute by any means. So as to maintain the political support of the members, leaders must do what they can to respond to members' wishes.

Good judgment demands that the experience and ability of members be factored into assignment decisions. Leaders in each party will also want to react to the decisions of the other party—to balance the knowledge and rhetorical skill of members of the other party, for example, with similar or counterbalancing qualities from their own party.

There may well be hardball trade-offs involved, too. For example, someone who has opposed the Speaker in a leadership selection struggle, or who has been publicly vocal about his or her displeasure with leadership's style or policy stance, is quite unlikely to be appointed as member and chair of his or her favorite committee. The committee assignment process is therefore a political exercise in which a variety of factors are balanced.

At times members have been transferred from committee to committee or the chair of one committee to the chair of another with no consultation and no advance notice. A former member of the House Republican leadership noted that former Speaker Bledsoe often consulted with other members of leadership or with a trusted veteran lawmaker before making his appointments. He assessed the abilities of various members and tried to give everyone at least one committee on their list of preferences. He also sought to provide assignments that helped members politically. Representative Chuck Berry, who followed Bledsoe, and Senate leaders including President Tom Norton, employed similar procedures and criteria.

There are examples of how committee assignments can be payoffs or punishment for support or nonsupport of leadership, the party, and its current policy preferences. Former Senator Martha Ezzard's policy orientation, out of tune with the leadership's, caused her to lose desirable committee positions she had once held. Jack Fenlon's policy orientation didn't fit in either. In 1988 he chaired the Senate HEWI Committee; one year later, he no longer did, although by 1991 he again chaired a committee. Farmer Lewis Entz was vice chair of the House Agriculture Committee in 1988, but he opposed the Republican efforts to override the Democratic governor's 1988 veto of the lotto bill and one year later found himself off the Agriculture Committee altogether. Representative Chuck Berry succeeded Bledsoe as Speaker and several Capitol veterans observed that his committee assignments said a lot about the sources of his support in the Republican caucus. Interestingly, in 1995 Speaker Berry put Representative Entz back on the Agriculture Committee—as chairman. As one House member commented, "If you're not in tune with leadership, you will get hurt."

There are also examples of how longevity, expertise, and hard work guide committee and chairmanship assignments. For years, Senator Al Meiklejohn chaired the Education Committee even though, as a moderate Republican, he often voted with the Democrats on critical bills, providing 4–3 margins. Many conservative colleagues would like to have had someone else chairing Education, but Meiklejohn's years of service and expertise made that critical position his until his retirement in 1996. A similar situation existed with Senator Dottie Wham's hold on the chairmanship of the Judiciary Committee. Her moderate and prochoice politics were a frustration for many hard-line conservative colleagues, to the point that she was opposed in the 1996 primary by a right-wing Republican. She was subjected to nasty negative attacks in the primary, which all but accused her of letting hardened felons out of jail. Still, her reserved demeanor, her competence, and her long-term record kept her in the Senate and in the chair.

<h2 style="text-align:center">COMMITTEE PERSONALITIES</h2>

Committees often take on distinct personalities. State Affairs was, for example, characterized by a former lawmaker as a place "for the hardball players. Leadership needs a place like that, though. You have to be open with what you do, but you also need a place to put the tough questions and make the tough choices." House Speaker Berry noted that it is understandable that State Affairs would play such a role, since its jurisdiction is broad and bills covering a wide range of subjects may be reasonably sent in its direction. For the 1997 and 1998 sessions Berry appointed a string of hard-right Republicans to State Affairs, prompting some to wonder whether the Speaker wanted a safe place for right-wing bills or a safe place for that group to play out its policy impulses, which would then be controlled elsewhere in the process.

The House and Senate Agriculture Committees also have unique qualities. As one would expect, they are dominated by legislators from the rural farming and ranching areas of the state and have, some say, a "cowboy philosophy." The 1998 House Agriculture Committee was populated by rural members Lewis Entz (chairman), Brad Young, Russell George, Carl Miller, Marylin Musgrave, Larry Schwarz, and Jack Taylor, and Western Slope member Kay Alexander along with veterinarian Steve Johnson and environmental boosters Dan Grossman and Mark Udall. The seven-member Senate Agriculture Committee was chaired by farmer-rancher Don Ament. Issues of water, taxes on agricultural materials and products, and land use are among matters central to the interests of these members, and they tend to stick together in opposition to their urban or suburban colleagues.

The thirteen-member 1999–2000 House Judiciary Committee was home for five lawyers. There were three attorneys on Senate Judiciary. All told, the two committees had twenty-one members, eight of whom were lawyers and ten of whom were women. The disproportionate number of women on the committee is understandable, as Judiciary Committees see many bills dealing with such women's and children's issues as divorce, custody, and sex offenses.

Judiciary Committees, like others, also have their own set of "groupies" that are seen in and around the committees each and every day. In January 1998, for example, representatives of these interest groups testified in House Judiciary: Colorado Trial Lawyers, Denver Police Department, Colorado Association of Sheriffs, Colorado Attorney General, Colorado Division of Criminal Justice, Governor's DUI Task Force, Mothers Against Drunk Driving, Adams County District Attorney, Colorado Public Defender, Colorado Defense Bar, Colorado Solicitor General, Colorado Coalition Against Sexual Assault, Colorado State Association of Teen Courts, Aurora Teen Courts, plus a string of health care groups and organizations. Birds of a feather, some say.

The House Committee on Business Affairs and Labor showed the same pattern. Members included Chairman Paul Schauer, an employee of Gates Rubber Company, Steamboat Springs businessman Jack Taylor, businesswoman Gayle Berry from Mesa County, computer businessman Ron May, computer consultant Brad Young, real estate businessman Andy McElhany, and others with business ties. On January 27, 1998, these groups testified on several bills before the committee: Post Properties, Colorado Homebuilders, Associated General Contractors of Colorado, Bell Plumbing and Heating, Rexall Plus Pharmacies, Colorado Retail Council, Eli Lilly Company, Colorado Association of Commerce and Industry, and a few others including pharmacy interests and Colorado government regulatory bodies.

And so it goes. Members, groups, and lobbyists alike gravitate toward the committees that handle the bills most closely associated with their interests and their pocketbooks.

Not surprisingly, House and Senate committees are not the same. The Senate is just over half the size of the House so naturally, given the legislature's parallel committee structure, the committees are smaller. They are also much less formal. With eleven to thirteen members per committee, House chairpersons tend to keep the sessions a bit formal. Witnesses and members alike are expected to speak "through the chair," and not just engage in conversation with each other as the impulse arises. In the Senate, on the other hand, members seem to "just sit around the table and chat," responding to each other and to witnesses directly and at will, and sprinkling hearings with good doses of jokes. The smaller size of Senate committees and the greater legislative experience of most senators combine to make the atmosphere more informal and relaxed than one finds on the House side.

Committee personalities and committee behavior seem also to be affected by gender. While there may well be a multitude of factors at play, gender is surely one of them in contrasting the 1998 House State Affairs Committee to the Senate Committee on Health, Environment, Welfare and Institutions. As noted elsewhere in this chapter, the 1997–1998 version of House State Affairs was virtually all men, conservative in the extreme, friendly to bills to ban or restrict abortion and to loosen the distribution of firearms, and not always cordial to witnesses. The Senate HEWI, on the other hand, had seven members, four of whom were women, including Chairwoman Sally Hopper. While House State Affairs hearings were sometimes nasty, Senate HEWI proceedings were invariably relaxed and friendly. Its policy predisposition was demonstrated in a 1998 bipartisan vote of 5–2 to kill a partial-birth abortion bill. The five votes came from two Democratic women, two Republican women, and one Democratic man. The two negative votes were those of the only two Republican men on the committee.

Some legislative observers suggest that the link between committee chairs and leadership is tighter in the House than in the Senate. Although there is no day-to-day direction of committee chairs, there are periodic meetings with leadership and regular contact throughout the session. The wishes of leadership on many of the more critical issues are no mystery. As one member commented, "Committee chairs, and members for that matter, all know how they got their appointments and they don't forget it. They pay attention to leadership." As a practical matter, leadership does not and cannot, either politically or legally, issue instructions to chairs or members on all subjects. But it gets its point across when it wants. Thus, in a recent session, Republican committee chairs got the message that too many Democratic bills had been passing. It was an election year.

Chairmanships

Committee chairmanships in the U.S. Congress change hands at what, until the November 1994 elections, seemed a glacial pace. There were several interrelated reasons for this. First, political careerism combined with the electoral success of incumbents to keep many members in Congress for decades. Second, the committee appointment system in Congress stressed seniority above all and thus members maintained what amounted to a right to return to their posts, election after election. Third, chairmanships are always held by members of the majority party, and the Democrats had ruled the House for most of four decades, and were dominant most often in the Senate as well. The Republican takeover of 1995 changed that, of course, but chances are that chairmanship turnover will be infrequent with that party too, their promises of change notwithstanding.

But it is an altogether different story in the Colorado General Assembly. Here, the pattern in committee chairmanships and vice chairmanships has been extremely fluid. One might even call it unstable.

Table 5.3 lists the chairs and vice chairs for each of the nine committees of reference, along with the Appropriations Committees in both the House and Senate, for 1991 and 1997–1998. In the 1997–1998 Senate, only three of the ten committees were chaired by the person who held the post six years earlier—long-term veterans Wattenberg (Business Affairs), Hopper (HEWI), and Wham (Judiciary).

What happened to the others? Bishop became Senate President Pro Tem, Bird retired from the Senate and ran for the Republican nomination for governor in 1994, Fenlon and Meiklejohn retired, Allison lost a primary race in her quest for reelection, Considine sought a U.S. Senate seat and lost, and Norton was elected Senate President. Even this fairly heavy turnover in committee chairmanships accelerated as the full impacts of term limits hit. Indeed, for the 1999–2000 legislature, just two of the Senate's ten standing committees retained the chairperson from the previous session.

There hasn't been much stability in the House, either. By 1997–1998, only two of the ten committees still had their 1991 chairs—veteran legislators Paul Schauer on Business Affairs and Grampsas of Appropriations. Six of the ten 1991 chairs were gone from the legislature entirely. Two of them later ascended to leadership slots—Foster as majority floor leader and Pankey as Republican caucus chairman. Another, Norma Anderson, later moved from the chair of Transportation to the chair of the Committee on Education and in 1997 she was selected as majority floor leader. At the end of the 1998 session eight of the ten chairs were term-limited, so chairmanship change moved even faster. For 1999–2000 just one committee retained its previous session chairperson. Thus, while the legislature is short on stability, it is not without opportunities for leaders to move members around and into open positions of influence.

Committee chairpersons differ considerably in their personalities and in the way they conduct business. Some are very warm and tolerant toward their fellow legislators and witnesses; others are brusque. With short legislative sessions and tight deadlines for dealing with bills, committee chairs must often limit testimony and prod fellow committee members to be brief and to the point with their questions.

In one key dimension, however, committee chairs tend not to differ. They guard their chairmanship prerogatives and defer to and protect those of the others. Reciprocity prevails.

Table 5.3—House and Senate Committee Chairs and Vice Chairs, 1991–92 and 1997–98

Committee	Position	Senate		House	
		1991–92	1997–98	1991–92	1997–98
Agriculture	Chrmn	Bishop	Ament	D. Williams	Entz
	V. Chrmn	Ament	Bishop	Jerke	Young
Appropriations	Chrmn	Bird	Lacy	Grampsas	Grampsas
	V. Chrmn	Taylor	Blickensderfer	Owen	Owen
Business Affairs	Chrmn	Wattenberg	Wattenberg	Schauer	Schauer
	V. Chrmn	Schaffer	Schroeder	Chlouber	Taylor
Education	Chrmn	Meiklejohn	Alexander	Shoemaker	Allen
	V. Chrmn	Ament	Arnold	Arveschoug	Dean
Finance	Chrmn	Fenlon	Coffman	Foster	Agler
	V. Chrmn	Schaeffer	Chlouber	Martin	Pfiffner
HEWI	Chrmn	Hopper	Hopper	Pankey	Epps
	V. Chrmn	Roberts	Congrove	B. Swenson	Morrison
Judiciary	Chrmn	Wham	Wham	Grant	Adkins
	V. Chrmn	Mutzebaugh	Mutzebaugh	Fish	Kaufman
Local Government	Chrmn	Considine	Dennis	Fish	Tucker
	V. Chrmn	Tebedo	Arnold	Entz	George
State Affairs	Chrmn	Norton	Tebedo	Ratterree	Salaz
	V. Chrmn	Owens	Duke	Duke	Paschall
Transportation	Chrmn	Allison	Mutzebaugh	Anderson	May
	V. Chrmn	Tebedo	R. Powers	Johnson	Swanson

COMMITTEE POWER

There may be little continuity in chairmanships in the Colorado General Assembly, but the chairs themselves have not wanted for power over the bills that come their way. Both the House and Senate rules give committee chairs the power to conduct the business of the committee. In practice, this has come to include scheduling bills when the chair wants to hear them (or, through 1988, not scheduling them at all), pulling bills off the table for any reason and at any time, accepting only certain motions on a bill, and limiting testimony on bills. For example, Senate Transportation Committee Chairman Mutzebaugh pulled a bill off the table to avoid a vote that might have killed it. Said Chairman Mutzebaugh, "I can take bills off the table any time because I'm the chairman."[3] House HEWI Chair Mary Ellen Epps did the same with Republican colleague Martha Kreutz's bill to require content labeling on cigarette packages. Epps said she took the action to buy time to assess the bill's fiscal implications. But Kreutz, who figured she had the votes to get the bill out of committee, saw the move as a desire to kill the bill. Said Kreutz, "I've never had anybody do that to me. I don't think that's a fair way to play the game."[4]

Committee procedures can be employed by chairpersons and party leaders to keep bills alive, as well as to kill them. For example, Senate Transportation Committee Chair Marilyn Musgrave refused to take a vote to kill a 1999 bill that restricted city use of photo radar. A motion to recommend the bill favorably had failed, but Musgrave then declined a vote on the question of finally killing the measure. Time passed, one vote changed, the bill survived, and it is now law.

Also in the 1999 session Senate leadership worked with Senator Norma Anderson to pass a bill that had already died in committee. The bill's purpose was to restrict the land-use control powers of local governments. Anderson's measure had died in the Local Government Committee. Following its demise, the same bill was introduced, after the deadline, with another bill number and sent to the Business Affairs and Labor Committee. It passed.

Committee chairs have killed bills they disliked in spite of their committee colleagues' favorable votes to send bills from committee to the floor by failing to sign and file the committee report until the legislative deadline for reporting bills out of committee had passed or until it was too late in the session to consider the bill on the floor. Such examples notwithstanding, the fundamental truth is that no one operates in a political vacuum and a persistent pattern of outrageous behavior could conceivably prompt the members of a committee to rebel. But since committee chairs are politicians and have a sense of the outer boundaries of their power, committee members rarely have to force the hand of their chair.

More common methods employed by legislators to pressure their colleagues to schedule bills include one-on-one persuasion and the mobilization of other opinion and pressure. For example, it is not unusual for legislators to work with lobbyists to build a backfire of constituent pressure in a chairperson's home district and thus prod the chair to move on a bill.

In the Appropriations Committees in both houses, chairpersons have used their powers to kill bills to enormous effect. In the 2000 session, 182 of the 468 nonbudget bills introduced into the House of Representatives had gone to that chamber's Appropriations Committee. Eighty-two had to stand scrutiny in the Senate Appropriations Committee as well. Of the 232 nonbudget Senate bills introduced, sixty-four went to the Senate Appropriations Committee and twenty-eight of these also went to Appropriations in the House.

The sheer volume of bills can create a bottleneck that the chairpersons can exploit to their political advantage. Sometimes there is no way to have full hearings on all these bills, especially with both the House and Senate adhering to firm bill-reporting deadlines. The chairs then can pick and choose among the ones to be scheduled. The others are postponed indefinitely (killed) or reported out too late for floor action.

This practice also provides others, including members of leadership, with political opportunities. The House Speaker or Senate President who wants to torpedo a bill can send it to Appropriations, as well as to the committee of reference, and be reasonably sure that the party colleague who chairs the Appropriations Committee (in the House, this is the Speaker's own appointee) will get the job done. The chair can simply keep that bill in the stack of literally dozens that are not scheduled, at least not until the very end of the session when they are, in effect, scheduled for demise. In similar fashion, chairs of other committees can choose to accept only motions to send bills to the Appropriations Committee with the expectation that they will die there. Majorities on committees of reference can collectively send bills to Appropriations when they want them dead but do not want to be on record as having manned the guillotine.

Indeed, statehouse veterans comment with some frequency that bills with no fiscal impact at all are nonetheless sent to Appropriations as a way to stop them. Former House Minority Leader Peggy Kerns complained, "The House Appropriations Committee is becoming the Rules Committee." Kerns wasn't alone. Joining her in complaint were Democrat Ken Gordon and Republican Bill Kaufman. Even Appropriations Committee Chairman Tony Grampsas said he didn't like his committee to be used as a garbage can for bills. "Don't give the decisions to us unless it's really dealing with money. I don't want 'em," said Grampsas.[5]

Grampsas and others on House and Senate Appropriations Committees may have said they don't want to be buried by an avalanche of bills, but increasingly they got them anyway. The TABOR Amendment limits state spending. The Long Bill usually budgets up to the annual spending limit. Cash funds as well as general fund tax money are subject to the TABOR spending limit. This has come to mean that any bill that involves spending, if it is to pass, will most likely require a cut someplace else. As a result, the Appropriations Committees have become killing fields. One state agency official commented during the 1998 session that "getting a bill through a committee of reference now is the easy part. It's Appropriations you've got to worry about."

In 1999 the legislature began to "set aside" some money earmarked for new programs adopted by newly passed legislation. House Appropriations Committee Chairman Steve Tool observed that this has lessened some of the inclinations to kill bills in the Appropriations Committees.

Representative Elwood Gillis, who chaired the House Appropriations Committee for a number of years prior to enactment of GAVEL, was famous for his use of the pocket veto. In one session, he refused to schedule hearings on bills to provide $35 million in state financing for a new convention center in downtown Denver. Gillis, like House Speaker Bledsoe, apparently wasn't sure the center would help people in rural eastern Colorado districts. In addition, Gillis said he wanted the state to control what the state paid for. He eventually relented, but not before drawing considerable fire. As the *Rocky Mountain News* editorialized:

> Like never before the state legislature has attracted charges this session of using high-handed undemocratic methods. In many states, Gillis could not have achieved such single-handed success—not even as the chairman of the committee through which the doomed legislation had to pass. But in Colorado it is different. Here, the committee chairman can simply refuse to hear a bill. Never mind that everyone on his or her committee would like to send the bill out on the floor for a general vote. That is just too bad.[6]

Like most of his colleagues chairing other committees, Gillis used his prerogatives well. When Democratic Governor Romer was pushing legislation to raise taxes to improve highways, Gillis was opposed and said he would not schedule hearings on the tax bill. He did eventually schedule them, but allegedly not until he had lined up the votes to kill the bill. And the bill did, indeed, die. A similar strategy was again employed later to halt movement of major highway legislation. And even though the GAVEL amendment prohibits committee chairs from simply refusing to hold hearings on a bill, committee chairs still find ways to scuttle them.

The interesting trip and eventual fate of a Senate bill designed to modify the formula used to divide highway funds among sixty-two counties (the City and County of Denver are excluded) provide another illustration of the power of committee chairs and the consequences of its use. Highway money is raised through taxes on fuel, vehicle registration fees, and other sources. The formula to allocate this money favored rural and sparsely populated counties. Suburban Republican Senator Paul Powers sponsored a bill to revise the formula, increasing the slice that the more urbanized Front Range counties would receive.

The bill was assigned to the Senate Transportation Committee, chaired by Senator Dave Wattenberg, whose district covered all or parts of seven rural and sparsely populated counties. Wattenberg scheduled hearings on the bill, but decided soon after they began that he had made a big mistake. When he discovered that the bill was likely to pass, he let it be known that, as committee chair, the only motion he would consider would be one to send the bill to the Senate State Affairs Committee. That committee was chaired by colleague Jim Brandon, whose district lay in the rural eastern part of the state and covered all or part of another eight counties.

Proponents of a revamped distribution formula managed to defeat a motion to send the bill to a certain death in State Affairs. But Wattenberg then pulled the bill off the table, with apologies to the people who had taken time to testify. "I apologize for hearing this bill," he said, "I should have handled it politically different." All this happened in February. Two months later, Wattenberg put the bill back on the table just long enough to entertain and pass a motion to postpone the bill indefinitely.

After Wattenberg pulled the bill off the table in the Transportation Committee in February, Senator Paul Powers sought an alternate route to change the distribution formula. By this time, the deadline for introducing bills was passed, but he asked Senate President Strickland for late-bill status for his measure and requested that it be sent to the Finance Committee, chaired by urban Senator Les Fowler. Strickland refused. Interestingly, Senator Powers had previously challenged Strickland for the Presidency of the Senate and had lost by just one vote. So much for the new formula.

The powers that reside with the House Speaker and Senate President on one hand, and with the committees and their chairs on the other, have often been used in tandem to prevent things from happening.

An illustration of the negative power of the nexus of leadership and committees is Governor Roy Romer's 1988 highway tax plan, contained in a bill sponsored by Democratic Representative JoAnn Groff. For several reasons, the Republican leadership disliked the measure. First, it would have raised taxes, and they did not want a tax increase bill to pass successfully out of a Republican-controlled legislature, especially in an election year. Second, if passed, it could have reflected favorably on a Democratic governor who was portraying himself as an energetic leader and was quite vocal about the need to invest in the state's physical infrastructure to boost the economy.

House Republican leadership handled the matter expeditiously and predictably. The Speaker sent the bill to three committees, including Representative Gillis's Appropriations. In the first committee, Transportation, the bill was largely gutted through an amendment by the Republican chair, who substituted his own tax plan. The bill passed out of this committee and went to Finance, passing there, too, though in further amended form. But in Appropriations, the next stop, it was killed. It was "postponed indefinitely."

The powerful combination of leadership and committees can be used to expedite a measure as well. Consider the fate of a House bill to expand the rights of parents to keep their children out of public schools and educate them at home. The bill died in the House Education Committee—not surprising, since these committee members tend to advocate public education. However, the bill came back the following year and went to State Affairs, sometimes described as "the Speaker's Committee." But it failed there, too. It returned one more time, in modified form, and was again sent by the Speaker to his State Affairs Committee, where it passed.

BILLS

Much of the work of the legislature goes on in committee hearings. Committees receive all sorts of bills. Many are actually adjustments to existing law, for there are laws on the books already that deal with virtually all imaginable subjects. Some bills are only one or two pages in length and simply change a few words in existing statutes. A good number are reruns, bills that have been introduced in one or several previous sessions but which, for any number of reasons, were not passed into law. Other bills are a hundred pages or more. More typically, they are relatively short, running from a couple of pages to two or three dozen pages in length.

Bills originate from a variety of sources. Every session, state agencies that administer the state's programs and enforce the provisions of law promote modifications or clarifications of existing statutes. Individual constituents will sometimes prevail upon a legislator to introduce and carry a bill, and the lawmakers may acquiesce, knowing the bill has no chance of passage, but hoping to show the constituents that "at least they tried." Representatives themselves often have their own agendas, such as preservation of environmental quality, the imposition of their religious values on others through law, placement of strictures on public employee lobbying, or improvement of the air quality along the Front Range.

Much of the impetus for new law or changes in current statutes comes to the legislature from organized interest groups, represented by lobbyists. Businesses want tax exemptions, doctors and insurance companies want limits on lawsuit awards, local governments want authority to create improvement districts, universities want expanded authority to manage their finances, Bronco owner Pat Bowlen wants taxpayers to buy him a new stadium, and so on. But since only legislators can introduce and carry bills, state agencies, interest groups, or private citizens must find legislators who will carry their water for them. And that is much of what one sees in committee hearings.

COMMITTEE HEARINGS

For each legislative day, there is a calendar in the House and another in the Senate that list the agenda for the day, including the bills scheduled for hearings in each committee. On one typical day in 1999, the House Business Affairs and Labor Committee listed three bills: HR 1344 sponsored by Representative King on "Interest on Life Insurance Proceeds," HB 1348 sponsored by Representative May on "Communication and Information Technology Committee," and HB 1352 by Representative Hoppe on "Discriminatory Pharmacy Co-Payments." The hearings were scheduled "upon adjournment" in the House that day. Since the House was first scheduled to hear five bills on third reading, twelve others on second reading, and proposed Senate amendments to fourteen House bills, adjournment for the day, and thus the hearings, would likely be late.

The scene inside committee rooms during hearings changes with the bills being reviewed and the level and the nature of interest in them. On a normal day, there may be a dozen or so people in attendance. Some will be members of the press, perhaps two or three of them reporting for the major Denver dailies. A few will be interns who are serving as staff aides for legislators. Others will be lobbyists, who make up a large slice of the Capitol population, and private citizens or state agency personnel, who are there to testify and provide information or monitor proceedings on bills that may affect their programs and agencies. Committee members sit at a long table in the center of the room. It is equipped with microphones, and all committee business is recorded on tape. The chair of the committee sits at one end and the legislators who are sponsoring bills up for review that day sit at the other. Visitors occupy chairs around the perimeter of the room.

The procedures that legislative committees follow are quite formal, although the behavior of the participants is not. Chairpersons announce the bill under consideration. Every member has a copy and so do others in the room if they have asked for one in the Bill Room. The sponsoring legislator, who has introduced and is "carrying" the bill, reviews it for committee members, describing its content and consequences and stressing the alleged need for the legislation. Sponsors generally bring others along to testify on behalf of the bill and answer technical questions—lobbyists, attorneys, financial experts, agency people, and others. Throughout the process, committee members may and do ask questions. The queries may be many or few, friendly or hostile.

Other citizens who are not part of the orchestrated sales force may also testify. And, at times, the opposition to a bill is as well orchestrated as the support. All one need do to testify is sign up on a sheet and speak when called upon.

A BILL TO PRIVATIZE

Testimony on a House bill designed to force the Denver-area Regional Transportation District (RTD) to "privatize," or sell its routes to private bidders, offers an apt example. The bill's sponsor, Representative Bill Owens, explained his measure and was followed by several private-sector "experts" who supported his arguments. One of his experts worked for the accounting firm of Price Waterhouse and described himself as a transportation cost expert. He claimed that his firm took no position on the bill, but that decisions should be made on the basis of "hard numbers." National studies, he said, showed that private ownership is best; therefore, the best way to improve the system would be to "privatize." Upon questioning, he could cite no examples of improvement or cost savings but maintained that "principles" pointed toward privatization.

Another witness was a transportation policy consultant from Los Angeles who had worked for that city's Mayor Bradley. He claimed that contracting is a viable approach that can save money. Next, a vice president from Greyhound Corporation told committee members, "I am the guy who puts rubber on the road" and claimed that his company could provide the same service as RTD for 35 percent less than current cost. For good measure, he also extolled the virtues of competition. Yet another witness, a consultant in the evaluation of businesses, added his support to the proposed bill.

An elected member of the RTD board followed the advocates. He was there, he said, to present the official RTD position, which, predictably, was in opposition to the bill. He claimed that the board wanted to explore privatization possibilities, but in a controlled and phased fashion, not all at once. He also stressed that there are no fully privatized systems in existence and, thus, no truly parallel experiences from which to learn.

By the time the RTD representative finished, most of the committee's eleven members had finally shown up. More testimony followed, and on subsequent days, RTD employees mounted a mass propaganda campaign against the bill. The governor announced that he would veto the bill as introduced by Owens. As a result, it was changed to provide for a partial and phased privatization plan. Eventually, it passed both the House and Senate and became law over the governor's signature.

Throughout the hearings, questions from Republican committee members were friendly when directed toward bill proponents and hostile toward those in opposition. For the Democratic members, the reverse was true. Committee hearings can make it clear how preset ideology shapes members' positions on individual bills and issues.

FOSTER AND HIS TRIAL LAWYERS

A more recent example was in the House Judiciary Committee where Republican Majority Leader Tim Foster was carrying a bill on behalf of Colorado's trial lawyers. The hearing left one wondering whether it was a legislative committee or a casino.

Foster's bill was designed to limit the extent to which the state and local governments in Colorado could claim sovereign immunity when sued by citizens for damages. As it stood, the state and its local entities cannot be sued unless they agree to be sued. One witness explained that this state of affairs is a holdover from the feudal system wherein the king simply asserted that he, the king, could do no wrong. This came about because actions of the nobility routinely harmed the peasants and the peasants would then come complaining to the king and ask for damages. The king finally tired of the claims and simply announced that the king can do no wrong, the government can do no wrong, so the king won't be sued.

Today governments can still only be sued if they agree to it, and the states have enacted legislation stipulating the conditions under which they are willing to be sued for damages resulting from their own negligent actions. Current law stipulates that liability is capped at $150,000 per individual claim, or $600,000 per incident. Foster's bill would have changed that dramatically.

His bill would have required governmental entities to modernize and upgrade their physical facilities, make them reasonably safe, and maintain them. The bill would have made public entities liable for acts committed by third parties, and it would have required the government to keep public premises and facilities safe. So, for example, if an injurious act was committed by a human, or if a loose dog in a city park bit someone, the expansion of the liability under Foster's bill might have made the government susceptible to suit.

Further, the legislation would have expanded the definition of a "vehicle" to include construction equipment such as backhoes and road graders that were off public roads, along with carts, boats, and snow-plows. An accident resulting from the use of such vehicles, even by a private party on public premises, could then make the government liable and subject to suit. Among the more controversial measures was one that would have made governments liable for damages for harmful actions by an employee or a volunteer who previously had been a convicted sex offender.

It was easy to identify the interested parties. The trial lawyers put Foster up to sponsoring the bill. Foster is a lawyer. Trial lawyers are interested in large slices of the legislative agenda in Colorado as trial lawyers are in all states. They are an ever-present lobby force. They pour a lot of money into legislative campaigns and they are well represented by their lobbyists.

It is always in the interest of the trial lawyers to expand the circumstances under which governments, or anyone else for that matter, can be sued. Trial lawyers make their money trying cases. The more cases they handle, the more people they represent, the more suits there are, and the more money involved, the better they do financially. They have an obvious interest in fighting any kind of tort reform that might squeeze down the circumstances under which a government can be sued. They have a similar interest in expanding the circumstances under which a government can be sued, and in expanding the amount of financial liability. They were not only supporting this bill, but in testimony their lobbyist himself called the Foster bill "the trial lawyers bill."

On the other side of the issue were both the state and local governments and the insurance industry. Local governments and state agencies obviously don't like to be sued, and insurance companies don't like to pay damages.

A string of local government officials was there to testify against the bill. One noted that in 1986 the legislature reformed the governmental immunity act to make it more difficult for people to sue Colorado state and local governments. As a result, insurance rates dropped significantly. This bill would push that trend in the opposite direction.

The proposed expansion of vulnerability for state and local governments to harm done by convicted sex offenders, witnesses claimed, would create a problem because no matter how hard schools and other governments try to check the background of employees and volunteers, including fingerprint checks through the FBI and the Colorado Bureau of Investigation, sometimes they are still unable to obtain the full picture and may end up being sued for not having data that they were simply unable to secure. Information, one witness said, simply slips through the cracks.

Opponents were similarly concerned about the expanded definition of "vehicle." Several witnesses used the snowplow example, noting that in bad weather, counties and cities are obligated to have equipment on the road in slippery and dangerous conditions when visibility is poor. Sometimes accidents happen. The consequences of covering vehicles beyond the normal licensed passenger car and truck, so as to include equipment like snowplows, could be to generate a blizzard, so to speak, of additional suits.

The bill as originally written represented a very significant broadening of liability exposure for the state and local governments. But when the hearings began the sponsor immediately proposed a "strike below the enacting clause" amendment. The effect of such an amendment is to kill the entire bill below the opening enacting clause, and substitute something else. That something else was a drastically shortened and much more limited bill. Opposition to the bill had obviously been voiced between the time the bill was drafted and the hearing, and changes had been made as a result.

This is common. Had Foster come forth and put the full original bill on the table it is clear that the opposition would have been even stronger.

When the opposition finished, the trial lawyers had their chance. Their case was opened by Jim Lee, former legislator, now a lobbyist. He began by explaining "why we came up with the bill that we did" and reviewed some of the elements of the original bill that had been eliminated in Foster's amendment. The point, clearly, was to persuade the committee that the trial lawyers had already done their fair share of compromising. Lee's remarks also highlighted the fashion in which legislators function as the mules for groups who seek to change law and expand their opportunities for financial advantage.

Lee went on to explain that in 85 percent of the cases where someone has been injured, sovereign immunity is invoked and the suit goes absolutely nowhere. In only 15 percent of the cases are citizens able to proceed and sue the government for damage. He argued that the whole system was tilted very heavily against the ordinary citizen.

Lobbyist Lee went on to ridicule the rhetoric of the opponents, claiming they characterized the bill as generating sweeping change. It wasn't sweeping change, Lee said, but only modest modification of the law. He employed tear-jerking language, referring to breadwinners and single moms who might have been damaged but were up against the monstrous government and were simply unable to sue. Lee said current law pits the family with a little budget against the big government with the big budget.

The lawyers' lobbyist was followed by Lee Anderson, president-elect of the state Trial Lawyers Association. Anderson proceeded to tell the committee and those in attendance stories about how citizens have been hurt by government trucks and by road graders but haven't been able to get a dime as a result.

Concerning the sex offender provision, the trial lawyers' president said that inclusion of this in the statute would constitute a statement to the children that "we care about you." He concluded his testimony by observing that "we haven't heard a lot about compassion here today, we've heard a lot about fiscal impact and a lot about cost, but not a lot about compassion." Anderson beseeched the members of the committee to consider the "ordinary citizen." He was, he said, "speaking for people who have no power," "for victims," and "on behalf of victims." There is "no victims lobby," the trial lawyer added. This bill would meet the needs and injustices in today's law.

It was interesting indeed to listen to the voices of the trial lawyers as they spoke to the committee on behalf of the poor and downtrodden whom they stand ready to help, and to represent, in tort actions for a paltry one third of all damage awards.

The fact that the system is knee-deep in lawsuits, some of which are triggered by attorneys looking for someone to represent, was not lost on committee members. One representative, Maryanne Keller, is a former city council member. She had earlier made the point that she feared this bill would open the system to even more "frivolous and outrageous" suits. She cited a number of instances in her own experience when her city had been deluged with suits of a frivolous, but nonetheless costly, nature. She was joined by Republican Marcy Morrison, a former county commissioner from El Paso County, who observed that "almost weekly my colleagues and I were getting certified mail from persons threatening to sue the county." There was clearly some sentiment on the committee to resist Foster and the trial lawyers, and it was equally clear that the resistance on the part of some of the members came from their own experience in elected positions at the local level.

When it was over the committee voted 7–6 favorably to move the bill to the Appropriations Committee. As it turned out the Appropriations Committee was the end of the road for this measure too. State agencies had estimated that enactment of the bill would cost at least $1.5 million in new money for the coming year. In the budget-tight Amendment One (TABOR) environment, bills of this nature are likely to die in the Appropriations Committee, as this one did.

The vote itself was interesting. As noted earlier there were four law-yers on the committee and one might have expected them to vote on the side of the Trial Lawyers Association. Indeed, three of the four, two Democrats and one Republican, did so. The remaining trial lawyer, Re-publican Russell George, voted no. One might also have guessed that Marcy Morrison and Maryanne Keller who had had experience at the local level would have no appetite for opening the system to even more suits. They too voted no.

But then what about the others? Professional Capitol sages out in the lobby gave this explanation: Republican Majority Leader Tim Fos-ter was carrying the bill and some members of his party just didn't want to oppose him. Republicans Vice Chair Tucker, Chair Adkins, and Martha Kreutz all voted for the bill, perhaps in deference to Foster. They may well have assumed that it would die in Appropriations anyway, and they were right.

It's reasonable to speculate that a number of factors in combination acted to move votes one way or another. The fact that some members were lawyers themselves made them sympathetic to the legislation. Others had been on the other side of the coin, having been sued by the trial lawyers in their capacities in local government, and were, as a result, resistant to the legislation. Indeed that's the way they voted. In the case of Adkins, Tucker, and Kreutz, the fact that the sponsor was the major-ity leader may have made the difference. It can't do members much good to vote against their own leaders unless there are some very good reasons for doing so.

When members are in the minority party, however, that incentive isn't present. And indeed, Democrats Knox and Rupert voted no. Thus the only Democrats who voted in favor of the legislation were trial lawyers.

If there was ever an episode that makes the legislative arena look and feel like a casino, this was it. Aligned on one side was the insurance industry, with big bucks at stake. Passage of this legislation would in-crease the vulnerability of their clients. Their cause was carried largely by the voices of local government. On the other side were the trial law-yers whose bread and butter comes from suing and doing so success-fully. The entire proceedings were laced with high-minded lingo, like protecting children, protecting the public interest, leveling the playing field, taking care of single mothers and poor families, and all that good stuff. Could any of this have to do with money?

When testimony is completed on bills, the committee chair typi-cally will place the bill on the table for amendment. This may be after very lengthy testimony; at other times, such testimony is limited because the committee chair does not have the time or does not want to take time to deal with the bill. Committee members are then free to offer amendments to the bill, and most often they do. After discussion of these amendments, roll call votes are taken on them and, after all efforts to amend the bill are completed, motions are made to act on the bill "as amended." These motions may be to pass the bill, and to move it to the Committee of the Whole for second reading floor action, to kill it by postponing it indefinitely, or to move it to another committee of reference or to the Appropriations Committee. Since 1989, the rules also allow any committee member to move to report a bill out at any time. But if this motion fails, the bill dies on the spot. Consequently, such efforts are rarely made.

Testimony can have a real impact on the fate of a bill, but so, too, can other factors, including members' concerns for their colleagues' views and for their own public images. A few years ago, a bill relating to athletics in higher education passed out of the House State Affairs Committee only to die on the floor. A legislator who privately opposed the bill but voted for it in committee commented that the bill sponsor needed a victory in committee to boost his morale, but that no one should worry as the bill would die on the floor. Similarly, a lobbyist who opposed a bill told fellow opponents not to worry because "we'll get it [the bill] in the Senate."

In another instance Colorado Springs Senator Ray Powers opposed a bill designed to give the state Air Quality Control Commission the authority to impose diesel emissions standards. However, when his effort to impose crippling amendments failed, Powers supported the bill, thus avoiding a recorded roll showing his opposition to a clean air measure.

Most of those close to Colorado's legislative process will assert that a bill's fate is usually determined well before hearings are even held. Votes counted by bill sponsors and lobbyists alike are fairly set well before any hearings, and the process is little more than a pro forma charade. A 1999 hearing in the Senate State Affairs Committee on a bill to ban payroll deduction of public employee association dues when some small portion was used in political campaigns provided a vivid illustration. Sixteen people testified; fourteen were opposed and two in favor. One of the two in favor was Barry Arrington, a former hard-right-wing legislator representing the Colorado Union of Taxpayers. Most of the fourteen opponents represented associations of students, teachers, and public employees.

The testimony was irrelevant from the start, and everybody knew it. A majority of the committee members represented the hard-core conservative wing of the Republican party. Their antipathy toward the politics of public employees was beyond doubt, and so was their vote.

Just the opposite was true of the four Democrats on the committee. The vote on the bill was 5–4 on party lines to send the bill to the Senate floor with a favorable recommendation.

Testimony could have consumed a minute or a year, with one witness or a thousand. It would not have mattered as preset and widely recognized ideology and political leanings predetermined the outcome. The real decision on the fate of that bill in committee was made by the Senate President when he sent it to State Affairs.

The general scene during hearings and the behavior of the people involved are less formal than the process itself. Staff members walk in and out constantly, delivering phone messages or notes from lobbyists and others who want to talk with members. Legislators themselves will wander in and out of hearing rooms to get coffee, return phone calls, or visit with lobbyists. They dash to other committees in the House or Senate where bills they are sponsoring are scheduled for hearings. Members of the press, persons there to testify or just observe, and staff members will enter and exit in similar fashion.

Committee meetings seldom start on time because members always seem to be buttonholed and delayed by lobbyists or colleagues while en route from the floor or their offices to the hearing rooms. And no one ever seems able to return from lunch on time. Some years back the Senate Education Committee was scheduled to meet at 1:30 P.M. to resume hearings on House Bill 1341, a major piece of legislation that dramatically altered the method of state funding of elementary and secondary education. The committee meeting started at 1:38 P.M., with just two of the seven members present—Senator Meiklejohn, the chair, and his colleague, Senator Fowler. Others arrived as follows: Considine at 1:45, Allard at 1:50, Mendez at 2:00, and Durham at 2:10. At 2:00, when Fowler left, Lee still had not arrived.

This is not unusual and probably cannot be avoided. On any given day, there are many activities going on simultaneously, and several may demand a legislator's attention at the same time. Furthermore, once lawmakers are familiar with a bill, additional testimony and discussion may be redundant. To the casual observer, however, the comings and goings may look odd, as when Senator Durham walked out of a hearing during testimony only to return shortly thereafter, and stayed just long enough to cast a negative vote. Committee hearings on a bill may be brief or they may run on and on. In one lengthy session, a legislative aide quipped, "I feel sorry for Madam Chair. She can't even get up to go to the bathroom."

There are times when witnesses and legislators alike get testy. In a committee hearing on a bill to revoke the driver's licenses of convicted drug dealers, witness Robin Heid told the Senate Transportation

Committee, "This kind of sarcastic ignorance of the U.S. Constitution is one of the most important problems facing us today. . . . In this legislature, in the United States Congress . . . we've got a bunch of smart aleck legislators wielding their power." Earlier in the same session, an Aurora policeman told the House Judiciary Committee, "Pardon my nervousness. I'd rather be out chasing a criminal, getting shot at." In yet another hearing, this one on property tax exemptions for church property, a representative of Baptist churches blurted out, "Whoever wrote that narrow word 'worship' in the state constitution should have been taken out and shot."

Members' comments to one another can be direct. In a Senate hearing on a House-passed measure to create chain prisoner gangs in Colorado, Senator Sally Hopper told the sponsor, "I'm really confused why in the heck we're doing it. Is it to get more people out in the fresh air? Is it to get more trash picked up along the highways?" "Senator Powers, I really admire you in a lot of ways, but I think this is the dumbest thing I've ever heard of."[7]

There are occasions, rare ones, when hearings take on the trappings of prematch World Wrestling Federation verbal exchanges. In 1997 the House State Affairs Committee held hearings on two abortion bills. Members of the committee included anti-abortionists Doug Dean, Mark Paschall, and Barry Arrington. Witnesses included Dr. Warren Hern, a Boulder physician who performs abortions, and Mr. Kenneth Scott, an avid anti-abortionist who, at the time of the hearings, was under a court-ordered restraining order for having threatened to kill Dr. Hern. At one of the hearings plain-clothed police personnel were stationed at the committee room doors.

Prior to hearings, Dr. Hern called a press conference to express his views and his opposition to the proposed anti-abortion bills. Representative Arrington took the microphone to call Hern a "hypocrite and liar." During hearings Representatives Paschall and Dean insisted on swearing in Dr. Hern and reminding him that false testimony constitutes perjury; swearing in witnesses is rarely done, and Paschall and Dean's action clearly suggested that Hern was not trustworthy. Some committee members were angered at Paschall's action and told him so. Others were simply embarrassed, and visibly so.

The behavior of the committee occasioned a column by *Rocky Mountain News* reporter Dan Luzadder entitled, "House State Affairs panel specializing in boorish conduct." Luzadder noted that the committee's behavior was keeping some folks from testifying for fear of being the subjects of attacks by some of the representatives.[8]

Occasionally, the lawmakers' behavior is polite in the extreme. Senate Education Committee Chairman Meiklejohn, seeing his senatorial colleague Harold McCormick enter a committee room, gallantly announced his arrival. "Ladies and gentlemen," he said, "Senator McCormick, President Pro Tem of the Senate, is here. Senator, welcome. Please participate in our proceedings." In the normal course of events, these gentlemen probably saw each other at least twenty times a day.

In hearings on a bill to raise taxes to improve highways, a Republican complimented a Democratic colleague for sponsoring a bill: "Thanks, JoAnn, for the guts to do something. This will not do much for her incumbency." In the same hearings, committee members danced around, trying to oppose the bill and simultaneously endorse its objectives. It was an election year, and the Republican committee majority was a conservative bunch. But the room was packed with folks who wanted road improvements, including a delegation of students and adults from Ponderosa High School in Parker where a number of young people had been killed on a very busy and narrow two-lane road. The concerns of the Ponderosa people had recently received extensive, statewide media attention, and in that committee room environment, no one dared to adopt an overt anti-improvement posture. To avoid that, the majority passed a substitute plan at half the cost and let the House Appropriations Committee kill it a month later.

The way in which legislators can function as the agents for other interests is sometimes rather transparent. In one hearing, a member of the press passed a note to a legislator asking that a question be posed to a witness. The lawmaker obliged, and the reporter proceeded to enter the response in his notes.

Curiously, legislators occasionally have trouble explaining the bills they sponsor and constantly have to deflect questions to the lobbyists in the room or ask that hearings on the bill be delayed until they can consult with someone who knows just what the bill means. A lobbyist commented about one instance when "I told my client to write out the script very carefully and simply, or the representative would get lost. And sure enough, when questions were asked, she did. She just never could understand that bill."

Sometimes, though, it is just the reverse. After a hearing, one freshman legislator told a senior colleague that, despite the fact that he didn't really like her bill, he voted for it anyway because "it was nice to see a bill carried by someone who knew something about it."

Members of the General Assembly become so accustomed to hearing testimony from lobbyists and others with personal or corporate interests in a specific bill that they can be caught off guard by someone with no apparent ax to grind. In a Senate committee hearing on a bill to restrict the authority of state agencies to engage in activities in competition with private businesses, a Mr. Lindsay from Northglenn appeared and signed up to testify. The committee chair asked Lindsay if he was for or against the bill and if he wished to suggest any amendments. Lindsay replied that he was just a citizen with a concern about legislation.

Lindsay spoke for a spell and then asked if the committee chairman had answers to his comments. The chairman replied that Mr. Smith, a lobbyist in the room, would respond. Later, a committee member asked the witness what he did for a living, to which Lindsay replied, "I start businesses and sell them. I'm just a country boy." The chairman added that "we hear a lot of that around here." No one ever figured out what Mr. Lindsay of Northglenn wanted; it was hard to imagine that he would trouble himself just to comment on a matter of public concern in the name of nothing more than good citizenship.

From time to time, committee hearings can provide good trivia. For example, the House Finance Committee held hearings on a bill to tighten the regulation of suppliers for games of chance and require those who sell "pull tabs" to register. Pull tab games were defined in the bill as "a game of chance commonly known as a 'pickle,' 'break open' or 'jar raffle,' for which tickets are preprinted with markings distinguishing winners and non-winners." In the course of discussion, the games were most often referred to simply as "pickles," but it was clear that many folks had no idea what a pickle was, if not something to eat. A committee member explained that the term originated in the days of barroom drawings where winning numbers were pulled out of a big glass pickle jar.

Most bills passed by committees stand a good chance of passing the floor, as well. Indeed, over two-thirds of the bills that make it through committee do pass in the full chamber, but a good many are amended on second reading or, occasionally, on third reading.

On the floor, committee members often become advocates for bills reported out of their committees. They know the bills well, and they have usually supported them and worked through compromises and amendments. Thus, they have an investment in the bills. As one legislator commented, "After twenty amendments you know a bill well." Support by committee members may cross party lines, too, for they know the bill when others may not; they are, therefore, in a strong position to influence colleagues who seek their advice and defer to their judgment.

There are times when bill sponsors seek to amend or even kill their own bills on the floor. This is most likely to occur when the original content of the bill has been diluted or when provisions that are offensive to the sponsor have been added. An example was a safe drinking water bill, sponsored by House Democrat Jeannie Reeser. Her bill had been gutted in the Agriculture Committee, and she and others successfully sought to restore the basic contents on the floor. Indeed, this bill had been sent initially to the Committee on Health, Environment, Welfare, and Institutions, where it was amended and passed, then sent to the now-defunct House Rules Committee to be scheduled for second reading. The Rules Committee, however, sent it back to Agriculture, which worked it over on behalf of some business and industry interests. But on the floor, the full body revived much of the original content.

CONFERENCE COMMITTEES

By the time they pass the second house, most bills—roughly 60 percent—have been altered from the form they were in when they passed in their chamber of origin. About three-fourths of the time, the first house will concur with the amendments made in the second chamber. But there are also many instances, especially in areas of highly controversial legislation, where an agreement is not so easily reached, and it becomes necessary to resolve the differences and make the bill palatable to majorities in both houses. Thus, another type of legislative committee is spawned—the conference committee.

Over the span of both the 1994 and 1995 sessions, 104 such committees were appointed. In twelve instances the original conference committee was unable to reach an agreement, and a second six-person committee was appointed to try to find agreeable middle ground. Each conference committee has just one bill to work on, one set of House/Senate disagreements to resolve.

When a bill returns to the house of origin, having been altered by the second house, the first chamber may, of course, accede to the changes. But if it doesn't, rather than simply let the bill die, it can establish a conference committee. The presiding officer, either the House Speaker or Senate President, then appoints three members to constitute that chamber's conference committee, and the second chamber is asked to do likewise. Together, these six members constitute the conference committee on the bill. A member from the first house, usually the bill's prime sponsor, serves as chair, having been so designated by the presiding officer when appointments to the committee were made.

The task of the six-member conference committee, then, is to focus on the disagreement between the two houses and work through a compromise that is saleable to the membership of both chambers. Before a bill is reported out of conference, there must be separate two-to-one majorities, or unanimity, within the group of three from each house. Conference committees are required to confine their deliberations to the points at issue unless they are given authority to "go beyond the scope" of the disagreements. This is commonly done and requires a majority vote in each chamber.

When majority support for a compromise version of the bill develops in both the House and Senate contingents, one or more members from each body meet with personnel in the Office of Legislative Legal Services to describe the compromise. The Legal Services staff will then prepare the report and have it signed by conference committee members. This report goes first to the house that did not request the conference, and, if passed there, it goes to the chamber that initiated the request and was the "house of origin." Either house may reject the report, holding to its original position. If one holds, the other may recede from its stance, and the bill will pass. Of course, if either house holds to an original position that turns out to be unacceptable to the other, the bill dies. If one conference committee member from each chamber so agrees, they may ask the Legislative Legal Services Office to prepare a minority report that will then accompany the majority report to the floors of the two chambers.

Members of conference committees include those most involved with the bill, and they often suggest to the Speaker and Senate President the names of members they'd like to see appointed to the Conference Committee. Usually the bill's sponsor is included, although there are exceptions, such as when a bill has been amended so dramatically that the original sponsor disavows the contents or even seeks to kill the bill. The Senate President and Speaker virtually never place on conference committees members who are opposed to passing the bill in any form, although there are exceptions. In 1998 Speaker Berry appointed Representative Ron Tupa to the conference on the Bronco Stadium bill even though Tupa was the most outspoken opponent in the chamber. The move astonished the bill sponsors, bill supporters, and even Tupa himself. Tupa ended up being outvoted in conference repeatedly on 5–1 votes.

Conference committees generally report their actions within a few days or weeks after receiving their charge, but must report within the last five days of the session. If they do not, or if they fail to respond to an earlier call by the full chamber, there are procedures in the rules to either force action or dissolve the committee. It is then possible to move to appoint a new conference committee.

Textbook references to conference committees often leave one with the impression that most bills end up in different form as they emerge from the two legislative chambers, and that it is always conference committees that work out the differences. But that is not the case. The 1995 and 1996 legislative sessions saw the passage of 620 bills, excluding midyear budget supplementals and resolutions. While the House and Senate versions differed on 381 bills, the disagreements were settled 277 times by the house of origin agreeing to the amendments made in the second chamber. As noted before, one or more conferences were required on just 104 bills out of the two-session total of 1,148 introductions and 620 passages. So while conference committees are very critical parts of the committee system and the legislative process, and while they are more frequently employed on high-stakes contentious legislation, most bills by far pass without them.

This should not be surprising. The legislative process at all points is characterized by endless informal hallway, lobby, and lunch discussions among members and interested parties. There is much communication, deliberation, and decision-making in committee and on the chamber floors, but there is much more that occurs constantly and informally. Thus, as one chamber amends the bills of the other, the bill's sponsors and others with stakes in the measures are, in all likelihood, aware of and involved in the activity. So it is quite natural for bill sponsors in the house in which bills originate to recommend to their colleagues that second chamber changes be accepted. After all, they were most likely aware of or a party to the decision to make the amendments.[9]

JOINT COMMITTEES

The Colorado statutes create several joint legislative committees, each with a special purpose. The Joint Budget Committee (JBC) will be discussed in Chapter 8 to give it the special attention it deserves. At this point, it is sufficient to note that the JBC is composed of six legislators, three from each chamber, who assemble the state budget each year and send it to the General Assembly for review, modification, and adoption. In 1985, the legislature established a Capital Development Committee, structurally modeled after the JBC. It, too, is a six-member joint House and Senate committee, with three members from each chamber. The task of the committee is to study the capital construction, controlled maintenance, and health and safety needs of the state, then project and rank priorities five and ten years into the future. This committee often travels throughout the state to conduct hearings and examine existing state facilities. It may solicit staff help from the Legislative Council, the Department of Administration, and the Office of State Planning and Budgeting. The committee's views of the capital needs of the state are forwarded to the Joint Budget Committee.

Before 1985, the JBC assessed and ranked the state's capital needs along with its other budget activities. The creation of the Capital Development Committee relieved the already overworked Joint Budget Committee of some of its responsibilities, but also took away some of its clout. This development did not excite the JBC members and staff personnel.

Three joint committees oversee important legislative service units. One of these, the Legislative Council, creates and oversees its namesake, the Legislative Council. The committee is composed of eighteen legislators. Six are appointed by the Senate President and six by the Speaker of the House. These appointments are subject to approval by the full chambers. In addition, the President, Speaker, and majority and minority leaders from each house are ex officio members. These six ex officio members, who are essentially the core of the legislative leadership, constitute the Legislative Council's executive committee and play a substantial role in setting the legislature's agenda, for interim committee work especially. A major task of the Legislative Council is to propose for House and Senate approval the name of a person to serve as director of the main research arm of the General Assembly, the Legislative Council. This individual, in turn, hires the rest of the council's staff personnel. The director, like the research unit itself, functions in nonpartisan fashion to serve the entire legislature.

Another such joint committee is the Committee on Legal Services. The membership structure of this committee is a bit unusual. It is made up of ten legislators, five from each house. For each chamber, there are two representatives from each party, plus the chairs of the Judiciary Committees. If possible, one member from each party in each house is an attorney. The prime task of the Committee on Legal Services is to recruit the director for the Office of Legislative Legal Services, who hires the legal and clerical personnel to staff the department. Among its drafting duties, Legal Services prepares bills and amendments in proper legal form and revises the state statutes as new laws are passed and old ones modified.

Finally, there is an eight-member Legislative Audit Committee. This committee is composed of two members of each party in both houses, with members nominated by the Speaker or the Senate President and confirmed by the full chamber. The committee recruits a state auditor and recommends that person to the General Assembly for appointment.

The state auditor, appointed for a five-year term, then staffs and oversees the State Auditor's Office, which conducts both fiscal and performance audits of state agencies. The Legislative Audit Committee is charged with overseeing the operation of this office, and, in the course of its oversight duties, the committee may recommend legislation to the General Assembly.

Each chamber has a committee on "services." These committees direct procurement of equipment, supplies, and so forth. In the Senate, the Services Committee is also responsible for checking Senate bills that are about to leave the chamber and House bills ready to enter the Senate for accuracy and proper form.

INTERIM COMMITTEES

In addition to the committees of reference, the joint committees, the service committees (all of which are permanent in nature), and the temporary bill-specific conference committees, there are special issue-focused committees established almost every year. These "interim committees" are created to give intensive examination to particular policy problems and report their findings, along with suggested remedial legislation, back to the General Assembly. Most of the work of committees of reference focuses upon rather narrow individual bills, but an interim committee may focus on broad topical areas, such as corrections, transportation, or education. In addition, interim committees occasionally may be convenient places to send politically hot topics.

Interim committees are joint House and Senate panels whose members are drawn from both parties and both houses and sometimes include private citizens, as well. They are usually established by joint resolution, with legislative membership generally ranging from fourteen to seventeen persons. Most of their meetings and work occur between sessions in the summer and early fall. The committees receive staff help from the Legislative Council and the Office of Legislative Legal Services. The product of their labors—summaries of findings and suggested legislation—is reported to the Legislative Council Committee, which, in turn, submits the report to the full General Assembly. Then, in the next legislative session, members of the interim committees sponsor and carry the bills that grew out of their study. Bills of greatest importance and those with the potential for favorable visibility are usually carried by the members of the majority party, often the interim committee chairs.

Legislators may or may not seek appointment to interim committees. Those with a special interest in a particular policy area will gladly serve on committees focusing on related problems. On the other hand, service on a panel that meets during the summer and early fall of an election year may not be attractive at all, especially if the policy area under examination is not of great interest to the legislator. Some recent interim committees include the Joint Review Committee for Medically Indigent and Illegal Aliens, which was composed of ten members and recommended four bills to the General Assembly; the committee on Long-Term Health Care Needs, which had fourteen members and suggested nineteen bills; the Committee on Juvenile Offenders, which had fifteen members and suggested seven bills; and the Committee on Water Quality and Water Resources, composed of fourteen members, which recommended eight bills.

COMPLAINTS AND REFORM

The committee system in the Colorado General Assembly has had its detractors. Not surprisingly, the Democrats, who have been in the minority for the last two decades, are often critics, but they have certainly not been alone. In the 1980s, a number of citizens' groups pressed for reforms, and members of the media have been critical as well.

No one disputes the need for a specialized committee system and a labor-divided legislature. Indeed, it would be impossible to conduct business any other way. It is certain aspects of the committee system, not the system itself, that have been under attack. The features of the system that have drawn the fire of critics have been the use of the so-called pocket veto by legislators who chair the committees and the selective referral of bills by the presiding officers. Some of the criticism and calls for change culminated in the 1988 citizen-initiated ballot proposal to amend the constitution and require hearings on all bills, thus outlawing the pocket veto. This measure, the GAVEL (Give A Vote to Every Legislator) amendment was passed by the voters overwhelmingly.

GAVEL began in 1988 as a House concurrent resolution carried by Democratic Representative Wayne Knox. It was designed to do several things: propose a constitutional amendment to require a hearing for every bill, prevent committee chairs from restricting applicable motions, and place restrictions on the use of the party caucus as a mechanism to bind members on floor votes.

The measure died on a party-line vote in the House State Affairs Committee. A total of twenty-three groups, including the PTA, the Colorado Senior Lobby, the League of Women Voters, the Council of Churches, the Citizens' League for Legislative Reform, and Colorado Common Cause, supported the resolution. Former House Speaker and Majority Leader Ron Strahle spoke against it, noting that with short legislative sessions and bill-reporting deadlines, it would be impossible to complete the work of the General Assembly without giving committee chairs considerable power to decide which bills would be heard. He also defended the caucus system, quoting former Democratic House Speaker and present lobbyist Ruben Valdez to the effect that "there is no way to write a budget on the floor."

The Republican majority on the State Affairs Committee succeeded in killing the Knox measure, but the coalition of reform groups prevailed in the end. They employed the initiative method, securing enough voter signatures on petitions to place the proposed constitutional amendment on the ballot. In November 1988, it passed by a margin of more than two to one.

There have been other complaints about the committee system, though none quite so broadly based as these. Democrats, for example, complain that the system is used to kill or gut their bills, especially in election years. The content of their bills, they say, is often excised and reinserted in similar bills carried by Republican legislators, particularly if the provisions are necessary and appear to be popular at election time.

They also claim that their bills have often been said to have fiscal impacts when, in fact, they do not and thus have been sent to the Appropriations Committees to meet certain death.

Even majority party Republicans have complained about the use of committees to kill bills. Bills designed to liberalize the right to carry concealed weapons have passed the House but died in the Senate Judiciary Committee, which has been chaired by moderate Republican Dottie Wham. Bills to expand charter schools or provide vouchers have expired in the Senate Education Committee. Until 1997 the committee was chaired by public schools advocate Al Meiklejohn. And increasingly members of both parties complain that the Appropriations Committees are used to kill bills for reasons that go beyond fiscal concerns. Representative Steve Johnson, for example, contended that his 1998 telemarketing bill, which passed successfully out of the House State Affairs Committee only to die in House Appropriations, was a victim of back-door lobbying. Both Appropriations members and lobbyists opposed to his bill confirmed his assertion.

There is little doubt that individual legislators can and often have employed their positions as committee chairs to thwart the will of the majority. And there is no way to deny the fact that the leadership and members of the majority party work the system to the disadvantage of the minority party. It is difficult, though, to structure a large deliberative body in a way that will get the work done without building in strategic positions of power. And it is unreasonable to assume that human beings who challenge one another publicly in elections and in leadership struggles will fail to use the positions they secure to impose their vision of the public good on others, meanwhile thwarting similar attempts by their rivals.

LEGISLATIVE OVERSIGHT

The General Assembly, through its committees, exercises what is termed "legislative oversight." The philosophy behind legislative oversight is simple: Since the impact of legislation is, in considerable measure, just what the implementing executive branch agencies make of it, the General Assembly should follow up on the laws it passes by checking to see what the agencies have done with them. Oversight review is often triggered by some specific concern of a legislator, by complaints from home district constituents, by crisis, or by lobbyists rather than by any broad oversight philosophy. There are, essentially, five ways in which the legislature engages in oversight: through audits; with JBC budget hearings; with review of agency rules; in the regular course of hearing bills and enacting legislation with formal hearings in committees of reference; and in interim committee studies.

The state auditor and his staff members are responsible for financial post-audits of state agencies and institutions. The results are reported to the Legislative Audit Committee. Sometimes, the auditor will, either at the direction of the committee or at his own initiative, conduct special audits or investigations.

Proposals for new law often emerge from the work of the auditor and the Audit Committee. Their audit reports may reveal conflicts between the dictates of the statutes and current practice in an agency. If the procedures being followed make more sense than those stipulated by current law, if the law is silent on an activity performed by an agency that seems necessary, or if some aspects of law seem to lack adequate rationale, suggestions for changes in the law will be developed. The auditor may suggest such changes in law or in practice, agencies may themselves request new authority or the deletion of some provisions of a statute, or individual legislators may see a need for changes. Members of the eight-person Legislative Audit Committee will then introduce and sponsor bills to effect the changes in law in the next legislative session.

Although the Joint Budget Committee is not charged directly and explicitly with the oversight of executive branch activities, it quite unavoidably reviews agency activity nonetheless. The JBC regularly communicates with state agencies as it assembles the annual state budget and considers supplemental requests each year.

The statutes instruct the Joint Budget Committee "to hold hearings as required and to review the executive budget and the budget requests of each state agency and institution." As it assists the committee in its work each year, the JBC staff reviews past budgets and new agency funding requests and provides briefings to committee members on agency functions, performance, problems, issues, and requests. In the process of assembling annual budgets, the committee holds hearings with agency personnel, which give representatives from the agency opportunity to tell their story and sell their programs to the committee. At the same time, committee members also have a chance to grill agency personnel.

The result of this interaction is that JBC staff personnel and committee members can review just about any aspect of executive branch activity they wish and probe as deeply as suits their fancy. When they like what they see, they can respond with enriched funding. When they don't, they can recommend funding cuts or budget-bill footnotes that place restrictions on agency operations. So, although the Joint Budget Committee is not, technically, an oversight body, its oversight activities can be significant indeed.

The Committee on Legal Services also exercises a type of legislative oversight involving the review of agency rules, primarily through the

Office of Legislative Legal Services that it oversees. Much legislation is written in a way that requires the administering agencies to create rules, regulations, and procedures to implement the programmatic or regulatory dictates of the statutes. These may involve charging fees, establishing reporting requirements, or specifying a certain level of compliance, with air or water quality standards, for example. These regulations are not the products of the legislature directly, but they do carry the force of law. Understandably and appropriately, the legislature wants to keep an eye on the rules to be sure they are in keeping with both the letter and the intent of the law.

When an agency writes a rule, it holds a public hearing and submits the proposed rule to the attorney general's office, where it will be reviewed in terms of its compliance with constitutional and statutory law. The rule is then published in the *Colorado Register*. It is also forwarded to the Office of Legislative Legal Services, whose attorneys also review it. If the lawyers have no problem with it, the agency is so notified and the rule becomes effective. If there *are* problems, Legislative Legal Services and agency personnel try to iron them out. If they do, the rule becomes effective. If they do not, it will be sent to the legislature's Committee on Legal Services, where a public hearing is held and attorneys for both the Legislative Legal Services Office and the agency argue their points of view. The committee then votes the rule up or down.

Each year, the legislature passes one massive bill that continues the life of agency rules, except those that the Committee on Legal Services has found objectionable. Should any rules, regulations, or procedures proposed for continuance be highly controversial, they can be allowed to expire simply by being excluded from the general bill.

The legislative review of rules is not a comprehensive oversight of the executive branch's implementation of law. But through the Committee on Legal Services and the Office of Legislative Legal Services that it oversees, one significant aspect of agency administration does undergo continuous legislative scrutiny.

Some level of oversight occurs in a continuous fashion as committees of reference hear bills each legislative session. As noted before, most bills do not create wholly new programs and policies, but extend, retract, or otherwise modify existing law. Consequently, committees cannot help but delve into current statutes and ask questions about the contemporary administration of these statutes as they go about their normal business each spring.

In addition, the joint rules of the Senate and House specifically assign oversight duties to each of the committees of reference. For example, the Senate Finance Committee is instructed to oversee the operation of the Departments of Revenue and Treasury. The House State

Affairs Committee has jurisdiction over the Departments of State, Military Affairs, Personnel, and State Planning and Budgeting. Committee members are charged "to keep themselves advised of the activities, functions, problems, new developments, and budgets of the principal department or departments of the executive department of state government which are within the subject-matter jurisdiction of each committee."[10]

The committees normally meet this charge by holding hearings where top personnel are invited to discuss the agency's current operations, directions, and problems. The hearings will sometimes be held before both the relevant House and Senate committees, meeting jointly, usually early in the legislative session before the committees become engrossed in their normal work of dealing with scores of bills. The testimony, questioning, or written materials that are submitted can be of consequence, leading to altered laws or budgets. But, often, the hearings are occasions to exchange pleasantries and barbs and to brief new legislators on state programs and activities; they also provide a forum for agency leaders to sell their programs.

The committee oversight function may change some as a result of a modification in the legislative rules that went into effect in 1999. Within the first two weeks of each session, committees are now required to include in their hearings with agency administrators a review of the budget information that the agency had earlier presented to the Joint Budget Committee. Following such "briefings," each committee may then forward its concerns and comments to JBC members. This process has the potential of impacting JBC budget decisions.[11]

Some legislation originates with the work of interim committees, which therefore become involved in legislative oversight themselves. Major problems, rather than individual bills or agency activities, are the focus of interim committee work. For example, the committees may look at corrections, education, or health. In the process, they will review existing programs and agency activity, thereby exercising some degree of legislative oversight on the policy implementation of the executive branch, even though this is not their main function.

There are, then, a number of places in both the statutes and the rules of the General Assembly where legislative oversight is mentioned, and there are many ways in which—in some fashion and to some degree—it occurs. But observation of the work of the General Assembly and conversations with legislators reveal that when compared to such matters as elections, budgets, interparty relations, struggles with the governor, and securing passage of one's own bills, legislative oversight is not a major agenda item for our lawmakers. They see more political currency in passing new laws than in probing the consequences of someone else's past actions.

NOTES

1. Dan Luzadder, "Did legislator violate state Constitution?" *Rocky Mountain News*, May 8, 1998.
2. *Rocky Mountain News*, February 14, 1994.
3. *Rocky Mountain News*, February 10, 1995.
4. Thomas Frank, "4 anti-smoking bills introduced," *Denver Post*, January 21, 1997.
5. Fred Brown, *Denver Post*, March 3, 1995.
6. "Tyranny of minority has earned the honor of legislative funeral," *Rocky Mountain News*, June 11, 1987.
7. *Rocky Mountain News*, May 8, 1996.
8. Dan Luzadder, "House State Affairs panel specializing in boorish conduct," *Rocky Mountain News*, February 8, 1997; see also Dan Luzadder, "Doctor, legislator get testy on abortion," *Rocky Mountain News*, January 21, 1997, February 11, 1997, and *Fort Collins Coloradoan*, February 2, 1997.
9. See John A. Straayer, "How Prevalent Are State Legislative Conference Committees," *Comparative State Politics*, April 1996, pp. 4–8.
10. *Colorado Legislator's Handbook*, Joint Rule No. 25.
11. Ibid.

6

Political Parties and Partisanship

The Colorado General Assembly is at one and the same time a highly partisan body and one in which the vast majority of the decisions show no party divisions at all. A simple examination of House and Senate journals reveals that most recorded votes are unanimous, or nearly so. A clear majority of all bills pass out of committee successfully, usually with minor evidence of party division. Much legislation is cosponsored, with members of both parties signing on either in the same chamber, or with a Republican sponsor in one house and a Democrat in the other. The 1996 and 1998 "Bronco Bills" were such examples; in 1996 the House sponsor was a Republican while in the Senate it was a Democrat, and in 1998 neither committee nor floor votes followed party lines. Legislative observers will routinely witness members crossing party lines for lunch or dinner or occasionally for more intimate forms of companionship.

But that's only half of the story. Leadership selection is strictly a high-stakes partisan matter. The House Speaker and President of the Senate are members of the majority party, selected on straight party-line votes. The floor leaders who control the daily schedule and the flow of business on the floor are selected by the majority party caucuses. Members are seated by party, with Republicans on one side of each chamber and Democrats on the other. In election years the majority party sometimes makes a conscious attempt to help its members pass bills, while denying legislative success to minority party members whom they hope to defeat in November. In the past, when the question at hand was an attempt by Republicans to override a veto by the Democratic governor, both parties usually closed ranks. On controversies over procedure, the majority party is rock-solid behind its leaders. Votes on issues of regulation, taxes and business, and labor often break along party lines. So do many votes on such issues as sexual preference and guns. Even on minor matters, such as office space and equipment, the majority party takes care of its troops and gives those in the minority party the leftovers.

WHEN PARTY MATTERS

Nothing is more important and nothing is more partisan in Colorado's legislature, or any other legislature for that matter, than the selection of institutional leadership. This is important and partisan because, as we learned earlier, the occupation of leadership slots means control of the agenda, and thus the policy, of the state.

The Speaker is the presiding officer in the House, and he decides the size of committees, who in the majority party will sit on them, and who will chair them. He decides which two majority House members will sit on the Joint Budget Committee. The Speaker decides which bills go to which committees and, in the process, can often seal the fate of the proposed legislation. The second in command, the majority floor leader, controls the chamber's schedule on a daily basis and thus, he or she too can play a major role in passing or killing bills. In the Senate the roles of majority party leaders differ a bit from those in the House, but the control of the majority party leadership remains firm here too.

All committee chairs are members of the majority party, and so too is a majority of the members of each committee. Committee chairs control committee agendas and schedules, and the majority party has the votes to work its will on bills.

The zeal with which the parties seek to capture a majority of the seats and the positions of leadership in the chambers, and thus influence over the state's policy, is displayed in a number of ways. Often, and in election years especially, the majority party will seek to deny minority party members legislative successes by killing their bills, and boost the legislative record of its own members. The point is to render those in the minority vulnerable to electoral defeat, and solidify the electoral position of the majority party members. Leading up to the 1994 election, for example, Democrat Bob Eisenach, who represented a politically competitive district, found it all but impossible to move his bills through the Republican-controlled House. He was defeated in November by conservative social agenda Republican Marilyn Musgrave. At the same time, the Republicans worked hard to help freshman Joyce Lawrence, who had won a seat in heavily Democratic Pueblo, get her bills passed. Indeed, at the start of the 1995 session one of Lawrence's bills was the first to pass the House, and the party, led by Majority Floor Leader Tim Foster, made a splashy public display of the event. Foster moved another bill down the schedule to make Representative

Lawrence's first, then commented that Lawrence had accomplished more in two weeks than her Democratic predecessor had in two years.

A Democratic challenge to Speaker Chuck Berry's Speakership, which was triggered by questioning of a procedural ruling, is another example of the perceived value of controlling leadership slots. In that instance the Republicans left the floor hurriedly to caucus, blasted the Democrats rhetorically, and brought retribution down upon the heads of the minority party by killing a major criminal code reform bill that had as its House sponsor the Democratic assistant floor leader, Peggy Kerns.

A similar majority party reaction occurred in 1994 in the Senate. There, Democrats on the Finance Committee took advantage of the absence of two Republicans on the seven-member committee, including the chairman, to "roll" the vice chairman, Jim Roberts. A bill sponsored by Democrat Linda Powers requiring bank payment of interest on house mortgage escrow accounts was on the table. Democrats, in the majority at the moment, moved to send the bill favorably to the floor. Acting Chairman Roberts pulled the bill off the table, planning to hold it from a vote until his fellow Republicans returned and were back in the majority. Citing the rules of procedure, Democrats forced a vote and passed the bill out of committee.

A few days later sponsor Powers asked that the bill be reconsidered in committee. It was, and Republicans killed it. Why? Because the Republican Senate leadership made it clear to the Democrats that they did not want their chairman "rolled," and unless the bill was returned to committee for its demise, Democrats could forget about the prospects of moving their bills successfully through the Senate. In both chambers, the majority party rules and has both the power and will to punish any challenge to its hegemony.

Senator Linda Powers felt the sting of partisanship again several years later. She lost her Senate seat to Republican Ken Chlouber in the November 1996 election. In 1997 she was nominated by the governor for a seat on the board of directors of the Colorado Compensation Insurance Authority. The Senate must approve such nominations. Its Business Affairs and Labor Committee deadlocked on her nomination 4–4, and thus her name went to the floor without a positive recommendation. Predictably Powers, a Democrat, was rejected by her former Republican colleagues.

Partisanship is also evident in the differential rates of success that members of the two parties have in moving their bills through the legislature successfully. In 1989 one-third of the bills with Democratic sponsors were killed in House committees compared to just 13 percent of those carried by Republicans. In the Senate, 10 percent of the bills with

Table 6.1—Bill-Passing Success (%)

| | House | | Senate | |
	Democrats	*Republicans*	*Democrats*	*Republicans*
1993	43.4	61.6	44.6	67.7
1994	42.1	63.0	50.0	72.7
1995	30.8	54.2	32.9	55.4
1996	44.0	59.9	40.9	62.9

Source: Colorado Statesman, January 10, 1997. Excluded are appropriations bills and bills recalled by their sponsors.

Republican sponsorship and 22 percent of those with Democratic sponsorship died by way of indefinite postponement.

The pattern continued. In the 1996 session, House committees killed 41 percent of the Democrats' bills, but just 26 percent of those whose prime House sponsor was a member of the majority party. Senate committees in 1996 sentenced 17 percent of the Republican-sponsored bills to death, as compared to 32 percent of those sponsored by minority party Democrats. Sometimes Democrat-sponsored bills are killed and parts then taken for inclusion in bills sponsored by Republicans.

Former Democratic House member Jerry Kopel, a twenty-two-year legislative veteran, examined the relative bill-passing success of members over a four-year period, 1993 through 1996. He found the same pattern, which is shown in Table 6.1.

A related indication of partisanship is the pattern of late bills. The Colorado General Assembly moves through its spring 120-day session with a series of deadlines. Those include dates by which bills must be introduced, passed out of committee and the full chamber in the house of origin, and dates by which bills must pass similar benchmarks in the second chamber. But the rules grant leadership the authority to waive some of the rules, including the deadline for submitting bills.

As with the rates of bill passage, permission from leadership to submit bills after deadlines, the granting of "late-bill status," shows a partisan pattern. During the 1996 session, thirty-seven House bills were introduced late, thirty-five of which were sponsored by Republicans. In the Senate, thirty-six majority party Republican bills were granted late-bill status as compared to just seven for the Democrats. In the 1998 session the late-bill numbers were 55–4 in the House and 27–7 in the Senate, in both cases favoring the majority party Republicans, and in 1999 the majority party advantage was 78–12 in the House and 37–6 in the Senate.

Jerry Kopel also studied the late-bill pattern for 1995, 1996, and 1997. He reported that over the three-year period there were 264 late bills. House leadership granted permission 136 times, 132 of those to majority party Republicans. In the Senate, there were 128 late bills, 109 for Republicans and just 19 for Democrats.[1]

The partisan tone of the legislature is also very evident in the voting behavior of members on bills that touch upon the core differences in the values of the two parties. The vast majority of all recorded votes on third and final reading are unanimous, or nearly so. But there are very important exceptions. Policy areas in which the parties differ relate to private property, business and labor matters, public employment, crime and corrections, and to some extent social issues such as sexual preference, abortion, and guns.

Bills that seek to limit the ability of government to promote land-use controls or environmental values at the expense of rather unrestricted use of private property generally find strong Republican support and Democratic opposition. Bills pitting labor against business, on workers compensation, or so-called right to work policies, for example, put the parties clearly at odds, with the Republicans taking the side of business. Similarly, the Democrats are much more likely to take the side of state or municipal workers, or the teachers, on measures relating to job security or due process in hiring and firing. Measures to loosen gun control or add controls on sexual preference and abortion are virtually always Republican bills.

On March 30, 1998, for example, the Senate conducted third and final reading roll call votes on seventeen bills. On six there were no negative votes, on two bills there was just one dissent, and on three more there were five or fewer "no" votes. Just three roll calls registered ten or more negative votes, and two of those showed evidence of a party-line split. One bill, which passed 24–11, with all eleven negative votes coming from minority party Democrats, addressed oversight of the Public Defenders Office. The other passed 18–14, with one Republican and one Democrat abstaining for reasons of conflict of interest. All eighteen positive votes were from Republicans and all fourteen "no" votes were from Democrats. The bill was on workers' compensation. So while the majority of bills passed that day showed no division between the parties, two bills did, and they were on crime and labor issues.

Floor patterns are reflected in committees too. Most bills pass out of committee successfully, especially in the house of a bill's origin, and do so with little or no party division. But it's not the same with all issues. As examples, the 1999 Senate Judiciary Committee passed, on a party-line vote, a bill to ban same-sex marriages. The Senate's 1999 State Affairs Committee killed a bill to provide some inheritance rights for gays, also along party lines. And the House Business Affairs and Labor Committee passed a 1999 "right to work" bill on a straight party-line vote.

The differences between the parties, and thus the importance of controlling the legislature to control policy, are powerfully illustrated by the way the parties split on interest group "scorecards." Following each legislative session a number of special interest groups examine the voting patterns of the members on selected sets of bills that are of particular importance to the groups.

Table 6.2 presents data from the scorecards of four groups, two of which are very conservative and two of which are generally considered to be more liberal. The two conservative groups are the Colorado Union of Taxpayers (CUT), whose policy preferences are for low taxes, low spending, and very limited government, and the Colorado Conservative Union (CCU), which is fiscally conservative and opposed to gun control and regulation of business, but is sympathetic to activist government in such social policy areas as abortion. On the more liberal side are the Senior Lobby, which champions the cause of senior citizens, and the environmental lobby, a coalition of groups that favor clean air and water as well as outdoor issues, planning, and land preservation policies generally.

The numbers in the tables show that there are very significant differences between the parties. The numbers represent the percentage of votes on which members voted in the direction preferred by the group. Republicans score high in the estimation of the two spendthrift groups, but low with seniors and environmentalists. The reverse is true with the Democrats. There are also some differences within each party along gender lines, although these differentials are somewhat mixed and are less distinct than the divisions between parties. Republican women are more inclined than their Republican male colleagues to support the seniors but they are just as conservative as the men on money matters, in the House especially. Further, the House and Senate differ, with the House generally being the more conservative fiscally, and less inclined to support the policy preferences of seniors.

The El Paso County delegation was singled out because it represents much of the hard-core conservative contingent in the legislature and within the majority Republican party. As the numbers show, the eight El Paso County House members and that county's four senators are much more conservative than the full chambers, more to the right of both the Republican party as a whole and the legislature's female contingent, and they vote in radically different fashion from the Democrats. They are friendly to the low-tax, pro-gun, anti-abortion folks, and less than supportive of senior and environmental interests.

Table 6.2—Interest Group Support Scores

	Environmental[1] Scorecard 1999		Senior Lobby[2] 1997		CUT[3] 1999		CCU[4] 1995	
	House	Senate	House	Senate	House	Senate	House	Senate
All Members	46.8	45.6	57.7	71.8	57.0	54.7	41.2	36.3
Republicans	18.8	17.0	39.4	57.4	80.1	80.6	56.2	54.0
Democrats	91.6	83.7	88.8	91.0	20.0	19.8	15.6	12.6
R - Men	19.6	17.5	34.4	51.9	81.9	81.7	55.4	57.3
R - Women	17.1	16.0	47.2	74.1	75.8	78.7	58.3	44.2
D - Men	91.9	82.2	91.1	91.0	19.7	23.8	16.3	12.3
D - Women	91.2	86.2	85.2	91.0	20.6	13.3	14.7	13.2
All Women	50.8	45.5	61.4	80.8	50.7	51.4	37.5	28.5
El Paso County Members	17.6	8.25	35.8	41.9	85.4	85.4	64.0	74.0

1. The Environmental Lobby is composed of sixteen groups, ranging from Clean Water Action and the Audubon Society to the Sierra Club and Trout Unlimited. Their policy concerns include air and water quality, controls on development, and outdoor and land preservation. There were eight votes on the 1997 scorecard, and the scores here represent the percentage of the votes on which members supported the lobby's position.

2. The Senior Lobby identified thirteen bills for its 1997 scorecard. Issues of concern relate to health care, insurance, finances, and the well-being of retired and elderly people generally.

3. Colorado Union of Taxpayers. CUT's scorecard contained a potential for twenty-one votes in the House and sixteen in the Senate. CUT generally opposes state and local spending and regulation, including welfare expenditures, and favors "tough on crime" legislation.

4. Colorado Conservative Union. The CCU scorecard contained a potential of thirteen House votes, and eleven in the Senate. CCU is antiregulation and anti-spending, favors minimal government, is for parental notification on teen abortion, and opposes gun control.

A look at individual rankings on two of the scorecards paints the same picture. In the seniors' rankings, the top ten were Democrats. For the Colorado Union of Taxpayers it was exactly the reverse with the Republicans as good guys and Democrats as the enemy. The same pattern held in the Senate. In both houses El Paso County members were well represented on CUT's list of friends, and metro-Denverites dominated its enemies list. For the seniors the legislative friends were mostly from the metro-Denver-Boulder region; none were from El Paso County.

One very revealing way to look at the difference political party can make is Senate District 14 in Larimer County. In 1995 it was represented by Bob Schaffer. Schaffer topped CUT's list of champions by logging an 87.5 percent score in support of the group's positions. During the same 1995 session Peggy Reeves represented a Larimer County district in the House. Her CUT support score was 15.0 percent, fifth from the bottom. In 1996 Schaffer went to the U.S. House of Representatives and Reeves won the state Senate District 14 seat. With this party change, the policy orientation of the district's Senate voice was turned on its head; the archconservatives lost a champion while the more moderate seniors and environmentalists gained.

Does party matter? Yes, it clearly matters on many very important policy questions, and it can also matter in matters of process and ethics. In 1998 the late veteran Republican House member and JBC Chairman Tony Grampsas was accused of ethical wrongdoing for allegedly holding up some state funds for the University of Colorado Health Sciences Center in connection with a faculty personnel matter. A citizen filed a formal complaint, prompting Speaker Chuck Berry to appoint a five-person investigating panel. The panel was composed of three veteran Grampsas associates, Republican House members Tucker, May, and Allen, along with Jim Dyer and Jeannie Reeser, the two Democrats who most habitually voted with the majority Republicans. Said one lobbyist, "Did you see the committee? Tony couldn't have done better himself."

The five-member panel found no fault in Grampsas's actions, and there was no reason to believe that the five were anything more than totally objective. But the composition of the panel itself points again to the advantages and results of party control.

There is also partisanship of a sandbox variety that shows itself in all sorts of little ways. Some years back, the House Speaker forbade Democrats from having food in committee rooms at lunchtime caucuses. The rationale given was that food might be dropped and soil the carpet. When Democrats insisted the rule apply also to Republicans, it was rescinded. Democrats have complained that they are on the short end of the stick with respect to copying equipment, office space, and secretarial help. At the start of the 1997 Senate, Democrats complained about their cramped quarters. Said Democrat Bill Thiebaut, "I was just furious when I walked in this morning and saw how cramped we were . . . we're all stuffed in here like a sardine can." Senate President Republican Tom Norton saw it differently: "I think it's a fair allotment of what we have available."[2] These kinds of slights tend to vary with the personalities and moods of those in leadership at any particular point in time.

In 1998 the House caught the partisan space-fight disease. Democrat Penfield Tate had moved his office setup into a storage closet that had been unused for a time. The Republicans, however, decided that the General Assembly's Doctor of the Day needed the space. The "Doctor of the Day" is the descriptor for physicians who volunteer a day of their time to be in the Capitol and attend to anyone who may be in need of medical care.

Tate and his Democratic allies saw his eviction as a tacky partisan move. Said Tate, "I mean, evicting a member of the General Assembly to make room for a Doctor of the Day? It just doesn't seem appropriate." Republicans saw it differently. House Majority Leader Norma Anderson commented, "He did not have authority from us to use that space. We have some members who have been ill, and we need a place where we can put a cot so they can lie down during the day to rest." As a counterproposal Tate suggested the doctor be assigned unused vault space. No dice, said the majority party.[3]

Sometimes partisanship can even be bipartisan. Wayne Knox, a public school teacher from Denver, served as a Democratic House member for well over two decades. Most of it was on the House Committee on Education. He was a tireless champion of the public schools. His tenure had to be frustrating, of course, because for all except two of his legislative years, Knox's party was in the minority and thus without any committee chairmanships but with a steady string of policy setbacks.

Al Meiklejohn, a Republican from Arvada, served a similarly lengthy tenure in the Senate. As a majority party Republican, Meiklejohn had considerable success with his policy initiatives, and for years he chaired the Senate Education Committee. He was "Mr. Education."

But Al Meiklejohn was a policy moderate and a friend of education, a policy area that consumes well over half of the state's general fund budget each year. What he valued and what he did meant spending money.

So in 1997 a bill was introduced to honor both Wayne Knox and Al Meiklejohn by naming college student scholarships after the two retired legislative veterans. The bill died in the House Education Committee; the *Rocky Mountain News* headline read "Political payback buries honor." The motion to kill the bill came from Doug Dean, an El Paso County representative and member of the majority party's right wing. His supportive hard-right colleague Barry Arrington, when asked if Meiklejohn's policy orientation affected the outcome, replied, "I won't ever lie to you and so I just won't comment."[4]

Reactions of legislators to partisan divisions vary. Some have cited the partisan nature of the General Assembly as a reason to quit. Democratic House members Peggy Lamm and Glenda Lyle chose not to run for reelection in 1996 and each cited excessive partisanship as one of the reasons. Lamm contended that the controlling Republicans worked to kill her bills, no matter their merit. Said Lyle, "Being in the minority is quite a disadvantage because there is so little we're able to accomplish."[5]

At the start of the 1996 session a number of Republicans wore buttons with the numbers 22/44 to symbolize the two-thirds count of Senate and House seats they would need after the 1996 election to have the ability to override any vetoes exercised by the Democratic governor. House Minority Leader Peggy Kerns commented, "I thought it was in extremely poor taste." House Democratic Caucus Chair Peggy Reeves added, "You don't want to set that tone."[6]

Members of both parties do acknowledge, however, that the parties differ in philosophy and policy preferences, and that the majority can and will use its superior numbers to get its way. Majority Floor Leader Tim Foster observed, for example, that the party system provides voting cues for the public.[7]

Not surprisingly, members of the parties differ some in their reactions to partisan behavior. Democrats tend to lament it, and argue that a bill's merits, not its sponsorship, should determine its success. Republicans contend that merit does indeed count, and that there is less purely partisan behavior than the Democrats claim. This difference should surprise no one.

When Party Doesn't Matter

The existence of the two-party system, media highlighting of party fights, the party-divided pattern of seating, and other displays of party division can give one the impression that virtually everything that goes on in the legislature reflects conflict between the two political parties. But actually, much of what happens is totally devoid of partisanship.

In the first place, much of the business of the legislature is routine or mandatory. Every year there are scores of bills that are just minor adjustments to existing law. Some, such as salary levels for judges or county officials, are needed to keep up with inflationary change. Some are "supplemental" appropriations bills, which provide needed mid-year adjustments in state agency budgets. Still others are grants of statutory authorization to state agencies to provide the legal basis for something the agency already does—collect a modest fee to cover the cost of processing various professional license applications, for example. Occasionally such bills will spark controversy, but most do not.

Similarly, some bills are proposed that adjust state statutes or budget numbers so as to comply with federal government mandates. Such bills may well trigger rhetorical flurries of attacks on Washington, but their mandatory nature generally means that interparty squabbling is muted. An example of such legislation is the law establishing the twenty-one-year-old drinking age. In Colorado and elsewhere these are state rather than federal laws, but they are enacted because of the threat of losing federal highway funds for failure to do as Congress dictated. Another example is "motor-voter" laws in which states, as directed by the national government, established voting registration opportunities in motor vehicle licensing offices and certain other state offices. A happier example for the states was the increase in the vehicle speed limit, which occurred after the national mandate was left out of the 1995 national transportation reauthorization legislation.

The nonpartisan nature of much of the General Assembly's business is reflected in the daily journals of House and Senate actions. One morning in a 1996 session, for example, the Senate passed twenty-eight bills on third and final reading. Sixteen passed unanimously. Three more were approved with just a single dissent, two with a pair of negative votes, and one each with five, seven, ten, thirteen, and fourteen dissents in the thirty-five-member body. Only four of the twenty-eight bills showed any pattern at all of party-line voting.

This same pattern is illustrated in Table 6.3, which lists a number of 2000 House votes and 1998 Senate votes. In each chamber these votes occurred on third reading, in rapid-fire succession, with little or no discussion, in a single half-day in the House and during two short Senate sessions. All the bills passed. Only two of the bills showed party-line division, one dealing with labor unions and one on conservation easements.

An especially vivid illustration of voting patterns was displayed on February 24, 1999, when the House passed seventy bills on third and final reading. Third-reading votes are almost always taken without debate, the debating and amending activity having taken place on second reading when the chamber dissolves itself into the Committee of the Whole.

On this day, thirty-four of the seventy bills were passed unanimously, eight had one dissent, and sixteen more drew from two to ten nays. Just twelve bills registered eleven or more negative votes. Eight of these were party-line votes. Party thus matters on many important issues, but just numerically; most bills meet little opposition at the final stage in the chambers.

Table 6.3—House and Senate Votes

House (Feb. 23, 2000)		Senate (Feb. 2 & 16, 1998)	
HB 1112	62–3	HB 1002	19–12
HB 1363	63–2	SB 43	31–0
HB 1333	62–3	SB 13	31–0
HB 1206	38–27	SB 35	31–0
HB 1343	58–7	SB 103	31–0
HB 1265	59–6	SB 38	30–1
HB 1322	34–31	SB 71	23–7
HB 1365	65–0	SB 12	31–0
HB 1349	48–17	SB 14	20–11
HB 1173	63–2	SB 107	34–0
HB 1174	65–0	SB 16	34–0
HB 1182	62–3	SB 8	29–5
HB 1191	55–10	SB 73	29–1
HB 1209	47–18	SB 46	34–0
HB 1211	61–4	SB 104	29–5
HB 1348	61–4	SB 45	29–5
HB 1353	34–31	HB 1031	34–0
HB 1258	53–12	SB 119	30–3
HB 1309	54–11	SB 147	23–11

Sources: House Journal, Feb. 23, 2000; *Senate Journal*, Feb. 2 and 16, 1998.

During one recent afternoon the House considered Senate amendments to twenty previously passed House bills. In every instance the majority accepted the House sponsor's recommendation to either accept Senate amendments or reject them and call for establishment of a conference committee. On ten of the twenty votes there was no dissent, and on only one bill were there more than twenty negative votes. It is true, of course, that many highly partisan legislative battles are won or lost in the process well before recorded votes are registered on the floor. Still, these figures show that the vast majority of the votes are on relatively noncontroversial questions and do not divide the members by party.

As noted, not all bills that receive unanimous or near-unanimous support, and not all votes to accept or reject amendments added by the other chamber, are without considerable controversy. Well in advance of a floor vote, a bill may have been the subject of intense disagreement, and a variety of compromises may have been negotiated or battles won or lost. Many critical decisions are made in committees, and most of the floor debate and amending activity occur during the second reading of bills, which is done in the Committee of the Whole. Thus, members may support a measure on the third and final floor reading, the only one in which individual votes are recorded, even though they fought to modify or defeat it at points earlier in the process. But the bottom line remains that a significant portion of a legislature's business does not divide the parties.

DIVISIONS BEYOND PARTY

We've noted so far that in many ways and on some issues, the members split along party lines. We've seen, too, that in strictly numerical terms most legislative actions show no party division at all. But there is also a significant amount of highly controversial legislation that divides members, but along lines other than political party. These nonparty fault lines include region or district, gender, ideology, and to some extent, even chamber.

There is one powerful factor beyond political party affiliation that will move a member's vote, and that is the perceived need to respond to the concerns and demands of constituents within the home district and thus "protect the locals." This is seen repeatedly in matters involving water and schools. Colorado is an arid state and water is precious—in the West, it is said, whiskey is for drinking and water is for fighting over. Population and industrial growth is mostly along the nine-county Front Range of the Eastern Slope of the Rockies. Much of the state's water, though, runs westward and toward the Colorado River. In decades past, a goodly amount of Western Slope water has been diverted across the mountains, eastward.

The Front Range interest in transmountain diversion has continued, and in 1996 it was evident in a bill designed to limit county government authority to deny Eastern Slope cities permits to construct water diversion projects. The cities of Aurora and Colorado Springs had wanted to build a project in Eagle County to divert water eastward, but in 1988 the Colorado courts had ruled that the county, which had denied a needed permit, did so under authority of state law.

A 1996 bill was introduced to strip counties of such authority. It was sponsored by the Senate President and supported by the thirsty cities. Colorado Counties Incorporated, the lobbying arm of the counties, opposed the bill, as did mountain and Western Slope interests generally. The state's municipal league, which represents cities on both sides of the continental divide, remained uncommitted. Pat Ratliff, who was then a lobbyist for the counties, argued that "this gets into local control for citizens. A permit process is meaningless if all you can say is yes." The cities saw it differently. Said the mayor of Aurora, "We're asking to bring back a level playing field."[8]

The bill was sent by the sponsoring Senate President to the Local Government Committee, which was chaired by a senator from Colorado Springs and whose membership was composed exclusively of Front Range members. The bill was passed out of committee and passed on the floor. In the House the bill also went to the Local Government Committee, but here both the chair and vice chair represented mountain or Western Slope districts. The bill, which had Republican sponsorship and which had passed successfully out of both a Republican Senate Committee and the Republican-controlled Senate itself, died in the Republican-controlled House Committee. Sometimes party matters, but when the vital interests of the folks back home are at stake, the region or district trumps party.

The same brand of local self-defense emerges in the financial high-stakes politics of school funding. Just over one-half of the money to run the state's elementary and secondary schools comes from state appropriations. The state's money is doled out to the scores of districts based upon a formula, the factors of which include student count, district size, and the number of "at-risk" students in each district. Needless to say, the selection and weighing of these factors are controversial.

Small districts seek an advantage, arguing that regardless of their low student numbers, every district has minimum fixed costs for physical facilities, administration, and so forth. Very large districts argue that sheer size forces up their administrative costs. Districts with larger than average numbers of troubled students seek extra funding for nurses, counselors, and other unique high-cost care and remedial activities.

Districts that are neither unusually small nor large, and which are blessed with relatively low numbers of troubled students, feel cheated since they receive little or no extra formula-based money beyond that which is generated by their student head count. They want the formula changed, and the districts that benefit by the formula currently in place do not.

Thus it was in 1995 that Republican Representative Steve Tool, who represents an area with a school district disadvantaged by the current formula, introduced legislation to add $6 million in the budget for fourteen school districts. These were districts, like his, that were disadvantaged for being middle-sized—neither too small nor too large to receive size-related funding bonuses. But the committee that examined his bill was heavily loaded with members from areas of large school districts and they liked the formula as it stood. The committee chair and the committee majority were, like Tool, Republicans. But again, region won out over party. The battle continued to rage through 1996 and 1997, and in 1998 some adjustments were made as a consequence to help the mid-sized districts.

The issue of deregulation of the electric utility industry, or "retail wheeling," as it is called, was on the legislature's agenda in 1997 and again in 1998, and it too illustrates divisions that fail to follow party lines. Retail wheeling would allow new companies to enter the retail market and purchase electric power from the generators, then send it to retail purchasers along existing power lines. Slowly, and eventually to a considerable extent, the state Public Service Commission would cease regulation of rates.

One might surmise that free market advocates within the Republican legislature would love the idea, and some do. But not all. Republicans who represent rural constituencies fear that upstart companies would "cherry pick" the better and more profitable customers, such as metropolitan-area large businesses and institutions—Hewlett-Packard, Coors, and large universities, for example. These volume customers would receive bargain rates, while the electricity costs to small, distant, and dispersed users would skyrocket. Small towns, farmers, and ranchers would be hurt.

An almost surrealistic 1997 Senate debate on the issue found party members borrowing lines from the other's ideological lexicon. Mike Feeley of Denver, the Democratic minority leader, argued aggressively for competition in the electric industry. Tilman Bishop, a Western Slope Republican, countered that the result of deregulation is that "the big get bigger and the little is no more." Hard-core right-winger Charlie Duke showed some populist colors, asserting that "the big fish are eating all the little fish and then sticking it to the consumer." "Do we need to be at the table when the meal is the consumer?" Duke inquired rhetorically.

Repeatedly in the debate, which was actually over a bill to study deregulation, Republicans with non-metro-Denver constituencies pointed to the consequences of airline and telecommunications deregulation as reasons to resist competition in the electric market. The customer "cherry-picking," they contend, generates hardships for their constituents. Party, ideology, free markets, competition—none of it matters when the well-being of the local district is at stake.

Yet another example is gun legislation. In both 1995 and 1996 measures to force county sheriffs to liberalize issuance of concealed weapons permits lost in political fights that pitted not the parties, but urban and rural members, against each other. One such 1996 bill died in the Senate Judiciary Committee when three urban Democrats joined two urban Republicans, including the committee chair, to defeat two Democrats and two Republicans, all from rural areas, on a 5–4 vote.

This scenario was repeated in 1998 on a House bill to make it legal to tote guns in motor vehicles. The very conservative House State

Affairs Committee passed the measure out favorably and the full House did likewise. Indeed, the bill's sponsor, Representative Mike Salaz, chaired the State Affairs Committee. But at the next stop the bill died. Senate President Tom Norton put the bill in the hands of the Senate's Judiciary Committee, which, while also under Republican control, was a politically moderate panel. Further, it was chaired by a moderate woman who represents an urban Denver district. Senator Wham and her Judiciary Committee colleagues were not interested in passing a state law designed to strip cities of the authority to control guns. Again, region and members' personal values mattered more than party as those closest to urban gang- and gun-related violence joined hands across party lines to oppose those whose connection to firearms related more to hunting and pickup truck gun racks than to drive-by target practice and convenience store heists.

Motives can be mixed in legislative voting and sometimes the actual reason for a vote is not clear except that it is tied to something other than political party. One example is a 1996 bill that was intended to force local schools to teach sexual abstinence as a part of their sex-education curriculum. The bill died in the House Education Committee on a 6–5 vote that crossed party lines. Four Democrats were joined by two Republicans, both of whom gave as their reason to kill the bill a felt need to preserve local control. They did not, they said, want the state intruding excessively into the curricular autonomy of local school districts.

On another bill, one designed to restrict municipal authority over air pollution, Republican Senator Sally Hopper joined Democrats to defeat the measure, saying that it went against her "Republican nature" to so restrict local control. The bill, of course, was sponsored by Republicans in both chambers; the Republican House had passed it, and all of Hopper's Republican committee colleagues supported it. When the bill was still in the House, Democrat Ken Gordon observed, "We say we don't want the federal government telling us what to do, but here we are telling communities what to do." And Republican Bryan Sullivant, in opposing the measure in the name of local autonomy, said that if the measure made it through the legislature he would ask the Democratic governor to veto the bill. It is difficult sometimes to ferret out the real motive behind members' votes, as lines such as "preserving local control" and "leveling the playing field" may be real, or may be offered just as rhetorical covers when one is departing from the preferences of party colleagues.

The 1998 version of the Broncos Stadium bill, SB 171, is one more example of extreme contentiousness and division, but not along party lines. To some extent the voting splits were regional, but it would be difficult to explain the voting with any single theory. Before ending up in a conference committee, the bill passed the Senate 20–15 and the House 38–26. The Senate's twenty "yes" votes came from seven Democrats and thirteen Republicans; in the House the thirty-eight-member majority was composed of fourteen Democrats and twenty-four Republicans.

But what is more interesting than the party division is the regional vote pattern. Twenty senators represent districts that fall within the stadium taxing district; eleven of them voted "no," nine voted "yes." Eleven of the senators whose constituents would not have to pay the stadium tax voted "yes," only four were opposed. The pattern in the House was similar. Representatives from within the taxing district split 18–18 while those outside the taxing area supported the measure 20–8.

From this 1998 Bronco bill episode one would be hard-pressed to find any single explanatory factor to account for the voting pattern. Some members argue that they had an obligation to let the people vote it up or down. Others were clearly cozy with the avalanche of lobbyists hired by the football club and others who stand to profit. Some are simply pro-sports enthusiasts. A cynic might conclude that the behavior is best explained by legislative compulsion to support the taxation of folks in someone else's district. In any case, political party affiliation provided no clue.

Among the most interesting sources of nonparty division, and for the Republicans the most troubling, is ideology. Increasingly, GOP fiscal conservatives and governmental "minimalists" in Colorado's legislative ranks have been joined by Republican colleagues who alternatively work to expand or contract the reach of state government as they seek to implement an ideologically rooted social agenda.

There has long been division within both parties. Democrats, in the House especially, have shown some low-key and muted splits along racial and ethnic lines, with minorities sometimes coalescing to support each other for leadership or Joint Budget Committee slots, or simply expressing displeasure with committee assignments. Occasionally, too, as a seemingly perpetual minority party, Democrats have expressed frustration in the form of schizophrenia with respect to preferred leadership style. Some time back, for example, House Democrats dumped the accommodating style of Minority Leader Bob Kirscht for the more fiery and confrontational brand of Federico Peña.

Similarly, Senate Republicans were badly split in the 1980s. While sporting a two-to-one numerical advantage over the hapless Democrats, they divided over a combination of ideology and personality. A group of conservatives supported then-President Ted Strickland, while a band of ultraconservatives featuring the likes of Steve Durham and Cliff Dodge both opposed the somewhat moderate policy stances of their fellow Republicans, and disliked Strickland personally.

While there have long been these divisions within the General Assembly, intraparty fissures took on a heightened character following the 1994 election, in the House especially. A new group of ultraconservatives with a social rather than strictly fiscal agenda was elected, and its members found each other in a hurry. Throughout both the 1995 and 1996 legislative sessions they caused considerable discomfort within House Republican ranks.

The group was relatively small, consisting of Representatives Congrove, Lamborn, Prinzler, Musgrave, Dean, and Paschall. Veteran Phil Pankey was somewhat of an elderly godfather to the group, and libertarian-leaning Penn Pfiffner was a sometimes fellow traveler.

The group drew attention early by holding unannounced meetings, which some said were in violation of the state's sunshine laws. Fellow Republican Lewis Entz, himself a moderate, referred to them as "bunnies" for their tendency to "hop up to the podium then scurry back to their holes."[9] Leadership had an early sense of the potentially divisive impact of the group, as Majority Leader Tim Foster cautioned in the initial Republican caucus meeting that the party would need to stay together so as to maintain control. Foster clearly sensed the potential danger to the party inherent in the combination of an oversized coalition (41–24 in favor of Republicans) and a true believer approach to politics.

The agenda of the bunnies, or "new House crazies" as some called them, included support for abortion restrictions, liberalization of concealed weapons permit laws, promotion of teaching sexual abstinence in the public schools, denial of state recognition of same-sex marriages, resistance to discrimination protection for gay and lesbian citizens, and lower taxes and spending generally. Their goals included a mixture of more government and less government—less government so as to pay fewer tax dollars, and more government to enforce preferred morals and lifestyle preferences on other people.

The political agenda of this group paralleled closely that of the Christian Coalition of Colorado. On the 1998 election season questionnaire that the coalition mailed to prospective legislators, the candidates were asked their position on abortion, tax revenue refunds, guns, marijuana, birth control, homosexuality, and parental control and discipline of children.

One example of the intraparty divisions that emerged was the split on a 1995 bill designed to extend penalties for so-called hate crimes against the elderly, disabled, gays, and lesbians. The bill was sponsored by Republican Ken Chlouber, a generally moderate member. It passed successfully out of the House Judiciary Committee on a vote that crossed party lines, but then died in the House Finance Committee. Said Republican Chlouber, "You can't beat up, harm, or hurt people simply because of who they are." His argument failed to move Republican colleagues Congrove and Lamborn, who claimed that the measure was redundant and that adequate protection already existed with law.

The presence of the social-agenda Republicans unsettled the party in other ways too. During the 1995 session, noises and gestures were made on the floor designating pleasure or displeasure with the outcome of votes on bills and causing colleagues to lament "childish behavior." On one occasion in 1966 an ultraconservative challenger to a moderate Republican member was brought in and invited to speak at a luncheon caucus. The plan precipitated a sense of outrage among members and the speech was not given.

A speech that was given, and which also provoked controversy, took the form of a prayer. Representative Mark Paschall was given the opportunity late in the 1996 session to give the opening prayer in the House of Representatives. He proceeded to include in the prayer what some viewed as inappropriate potshots at abortion, multiculturalism, and gays and lesbians. Some members walked out of the chambers, and even many of those who did not, some in his own party, expressed the view that Paschall ought not employ the occasion of a prayer from the podium to express private policy preferences.

The reactions of his colleagues, Democrats and Republicans alike, did nothing to mute Paschall's zeal. In a prelude to the 1998 session, Representative Paschall sent a mailing to members of the Colorado Christian Coalition asking for support in his efforts to ban abortions. Wrote Paschall, "Dear Sisters and Brothers: When I became a State Representative I knew that I would succeed by God's power and the willingness of His people to do His work."

The 1995 and 1996 legislative activities set the stage for intraparty fights in the 1996 August primaries, as additional ultraconservatives emerged to challenge Republican moderates in both the House and Senate. Representatives Marcy Morrison, Martha Kreutz, Bill Kaufman, Russell George, and Ken Chlouber were among those derisively deemed by the ultra-right to be moderates—sometimes called RINOs (Republicans In Name Only). Morrison, along with House Republicans Bryan Sullivant, Jeanne Adkins, and Gary McPherson, faced challenges from the right. So did Republican Senators Elsie Lacy, Dottie Wham, and Ray Powers.

Lacy, chair of the Joint Budget Committee, was a target because of her earlier support of the "bubble bill," which provided a zone of protection in and around abortion clinics. Dottie Wham's sins were multiple, for she chaired the Senate Judiciary Committee, which sometimes functioned as a roadblock to pro-gun and anti-abortion advocates. Indeed, in the 1996 primary election she was subjected to a barrage of nasty attacks. One suggested that she was responsible for the movement of convicted felons into the district's neighborhoods. Others, attacking her on the issues of abortion and taxes, were mailed into the district by groups in Virginia.

Moderate Republicans, it seemed, were more worthy of political rebuke and challenge by the right than were the Democrats. A publication issued by the Colorado Conservative Union featured a front-page "wanted" poster with the pictures of moderate House Republican Russell George and moderate Senate Republican David Wattenberg. Their crimes were having voting records deemed too liberal by the Conservative Union. George, a very able and articulate lawyer, and Wattenberg, a crafty and seasoned rancher, were effective for the wrong causes, it seemed. So too were twenty-year veteran Republican Al Meiklejohn, who for years had chaired the Senate Education Committee, and other influential moderate Republican Senate committee chairs like Dottie Wham and Sally Hopper.

Both before and throughout the 1998 session, stories circulated that a number of Republicans who voted "wrong" on a 1997 abortion bill would be targeted in 1998 primaries by the party's right wing. Indeed, the Christian Coalition produced a list of them, entitled the "Fake Fifteen."[10] Tambor Williams of Greeley and Marcy Morrison from Manitou Springs in El Paso County were among them. Both chose to seek access to the August 1998 primary ballot by way of petitions rather than in the April party caucuses in which the religious right planned to seek control. During the primary nomination season, Williams's right-wing opponents labeled her as "cunning, deceitful, unloyal, a wolf in sheep's clothing," and chastised her for not honoring "God's miracle of newborn life."[11]

There were shades of a moderate versus ultraconservative split in the Senate too, but it was less pronounced than in the House. Four Republican senators stood apart from the others for their views on social and fiscal issues. These were Bob Schaffer, Charles Duke, Mike Coffman, and Mary Anne Tebedo.

They worked both within and outside of the chamber to promote themselves or their politics, although they were not much of a united force within the Senate. Duke was long a darling of the nation's anti-government militia types, and following the 1996 session he attempted to mediate between the FBI and Montana "Freemen." He ran an abortive campaign for U.S. Senate. Schaffer spent much of his time promoting himself for the U.S. House of Representatives. He drew some media attention by seeking to manipulate a committee schedule so as to tie up the time of his U.S. House seat rival, Senator Don Ament, in a ploy that backfired, and by referring to single-payer health insurance plans, like the Canadian one, as a "fascist economic model."[12] Mary Anne Tebedo's fame was increased through the activities of her daughter, who refused to recognize the legitimacy of the current government and spent time in jail for her efforts, and her son, who for years was on the forefront of anti-gay activities.

The Republicans' ideological split has gone across legislative chambers and clear outside the General Assembly itself. In 1998 moderate Denver Republican Senator Dottie Wham, along with moderate Fort Collins Republican Steve Tool, sponsored a bill to allow local governments to provide needle-exchange programs for drug addicts to reduce the spread of AIDS and other blood-related diseases. Among the prime motivations was a desire to halt the transfer of AIDS to the helpless children of the adult carriers.

Senator Wham successfully guided the bill through the Judiciary Committee, which she chaired, and, with the support of Democrats and a handful of fellow Republicans, she got it through the full Senate. But that was the end of the line. In the House Committee on Health, Environment, Welfare, and Institutions, Wham and Tool's fellow party members killed the bill on a party-line vote. The action prompted Dr. Matthew Hines, a Colorado Springs physician, to exclaim, "Seven to four! This issue is all about politics. Which of these Representatives are going to vote for public health. And which are going to vote against women and children, who will die."[13]

Between the time the Senate passed the bill and the House committee killed it, Colorado Republican Party Chairman Steve Curtis took the issue beyond the legislature and to the full party and larger public. At a party meeting Curtis said, "Anybody who votes for something as un-Republican as a needle-exchange bill is asking for a primary."[14]

Curtis's remarks were widely reported and highlighted the party split, and they triggered angry responses from Republican officeholders. "Let's have the testimony. I'll take my licks from my constituents," said Representative Marcy Morrison.[15] Her colleague, Republican Representative Gary McPherson, commented, "It's inappropriate for the state chair to tell legislators how to vote on issues." "I'm offended," added Republican House member Joyce Lawrence.[16] Senate Republican David Wattenberg was more pointed: Curtis, he said, "is a silly son-of-a-bitch," and Wattenberg characterized his actions as "asinine, autocratic."[17]

Steve Tool, House sponsor of the now-dead needle bill, got his shot a month later at a Republican House caucus luncheon. After exchanges of comments on the issue Tool told Curtis, "If you want to get involved in issues, run for office."[18] In neither the House nor the Senate have the ultra-right social-agenda contingents taken charge, but in the House they appeared to have had the larger impact. They clearly caused discomfort, especially in foreshadowing primary challenges to moderate Republican colleagues. They've also drawn attention to the voting records of others, and sought to taint some of them as too liberal for true-blue Republicans. In the eyes of some observers, past House Democrat Minority Leader Peggy Kerns among them, they've pushed the chamber as a whole further to the right. They've forced votes on gun, abortion, and sex-education issues, for example. These are issues members often prefer to avoid.

The fracture in the Republican party continued to be evident in the 2000 session. The extreme right element in both chambers gave Governor Owens and moderates a hard time on the governor's gun control and education reform proposals. Indeed, on some measures the politically ambitious House floor leader led the right wing against the bills of his own Republican House Speaker and spent some time counting Republican votes in anticipation of attempts to override possible vetoes by his own Republican governor.

Frequently members will divide, or come together, along lines of gender, although this seems to be less frequent than was the case some years ago. Women, more than men, show an interest in promoting legislation dealing with children, families, and health care. A few years ago, for example, Republican women in caucus joined together to force a change in the budget as proposed by the Joint Budget Committee to fund mobile mammography facilities in rural Colorado. Recently, too, a cross-party group of women legislators met informally to trigger some movement on a major school funding bill that had stalled. In Senate floor debate on the 1998 K–12 school funding bill, Senator Mutzebaugh moved to eliminate all funding for "at-risk" students. *Denver Post* reporter Peggy Lowe wrote, "Most of the female senators marched to the podium to oppose it." "I am stunned that we are going to do this . . . to hurt at-risk children," was Senator Pat Pascoe's response. Added Senator Peggy Reeves, "We've got to do things to help these children move ahead." Senator Dottie Wham suggested that Mutzebaugh made the attempt to help his own school district.[19]

The gender bond is dissolving some as more and more women are elected. With their increased number comes an increase in the diversity of their backgrounds and value systems. Women who come to lawmaking from backgrounds similar to those of men, law or small business, for example, often display policy preferences similar to those of their male counterparts on issues of finances, property, and so forth.

The Colorado Union of Taxpayers, for example, listed Vickie Agler and Mary Ellen Epps among its top ten fiscal conservatives in 1995 in the House of Representatives. For 1998, five of CUT's top ten fiscal conservatives were women, and on CUT's scorecard they were more conservative than their Republican male counterparts. The more liberal environmental lobby included Epps, House members Dorothy Gotlieb and Marilyn Musgrave, and Senator Mary Anne Tebedo on its list of legislators, the least supportive of environmental measures in 1977. As data in Table 6.2 show, women overall are a bit more friendly to the causes of seniors and environmentalists, and less cozy with the most conservative interests. Still, feminine connections exist across both party and chamber lines, and sometimes make a difference in policy results.

Occasionally there are political actions driven by neither party, nor ideology, nor region, nor reason. In 1998 in the midst of a series of fast-moving third and final reading votes on the chamber floor, Senator Ray Powers came to the podium to speak on a bill. Said Powers, "My seatmate [Senator Jim Congrove] told me this was a bad bill. I was set to vote against it until I realized it was my own bill."

Finally, there are times when institutional structure seems to promote division. Past House Majority Leader Tim Foster, for example, said this about the Senate: "I think we can talk about the cave of the winds and the house of the living dead with impunity."[20] On another occasion Foster resisted sending a bill, on which he was a party, to a conference committee with the Senate, saying that he didn't want to "suffer the brain damage" associated with interaction with senators.[21] Off the record some Democratic senators have referred to their own governor as "worthless" and "a backstabber" for his willingness to work with the Republican majority.

So legislatures, the Colorado General Assembly included, are houses of conflict. This should not be surprising, and in a pluralistic society we might well be disturbed if it were otherwise. Why, for example, would we want a representative body to be anything other than reflective of the citizenry that members were selected to represent?

The General Assembly is organized along party lines, and on many fundamental matters the members are divided along party lines. But such is not always the case, and as we have seen, ideology, region, ethnicity, personality, and even institutional configuration can generate splits where members coalesce across, rather than along, party lines.

Political scientists have long advocated what they call a "responsible two-party" system. Such a system consists of two competing political parties, each internally united in policy preferences and platform and held together by leadership. The parties are internally cohesive and offer the voters alternative policy directions. Voters take their pick of party, and thus policies. If the winning party delivers the goods and the voters continue to like what they see, the party is returned to office. If not, the incumbent party is displaced by the other one. The voters know where the parties stand and they know whom to hold responsible.

With one-party domination of the Colorado General Assembly for well over two decades, one might expect that the voters could easily figure out who is in charge and whom to thank or blame for the policy results. In some measure they can; what we have by way of tax, education, transportation, environment, and crime policy has come to us when Republicans, not Democrats, were in control.

But which Republicans, and have they really been in control? For most of the 1990s the majority has been cohesive on some issues but not others. Divisions based upon ideology or region or gender have contributed to the absence of strong party leadership and party cohesion. Disagreements on regulation, needle exchange, and abortion are examples.

All through the 1998 session, virtual chaos reigned on matters of taxes and the budget, and it continued through 1999 and 2000. Members and leaders in both houses were at odds with each other and the two chambers were in disagreement as well. Much of the chaos was the result of the TABOR amendment, which has made the entire voting public party to the formation of state fiscal policy. Political scientists' ideal two-party model is not to be found in Colorado—a ragtag version perhaps, but not one with discipline.

NOTES

1. Jerry Lopel, "Abuse of 'late bill' system is in full gear." *The Colorado Statesman*, March 27, 1998.
2. John Sanko, "Senate Democrats fired up about cramped quarters," *Rocky Mountain News*, January 9, 1997.
3. *Rocky Mountain News*, January 30, 1998.
4. Dan Luzadder, "Political payback buries honor," *Rocky Mountain News*, January 14, 1998.
5. *Capitol Reporter*, April 1, 1996.
6. *Denver Post*, January 11, 1996.
7. *Capitol Reporter*, April 22, 1996.
8. *Rocky Mountain News*, January 23, 1996.
9. *Capitol Reporter*, April 10, 1995.
10. "Williams says she's a target," *Fort Collins Coloradoan*, October 6, 1997.
11. Burt Hubbard, "Open season on Republican moderates," *Rocky Mountain News*, May 11, 1998.
12. *Denver Post*, April 20, 1995.
13. *Rocky Mountain News*, March 10, 1998.

14. Michelle Daly Johnston, "GOP chair's remarks stir up a hornets nest," *Denver Post*, March 1, 1998.
15. Ann Schrader, "Needle-exchange issue still hot," *Denver Post*, March 3, 1998.
16. Ibid., *Denver Post*, March 1, 1998.
17. Ibid., *Denver Post*, March 3, 1998.
18. Michelle Daly Johnston, "State GOP chief appeals for unity," *Denver Post*, April 8, 1998.
19. *Denver Post*, April 11, 1998.
20. *Rocky Mountain News*, March 15, 1996.
21. *Rocky Mountain News*, February 3, 1995.

7

The Money and Power of the Third House

An opening pastoral prayer in the General Assembly went like this: "God bless those who don't have lobbyists." The director of Colorado Common Cause observed, "It's no secret that the most underrepresented sector of society in Colorado are the people."[1]

There is a good deal of folklore about the interest groups and lobbyists who inhabit the Capitol. Collectively, they're sometimes called the "third house" of the legislature, and lobbyists are often referred to as "hired guns." Tales of the rare instances of bribery and arm-twisting persist and often grow with the telling, thus contributing to a skewed public image. But in truth, there is very little underhanded or under-the-table dealing among lobbyists and legislators. Most of what goes on is done in the light of day for all to see, although the financial aspects of interest group and lobbyist activity that are available in public records are incomplete and can be misleading. Still, anyone snooping for lawbreakers will find little to report.

The story of interest groups and lobbyists is not a story about crooks. It is a story about power. These groups and individuals are integral parts of the legislative process, and their influence on the public policy of the state is enormous. They provide a large portion of the money that funds legislative campaigns. In the understaffed legislature, they provide a major slice of the information that lawmakers use in decision-making. They outnumber the legislators six to one, and many are career lobbyists, living much of their lives in the Capitol, year after year. They come to know the process and policies inside and out. Legislators, on the other hand, are a much more transient sort, here today and gone tomorrow—unless, of course, they become lobbyists. With the full impact of term limits in effect since 1998, the legislators, in the

House especially, are short-timers in an institution full of career influence peddlers.

LOBBYING AND THE LAW

State law governs some of the practices of interest groups and lobbyists. It identifies professional lobbyists as individuals who seek to influence the decisions of the governor, lieutenant governor, legislature, boards, commissions, or rule-making body on behalf of others, and for pay.

Professional lobbyists must, by law, register with the secretary of state's office, providing personal information and the names of the individuals or organizations they represent. They must report the persons or organizations for whom they work, as well as those who pay them, if different. They are required to file monthly and year-end formal statements listing the amounts and sources of their income. They must report their expenditures, identifying persons on whom money is spent for entertainment and gifts, media costs, and other expenses. In addition, professional lobbyists are required to indicate the legislation, rule, issue, or vote they are seeking to influence. When a professional lobbyist's work is dormant (between legislative sessions, for example), this, too, is reported on a special form. The law specifically prohibits contingency lobbying, which is an agreement between employer and lobbyist to make payment only upon successful achievement of a designated legislative outcome. It also prevents lobbyists or groups from making contributions to members or candidates when the legislature is in session.

Persons classified as volunteers have been exempt from these rules but they must register with the chief clerk of the House of Representatives and the secretary of the Senate. Volunteers are defined as persons who receive no remuneration for their efforts, save for reimbursement of actual costs. People representing church, civic, and reform groups, such as the League of Women Voters and the PTA, fall into this category.

Many of the roughly 600 lobbyists registered in Colorado are employees of state agencies, and the law treats them in a special way. Each agency is, by law, allowed to designate one employee as its legislative contact. These contacts must then register and provide periodic reports on any costs incurred by the state for their legislative liaison work. They must report the legislation of interest and estimate the time spent in lobbying activity.

Failure to comply with the legal reporting requirements can result in temporary suspension of a lobbyist's license and, in extreme cases, fines, time in jail, or both. There have been a few suspensions in recent years.

The law also requires that some interest group expenditures related to elections must be reported. Legislative candidates themselves are required to file a series of contribution and spending statements for each election, thereby disclosing the identity of donors. In addition, some donors must report, as must organizations that seek to influence an election for an office or a ballot issue.

Persons organized as political action committees (PACs) must also report their receipts and expenditures, unless they take in less than $250 per year. Included are corporate PACs, union PACs, and political education committees. They must list in the public record the names and addresses of donors who give the PAC $25 or more in cash, or $100 of in-kind contributions. These PACs must provide the same information about those to whom they give $25 or more.

There are some reporting requirements associated with both lobbying and spending to influence electoral outcomes, but there are no expenditure limits. Individuals, groups, and corporations are free to spend and lobby as they please if they comply with the reporting laws and thus leave a public trail of their actions.

ETHICS RULES

Apart from these legal dimensions of the lobbying enterprise, there are some ethical considerations as well. Seldom is a bill without its interest group supporters and opponents, and never does a legislative day go by that the Capitol hallways and coffee shop are not filled with lobbyists. No legislator can get through a day without receiving a healthy dose of lobbyist opinion and advice. Millions of dollars are spent trying to affect the formation of public policy and the outcome of legislative elections. The stakes are high, and the legislative pace hectic. It is no wonder, then, that the behavior of the hundreds of participants in this process will raise some ethical questions, even if the process is, by and large, legal and above board.

Lobbyists are constantly concerned about legislators' stands on issues; occasionally, they can't resist the temptation to glance at materials on a lawmaker's desk. Lobbyists are paid to get bills passed or stopped, so one should not be surprised to hear them stretch the facts from time to time. These interest group representatives are in the Capitol all day, every day that the General Assembly is in session. Some pragmatic problems arise—where do they hang their hat and where can they find a phone? In recent years, places have been designated for lobbyists to leave clothing and working materials, and there are public pay phones available. Additionally, modern cellular phones are ubiquitous. Still, there is some unauthorized use of legislators' facilities. And since being on top of the latest information is the name of the game, eavesdropping is bound to occur.

Occasionally, basic rules of conduct, such as getting permission before using facilities and equipment, reading only authorized materials, and treating people in a civil fashion, are violated. In fact, at one point, they were violated frequently enough that the House and Senate leadership appointed a committee of lobbyists to develop a code of ethics, and following that the General Assembly adopted guidelines for lobbyists. The guidelines prohibit deceit and threat, known issuance of false information, hiding of information, efforts to tamper with the internal organization of the legislature, use of state equipment, and more. The measure also gives the leadership of the General Assembly authority to investigate violations.

Lobbying ethics are a sensitive matter in the legislature, as ethical breaches can both ruin a lobbyist's career and be politically costly to legislators. A 1999 blow-up over an allegedly forged letter provides a vivid example. At the request of local drug stores, Representative Diane Hoppe sponsored a bill to prevent health insurers from providing discounts to patients who purchase drugs by mail. A letter from an Arizona discounter appeared and was distributed to lawmakers, which suggested that mail ordering saved nothing. This message from a mail-order discounter was counterintuitive and raised suspicions concerning its authenticity. Amidst suspicions of forgery, legislative leaders quickly promised an investigation. "It's the most serious ethics crisis involving lobbyists in almost a decade," stated Senate Majority Leader Tom Blickensderfer.[2]

The issue of ethics can extend to legislators' behavior toward lobbyists, as well. For example, in attempts to raise funds for causes they supported, some legislators have leaned on lobbyists to make contributions. In one publicized instance, two legislators tried to sell $500-per-couple tickets to a dinner benefiting a program of the University of Colorado's Graduate School of Public Affairs. This obviously puts both the lobbyist and the lawmaker in a peculiar position. The lobbyist wants to be influential in the Capitol, and saying "no" to legislator solicitations does not help. And the lawmaker is supposed to represent constituents. What, then, does the legislator do when a lobbyist, implicitly to be sure, wants the favor returned at decision time on some bill?

In another fund-raising venture, Senator Marilyn Musgrave highlighted the mix of the roles of lawmaker and lobbyist. Clearly a senator is an elected lawmaker. But during the 1999 legislative session Musgrave sent out a letter urging gun enthusiasts to send money to the Rocky Mountain Gun Owners, a lobbying group, and another to persons on the Christian Coalition mailing list pushing contributions to help "prepare to battle the homosexual lobby."[3]

In yet another instance, a former Republican representative, senator, and Joint Budget Committee chair secured information from the

Legislative Council that was passed on to the state Republican party and used against a Democratic incumbent House member in an election. At the time, the information thief was on the payroll of the City and County of Denver as a lobbyist, and his partisan actions stirred a storm of protest and raised serious ethical questions.

A more recent controversy involved suggestions of trading promises for votes on the 1996 bill that established the metropolitan stadium district. The measure, called the "Bronco bill," passed by one vote in each chamber. It might have died in the House except for the votes of Representatives Romero and Chavez, who came over to the Bronco side after Bronco owner Pat Bowlen promised, in writing, to ensure the use of minority contractors in constructing the stadium. It mattered not that the district board would be a public body and the stadium a public facility, not Pat Bowlen's. The promise got the votes.

It is not easy to tell when there are genuine ethical lapses, and when circumstances that seem questionable are matters of mere coincidence. In 1997, for example, the Legal Services Committee determined that records of patient abuse in hospitals could remain secret, as Colorado's law now reads. It turned out that the attorney who argued that position before the committee had, along with her husband, contributed $72,000 to the Republican party in recent years. When the state Common Cause director suggested a link between the money and the vote, committee member Jeanne Adkins exclaimed, "He's implying that my vote is bought and paid for? Absolutely offensive. It questions my integrity. It's incredible."[4]

Finally there is simply the matter of the personal closeness that develops among legislators and lobbyists. They spend countless hours together, in the same Capitol building and in dozens of breakfasts, lunches, dinners, and fund-raisers. Occasionally the togetherness is much less than arm's length and can't help but impact the votes of the legislator.

Recent efforts to place additional ethics parameters in state statutes for the lawmakers themselves have been unsuccessful. In 1996 both chambers passed a measure designed to prevent state employees from working as lobbyists for private firms they had regulated, for a period of six months after their state employment ended. It died when efforts were made to include legislators in its coverage. A similar measure died in the 2000 session. Many legislators move immediately into the lobbying business when they leave the legislature, and they've been loathe to deprive themselves of that option.

While problems of political ethics will never be fully resolved, codes of ethics that provide guidelines can help. So do the informal norms; in fact, these may be the more powerful. If word gets around that certain lobbyists snoop, give misleading information, or use bad taste in personal interactions, their reputations will fall. And both lobbyists and lawmakers will tell you time after time that your reputation and your word are all you've got.

THE RANGE OF INTERESTS

The range of groups and organizations that lobby under the gold dome is enormous. It includes business and industry, unions, professions, local governments, state agencies, and the governor of the state. Organizations include the Colorado Association of Commerce and Industry, the Colorado Association of Realtors, the Colorado Association of Tobacco and Candy Distributors, the Colorado Bankers Association, the AFL-CIO, the Colorado Education Association, the Colorado Dental Association, the Colorado Municipal League, Colorado Counties, Inc., the Colorado Commission on Higher Education, Colorado State University, and the governor's office. When bills to establish disclosure of information on home sales are discussed, the realtors take notice. When there are proposals to expand the scope of dental assistants' duties and responsibilities, the dentists come alive. Any time there are questions of taxation, business and industry lobbyists go into action. When the legislature talks of tinkering with property tax reductions, cities and counties turn up the heat. Representatives of higher education are awake year-round, looking for ways to protect state appropriations. Professions want to be licensed to restrict competition, but are less sure that they like the accompanying regulations.

Here are just a few examples, from a recent session, of the range of interests and the nature of the political conflicts that emerge. Year after year, it seems, the optometrists are at political war with the ophthalmologists. This is not unusual, as professions fight with each other all the time in their efforts to use the law to protect their definition of public health and safety, along with their pocketbooks.

Ophthalmologists are medical doctors with medical training; optometrists are not. As in other states, Colorado's medical practices act establishes educational and experiential qualifications for medical practitioners, and stipulates in law who can do what. The medically trained ophthalmologists may do things that optometrists may not. For example, for years the MDs could use drugs to dilate eyes for examinations but optometrists, by law, could not. The law was changed some years ago and now optometrists may administer the dilating drug, and some other medications as well.[5]

A recent fight was over the optometrists' desire to be allowed by law to perform corrective laser surgery. The practice of making small incisions on the cornea to correct vision and reduce or negate the need for glasses has expanded enormously in recent years. At a cost of $1,000 to $2,000 per eye, it is a lucrative business.

Optometrists contend that the surgery is simple, and they can do it safely. Ophthalmologists disagree, and contend that such procedures, in the hands of people without medical training, are a danger to public health and safety. Optometrists contend that providing, in law, a monopoly for ophthalmologists on the process is a danger to the public's pocketbooks.

The political fight floats on a sea of public interest rhetoric—protection of public health and safety versus protection of the consumer through increased availability of the service and competition. Clearly there are both medical and economic dimensions to the issue. The public is not well served if those performing medical procedures are not competent. But neither is it well served if prices are inflated in a million-dollar industry through unneeded legal protection of a lucrative market for a select few.

Who is right and who is wrong? Legislators can find whatever answer they want. There are both medical people and lobbyists on both sides of the issue, and they all come armed with studies and arguments to prove their case.

Then there are the chiropractors and the veterinarians. Some chiropractors have discovered that the adjustments they administer to fellow humans also work on their pets. This practice was of little concern to the veterinarians as long as the animals belonged to the chiropractors themselves. But they took notice when the practice became commercialized. When, in 1995, the law regulating chiropractors was up for renewal, the veterinarians lobbied to adjust the law to prevent paid chiropractic work on animals in the absence of consultation with a vet.[6]

There's more. In the years since it has become a cultural norm for women to seek the care of a medical doctor for births, midwives have continued to assist women in the process. For years, Colorado's medical practices act made it illegal for persons without a certain minimum level of medical education and experience to assist in the birthing process. Medical doctors and certain nurses possessed the training and experience to qualify.

But many women who were assisting at births, especially some in rural and heavily ethnic communities, did not meet the formal requirements. Still, they had assisted in dozens, sometimes hundreds, of deliveries. Technically, they were in violation of the law. In some instances, such assistance was given because legally qualified medical help was either too distant or too expensive. Sometimes, lay midwife help was given as part of a cultural tradition passed on through the years. And further, there was a growing interest, generally, in use of the services of midwives as alternatives to MDs or licensed nurses.

Lay midwives and their past and prospective patients wanted the law changed to allow expanded use of midwifery services. Medical doctors wanted the law to remain unchanged. The former cited case after case of success. Doctors told horror stories of childbirth tragedies that could have been prevented by the presence of someone medically trained. Some testimony and lobbying focused upon public health and safety. Some centered on the psychological benefits to the mother produced by the presence and warmth of the midwife. Some centered on the high cost of medical doctors and hospitals.

The MD–lay midwife struggle went on for years. Finally, in the early 1990s, the law was changed to allow midwives to practice.

Professionals aren't the only ones who hire lobbyists and fight to write laws that advance their values and their bank accounts. So do businesses. In recent years the "brew-pub" industry has blossomed in Colorado, and has cut somewhat into the profits of such large producers of suds as Coors and Anheuser-Busch. Further, by state law, liquor stores are closed on Sundays, but until recently the law allowed brew-pubs to make Sunday sales to the public. Much to the chagrin of the brew-pub owners, that has now changed. A 1996 bill was introduced, and passed, that both stopped the Sunday sales and limited the amount of beer the small brewers may sell to liquor stores.

The 1998 session saw a contest involving auto insurers, health insurers, and trial lawyers. Representative Jennifer Veiga introduced a bill designed to lower the state's minimum mandatory insurance levels. The rationale was to thus lower premiums with the expectation that more affordable rates would lower the number of illegally uninsured motorists.

The auto insurance companies liked the idea; trial lawyers and health insurers did not. The lawyers' argument was that rates would not fall much at all since the bill would affect personal injury coverage only. Health insurers argued that the bill would result in cost-shifting. Where auto personal injury coverage was too low to cover all medical costs in an accident, the cost would shift to medical policies or the pockets of the persons involved.

In support of the measure, Representative Veiga observed that the bill's rates were set after careful study by an interim committee. Opposing the bill, Floor Leader Norma Anderson noted that "the auto insurance people love this bill. The health insurers don't like it. I'll tell you why. It's a cost-shifting bill." Minority Floor Leader Carol Snyder added, "There are a certain number of deadbeats who will not buy auto insurance if the cost is $1 a year." Speaking for the trial lawyers, lobbyist Tom Bastian commented, "It cuts that tiny amount you pay for personal injury coverage by 50 percent. You still have liability, collision, uninsured and all the rest—and they make up the lion's share." Bastian's trial lawyers make a living trying cases, many of which involve personal injury damages paid for by auto insurance policies.[7]

Over the course of several sessions the operators of private prisons have spent heavily to lobby lawmakers to pass bills in some instances and kill them in others. Rebound Corporation, which ran a private prison in Brush, paid a quarter of a million dollars over several years to lobbyists Diane Rees and Frank DeFilippo to support legislation creating a juvenile boot camp and to fight measures to expand state-run facilities. Clearly, more state prison capacity means less business for private prisons.

In 1998 Rebound needed more than just lobbyist help to move or kill bills. Rebound's Brush facility became the center of legislative attention when a Utah youth committed suicide and the facility was bombarded with allegations of staffing and clinical inadequacies, harassment of inmates, and sexual relations between staffers and prisoners. The state eventually closed the facility.[8]

When businesses fight with each other, and the battles are constant, the cry is always to "level the playing field." Leveling the playing field is, of course, slang for changing the law so as to give one interest or another a legally concocted economic advantage over competitors. Somehow, even after decades of effort to create truly free enterprise and fair competition, the field remains tilted. Which way the tilt goes depends upon whose lobbyist and whose statistics are believed.

Private-sector professionals and private enterprises are not the only ones who struggle to mold the law in their favor by leaning on the elected representatives of the people. So do governments. In recent sessions there have been multiple attempts to enact what is called "takings" legislation. Such laws would make it easier for owners of private property to collect compensation from cities and counties for reductions in the market value of their property caused by zoning decisions or public-benefit restrictions on use of the property. Some property owners argue, for example, that requirements to set aside some portion of a property for a public purpose as a condition for receipt of a development or building permit is a "taking" of property. So too, some say, are restrictions on land use for environmental protection purposes.

Cities and counties oppose such legislation, arguing that it represents state-level preemption of decision-making prerogatives that properly belong at the local level. City and county lobbyists, and there are many of them, argue that state lawmakers who complain bitterly about federal intrusion into the public policy affairs of the states ought not do the same to the locals. As one local government lobbyist commented, "Local control to these guys seems to mean controlling the locals."

The political game is clear. Property owners, often developers or farmers who have had decisions by city or county officials go against them, move on the state level asking that the state deprive the local officials of the ability to render what are considered to be economically disadvantageous decisions. Notions of local control are sacrificed at the altar of profit.

Cities and counties, along with special districts and the schools, organize collectively to lobby the legislature. The cities' organization is the Colorado Municipal League—the CML. The league maintains a suite of offices and a staff just a few blocks from the Capitol. During the year, CML conducts workshops for both elective and appointed city officials and employees on a wide range of topics, including legislation and legislative relations. The league is necessarily concerned with bills involving taxation, employee pay and pensions, zoning and land use generally, public utilities, roads and traffic, elections, and much more.

Besides meetings and workshops, CML staff communicate with city officials through a "Statehouse Report," which tracks the legislative session, providing brief analyses of bills, the league's position on each, the bills sponsors, and the CML lobbyist who is working the bill. Like Colorado Counties, special districts, and the schools, the league maintains a full-time presence in the legislature with a contingent of six lobbyists.

The lobbying position of CML and the other associations of local government is interesting. On the one hand, their lobbyists are much like the legislators themselves; they are spokespersons for the citizens of Colorado. Cities, counties, special districts, and schools are created in law by the state, for the state. They are the people's governments. Local officials and thus their collective organization and lobbyists are, like legislators, working for the public and are ultimately responsible to it through the electoral system. Legislators and the locals thus are, or should be, comrades.

But in the legislature it is not always viewed that way. For legislators whose feet, finances, and heads are firmly planted in private-sector philosophy, and for private interests who may not like government regulation in such areas as land use or utility provision, local governments and their lobbyists look like just another set of special interests. One of the challenges local government lobbies encounter is to present their cases as the cases of "the people," the same people to whom legislators must report. It often helps the cause of local interests to have members of the General Assembly arrive with some elective local government experience. It also helps to maintain good communication between local government lobbyists and local officials so that the officials from back in the home district can carry the desired messages to the Capitol.

Among the more numerous and visible interests in the legislature are the schools. Local school boards, associations of school executives, teachers and board members, community colleges, universities, students—they all find their way into the Capitol to lobby.

The reasons for their interest in the work of the legislature are clear. Roughly one-half of all the money that runs Colorado's 176 local school districts is appropriated by the state legislature. Most of the rest comes from the local property tax, and state law sets the permissible parameters of that tax. Much of the money that runs the public colleges and universities is appropriated by the legislature, too.

Besides providing money, it is the state legislature that creates the organizational system of education at all levels. The legislature can and does prescribe some curriculum requirements, as well as systems of tests and measures of student progress. Systems of teacher licensing and tenure are creatures of state law.

So it is no wonder that the districts, schools, and employee groups spend millions of dollars each year on lobbyists and propaganda to seek favorable legislative action. Their existence, programs, and cash flow depend on it.

Sometimes school interests lobby together and sometimes they do not. On matters of teacher tenure and due process, teachers, school executives, and the school boards may well take opposing positions. But other times, such as when the budget is at issue, they stand together, and united they are more effective. Late in the 1998 session, for example, the state associations of school executives, the teachers association, and the association of school boards were together in their push for a higher inflation increase than the one proposed by the House in its version of the school finance act. The education lobby did not get everything it wanted, but its united front did produce some increase.

From time to time questions have arisen on the matter of using public resources to lobby public decision-making. Few politically knowledgeable people will dispute the need for cities, counties, schools, special districts, and both state executive and judicial agencies to maintain effective, continuous communication with the fount of their existence and policy directions, namely, the state legislature. But how much do they spend, and what do they do?

Some years back, executive branch agencies were instructed to designate one employee each to be the point person, the legislative liaison. The purpose was to keep agencies from swamping legislators with advocates for agency programs and budgets on public time and money. The cities, counties, schools, and special districts pool resources to communicate with each other and the legislature through the mechanism of state organizations—CML for example.

But beyond these organizations, some local governments have hired additional private lobbyists, and this has raised questions as to its need and propriety. The *Denver Rocky Mountain News* reported in 1999 that "twenty-three local governments, school districts and state colleges hired lobbyists this year." In one instance, Glendale, a city of roughly 4,000 people, contracted with lobbyist Bill Artist to the tune of $140,000.[9] The issue has never been the need for intergovernmental communication and liaison. Rather, when public-public lobbying is questioned, it is a matter of style and cost.

Many longtime statehouse observers believe that there has been an increase in the number of interests represented in the legislature, including the appearance of some rather rigid, single-issue groups. Some say there has also been a change in the lobbying environment. Many organizations have long sent their own direct-hire employees to the legislature to represent group interests. But others have linked up with the growing number of contract lobbyists, who represent several clients on a fee basis. This is an efficient way for many organizations to operate, of course, as it gives them eyes and ears in the Capitol without having to pay someone on a full-time basis. Some groups send volunteers to the Capitol and are concerned with a rather narrow range of issues—prochoice and anti-abortion groups and some religious and environmental concerns are examples.

There are interests centered well beyond the state of Colorado that maintain a presence in the Capitol. The National Rifle Association has a statehouse lobbyist and regularly pushes a legislative agenda. When gun control legislation was introduced following a series of murders in the Denver area committed by a drug-influenced individual with a stolen automatic assault rifle, the association, its membership, and its lobbyist came alive with a vengeance to fight off any public weapons control whatsoever. Indeed, between 1992 and 1994 the NRA pumped $40,000 or more into the campaign coffers of legislative candidates. Forty-three lawmakers, all but three who were Republicans, received donations ranging from $250 to $1,000.[10]

National tobacco interests have been active in Colorado's legislature recently, and they push their agenda through the work of locally hired lobbyists. During the 1996 session a measure to restrict smoking in the chambers was opposed by tobacco interests, while one that would have preempted local cigarette sales restrictions to minors with a statewide measure was supported by the tobacco people. The tobacco interests, including Philip Morris, R. J. Reynolds, and the Tobacco Institute, employed a bevy of well-known statehouse regulars, including Wally

Stealey, Ruben Valdez, and Pancho Hays. Tobacco also pumped money into legislative campaigns. In addition to the gun and tobacco lobbies, businesses such as US West, United Airlines, Ford Motor Company, and Exxon are represented by lobbyists in the Colorado General Assembly.

WHO IS INFLUENTIAL?

There is broad agreement on the tactics and styles that make for successful lobbying. There is less agreement, however, on who the most influential interest groups are. Some observers cite government and government-related groups—the Colorado Municipal League, Colorado Counties, Inc., and colleges and universities, along with the Colorado Education Association and CAPE (the Colorado Association of Public Employees). Cities, counties, and institutions of higher education throughout the state can use their elected officials and top administrators to call upon the legislators and press for their collective interests. Colorado's thousands of teachers and state employees can grab the ears of their local legislators in every corner of the state. Given their sheer numbers and the fact that statewide organizations are already in place, these governments and government employees can be powerful forces indeed.

But to some extent, the potential influence of governments and their employees is muted by an attitude and orientation that have been in place in the Colorado General Assembly for decades. Many of the Republicans controlling the legislature have been very conservative on fiscal matters. As a result, some of them have been suspicious of government programs and employees; some have even been frankly hostile. During the 1980s, the mood of the Reagan administration at the national level reinforced this attitude to some extent, so there has been an inclination, year after year, to minimize government and hold taxes and spending down as much as possible. This attitude became even more pronounced after the 1994 election, when the Republican capture of the U.S. Congress was reflected in an enlarged Republican majority in Colorado's House and the election of a conservative social-agenda group willing to cut government wherever it was found. So the wants and needs of cities, counties, schools, and state agencies have not always been met gladly.

The "iron triangle" phenomenon, so prevalent in Washington where congressional committees or subcommittees join with specific agencies and selected interest groups to monopolize policy-making in their narrow areas of interest, is much less in evidence in the Colorado General Assembly. For the most part, the majority party looks for ways to reduce the scope of government programs and duck new expenditures, and committees typically do not act as the unabashed advocates and protectors of selected agencies or local governments. Nor can legislative committees be sure that their handiwork will receive the stamp of approval on the floor.

Most knowledgeable observers of the Republican-controlled Colorado General Assembly cite business and industry groups as the most powerful interests in the past decade or so. Consequently, the legislature has been oriented toward the business and private sectors; the political environment, quite simply, has been very friendly to business. The wave of interest in "privatizing" some of the functions of government is a manifestation of this orientation. So too is the interest in "takings" legislation designed to weaken local government's land-use powers in relation to private property. In addition, business and industry interests have been generous in funding legislative campaigns and have concentrated their money on incumbents and Republican candidates.

For some years, CACI (the Colorado Association of Commerce and Industry) was cited as a very powerful group. More than one legislator has said that, in effect, CACI just walks in and gets what it wants. Following the 1999 session, CACI Executive Director Sam Cassidy said frankly that the legislature had been very good to business. Other significant business and industry bodies include the Greater Denver Area Chamber of Commerce and Colorado Concern, a collection of some fifty wealthy and influential businessmen. US West and Adolph Coors Company are ever-present, both with their lobbyists in the Capitol and their money in campaigns. The same is true of the construction, transportation, and insurance industries; the farm and ranch businesses; the realtors; the apartment owners; and others. Some say that agricultural interests are especially influential because they have historically had good lobbyists and have been able to channel their concerns to the House and Senate Agriculture Committees, which tend to be packed with rural legislators. One veteran legislator summed it up: "Lobby influence depends on the issue and the group. CACI can have anything it wants because its values coincide with those of the Republican party. The trucking industry gets its way too. So does the Cattlemen's Association, because people accept their values and they have good lobbyists."

Who Are the Lobbyists?

Some interests send their own employees to the Capitol. State agencies designate certain employees to be legislative liaisons. The Colorado Education Association, the Colorado Municipal League, the Colorado District Attorney's Council, and many others put people directly on their payrolls to represent them and perhaps perform other functions, as well. The Colorado Education Association, for example, has several employees who lobby for the teachers' group, and so do the cities of

Denver and Colorado Springs. The Municipal League sends six direct-hire employees to the Capitol.

A very large and growing number of interests hire contract lobbyists to speak for them, just as one buys the time of such other professionals as attorneys and mechanics. And just as they can change doctors and lawyers, clients can fire their lobbyists.

David Rice was long referred to as the king of the lobby corps. He first lobbied in the Colorado General Assembly in 1943. He returned in 1949 after World War II and on a part-time basis he lobbied until 1997—a career that spans more than forty years. Rice passed away in 1998. As the ultimate tribute to David Rice, his friend and fellow lobbyist Danny Williams said, "He could do more on the phone from his hospital room than most of us can do in person."[11]

Rice's main task over most of his lobbying career was to represent the interests of the Colorado Cattlemen's Association, but he had other clients, too. In 1997 he still represented the Cattlemen's Association, Colorado Counties, Inc., the Colorado Woolgrower's Association, and United Track Racing.

David Rice was always a "down home" country boy. He was friendly and easy to talk with and often had a joke to tell. Rice was not intense and did not deal in information overload—a note, maybe, plus a few words, but no stacks of statistical data. Indeed, Rice's notes to himself were often written in ballpoint pen on the backs of his hands—not napkins, but his hands.

Rice peddled smiles, easy conversation, and reliable information for over fifty years and saw over a thousand lawmakers come and go. The legislators, not David Rice, were the newcomers. Everyone knew him, and everyone trusted him. He represented interests with deep roots in the economy and the cultural values of Colorado and the West.

Hays, Hays & Wilson is one of the largest contract lobbying enterprises in the state. Frank Hays Sr. was a former Republican lieutenant governor. His son Frank, "Pancho," now runs the firm. James Wilson, now deceased, was a former reviser of statutes in the Colorado General Assembly. The organization has taken on other lobbyists in recent years, including Karen Reinertson, who is a long-standing regular in the Capitol and once served as Democratic Governor Roy Romer's chief budget officer. Often affiliated with Hays is lobbyist Bill Artist, a past member of House Republican party leadership. Others who work with Hays are longtime lobbyists Lynn Young and Becky Brooks. The folks in Hays's outfit have been well placed politically and they make good money selling their history and their contacts.

The 2000 secretary of state's list of lobbyists showed Hays and his associates representing over three dozen separate interest groups. Most were listed as clients by all three lobbyists, although a few were listed by just one or two of them. The names and addresses of lobbyists' clients can also be found in the lobbyists' financial reports, which are kept by the Colorado secretary of state. Those records showed that Hays, Hays & Wilson served clients in Michigan, New York, California, Virginia, and the District of Columbia, as well as those based in Colorado.

Another large contract lobby firm was that of Wallace and Michelle Stealey. Wally Stealey is a former professor of political science at the University of Southern Colorado in Pueblo. Before getting into the lobbying business, he worked on the staff of former Democratic Governor Richard Lamm. The Stealeys' list of clients, totaling more than forty, is at least as lengthy as that of Hays, Hays & Wilson, and it is interesting to note that it contains many of the same parties. Indeed, the Stealeys and Hays, Hays & Wilson are located in the same Capitol Hill office suite. So are several other veteran lobbyists. Some interests obviously want to be well covered. Stealey retired from active lobbying in 2000 and his firm was taken over by veteran lobbyist Becky Brooks.

Other very successful lobbyists serve lengthy but somewhat less gargantuan client lists. Danny Tomlinson once lobbied for US West and now works on his own or sometimes works as a partner with Bob Ferm on certain matters. Peg Ackerman, who holds a Ph.D. in chemistry as part of her background and also runs a publishing and consulting enterprise, has a number of law enforcement groups on her client list. And Peter Minahan, who lobbies in concert with his wife, is a former Republican House member. Their client lists are representative of the lists of many other lobbyists, and are shown in Table 7.1.

Just as contract lobbyists serve many clients at once, so, too, do some interests cover the waterfront by hiring several lobbyists. The Colorado Association of Homebuilders lists two lobbyists and the Colorado Bankers Association lists six. Colorado Counties, Inc., has eight of them. The Colorado Municipal League has six people representing them in the General Assembly, all direct-hire league employees. US West Sprint lists thirteen, including Pancho Hays and Karen Reinertson.

Increasingly, it seems, the ranks of the lobby corps have been swelled by the inclusion of former legislators. Lobbying can be a logical occupation for former members of the General Assembly since they know the process and people well, and thus have ready access to the ears of former colleagues. Furthermore, until 1999, legislators earned just $17,500 per year, plus expenses. But lobbying can be very lucrative indeed.

The secretary of state's 2000 directory of registered professional lobbyists listed twenty-five people who were former legislators. They are identified in Table 7.2, along with their former position in the General Assembly and party affiliation.

Table 7.1—Lobbyist Client Lists (2000)

Margaret E. Ackerman
    American Mobile Home Association
    Colorado Association of Commerce and Industry
    Colorado Community Corrections Coalition
    Colorado Coroners Association
    Colorado County Treasurers Association
    Colorado State Association of County Clerks & Recorders
    County Sheriffs of Colorado, Inc.
    Natural Fuels Corporation
    Vanatta Sullan Sandgrund and Sullan
    Wembley USA Inc.

Peter M. Minahan
    Colorado Communique, Inc.
    Atmos Energy Corporation
    Auto-Matic Credit
    Colorado Financial Services Association
    Colorado Optometric Association
    Colorado Orthopedic Society
    Colorado Veterinary Medical Association
    Denver Regional Council of Governments
    McLeod USA
    Nextlink Colorado LLC
    Unilicorp United d.b.a. Peoples Natural Gas
    Workers Compensation Education Association
    Youthrack, Inc.

Danny L. Tomlinson
    Alliance of American Insurers
    American Family Life Assurance Company
    Bighorn Action, ORG
    City of Westminster
    Colorado Grain & Feed Association
    Colorado Insurance Coalition
    Colorado Self-Insured Association
    Colorado Society of Certified Public Accountants
    Colorado State University System & Foundation
    Creekside Coalition
    Denver Dumb Friends League
    Economic Developers' Council of Colorado
    Green Industries of Colorado (Greenco)
    Hall & Evans, LLC
    Hanifen Imhoff, Inc.
    Health Management Systems, Inc.
    Kansas Builders, Inc.
    Medical OPS Management, Inc.

Source: Secretary of State, 2000.

Table 7.2—2000 Lobbyists Who Are Ex-Legislators

Lobbyist	Party	Former Position(s)
Bill Artist	Republican	House, Asst. Majority Leader
Bev Bledsoe	Republican	House, Speaker
Jim Brandon	Republican	Senate
Sam Cassidy	Democrat	Senate
Maggy Christiansen	Republican	House
Frank DeFilippo	Republican	House, Committee Chair
Steve Durham	Republican	Senate
Don Eberle	Democrat	House
Faye Fleming	Republican	House
Joan Green	Republican	House
JoAnn Groff	Democrat	House
Gwenne Hume	Republican	House
Joan Johnson	Democrat	Senate
Bob Kirscht	Republican	House, JBC Chair
Peggy Lamm	Democrat	House
Jim Lee	Republican	House, Senate
Don Mielke	Republican	House, Committee Chair
Peter Minahan	Republican	House
Betty Neale	Republican	House, JBC
Chris Paulson	Republican	House, Floor Leader
Paul Schauer	Republican	House
John Singer	Republican	House
Dick Soash	Democrat	Senate
Ruben Valdez	Democrat	House, Speaker
Danny Williams	Republican	House, Committee Chair

Source: Secretary of State, 2000.

A substantial portion of the lobby corps is female. Of the over 500 registered professional lobbyists, almost 40 percent are women, and many of these are among the best and most influential.

Many lobbyists are in the business on a part-time basis, or they only show up on occasion to represent their employers. Most Capitol observers agree that, among the hundreds who are registered, just two or three dozen lobbyists constitute a full-time and very influential set. Pancho Hays, Steve Durham, Danny Tomlinson, Bill Artist, Ruben Valdez, Frank DeFilippo, Jim Christiansen, and Jerald Johnson would have to be included on such a list. So would Lynn Young, Bonnie Geiger, JoAnn Groff, Jeanne McEvoy, Flo Mendez, Freda Poundstone, Becky Brooks, Diane Rees, Cathy Walsh, Karen Reinertson, and Peg Ackerman.

And there are influential husband-and-wife teams, including Bob and Linda Kirscht and Beth and Peter Minahan. Like the legislature itself, the lobby corps is becoming a coeducational community.

The employment of former legislators as lobbyists, though very common, can become controversial at times. Just before the 1988 legislative session, veteran legislator and former JBC Chairman Cliff Dodge resigned his Senate seat to take a lucrative position as lobbyist for the City and County of Denver. Dodge negotiated with the City before resigning his Senate (and JBC) seat, and the House Speaker called the City on Dodge's behalf. Whether that foreclosed the City's option to reject Dodge in favor of someone else is a matter of speculation. But an editorial in the *Rocky Mountain News* raised questions of political conflict of interest since Dodge could have stayed in the Senate and on the Budget Committee and voted on decisions affecting Denver had he not been hired.

There is also some concern about the propriety of allowing former legislators to enter the lobbying business immediately after leaving the General Assembly. Clearly, ex-legislators are well positioned. They know the process and the lawmakers. Indeed, they are close personal friends and party comrades with many of them. Does this set the stage for the inappropriate peddling of influence? Opinions differ on the subject.

Some lobbyists who are not former legislators dislike the practice because it presents them with additional and often effective competition for clients and perhaps more opposition on certain bills, as well. Without doubt, past lawmakers like Bob Kirscht, Bill Artist, and Ruben Valdez are tough rivals in the lobbying game.

Making Money as a Lobbyist

There is a lot of money to be made in the lobbying business, although it is a bit difficult to figure out just how much. For example, two of the largest lobbying firms are Stealey and Associates, and Hays, Hays & Wilson. As of the end of 1995, Stealey and Associates reported gross receipts of $866,734.[12] At the start of the 1998 legislative session in mid-January, Stealey reported estimated gross income for the tax year of over $700,000 from a listing of thirty-two clients. They are shown in Table 7.3. Stealey listed 228 bills as objects of his attention on behalf of those who were paying him.[13] More bills were introduced later and his list grew.

Through November Hays and his associates had billed clients for $425,623 for 1996, and Pancho Hays had been paid $148,471. Early in the 1998 session, Hays's receipts again topped $400,000.[14] Another well-known lobbyist, Bill Artist, reported income of $173,329 for 1995 and $186,997 for 1997; Jerald Johnson reported a 1997 gross income of $187,500.[15]

Table 7.3—Stealey's 1998 Paying Clients

Client	Estimated Fee
Archer, Daniels, Midland	$25,000
Artist and Associates	30,000
Casino Owners Assn., Colorado	35,000
City of Trinidad	15,000
Colorado Auto. Free Trade Assn.	15,000
Colorado Education Association	49,000
Colorado Plumbing, Heating, Cooling Contractors	600
Colorado Radiological Society	12,000
Colorado St. Pipe Trades Assn.	7,500
Community Corrections Services, Inc.	10,000
County of Pueblo	25,000
EQUUS Farms	30,000
Ethanol Management Co.	8,400
First American Railways, etc.	12,500
Forbes Trinchera Ranch	24,000
Hays, Hays & Wilson	18,000
Health Insurance Assn. of America	27,000
Independent Bankers of Colorado	25,000
International Brotherhood Elec. Wkrs.	7,500
Klode Salvage Dist. Center	20,000
Merk and Co.	24,000
Newmont Gold Corp.	36,000
Prudential Ins. Co. Am.	25,000
Rio Grande Water Cons. Dist.	12,000
RJR Tobacco Co.	62,000
RRK Enterprises, Independence House	10,000
Seagram and Sons	20,000
Taubman Company	12,000
Towing and Recovery Pros	20,000
United Title Companies	15,000
US West	36,000

Source: Colorado Secretary of State, 1998.

It is sometimes a challenge to determine how much of the gross receipts of lobbyists are reasonably identified as income. In 1995, for example, Stealey reported expenditures of $40,613 for gifts and entertainment, and another $375,535 for all other expenditures. These expenditures, in Stealey's case as with other lobbyists, include rent for office space, payments to other lobbyists, supportive personnel, and similar costs of doing business. It is not at all unusual for lobbyists to report expenses totaling one-third to one-half of their gross receipts, but since personnel versus business costs for such items as office space, transportation, meals, and drinks can be differentially calculated, it is difficult to figure the true income of lobbyists, or to compare them. It is clear, though, that the several dozen lobbyist regulars in the Capitol are not poor.

Both the lobbying and the profiting from peddling influence can be a team sport. That is demonstrated by both the physical and financial connections among these agents of special interest. Suite 900 at 1301 Pennsylvania Street, for example, is a popular launching spot for the representatives of scores of paying clients.

Bill Artist, former House Republican assistant majority leader, lists his lobbying operation address as Suite 900, 1301 Pennsylvania Street. He represents nearly twenty groups, ranging from the Denver Broncos to the City of Sterling, and Hays, Hays & Wilson. Hays, Hays & Wilson have the very same address and the same phone number. On their list of over thirty clients is J. William Artist and Associates, and Stealey and Associates. The address of the offices of Stealey and Associates is also 1301 Pennsylvania Street, Suite 900.

The Pennsylvania Street address is clearly popular. Besides being the office of Bill Artist, Pancho Hayes, and Wally Stealey, it is the office location for lobbyists Becky Brooks, Chris Chandler, Matthew Flora, Chuck Ford, Karen Reinertson, Joan Solem, Michelle Stealey, and Lynn Young.

LIVING TOGETHER

Being office complex roomies is not the only way lobbyists get together. They help each other lobby and get on each other's payroll too. In 1997, for example, Jerald Johnson paid former legislative liaison for Governor Romer, now lobbyist, Cathy Walsh $20,000. Johnson's receipts included $25,000 from Wally Stealey.

Togetherness at the Capitol goes beyond office suites and payrolls. Lobbying is their profession and livelihood. The place of work during the most important time of the year is under the gold dome on East Colfax Avenue in downtown Denver. So they see each other daily, year after year. They eat together, drink together, focus their attention on the same bills, the same committees, the same legislators, and each other. They share stories, gossip, and information, and sometimes they hide it. For lobbyists, the "public" becomes their clients and the other lobbyists.

And that can easily become the public for senators and representatives as well. As a 120-day legislative session drags on; as lawmakers' twelve- to twenty-hour days become a blizzard of bills, conversations, victories, defeats, and compromises; and as they are endlessly the target of persuasion artists, the views of the lobby corps can look and sound like those of the Colorado public.

One legislator told another recently that his telemarketing bill "didn't have a chance; everyone is against it." To the query "Are you hearing from your constituents?" the response came, "No, but all the lobbyists don't like it." He was correct; the lobby corps killed it in House Appropriations.

For better or worse, and probably for worse from the public's standpoint, the people one works with and interacts with daily tend to be more persuasive than those who are at a distance. The voters are at a distance, preoccupied with family and work. The lobbyists are immediate and constant, preoccupied with delivering for their paying clients. As the pastor prayed, "God bless those without lobbyists."

Lobby Tactics

Frank DeFilippo is a lobbyist. At one time he was a Republican member of the House, and chaired the Senate Affairs Committee. After serving several terms as an elected representative, DeFilippo began exploiting his legislative contacts and knowledge of the lawmaking process on behalf of paying clients. Frank DeFilippo spent some of his revenues on other people's coffee, rolls, lunches, drinks, and dinners— lots of other people. From January to June, some years back, he dined sixty-eight times with sixty different lawmakers, and when he ate with Representative Bledsoe, who was the Speaker of the House at the time, he dined with Mrs. Bledsoe, too. Twenty-three of these people were senators, and thirty-seven were members of the House. Nine were minority party Democrats; the remaining fifty-one were members of the majority party, which is also DeFilippo's party. A few years later Speaker Bledsoe, like Frank DeFilippo, left his elective seat and became a lobbyist—in a lobbying firm as a partner with DeFilippo.

Happily for hungry legislators, Frank DeFilippo isn't the only one who is willing to buy food. In the first two months of the 1998 session, Wally Stealey picked up the tab for Senator Don Ament four times to lobby him for four different clients; the total cost was $143.77. Other Republicans similarly fed were Senator David Wattenberg and Representatives Dave Owen and Brad Young, several times each. Stealey's bipartisanship showed as he also dined with Democratic Senators Mike Feeley, Rob Hernandez, and Jim Rizzuto, and Representatives Bob Hagedorn and Paul Zimmerman.

That's the nature of the game, of course. Lobbyists who simply show up in the Capitol on decision day, introduce themselves to harried lawmakers, and ask for consideration of their clients' positions don't accomplish much. Indeed, no smart lobbyist would even think of operating that way. Rather, DeFilippo, Stealey, and other successful players of the influence game operate much like successful people in any line of work. They do their homework. They make themselves and their clients known to lawmakers well in advance of decisions. They establish comfortable interpersonal relations outside the context of legislative votes, without asking for anything.

Requests to legislators for consideration of a client's concerns and desires can be made quietly at a later time—often with good results. And if relationships of trust and mutual respect are established, lawmakers will, in almost reflex fashion, want to hear the lobbyists' views before committing to positions or casting votes. It is not at all unusual for legislators to ask lobbyists in committee hearings and elsewhere if they've worked matters out with other groups and lobbyists; if the answer is "yes," the lawmakers' comfort level rises. The coffee and beer that Frank DeFilippo and his colleagues buy with portions of their income do not directly purchase any votes, but they *do* guarantee access to the ears of many lawmakers.

A legislator described the effectiveness of developing personal relations this way: "[Colorado Cattlemen's Association lobbyists] Rice and Christiansen are influential, and that tracks in large measure to their close personal ties with the Speaker. If they don't want a bill to get out, it won't get out."

One of the truly great displays of effective lobbying, albeit somewhat unusual, took place during a Senate hearing on a bill to transfer a slice of state land to the City of Pueblo for use as a neighborhood municipal park. There was considerable opposition among the senators, as they were uncomfortable about piecemeal disposal of state property in the absence of a full state plan to guide such land decisions. Their comfort level rose perceptibly, however, when an eleven-year-old approached the committee with hand-drawn pictures showing how she and other children in the neighborhood envisioned the park. One senator even asked the child if she would draw pictures for some of his other bills. The little girl's bill became law.

Another noteworthy display of lobbying occurred late in the 1996 session; to some observers it was a thing of beauty while to others it was proof positive that the system was corrupted by big money and inside games. The occasion was the introduction and passage of what was known as the "Bronco bill." This is not to be confused with the 1998 version of the "Bronco bill" wherein the financial stakes for taxpayers were raised considerably.

The Bronco bill passed both houses by the narrowest of margins—33–32 in the House and 18–17 in the Senate. Both the supportive and opposition coalitions crossed party lines. The final compromised version of the bill passed both chambers on the final day of the session. The governor signed it into law.

The Bronco bill established a six-county Denver-area metropolitan stadium district. The district has a governing board composed of people appointed by the governor, Denver's mayor, and others. The task of the board was originally to conduct an election, in November 1997, in the six-county area, asking voters if they would authorize continuation of an existing sales tax to fund a new football stadium for use by the Broncos. The tax was already in place and paying for Coors Field, which is used by the Colorado Rockies baseball team. In addition, the stadium district board was charged with choosing a site for the new facility should the voters say "yes."

The bill was pushed by Bronco owner Pat Bowlen. Bowlen claimed that the existing Mile High facility was too old and in need of expensive repairs, so much so that it made sense to just abandon it and build another stadium. Additionally, Bowlen claimed that he needed more profits to make his team competitive. He wanted to increase his take with more luxury boxes and concession and parking income.

The Bronco bill made it through the legislature in the waning hours after an unprecedented and expensive lobbying effort. At the start of the session, no legislator would serve as the bill's sponsor and, indeed, none did until very late in the session. Finally, House Republican Vickie Agler and Democratic Senator Ed Perlmutter agreed to be the sponsors. The acquisition of sponsors came after allegedly secret high-priced luncheon meetings with lawmakers, paid for by millionaire owner Bowlen. The bill was introduced on the 100th day of the 120-day legislative session and thus required, and received, a grant of late-bill status by the legislature's leadership.

Bowlen reportedly spent roughly $125,000 on paid lobbyists to lean on the legislators. The Hays, Hays & Wilson firm received $80,000. Besides Pancho Hays, the paid persuaders included Bill Artist, past Republican legislator; Wally Stealey, longtime lobbyist and past aide to former Governor Richard Lamm; Porter Wharton, a Bronco operative; and Steve Farber and Gary Reiff, who work with the law firm of Hyatt, Farber and Strickland. Reiff worked previously on the campaign of Governor Roy Romer, and Strickland was a 1996 Democratic candidate for U.S. Senate. The pressure team was clearly both expensive and bipartisan, featuring lobbyists with deep roots in both political parties.

Did Patrick Bowlen's minions do a good job of educating legislators on the public benefits of the Bronco bill? Or did a crowd of inside politicians twist rubber legislative arms that reach out each election year for lobbyist help in securing interest group campaign contributions, in a quest to convert public money to private gain? It depends on one's perspective.

To some legislators, this was a good bill, one clearly in the public interest. Their support was support for the public good, not for lobbyists or millionaire sports moguls. Representative Bill Martin said that the Broncos were the international figurehead for the state. Bryan Sullivant touted the promotional value of the team for the ski industry. Doug Dean was emphatic that the state could lose the team if voters failed to pony up for a new stadium. Martin, Sullivant, and Dean all represented legislative districts outside the six-county area.

Other lawmakers saw it differently. Ron Tupa, whose Boulder County district lay within the stadium district, termed the bill "corporate welfare at its worst." Ken Chlouber, whose House local government committee held hearings on the bill, observed that "it's almost like the Broncos have turned the joys of football into prostitution." Senator Mike Coftman, also representing constituents within the district boundaries, noted that "the Bronco bill would never have been done without the level of lobbying."[16]

Public opinion seemed to be similarly divided. The *Rocky Mountain News* reported reactions on both sides of the issue.[17] Those in favor of the bill claimed that the project would "enhance the area" and mean some employment. One respondent simply "loves the Broncos." Others feared the Broncos would leave if Bowlen did not have his way.

Those on the other side cited more pressing needs for public money, including schools, teachers, roads, playgrounds for children, and juvenile facilities, not millionaire professionals. Others noted that this was one more case of someone wanting to stick their nose in the public trough, and that the public doesn't pay the costs of facilities for other businesses. *Denver Post* sportswriter Mark Kiszla wrote, "not too good at football any more, the Broncos have taken up extortion."[18]

Many legislators explained their supportive votes as endorsement of democracy, and not necessarily related to the team, the stadium, or the costs to the taxpayers. The legislative decision, many said, was simply whether or not to let the voters in the six-county area decide and, anyway, "What's wrong with democracy?"

Like so many aspects of political life, and life generally, reality is in the eyes of the beholder. Was the passage of the Bronco bill a victory for democracy, an act opening the door for the people to decide whether or not to be partners in supporting the joys of Sunday recreation and bolstering community pride? Or was it legislative abandonment of the responsibility of elected representatives to protect the public from private interest vultures who make millions by taking dimes and dollars from kids and day-laborers? And was this episode an example of good citizens

exercising their constitutional rights to speak and to petition government, or was it the product of pressure peddlers and election propagan-
dists helping millionaires put the cost of doing business on the taxpayer
while privatizing profits?

In the real day in, day out world in the Capitol, there are some very
routine and tedious dimensions to the work of the lobbyist. At any
point, most of them may be tracking a dozen bills or more, all at various stages in the legislative process. Some of these will be in the House,
and others in the Senate. Some will be in committee or waiting for
hearings. Others will be pending scheduling for second or third reading
on the floor. When a bill encounters opposition, the lobbyist will scramble
to gather support, try to reduce the resistance, or search for compromise. There will also be bills a lobbyist opposes, and time must be spent
seeking help from legislators to stop or modify them.

Lobbyists move through the Capitol all day, observing the action in
committees and on the floor, buttonholing lawmakers, talking with
other lobbyists, calling clients, working with staff members who are
drafting bills and amendments, and drinking lots of coffee. As they
track and seek to influence the fate of bills, they carry along check sheets
or notebooks listing these bills and the names of legislators on the relevant committees. As legislators indicate how they will vote on bills,
the names on that list are marked accordingly.

There is little glamour to this part of the job. It is a matter of bending the lawmakers' ears, seeking commitments, and keeping score.
Increasingly, it seems, some lobbyists find the job too difficult and tedious. Some say it just isn't fun anymore, with an endless flow of new
legislators to approach, more ex-legislators in the lobbying game, and
growing competition. But money can often compensate for glamour.
As Lynn Young quipped when asked if she was looking forward to the
end of the 1999 session, "Yes, but where else can I make this much
money?"[19]

Given the good money to be made in the lobbying business, the
competition is stiff. Some people believe that the increase in legislators
entering the game has not only added to the competition but may underpin some of the ethics problems cited earlier, as well. There are stories
of lobbyists sitting around a large table with other lobbyists and legislators, then using the experience to sell their wares to potential clients and
secure contracts by saying, "I have breakfast with the Speaker."

Often, intrusion and pressure by lobbyists get the best of lawmakers. Indeed, to escape constant interruption by lobbyists who should
know when to back off and to find time to think and do some desk

work, legislators have been known to sneak to their offices, lock their doors, and work with the lights off.

Some lobbyists seem to be connected more comfortably with one party or one house, due, no doubt, to the political background and policy orientation of the client group and lobbyist. Lobbyists who are former legislators will, of course, have strong ties to one of the parties. Lynn Young and Freda Poundstone are long-standing activists in the Republican party. Pancho Hays, Bill Artist, and Bob Kirscht also have had Republican connections. Ruben Valdez, Wally Stealey, and Karen Reinertson have Democratic histories.

Similarly, some groups tend to be more comfortable with the political orientation of one party. For example, Adolph Coors Company is headed by a prominent and very conservative Republican. It would truly be amazing if the Coors lobbyists focused their attention on Democratic lawmakers. The reverse is true of the Colorado Education Association, which naturally supports state spending on education. Consequently, in a Republican-controlled legislature that has been reluctant to loosen the state pursestrings for well over a decade, the teachers are more comfortable with the Democratic party.

Lobbyists will sometimes hire other lobbyists to work on certain legislators on particular bills, and it is not unusual to see income from one lobbyist listed on another lobbyist's financial report. This, again, reflects the fact that some are better connected with House members or Senate members, with Democrats or Republicans, with rural or metro lawmakers.

It should be noted, too, that communities are formed in legislatures, as in any society. Lobbyists who regularly work together and with the legislators get to know one another very well, both in the Capitol and beyond. This can engender both influence and enmity.

There is no doubt that good information, persuasively but economically presented by someone who is trusted and has a reputation for honesty and reliability, is a winning ticket. Legislators are terribly busy, for everyone in the world wants a piece of their time; therefore, a group spokesperson who has easy access and can communicate quickly is at a premium. Legislators who have been burned by relying on bad information from a certain source will not go back. Nor do they want to sift through stacks of paper or be badgered constantly and unduly pressured.

When contract lobbyists take on a dozen, or a score, of clients, there is the clear potential that two or more of them will end up on opposite sides of a given issue. Furthermore, the lobbyist may not agree with every client's position. These are simply problems that all lobbyists must work out for themselves. Some will interview potential clients in advance to determine if their interests and philosophies are compatible.

Both legislators and lobbyists are aware of the potential conflicts and often recommend against taking on clients when such difficult situations are likely to arise.

House Majority Leader Chris Paulson said of lobbyists, "The most effective ones are the ones who give you straight information rapidly." And lobbyist Bob Ferm commented, "We act as staff, we really do."[20] Former Senator Tom Glass said that his constituents seldom have views on the issue or know how he votes, but lobbyists "get information to you in 10 minutes."[21] Former House Speaker and Majority Leader Ron Strahle noted, "They don't give you the hard sell, generally speaking."[22]

Relationships among legislators and lobbyists are almost always cordial, sometimes even incestuous, as over the years they eat, drink, and work together. But it isn't always. When he was House Speaker Pro Tem, Paul Schauer said of a lobbyist who had suggested a link between his vote and campaign money, "I told him to stick his head where the sun don't shine."[23] Another legislator who is now a lobbyist herself, when it was suggested that she had "been rolled" by a lobbyist, resolved never to have anything to do with him again.

Two 1998 actions in the Senate also demonstrate that there are exceptions to the normal comradeship among members and lobbyists. Antilabor "right-to-work" lobbyist Guy Short, who had a history of opposing moderate Republicans while promoting right-wingers, drew the ire of moderate David Wattenberg. From the lectern in the Senate chambers, Wattenberg referred to Short as "that silly son-of-a-bitch standing by the glass." The "glass" refers to the area just beyond the rear of the chambers, the "lobby," where lobbyists gather, mill around, and converse with each other and with members when the bodies are in session.

While Wattenberg's rhetorical target was individual and personal, Senator Elsie Lacy blasted lobbyists with a broader brush. In alternate years Lacy chaired the Joint Budget Committee and in that capacity she, as well as her JBC colleagues, were twenty-four-hour-a-day targets of every imaginable group and agency seeking enriched funding. Midway through one session, she'd had enough and exhorted the supplicants to "get out of the faces" of Budget Committee members. She went on to finger the lobby corps gathered outside the chambers, saying, "everybody's like a bunch of vultures out there." She went on, "there is no money."[24]

Of course later in the session, Lacy served as prime sponsor of the so-called 1998 Bronco bill. In that capacity she worked intimately with one of the largest teams of lobbyists ever collected to work on one bill. The measure was designed to pave the way to put hundreds of millions of tax dollars into a new football stadium.

Legislators are short on staff and long on the need to make tough decisions on complicated and controversial issues. They value sources of good information. As a result, lobbyists who generate long-run access and influence do well. Some of the more successful ones will stay in touch with legislators even when there are no pressing issues at hand. They will often provide information and opinions on both sides of an issue or alert the lawmaker to sources of possible opposition. The legislative process is not a one-inning ball game, with a winner and a loser. It is more like a never-ending game of craps, where winners and losers change continually; if you play all your chips in the wrong place and wrong time, you're out of the game.

In addition to tracking bills for their clients and communicating concerns and information to lawmakers, lobbyists orchestrate testimony by clients, supportive citizens, and experts for committee hearings. They sometimes testify themselves, but as often as not they simply make the arrangements and do their own communicating with legislators privately.

Orchestration of political information and pressure is not confined to hearing-room activities. Very often, lobbyists will organize a blizzard of legislative calls and contacts. On a bill impacting cities, for example, they may have city council members, mayors, city managers, and community leaders from city after city lean on the lawmakers from their region in one way or another. Not infrequently, legislators themselves are parties to such networks. A representative whose bill is hung up in a committee may try to move it along by soliciting the help of lobbyists and their contacts and building a constituency backfire under a committee chair and other legislators. There are times when it isn't clear who is lobbying whom in lobbyist/legislator relations.

Timing is important in the orchestration of district- or statewide pressure on legislators. Lawmakers deal with so many bills, which are often amended over and over again, that if a wave of constituents calls too far in advance of a decision, it may lose its effect. Unless contacts are made fairly close to decision time, some lawmakers will either forget or be successfully counterlobbied in the interim.

Letter-writing and rallies at the Capitol are also instruments used by individuals and groups to influence policy. Some letters work, and some don't. When individual citizens write concise and thoughtfully prepared letters, they are read and usually draw a written response or a call. They sometimes affect legislator behavior, as well. Legislators care about their constituents, whether out of a sense of duty or a concern for reelection or both. They will read and sometimes reread a handwritten constituent letter, check the name and address carefully, and wonder how many others in their district feel the same way about the issue in question. Similarly, constituent letters or phone calls asking for help, in dealing with a state agency for example, usually receive a helpful response.

But there are forms of written communication that do not work. One is the mass-produced form letter. RTD employees once blitzed lawmakers with preprinted cards, and some state classified (civil service) employees sent legislators swarms of mass-produced letters with their opinions about pay raises. Most of this material goes quickly into the trash and leaves legislators wondering about the political savvy of those in charge of such mass-production enterprises.

Senator Sally Hopper successfully sponsored a bill that restricted the sale and rental to minors of films depicting cruel and violent scenes. She was prompted to examine such films and then carry the legislation, she said, because of a single letter from a mother in her district. She also admitted that she generally does not even read mass-produced or unsigned letters.

In some instances, state employees will use state resources to lobby their legislators, and this boomerangs badly. The many state employees can have considerable clout. But communications from them using state letterhead and state postage are politically worse, by far, than no message at all—especially in an assembly where many members are already suspicious of state programs and employees.

Legislators do not take kindly to written threats or distasteful and uncivil messages. This does not occur with great frequency, but there are times when citizens, and occasionally even a lobbyist, will foolishly and ineffectively communicate direct or implied political threats or fire an emotional and tasteless cannon at a legislator. Amateur or single-issue lobbyists are much more apt to do this than are the contract lobbyists and the old pros. Douglas Bruce, author of a 1988 tax-limit constitutional proposal, told a Senate committee that he might target some legislators for recall efforts. Senator Sally Hopper responded, "I don't react well to threats. This really makes me mad."[25] Politically, threats can backfire.

In a truly class act a few years back, a senator responded to a series of unusually hostile letters from a citizen in this fashion:

Dear Ms _____:
   I thought you would like to know some lunatic is using your name and stationery to send threatening, tasteless and obnoxious letters to me.
   As a protection for both you and me, I am following the procedure we normally use and turning the letter over to the Colorado State Patrol.
   Sincerely,
   State Senator

Capitol Building rallies, by themselves, rarely influence policy. But used in conjunction with other pressure techniques, they can help the cause of a group. Elderly citizens seeking legislative assistance with their heating bills and depositors at failed industrial banks seeking remedial legislation staged rallies on the Capitol steps. Both were successful in generating legislative relief. But it would be a mistake to attribute the success to the rallies alone. The gatherings did generate some statewide print and video news coverage, but group members also contacted law-makers personally and worked directly with them to develop the remedial legislation.

The legislature passed a bill expanding the opportunities for parents who wish to keep their children out of public or licensed private schools and educate them at home. On the day of the hearings, the Capitol coffee shop and the committee room were full of mothers and fathers and freshly scrubbed kids. It all made for nice press pictures and stories, and it may have helped in a very marginal sense. But it is the prehearing groundwork and continuous lobbying that get the job done; a good show, alone, cannot.

The influence of interest groups and their lobbyists is probably never more direct than when they participate in the writing of bills or simply do the drafting themselves. The Office of Legislative Legal Services, of course, actually writes the final bills, but materials come to them in forms ranging from the verbal expression of an idea to detailed drafts prepared by interest group attorneys. Often, a legislator will simply commission a lobbyist to work directly with a staffer and other legislators to draft acceptable compromise language.

Pointed examples of the very direct role a group can play in framing proposed legislation are found in three bills written by the National Rifle Association. The *Denver Post* reported that these bills were unveiled by the group at a press conference where their legislative sponsors did not even appear. In the end, only one of the bills made it all the way through the legislature, and then only in amended form, and it became law without the governor's signature. But no one pretended that the bills were anything other than the work of the NRA. The Republican representative who sponsored one of them was asked about the interest group's authorship. He responded, "It doesn't bother me . . . the NRA has 50,000 members in Colorado—many of them are my constituents."[26]

This is not an uncommon scenario. The same *Post* article also noted that "the Colorado Medical Society wrote the first draft of a sweeping package of medical malpractice insurance reforms," and the lotto measure that was so hot in 1988 "was written by the law firm of Davis, Graham & Stubbs, under the direction of cities, counties, special districts and lottery vendors." In another report on lobbying in the

General Assembly, the *Post* stated, "It's not unusual for a state legislator to freely admit that 'I'm carrying this bill for so and so,' naming a special interest such as the trucking industry, apartment owners or a medical group."[27]

Interest groups and their Capitol lobbyists don't just bring requests for legislation to legislators; they sometimes have their own lawyers write the measures. As the process moves along, lobbyists will commonly be the origin of amendments. In one 1999 Senate floor session, Senator Rob Hernandez moved an amendment that was favored by lobbyists, to which his colleague Elsie Lacy remarked, "Wait a minute, you have an amendment for lobbyists?"[28]

On a 1999 gun measure House Majority Floor Leader and bill sponsor Doug Dean said he'd bring his bill up for floor debate when NRA members would be around to talk with legislators.[29] In Senate debate on a 1999 workers' compensation bill, sponsor Ken Arnold exited and reentered the chamber to get information from lobbyists as he answered other senators' questions. Interactions of this sort are routine.

There are times when the effective "ownership" of a bill by an interest group is, or perhaps should be, an embarrassment to a lawmaker. It is commonplace for sponsoring legislators to introduce a bill briefly in committee and then call on a string of lobbyists and experts to explain what it means, what it does, and why it is needed. But, at times, legislators are simply unable to answer questions about bills they are sponsoring and are forced to refer questions directly to lobbyists. An observer said this about one legislator: "You wonder how this person gets bills. Lobbyists explain the contents over and over and she still stumbles through the contents."

There are even times when it is unclear who the lawmaker is. All legislators work with lobbyists to try to pass some bills and kill others. But some let the lobbyists do most of the work—deal with the drafters to get bills written, pressure other legislators and lobbyists, orchestrate district pressure on colleagues, arrange for testimony, work out compromises with other groups and other legislators, and handle all the committee and floor vote counting.

Proposed legislation will often pit interest groups and lobbyists against each other. This was the case in a struggle that developed between physicians and insurance companies on one side and attorney groups on the other. The issue in contention concerned a proposal to place a dollar lid on the size of medical malpractice jury awards. The physicians and insurance companies attributed some of the escalation in malpractice premiums to high jury awards and expressed concern that the exorbitant premiums could cause doctors to abandon some specialties. The lawyers argued that a patient who is medically mistreated has every right to whatever compensation a jury of peers deems appropriate.

Groups and their lobbyists sometimes luck out and escape the need to contend with pressure from the other side. In the midst of a recent session, a half-dozen lobbyists were leaning against the brass rail, discussing a bill. One asked, rhetorically, "What'll we do if some consumer group gets wind of this?" Another responded, "They'll never even know the thing [the bill] is here." This is, of course, why it often pays interest groups to invest in the services of a contract lobbyist who is under the gold dome every day and who *does* feel the wind.

Term limits have had an impact on lobbying, just as they have on other aspects of legislative life. The strategy of some veteran lobbyists was to forge close ties to those in leadership positions and count on these legislative leaders to help pass or kill bills through such tactics as strategic committee assignment. But as term limits have pushed leaders out, these connections no longer exist. This works to the advantage of newer, younger lobbyists as the "inside track" of the old lobby vets disappears.

FREEBIES

An article in the *Rocky Mountain News*, "Free Eats, and more," read: "Colorado legislators could eat for days without paying for a single meal, but most learn that time with their families is more valuable than free eats." Another one carried this headline: "Contrary to popular belief, there is a free lunch," and then went on to say,

> Legislators never have to worry about going hungry. Lobbyists see to that. Breakfasts are a daily event at the statehouse, and there's usually a line of lobbyists ready to pop for lunch, dinner or drinks. Need a ticket to a Denver Nuggets or Colorado Rockies game? How about a College bowl game? Passes to Sea World? A nice bouquet of roses? Tickets to Water World? A 10-pound bag of potatoes?[30]

The vast majority of states now have legal limits on the value or kinds of gifts that groups, lobbyists, or individuals may present to lawmakers. Some are very restrictive, as in Massachusetts and Wisconsin, which operate with a "not even a cup of coffee" rule. But Colorado is without prohibitions. Coffee and a lot more, ranging from fat-filled pastry to health-friendly juice and fruit, are available free to lawmakers first thing in the morning throughout the legislative sessions. So is lunch, as is dinner, and so are drinks. Table 7.4 lists those picking up the meal or cocktail tab for two sample weeks during the 1998 and 2000 sessions.

Former House Speaker and Majority Leader Ron Strahle once commented, "We have a few people who are enchanted by the prospect of a free meal. . . . As you're there longer and longer, you appreciate being able to stay in your apartment and throw a hamburger on the stove and take off your shoes."[31] Former Senator Linda Powers said, "In the event I wanted it, I could go an entire session without ever paying for dinner or a drink."[32]

These comments bespeak both an unavoidable political reality (the way in which money is used to purchase nice things for legislators and thus create friendly relations) and a potential for the representative role to be perverted through the substitution of cash for constituent interests and lawmakers' judgment as the force driving decisions. It is hard to argue that buying a legislator a cup of coffee and discussing an issue is wrong. After all, what kind of a democracy would prohibit private citizens doing that? And who can fault a $50 donation to a candidate to help pay for a newsletter to constituents? But what about the gift of a car or a $100,000 corporate check to finance a candidate's media blitz? Perhaps it's clear in the case of the car, if it is a personal gift and not intended for use in a campaign or running to and from the Capitol. But as the numbers and values rise, so do the qualms about the mix of gifts and politics.

In addition to the food and drinks that are always in plentiful supply, members of the General Assembly are on the receiving end of commodities ranging from coffee mugs and pie to a $2,000 trip to the Super Bowl. The Colorado State University alumni association provided the coffee cups. A children's advocacy group gave each legislator a pie. Pfizer Pharmaceutical paid for the football outing. The University of Colorado routinely provides football game tickets along with food and drinks for legislators. The Colorado Rockies and Ski Country USA treat lawmakers to free ball games and ski outings. So do Coors, US West, and others with a clear stake in public policy.[33]

In August 1989, Senate President Ted Strickland, Senate Transportation Committee Chairman David Wattenberg, and Republican Representative Tom Ratterree played golf with US West lobbyist Stan Sours in the International Golf Tournament at Castle Pines, Colorado. The entry fee was $2,000 each. US West paid.[34] More recent free adventures included a trip for the members to Belize, and visits to the Rockies Tucson spring training for the two prime sponsors of the 1998 Bronco stadium bill, Senator Lacy and Representative Douglas Dean, who had earlier visited Belize. They were joined in Tucson by Representative Jennifer Veiga, who later was Dean's choice, albeit unsuccessful, as his House comrade on the 1998 Bronco bill conference committee.[35]

Table 7.4—Interest Group–Sponsored Functions for Legislators

	Breakfast	Noon Luncheon	Cocktails/Dinner Hour
Week of January 10 (Monday) – January 14 (Friday), 2000			
Jan. 10	Focus on the Family	Public Employer Retirement Association	Colorado Timber Association
Jan. 11	Northern Colorado Social Legislation Network and Catholic Charities	Party Caucus Luncheon	Colorado Community College
Jan. 12	Pinnacol Assurance	American Electronic Association	Colorado Wildlife Commission
Jan. 13	Signal Behavioral Health Network	Colorado Psychiatric Association	Colorado Chiropractor Association
Jan. 14	Association of Collection Agencies	Colorado Dental Association	No event scheduled
Week of February 23 (Monday) – 27 (Friday), 1998			
Feb. 23	Colorado Grain and Feed Assn.	Mental Health Association	Rural Electric Association
Feb. 24	Advisory Council on Adolescent Health	Party Caucus Luncheon	Women in Government Meeting
Feb. 25	Farmers Insurance Group	Colorado Beer Distributors Association	Colorado Women's Bar Association
Feb. 26	Colorado Developmental Disabilities Planning Council	Colorado Libraries Association	Colorado Counties, Inc.
Feb. 27	Colorado Assn. of Homebuilders; Colorado Mfg Housing Assn.	Two candidate kick-off events	Natural Fuels Corp.

Every year, Colorado Ski Country USA takes lawmakers skiing. Stock show admissions, basketball game tickets, and invitations to concerts come along regularly. Tobacco giant Philip Morris is among the prime hosts.

Do such gifts buy votes? Reform groups think they do; legislators say no. Representative Steve Johnson said of Coors hockey tickets, "These are good seats." He concluded, "I think they want access. But none of them are going to affect my vote. Every legislator has to decide, are they going to feel obligated? I don't. I vote with the folks some times and not at other times."[36] Still no one argues that the gifts diminish access to legislative ears.

Interest Group Money in Elections

Over the years, the really big money has not come in the form of roast beef sandwiches, scotch, or sacks of onions. It has come in cash— thousands upon thousands of dollars of it given to candidates for state legislative office, mostly incumbents. Colorado Common Cause conducted a detailed study of campaign contributions in the 1992 election and discovered some interesting patterns.

First, running a state legislative campaign is not cheap. In 1992 the average amount raised by House candidates was over $20,000, and for the Senate it was $25,000. These numbers are up from roughly $12,000 for the House and $19,000 for the Senate in 1982 and 1984.

Second, Common Cause reports that "money matters." That is, the odds of winning clearly increase with the amount of money raised. For example, for those who raised less than $10,000, just a quarter of the House candidates won, and 18 percent of the would-be senators pre-

Table 7.5—Odds of Winning, by Amount of Money Raised—All State Legislative Candidates, 1992

Amount Raised	House Races	Odds of Winning	Senate Races	Odds of Winning
$0–$9,999	36 ran/9 won	25%	6 ran/1 won	18%
$10,000–$19,999	22 ran/15 won	69%	7 ran/3 won	43%
$20,000–$29,999	34 ran/24 won	71%	8 ran/6 won	75%
$30,000+	23 ran/17 won	74%	9 ran/8 won	89%

Source: PAC in the Saddle Again. Denver: Common Cause, 1992.

vailed. By contrast, three-fourths of the House candidates and four-fifths of the Senate candidates who raised over $30,000 won.

Where has the money come from? Not primarily from individuals or the political parties. Rather, almost sixty cents of each dollar was donated by political action committees. The interests behind the PACs are, of course, the same ones who hire the lobbyists.

It is well known that PACs, like gamblers, seek to place their bets on winners. It is therefore not surprising that they gave most heavily to incumbents and to Republicans. Incumbents win most often, and Republicans are Colorado's legislative majority party. The incumbents received six times as much money as did challengers, and Republicans beat Democrats at the PAC money game by almost two to one.

The bottom line is this: Candidates need a lot of money to win. Most of the money comes from the same interests that fuel the lobbyist corps. These interests give most heavily to incumbents who have the best chances of winning, thus further increasing their advantage, and to Republicans who not only win more often than Democrats but who also control all the formal levers of power in the state's policy-making body. Following the donations and elections, the interest group lobbyists supply the winners with gifts, food, information, and suggestions of what bills to introduce and how to vote.

Who are these groups? There are literally scores of them, representing big business and small businesses, big banks and little ones, all the professions from lawyers to eye doctors, workers, churches, the manufacturers of booze and smokes, and more. In Table 7.6, Common Cause lists the top twenty contributors to legislative campaigns for 1992.

In 1996 the legislature enacted into law some modest limitations on political contributions. The law took effect in 1997. It limited gifts

Table 7.6—Top PAC Contributors, All State Legislative Races, 1992

1. Colorado Trial Lawyers Assoc.	11. Philip Morris
2. Colorado Realtors	12. Colorado Professional Firefighters
3. Colorado Education Association	13. Amoco
4. AFL-CIO/COPE	14. Coors
5. Colorado Construction	15. Southland
6. Colorado Medical Society	16. Metro Housing
7. Colorado Public Affairs Council	17. Colorado Concern
8. Teamsters	18. Hospital Express Legislative
9. Colorado Independent Bankers	19. Tobacco Institute
10. US West	20. Colorado Chiropractors

from individuals, PACs, and candidate campaign committees to state
Senate candidates to $1,000, and $500 to candidates for House seats.
The political parties were limited too, but at a much higher level. Contributions from parties were capped at $40,000 for Senate candidates
and $20,000 for House candidates.

In November 1996, the voters did the legislature one better. They
passed an initiated statute that clamps down on campaign contributions even tighter than did the 1996 legislative action. Individual and
PAC contributions to House and Senate candidates were capped at $200
per election cycle. Other candidates, corporations, and unions were prohibited altogether from contributing. In 1999 the court voided portions of the 1996 law, and in its 2000 session the legislature enacted a
whole new campaign finance act, which elevated the level of permissible individual contributions to $1,250 for House candidates and
$1,500 for Senate candidates. It also eliminated the ban on union and
corporate giving.

The flow of interest group money into candidate campaign coffers
is not always initiated by the groups or their lobbyists and other strate-
gists. Indeed, as often as not, it is in response to the request, and sometimes outright pressure, of the candidates themselves or the parties. The
parties throw fund-raisers ranging from New Year's Eve events to chili
cook-offs and "invite" lobbyists to attend, for a price. At a Republican
"dessert auction," for example, lobbyist Pancho Hays coughed up $500
for a cake baked by Representative Paul Schauer and tossed in the face
of Schauer's colleague, Ken Chlouber.[37] Indeed, whether it is a political
party event or a fund-raiser for a particular candidate, the lobbyist list
is often a prime source for "victims" to be included on the invitee list.

In preparation for election or reelection, candidates routinely send
out letters soliciting money from political action committees. Challengers who lack either electoral or lawmaking records generally send with
their request portfolios of materials describing their campaign plans and
touting both their abilities and chances for success. Veteran lawmakers
sometimes dream up schemes designed to give the completely naive the
impression that they're not simply begging for money. Republican Penn
Pfiffner, for example, invited lobbyists to an event that featured not
only him and something to eat, but a presentation of political views
given by other lobbyists—an educational panel of sorts.[38] Legislative
veteran Jeanne Adkins offered lobbyists a legislative directory, which
she published, at a discount price.[39] Whether in the form of bargain
prices for a variety of products or short and sweet requests for cash,
it's not a one-way street. PACs and lobbyists give, but the candidates
ask.

HOW POWERFUL?

Just how powerful is Colorado's legislative "third house"? People will offer a variety of answers to the question. A *Rocky Mountain News* headline read "Lobbyists get their way at capitol."[40] The article cited the large amounts spent by such successful interests as Envirotest Systems, Inc., which does the auto emissions testing in the state, the teachers association, banks, and telecommunications firms. These groups spent tens of thousands of dollars on lobbyists to promote or defeat legislation.

There is considerable public opinion to the effect that big-money interests get their way and that there is simply too much money in politics. The extremely low level of confidence that the public has in its policy-making bodies may well be a result of the broad view that money and lobbies run the show. Certainly former Common Cause Director Rick Bainter feels that way. He commented that while the big-money interests can spend freely to seek to influence the content of public policy, "Citizens or consumer groups or single mothers who are worried about child care issues, they don't have $70,000 to hire a lobbyist."[41] Eric DeGraff, a businessman and member of the conservative Colorado Union of Taxpayers, put it a little differently: "Us working stiffs can't afford to hang around the Capitol. By the time we're through working for a living, we're too infirm to go down there."

Legislators, though, have a different opinion. They will actively solicit campaign contributions from the organized interests who have money to give, and they freely admit that the money generally buys the giver a guaranteed shot at bending the lawmaker's ear. But almost universally, legislators deny that money buys votes. The words of Representative David Owen are typical: "you can take them or leave them."[42] Senator Joan Johnson's comments reflect the same viewpoint:

> A lunch or dinner, a coffee mug, a piece of pottery, a pen, a box of candy, flowers—it's all nice, but it doesn't mean that anyone here is going to vote for or against something. If you have a sense of ethics, which most of us do, you're not going to be unduly influenced by these things.[43]

We are left, then, with this interesting question: If the lawmakers are correct in their assertion that money does not buy votes, and if businesspeople, labor leaders, and professionals are not foolish, how does interest group money get into campaigns? Clearly the donors must believe that their money has an impact on something. Otherwise, wouldn't they give their money to youth baseball instead?

NOTES

1. *Denver Rocky Mountain News,* March 7, 1999.

2. *Denver Rocky Mountain News,* April 23, 1999.
3. *Denver Rocky Mountain News,* March 31, 1999 (Peter Blake column).
4. Michael Romano, "Secrecy backer enriched GOP," *Rocky Mountain News,* January 10, 1997.
5. *Rocky Mountain News,* February 5, 1996.
6. *Rocky Mountain News,* February 1, 1996.
7. *Denver Post,* February 18, 1998.
8. Burt Hubbard and Lou Kilzer, "Youth prison uses lobbyist," *Rocky Mountain News,* April 19, 1998.
9. *Denver Rocky Mountain News,* January 24, 1999 (Peter Blake column).
10. *Denver Post,* August 27, 1995.
11. Andrew Simons, "Ranching lobbyist David Rice dies at 81," *Denver Post,* March 17, 1998.
12. Secretary of State records.
13. Ibid.
14. Emily Narvaes, "Under the dome," *Denver Post,* January 5, 1997.
15. Secretary of State records.
16. *Denver Post,* April 30, 1996.
17. *Rocky Mountain News,* May 12, 1996.
18. *Denver Post,* April 30, 1996.
19. In conversation with author.
20. *Rocky Mountain News,* February 1, 1988.
21. Ibid.
22. Ibid.
23. Ibid.
24. "Lacy scolds hungry lobbyists," *Denver Post,* March 18, 1998.
25. *Rocky Mountain News,* February 28, 1989.
26. *Denver Post,* February 21, 1988.
27. Ibid.
28. *Denver Post,* date uncertain.
29. *Rocky Mountain News,* March 19, 1999.
30. *Rocky Mountain News,* January 1, 1996.
31. *Rocky Mountain News,* February 1, 1998.
32. *Rocky Mountain News,* January 1, 1996.
33. *Rocky Mountain News,* January 7, 1996.
34. *Rocky Mountain News,* October 20, 1989.
35. Thomas Frank and Ricky Young, "Lawmakers: We take gifts but aren't on the take," *Denver Post,* February 15, 1998, and Peter Blake, "A GOP recall? Don't count on it," *Rocky Mountain News,* March 11, 1998.
36. Thomas Frank and Ricky Young, "Lawmakers: We take gifts but aren't on the take," *Denver Post,* February 15, 1998.
37. *Rocky Mountain News,* January 10, 1994.
38. *Rocky Mountain News,* December 17, 1995, and January 7, 1996.
39. *Rocky Mountain News,* January 10, 1994.
40. *Rocky Mountain News,* May 14, 1995.
41. Ibid.
42. Ibid.
43. *Rocky Mountain News,* January 1, 1996.

8

Legislative Budgeting in Colorado

Budgets have often been called statements of public policy priorities expressed in numbers, for they very clearly demonstrate what decision makers think is worth paying for and what is not. For employees of public agencies and the beneficiaries of their activities, appropriations are the lifeblood of public programs. Those who have spent any time in political or organizational life know that control of the budget—virtually any budget—means control of the power.

The story of public budgeting in twentieth-century America has, in substantial measure, been the story of a growing executive role in the process. In the 1920s, the national government moved from what is called a "legislative budget" to an "executive budget." Most states followed suit.

Under the legislative budgeting system, government agencies submitted annual requests directly to the legislature or one of its committees for review and inclusion in the budget. In the now common executive budgeting system, however, agency requests are funneled through the office of the chief executive en route to the legislature and are massaged and melded with other requests into a single document that reflects the priorities of the chief. The rationale for the new system is to allow presidents, governors, and mayors to better coordinate overall policy implementation and mold budgets to their policy goals. It is neither surprising nor unintended that the new process has also meant increased power for chief executives and diminished power for legislatures.

Following the national model, many states and local governments have moved to executive budget processes, too. At first blush, Colorado appears to be one of them, but this has been largely a change in name only. In practice, Colorado's budget process is very legislative centered and minimizes the role of the governor. A document entitled "An Introduction to the Colorado Legislative Process" that was prepared for new lawmakers by the Legislative Council states:

> Very few state legislatures exercise the degree of "power over the purse" that is observed by the Colorado General Assembly. Most legislatures go through the motions of budget review with the executive branch making budget decisions and the legislators following the executive's lead. Colorado's legislative budget procedure, directed by the Joint Budget Committee and the Capital Development Committee, provides the discussion and review of executive branch operations that the General Assembly believes is necessary to foster efficiencies and uphold the separation of powers.

One past chairman of the legislature's Joint Budget Committee (the six-member group that monopolizes budgeting power in Colorado government) said, "The governor develops a budget and the legislature ignores it." Another former JBC chairman commented, "The governor's budget ends up on the round file, although it is used to find places to cut." Senator Elsie Lacy, the 1997 JBC chair, said of Governor Romer's budget that "her first inclination was to toss it into the trash." Romer himself has complained about this state of affairs: "This particular governorship is one of the weakest in the United States in terms of its statutory or constitutional authority."[1] Republican Governor Bill Owens had better access to the ear of lawmakers, but the keys to the state vault remain legislative.

The state agencies know this, of course, so they attempt to deal effectively with the JBC—they know where the budget power lies. The governor's priorities sometimes get lost in the process; therefore the JBC and, hence, the legislature become all the more powerful. Some observers argue that the governor and his budget office, the Office of State Planning and Budgeting, play a growing role in influencing legislative appropriations, but it is the legislative—not the executive—branch that is unmistakably the dominant force in the process. Whatever impact the governor has on the budget comes from the agencies' adherence to his preferences and limits on their programs as they prepare annual requests for the budget assembly by the legislature.

THE FALSE APPEARANCE OF EXECUTIVE BUDGETING

A review of certain constitutional and statutory provisions and a superficial glance at the activities at the start of a legislative session would not suggest such extensive legislative budget control. Colorado governors do go through some of the activities associated with executive-centered budgeting processes, which may add to the appearance, false though it is, that Colorado's chief executives are the major players in the budget game.

The governor dutifully addresses a joint session of the General Assembly's two houses to set forth views on the state's major problems, needs, and priorities. Indeed, Article 4, Section 8, of the Colorado Constitution says, "He shall, also, at the commencement of each session, present estimates of the amount of money required to be raised by taxation for all purposes of the state."

By statutory requirement, the governor submits a budget to the legislature annually. The Office of State Planning and Budgeting (OSPB) is charged with collecting and reviewing all agency budget requests and assembling this budget, then communicating to the JBC, the legislature, and the public the governor's annual executive budget proposals. Then, "after legislative review and modification, if any, of the budget and appropriation of the moneys thereto, the governor shall administer the budget."[2] Even the statutory charge to the Joint Budget Committee suggests a prominent gubernatorial role in the process. The JBC is "to hold hearings as required and to review the Executive budget and the budget requests of each state agency and institution."[3]

All state agencies, then, save for elementary, secondary, and higher education, and judiciary, along with those headed by directly elected officials, send their budget requests through the governor's OSPB. The requests are reviewed and receive the blessing of the governor. From there, they are sent to the legislature's JBC in aggregated form.

For years, under Governor Richard Lamm, agency requests were largely "wish lists," with totals well beyond anything one could reasonably expect from the legislature. This did little to make the Joint Budget Committee take the executive's budget requests seriously. Under Governor Roy Romer, agency requests were screened more carefully and were more realistic. Nonetheless, they still constituted just one source of data used by the staff as it built annual budgets. The same was true under Governor Owens. And, since state agency personnel knew this, they paid some attention to the governor's apparent budget role, but then proceeded to deal directly with the legislature and its budget committee.

This process *does* give the governor a chance to express policy and budgetary preferences. It also gives the chief executive a certain amount of publicity and, thus, an opportunity to impact public opinion. But the bottom line is that, in Colorado, the state budget is the product of the legislature, not the executive, and the legislature guards its budgetary power jealously and effectively.

The legislature's control of the budget process means, too, that the influence that the governor's policy preferences have on budget decisions must be felt far in advance of the submission of a formal budget document as called for in the constitution; much of it comes very early in the process when the governor's preferences are communicated to agency heads as they prepare requests for the legislature.

CONSTRAINTS ON THE LEGISLATURE

While in the context of Colorado state government itself the General Assembly remains the dominant branch, it has increasingly become constrained by both statutory and constitutional provisions of law. Indeed, one might now question the extent to which representative democracy operates with respect to fiscal matters. The statutory strictures have come in the form of spending limits that the General Assembly imposed upon itself. The constitutional noose is what is termed "Amendment One," otherwise known as "TABOR" or the "Bruce" amendment.

Going back into the 1970s, the legislature voluntarily tied its own budget hands with a statutory spending limit called the "Kadlecek" amendment after its sponsor, JBC member and Democratic Senator Jim Kadlecek. This statute capped each year's budget at 7 percent over the budget of the previous year, no matter the rate of inflation or the availability of tax revenues.

More recently the legislature once again limited itself by statute through what is called the Arveschoug-Bird provision. This limit is even lower than the 7 percent Kadlecek measure, limiting each budget to either 6 percent more than the prior budget or 5.5 percent of state personal income, whichever is least. This recent (1991) Arveschoug-Bird restriction applies to general fund operating appropriations but does not cover spending for such capital items as highways, prisons, or other state facilities.

Overlapping these statutory limitations are those embedded in Amendment One, which is actually Section 20 of Article 10 of the state constitution. It is commonly referred to as TABOR, the acronym for Taxpayers' Bill of Rights. This limit was proposed and pushed by Douglas Bruce, a transplant from California who now resides in Colorado Springs. Bruce is an avid antigovernment activist, and Amendment One, adopted by the voters in 1992, was his third attempt to tie the hands of state government.

Amendment One limits spending in any one fiscal year to the prior year's level plus the combined percentages of inflation in the Denver-Boulder area, and statewide population growth. It covers all state spending, including such cash revenues as college tuition and hunting license fees, and expenditures for such capital projects as roads and schools. Further, Amendment One bars the legislature from raising the level of existing taxes, renewing an expired levy, or initiating new ones. The legislature is free to cut taxes, and while moderates in both parties are wary of eviscerating the state tax base, in each legislative session since the adoption of Amendment One fiscal conservatives in the legislature have sought to do so. But any tax increase, either state or local, must be approved by the voters in the jurisdiction involved.

Amendment One has been enormously controversial, and it has altered both the role of the legislature in the state and procedures within the legislature itself. One major criticism is that the people's representatives are no longer able to make tax and spending decisions they deem necessary to address the state's problems and needs. Rather, they must toss to the public, which may be wise but which is generally unfamiliar with the current state of affairs, complex public policy choices. The results, critics allege, are either inadequate funding of needed programs or decisions not rooted in a solid information base.

Within the legislature, the role of the Finance Committees has changed. Historically, Finance Committees, or Ways and Means as they are often labeled, consider bills that raise revenues—tax legislation, in other words. Now under Amendment One, Finance Committees may recommend bills designed to cut taxes, but not bills that would raise them. This also means that any integrated plan to revamp the tax structure by raising some taxes and lowering others is out of the hands of the people's representative body. Instead, voters, from students to cab drivers to brokers, will decide.

TABOR has also changed the role of both the Appropriations Committees and the Joint Budget Committee. Since TABOR, the Appropriations Committees have increasingly become bill graveyards because any measures with positive fiscal impacts will affect other parts of the budget in negative fashion. In 1999, $10 million was "set aside," outside the long bill, for new programs resulting from new legislation. This took some pressure off the JBC to kill bills that triggered spending. Still, the JBC, as it produces a budget that must balance the dictates of the 6 percent limitation, TABOR's strictures, and the flow of cash funds, has become ever more influential in relation to the full legislature. The complexities and consequences of TABOR and related budgetary restrictions are discussed in more detail later.

Clearly, it is still the General Assembly that assembles and passes upon the annual budget, and as between it and the governor, the legislature dominates. But the fiscal latitude, and thus the policy latitude, of the body is highly restricted.

PARTICIPANTS IN THE BUDGET PROCESS

Many actors and groups are parties to the process. These include the Joint Budget Committee, its staff, and the party caucuses, as well as the

House and Senate Appropriations and Finance Committees, the Capital Development Committee, the Colorado Commission on Higher Education, the Transportation Commission, the Office of State Planning and Budgeting, and the Legislative Council. The GAVEL amendment adopted in November 1988 has placed some restrictions on the operation of party caucuses, and altered their role.

JOINT BUDGET COMMITTEE

The Joint Budget Committee was established in evolutionary fashion in the late 1950s and 1960s as a legislative effort to develop budgetary expertise independent of that possessed by the executive branch. It was formalized in statute in 1973. With six members, three from the House and three from the Senate, it is generally considered to be the most powerful committee in the legislature. Since it is the committee that handles the money, appointments to the committee are prized.

The statute that creates the JBC reads:

> There is hereby established a joint committee of the Senate and House of Representatives officially known as the Joint Budget Committee, and to consist of the Chairman of the House Appropriations Committee plus one majority party member and one minority party member thereof, and the Chairman of the Senate Appropriations Committee plus one majority party member and one minority party member thereof.[4]

The Republican party has been the legislative majority party for decades and as a result, two of the three members from each house have been Republicans.

The two Republican House members are appointed by the Speaker. The Democratic member is technically designated by the minority leader and appointed by the Speaker, but, in practice, House Democrats elect their JBC member. In the Senate, the two Republican JBC members are elected in the party caucus. The Senate Democrat is named by the minority leader.

Membership on the Joint Budget Committee is linked to membership on the Appropriations Committees of each chamber—the three JBC senators also sit on the Senate Appropriations Committee, and the three JBC representatives sit on the House Appropriations Committee. Since all bills that appropriate funds go through Appropriations as well as one or more committees of reference, this membership linkage provides continuity to the entire budget process. The chairmanship of the JBC shifts each year between a senator and a representative.

This crossover in membership between the two Appropriations Committees and the Joint Budget Committee, coupled with the appointment power of the House Speaker and Senate majority leader, concentrates power in the hands of just a few legislators. The Senate President, House Speaker, and the two majority floor leaders control much of the General Assembly agenda and, along with the four majority party JBC members, they can, through the Appropriations Committees, determine the fate of much of the proposed legislation and dominate the budget process as well.

JBC STAFF

The Joint Budget Committee is served by a fairly small but very influential staff. The six-member committee hires a staff director who is responsible for hiring additional analysts and clerical staff and, according to the statutes, preparing reports and recommendations. The director and staff collect and assemble data and formulate requests for state funding to be analyzed by the six committee members. The JBC staff is composed of about fourteen full-time people, including the director, budget analysts, administrative secretaries, and a receptionist. They are not part of the state classified personnel system, but are employees of the General Assembly. Their responsibilities and salaries are established by the legislature.

The analysts who work on the budget recommendations that go to the JBC itself are drawn from a variety of backgrounds. The past and current chiefs of staff say that they look for people with analytical skills, who are comfortable working with numbers, and who have experience in developing and defending recommendations publicly. All staff analysts have at least a bachelor's degree, and may have master's degrees. Degrees in public administration are common and prior professional experience the norm.

The perspective that JBC analysts bring to their work is not prescribed for them, one former staff director contended, noting that their task is to analyze, not recommend. "Nobody voted for us," he said in describing the staff's obligation to avoid using their role to shoehorn personal preferences into state policy. But, at the same time, staffers must manipulate data and present JBC members with feasible alternatives, and anyone with political experience knows full well that influence does, in fact, accompany the generation of data and alternatives. Indeed, in the late 1980s, when asked whether Speaker Bledsoe, Governor Romer, or Staff Director Robert Moore had had the most impact on state policy, several people in both the legislative and executive branches picked Moore. Chuck Berry, who followed Bledsoe to the Speaker's position, recounted a comment made by Governor Romer: "When I'm done being governor in this state, I'm going to get a position of real power. I'm going to become a JBC analyst."[5] Even if Romer meant it as a joke, it is still testimony to the power that is wielded by those involved in budgeting and the control of information.

The staff of the JBC is, thus, an important and influential element in Colorado's budgeting system. However, JBC members themselves may or may not have expertise in budgeting, and they come and go with some regularity. For example, between the 1987 and 1988 sessions, two of the Senate JBC members resigned from the General Assembly; when the 1987 session began, only one person on the six-member panel was a carryover from the 1985 and 1986 sessions. In 1989, there was yet another new member. Following the 1998 elections, term limits dictated that all three House JBC members were new to the committee, as was one of the three JBC senators. New legislators often bring fresh ideas or new programs they care about and hard questions on existing programs and agencies. But, inevitably, they are also new to the JBC's complex procedures and must go through a learning phase before they truly think and act independently.

The staff, on the other hand, does not turn over so rapidly; indeed, Robert Moore served a full decade as director and was intimately familiar with every nook and cranny of the budget. His successor, Kenneth Conahan, was a staff analyst under Moore and he too has been the staff director for over a decade. Consequently, although many legislators on the JBC may be smart, hardworking, and fast learners, they are highly dependent upon their staff for information and advice.

Though the enormous influence of the staff remains under the directorship of veteran staff member Kenneth Conahan, the style has changed some. As one JBC member noted, "Moore played things close to the vest. Conahan is more open." The relations between the OSPB and JBC seem to have improved somewhat. That change may be partly due to the staff change, as well as to the improved accuracy of OSPB's revenue estimating and, in 1999, to the presence of a Republican governor.

MAJORITY PARTY CAUCUSES

Major participants in the Colorado budget process also include the party caucuses in the House and Senate. As noted before, both parties in both chambers have, for years, caucused from time to time to discuss problems and issues and establish party positions. But none of the caucuses are as significant as the meetings of the parties—the majority party especially—on the "long bill," the recommended budget bill prepared annually by the JBC. In the midst of the spring legislative session—after the JBC and its staff have analyzed data and budget requests, held hearings with agency personnel, set recommended budget figures for the coming year, and, in the process, sought to match anticipated revenues with recommended appropriations—the budget is sent over to the legislature in the form of one big "long" bill. The budget is introduced like any other bill and assigned to the Appropriations Committees. From there, it is reported out to the full House or Senate. It begins in the House in even-numbered years and in the Senate in odd-numbered ones.

But this formal process masks a most critical point, for between the time the budget bill reaches Appropriations and when it is reported to the floor, it spends a few days in lengthy sessions of the party caucuses. These groups prepare to propose on the floors any adjustments they desire and try to ensure that thirty-three members in the House and eighteen in the Senate will agree to the bill's contents and support it. With its numerical advantage, the majority party maintains control of the state budget, and the majority party caucuses can become real decision points. There are occasions when the minority party's proposals for alterations in the JBC budget are adopted, but in large measure floor action is pro forma. The budget tends to remain much as proposed by the JBC and most of what little change is made is in response to the desires of the majority party members.

APPROPRIATIONS COMMITTEES

The House and Senate Appropriations Committees play a role in the budget process since the long bill is assigned to them each year and they report it to the floor. But, in fact, their work on this measure has been preempted by the majority party caucuses.

However, there are other bills with financial implications that also flow to Appropriations. In every legislative session, all bills with any fiscal implications automatically go to the Appropriations Committee, as well as to one or more committees of reference. In 1996, for example, the House committees held hearings on 360 bills, plus eighteen more that provided midyear supplemental appropriations for state agencies. One hundred and seventeen of the 360 were also sent to the House Appropriations Committee, as were all eighteen supplementals. Beyond that, House Appropriations heard fifty-four of the Senate's 237 bills. The Senate's own Appropriations Committee heard eighty-seven bills that originated in the Senate, and fifty-six that came over from the House. For 1998 these numbers declined some, but Appropriations remained a very busy committee and the end of the road for dozens of bills.

The tasks of the two Appropriations Committees is, technically, to examine bills for their fiscal consequences, and in 1999 they did just that. But sometimes the committees will explore the substance of bills too, thus duplicating the work of committees of reference. This, plus the spending limitations imposed on the legislature by Amendment One and the General Assembly's own 6 percent limit on annual budget growth, make the Appropriations Committees quite powerful. They can, and do, kill dozens of bills on the rationale that the money just isn't there to fund them.

The House and Senate Finance Committees play a role in the state budget process, too, albeit one that is quite different from that of Appropriations. Finance Committees are committees of reference and are typically assigned bills that deal with revenue generation, rather than financial appropriation. Legislative Council publications describe the subject matter of the Finance Committees as taxation, property tax relief, and school finance. In a recent session, bills heard by the Senate Finance Committee included gas tax exemption for government entities, tax credits for business research and development in enterprise zones, collateral for financial institutions, and funds relating to workers' compensation, the Colorado lottery, and property tax valuation.

As noted previously, the role of the Finance Committees changed significantly after the 1992 voter adoption of Amendment One. Amendment One requires a citizen vote on the adoption of any new tax, the continuation of one that expires, or an increase in any existing levy. Historically this was the job of the legislature and its Finance Committee. Since 1992, the Finance Committee's tax-related role has been reduced to considering tax cuts and some measures dealing with fees.

CAPITAL DEVELOPMENT COMMITTEE

In 1985, the General Assembly created a Capital Development Committee that is structurally patterned after the JBC. It is composed of six members, three from each chamber. Like the JBC, it has membership from both political parties, selects its own chairperson, and establishes its own operating rules. The statutory charge to the CDC is to study state agency requests for capital construction, maintenance, and capital asset acquisition; to hold hearings on these matters; to forecast state needs and prioritize them; and to forward findings and recommendations to the JBC. The committee receives staff assistance from the Office of State Planning and Budgeting, Legislative Council, and other offices that provide such help to the legislature.

The establishment of the CDC cut into the terrain of the JBC and OSPB to some extent and reportedly created some hard feelings. The JBC still has major control over the budget, though, as CDC recommendations to the JBC are just that—recommendations. CDC priorities are usually proposed for funding by the JBC only after other needs are covered.

COLORADO COMMISSION ON HIGHER EDUCATION

The General Assembly passed legislation in 1985 to modify and enlarge the role of the Colorado Commission on Higher Education. The commission was not and is not a "super board" that governs the state's colleges and universities, but serves to provide some coordination of programs and budgets. Among significant changes, the 1985 legislation gave the commission authority to develop a formula to distribute higher education funding among the many state colleges and universities.

Prior to the passage of this legislation, usually referred to as House Bill 1187, each of Colorado's many colleges and universities was funded separately and directly through an appropriation in the long bill. Since 1985, however, the CCHE makes a single, lump-sum request for all institutions of higher education, and the JBC and the legislature, in turn, make a single, lump-sum appropriation. The money is then divided by the CCHE formula, which is tied to student count and type of educational program and, since 1999, a series of so-called quality indicators, which actually measure quantity. The funds are forwarded to the governing boards, which allocate them to the institutions under their respective jurisdictions, again using the formula as a guide. The passage of HB 1187 clearly modified the role of the JBC and legislature in the budget process as it relates to higher education, and it expanded the role of the CCHE in this large portion of the state budget. The legislature has, however, had to regain some of the control over higher education that it gave away with HB 1187. With tuition revenues defined as cash funds and counted against the annual TABOR spending limits, the legislature has had to take a more specific and intrusive posture with respect to college and university budgets. In addition, it has embedded policy directives in budget bill footnotes.

STATE TRANSPORTATION COMMISSION

The State Transportation Commission is an eleven-person body whose members are appointed by the governor and confirmed by the Senate. The Transportation Department is supervised by a director, who is also appointed by the governor and confirmed by the Senate. The administration of the department and its budget is almost entirely out of the hands of the legislature. The bulk of the funding for Colorado's roads is derived from fuel taxes and federal appropriations and is controlled by the commission; indeed, almost all of the department's budget, which exceeds $900 million annually, is outside the control of the legislature. The department's money does appear in the budget, but in a purely pass-through form. Historically, the legislature has sought ways to gain expanded and specific control over the department's budget.

OFFICE OF STATE PLANNING AND BUDGETING

According to the statutes, the Office of State Planning and Budgeting (OSPB) would seem to play an important role in the state budget process. But its role is actually quite limited. The OSPB is the governor's budget staff arm; its director is appointed by the governor and is a member of the cabinet. The OSPB collects state agency budget requests annually and reviews and compiles them into a single document that becomes the governor's budget recommendation. But in practice, the legislature creates its own budget with the help of its own staff. The product of the OSPB is one piece of data that is used along with many others by the JBC staff to build a proposed budget. The staff also considers prior budgets and footnotes, appropriations reports, and statutes, and consults with agency personnel.

Until 1989, the OSPB was responsible for preparing "fiscal notes" for the legislature on all bills that appeared to have a potential impact on the revenues and expenses of any state agency or local government. However, the 1988 General Assembly transferred that responsibility to the Legislative Council. With the JBC staff creating its own version of the budget each year and with its fiscal impact responsibility taken away, the OSPB is less central to the state budgeting process.

After the election of Roy Romer in 1986, efforts were made to improve and enhance the role of the executive branch in the process. Agency budget requests were given a ceiling by the governor and funneled through the OSPB, which sought to turn its relations with the JBC and its staff from adversarial to cooperative. It also attempted, with some success, to upgrade its credibility by improving the accuracy of its annual revenue forecasts. That has continued with Governor Owens.

LEGISLATIVE COUNCIL

The Legislative Council, whose prime functions have been to serve as the legislature's research arm and to provide staff help to legislative committees, has come to play a role in the budgeting process of late. The legislature has, for years, looked to the Legislative Council for estimates of state revenues as it assembled the budget each spring and struggled to match state appropriations with anticipated revenues. The OSPB provided revenue estimates, but under Democratic administrations they were usually seen by members of the majority party as overly optimistic and, in any case, they came from "the governor's people." Legislators thus called on the Legislative Council for "second opinions." Now that the legislature has shuffled the responsibility of estimating the fiscal impact of bills and generating revenue estimates, the Legislative Council has clearly come to play a larger role in the budgeting process.

One price of this expanded role has been increased pressure on its staff. With roughly six persons assigned to the fiscal note process, they average over 100 notes each, and must prepare most of them very early in the session so that committees can meet the deadlines for reporting bills out to the floor.

One additional feature of the state budgeting process bears mention at this point—the fact that nearly one-half of the state budget is either not controlled or only partially controlled by the legislature. Most of the Transportation Department's budget of over $900 million is under the control of the Transportation Commission, not the legislature. That amounts to almost 8 percent of the state operating budget. Nearly $1.46 billion more supports higher education, and, although the legislature determines how large that number will be, it is, by law, appropriated in lump-sum fashion to the CCHE, which then distributes it according to a formula that it, not the legislature, has created. Another huge sum, over $2 billion, is allocated to the state's elementary and secondary schools—again, by formula, but in this case it is a legislatively created formula. Fundamentally, then, despite having tightened its grip on the budget process by minimizing the executive's role, the legislature still finds itself sharing influence on allocations with others. On top of this, of course, the legislature's revenue-raising and spending authority is constrained both by its own statutory limit and by Amendment One.

THE BUDGET-MAKING PROCESS

In some respects, budgeting is a year-round activity. The fiscal year runs from July 1 to June 30 of the following year, and the first steps in constructing a budget for one fiscal year actually begin over twelve months in advance. As one fiscal year begins, plans for the next one are well under way. And at the same time that hearings are being held for a budget that will take effect six or eight months down the road, adjustments for the current year are being made.

For the JBC members and especially for the staff, budgeting is a full-time job. Staff members monitor the spending activities of agencies throughout the year. They may travel across the state, visiting state facilities and agencies and meeting with personnel. Data gathering and the analysis of patterns of funding and spending are continuous activities.

JUNE

The budget cycle begins formally in the month of June, a full thirteen months in advance of the July 1 start of a fiscal year. It does not end until fifteen months later, in August, when the books on the fiscal year that ended on June 30 are officially closed.

In June, the governor's budget arm, the Office of State Planning and Budgeting, issues budget instructions to the state agencies. Agency budget requests are submitted to the OSPB in August and, after review and possible modification, they are forwarded to the JBC by a statutorily set deadline of November 1.

Under Republican Governors Love and Vanderhoof, agency requests were not reviewed and cleared by the executive branch prior to being submitted to the JBC in November. But under Governor Romer, the requests of agencies he directed were cleared by both the OSPB and the chief executive. In some years agencies were given a "mark," indicating how much they may request, and the requests were studied to ensure that they were in line with the governor's program. Like the elective offices of attorney general, secretary of state, and lieutenant governor, the Education and Judicial Departments are not "cabinet" departments under the governor's control, and they did not fully comply with this part of the process. They did provide request numbers for inclusion in the OSPB-prepared governor's budget, but more importantly, they also dealt directly with the JBC. Governor Owens, too, has employed a heavy hand in tailoring agency requests. It is at this very early stage in the budget process that the governor may influence the budgetary outcome by shaping the agency requests that go to the JBC.

By November 1, then, agency budget requests are in the hands of the JBC and its staff, having arrived after an OSPB screening. Again, it can appear to this point that at least some pieces of the Colorado budget—those of agencies that channel requests through the OSPB—are formulated by a process in which the governor and his budget staff play a central role. But that is not the case. The JBC staff will look at the agency requests as submitted through the OSPB, but these requests constitute just one of several sources of data as the budget proposal is developed.

NOVEMBER

In the months leading up to the November 1 deadline, and in November and December when agency requests are in and hearings with agencies are going forward, JBC staff analysts will have studied past budgets and requests, earlier staff recommendations, audits, appropriations, and interim committee reports and statutes. They will have talked with agency personnel and others. Their information base will be substantial and will underpin both the briefings they will make to JBC members and the staff recommendations they will develop.

Staff members and legislators alike have commented that it isn't always easy to obtain all the data they would like to have. Staff members do come to know which agencies and which people within them will provide reliable information. It used to be said that institutions of higher education are among those that are hardest to get such data from; "they don't always provide what is requested, and, when they do, it is often only what was asked for and absolutely nothing more," said one JBC staffer. The former Department of Health was cited as another. One former legislator laughingly noted the problem of getting to the bottom of the Health Department's budget: It is so large, with so many sources of revenue and so many budget categories, that it was all but impossible to pin down the director and find the bottom line. "The director would tell us anything we wanted to hear and agree to do anything we asked," he said, "but we knew damn well that when he left he'd go back and do whatever he wanted and we'd never be able to sort it all out." More recently the particular agencies that make it difficult to gather complete and reliable data have changed with time and the personality of the director.

The briefing materials that staffers prepare for JBC members list budget issues and, perhaps, some nonbudget matters that are known to be of interest to JBC members or other legislators. They will also contain prior-year budget figures and revenue estimates and the staff's analysis of important issues and agency requests. And they will show the staff's recommendations for the coming year. Various sections of the budget are assigned to different staff members. The JBC is briefed by staffers concerning each agency; the committee then decides what topics it wishes to discuss with agency personnel as the budget hearings proceed.

Budget hearings are held from November to January. Agency personnel are informed in advance of the issues and problems that the committee wishes to study. JBC staff members sit in on the hearings, armed with their data and analyses and prepared to defend their conclusions and recommendations.

JANUARY

Preparation of the budget for the coming fiscal year resumes in January. The governor delivers a state-of-the-state address outlining his priorities and provides a summary of his budget requests. The General Assembly examines Legislative Council, OSPB, and JBC revenue estimates for the coming fiscal year and adopts a "budget resolution" that stipulates the state's anticipated revenues against which they will budget. The state may not, by law, go into debt.

The recommendations from the Capital Development Committee and the results of an annual salary survey are forwarded to the JBC, as well. The salary survey compares the wages of state employees to those of private-sector employees in similar jobs and provides the basis for decisions on salary increases for state employees who are part of the Classified Personnel System.

The JBC shifts gears sometime in the month of January, taking up agency requests for changes in the current year's budgets. These supplementals, as they are called, can be positive or negative; that is, they can call for increased or decreased funding. Although those initiated by the agencies are never negative, JBC staff members search for places to recoup funds, generally with some success.

Agency supplemental requests are approved by the governor prior to review and recommendations by the JBC staff. Factors that the committee weighs in judging midyear supplemental funding requests include errors in the original budget, unanticipated changes in workload, acts of God, and new data. Later in the session, the JBC formally makes decisions on supplemental requests, and, where they are positive or negative, bills authorizing the changed levels of funding are introduced and sent to the Appropriations Committee. They typically pass both chambers with no difficulty.

In January and February, the JBC sets the figures that will appear in the budget it recommends to the full legislature. By this point the committee has had full briefings by staff members and has held budget hearings with agency personnel. It has had an opportunity to pursue whatever questions members may have and obtain whatever data they want. CDC recommendations and salary survey results have also been received. As the process moves along, the JBC provides briefing papers to keep legislators informed of budget activity and solicits input from them.

With ongoing staff briefings and recommendations, committee members progress through the budget section by section. They may vote to accept staff recommendations or they may modify them. The committee tries to address the needs of each agency at this stage to prevent a too-generous funding of those treated early in the process and a squeezing of others treated later to make up for a shortfall. When the committee has gone through all sections of the budget, it will then "come back" through the sections to make whatever adjustments are needed and ensure that recommended appropriations balance against anticipated revenues. In the "come-back" process, agencies are allowed to see the tentative budget numbers and argue their cases if they choose. Some years ago, the committee and its staff kept the agency numbers secret until the bill was introduced, although they were commonly leaked to agency personnel by JBC members.

Throughout this process, party differences among the JBC members fade somewhat. The chairperson and majority party members will stay in touch with the leaders of their respective houses and with their party, though not necessarily on a daily basis. And in difficult times or in times of crisis, the link with leadership will tighten. But, like any small group of people who must work together closely for an extended period of time, the JBC members come to share some values and viewpoints. They all must wrestle with the same overriding problem, namely, how to fund legitimate program needs when costs far outrun available resources, and how to stay within the statutory and constitutional spending limits.

In addition, members of such small groups tend to develop an institutional loyalty of sorts and become defenders of their unit. Certainly, party and philosophical differences don't disappear, the influence of leadership isn't rebuffed, and all committee votes aren't unanimous. But the rough edges of party division are often smoothed out and all members can impact budget discussions in meaningful ways.

The committee and its staff are lobbied as they set figures, as they have been throughout the weeks and months preceding that stage. They are lobbied by agency personnel, by lobbyists, and by their colleagues in the legislature. Agency people and lobbyists have obvious interests to push; for agency folks, it is their programs, and for lobbyists, their clients. In recent years, the JBC even set aside time specifically to give agency people and others the chance to visit with the committee members and express their views.

Legislators have objectives, too. Some will have interests in particular programs—in mental health or preschool programs, for example. Others will have home district interests to defend—state fairgrounds, or a university located in their district that they want to see generously funded. So, they visit with their colleagues on the JBC, and they talk with members of the staff throughout the budget-making process. This sort of continuous communication with the legislature's main budget committee, especially by agency people, is further evidence of the legislative-centered nature of Colorado's budget process and of the freedom that executive branch personnel feel in going directly to the legislature.

MARCH

Once the budget numbers are set, the adjustments made, and the document reviewed intently, a narrative is written to accompany the long bill and provide a section-by-section explanation. The narrative is addressed to the members of the General Assembly, but it really is directed to the majority party caucuses. It explains the numbers in the bill, briefly explores the reasoning behind them, and discusses the differences, plus or minus, from the funding of the prior year.

Three important features of the budget process are worth noting at this point. First, much of the budget is driven by formula. The CCHE uses a formula to construct the higher education budget. The elementary and secondary education budget, the single biggest slice, is assembled by a formula. And case- and patient-load formulas drive some of the figures for social service and health programs.

Second, the JBC must address broad policy issues and make choices and assumptions on the front end of the process. Where will priorities lie for the coming year—in the public schools, with highways, prisons, universities? Will per diem and mileage allowances for employees on state business be increased? At what rate will the state reimburse counties for housing state prisoners? The answers to these questions and many more like them will impact the budget's bottom line.

Third, appropriations may not, by law, exceed statutory or constitutional limits, but they may not exceed revenues either. But what will the revenues be? How much will the state collect in income and sales tax? Will the economy be healthy? Will it snow enough to ensure a good ski tourist season? Whose estimates should be believed—the OSPB's or the Department of Revenue's or the one developed by the Legislative Council? How much of a reserve should be kept? These are difficult and slippery questions, but they must be answered, often several times along the way.

In mid- to late March, the long bill is introduced in the House in even-numbered years or in the Senate in odd-numbered years. The bill is referred to the Appropriations Committee, where it sits for a few days while it is scrutinized in a most critical forum—the party caucuses.

For years up to and through 1988, when the long bill emerged from the JBC, the majority party members caucused in day-long sessions until the group had worked its way through the entire budget bill, using a set of formal rules and taking formal ballots until there were thirty-three supporting votes in the House caucus and eighteen votes in the Senate caucus. (Recall that thirty-three and eighteen are the magic numbers needed to provide absolute majorities in the sixty-five- and thirty-five-member houses.)

The majority party, and especially its leadership, wanted the votes in line before going to the floor for two reasons. First, it was a quicker and more orderly way to deal with the budget. Second, as one lobbyist quipped recently, "This process is all about power—absolutely nothing but power. That's why they hate GAVEL so much. They're afraid of losing some power!"

The caucus chair presided at the meetings, which were attended virtually the entire time by all majority party members. Legislators in the minority party often met, too, but they really had no decisions of consequence to make on the budget. In the majority caucuses, the two JBC members from their party, with the indispensable help of JBC staffers, explained and defended the numbers and rationale as the group proceeded, section by section, through the budget.

The majority parties in the two caucuses followed slightly different rules for dealing with the long bill. In the House of Representatives, a vote of 60 percent of those present and voting was required to alter the recommendations of the JBC, and thirty-three votes were required to "close," or agree to, a section. A section is a part of the budget dealing with one agency—education or corrections, for example. In the Senate, JBC recommendations could be changed by a simple majority, with eighteen votes needed to close a section.

With the 1988 passage of the GAVEL amendment, the members' floor votes may no longer be bound by caucus decisions, but this has not eliminated majority party caucuses as critical junctures in the budget process. The formal rules and votes are gone, but members continue to caucus, discuss the budget, and voice their agreement and disagreement with the JBC recommendations. The sentiment of members, as expressed in straw votes, is often translated into formal decisions in the Appropriations Committees and on the floor, where the bill goes next, by united majority party voting.

In some years, the majority party holds together and steadfastly rejects any and all budget amendments proposed by members of the minority party. But other times a few adjustments sought by the minority party receive the support of a majority on the floor. It tends to hinge upon the personal relationships among majority and minority party members at the time, those in leadership positions especially.

The bill as it comes from the JBC has always been changed to some degree in the caucuses, but rarely in major ways. The JBC is powerful, and its versions of the budget fairly well establish the ultimate configuration. It is a lengthy and complicated bill, and the JBC members are intimately familiar with its contents, while others are not. And recommended appropriations are balanced against anticipated revenues and the legal spending limits. If members wish to approve additional spending, it has to come from another place in the budget. If not, the revenue projections have to be increased or the planned reserve has to be lowered. Members who wish to lower some recommendations are countered by their JBC colleagues, who generally have the distinct edge in information or know very well why each number is set as it is.

Caucus discussions are interesting. The reliability of the revenue estimates is always questioned, and every year there are some members who seize the opportunity to preach about fiscal frugality, the evils of big government, and the tax burdens faced by their constituents. And there are always those who wish to increase funding in some area dear to their hearts or to build some facility within their district. The task of the JBC members is to answer the questions, rebut the criticisms, and defend the work of the committee as expressed in the long bill. In a recent House caucus, two representatives chimed in about the desirability of reducing the revenue estimates by $100 million, just to be safe. The JBC chairman responded that "if you do, we'll have to cut programs and some of you are bringing in new bills with new costs at the same time."

When changes to the long bill have been made in caucus, they have generally been quite small, at least in relation to the size of a budget of over $9 billion. In 1994 the House debated proposed amendments to the long bill one full day and ended up making changes that amounted to one-tenth of 1 percent of the budget total.[6] In 1996, House members debated the budget bill on the floor for just three hours, approving eighteen of forty-three amendments that were proposed and, again, changing the JBC's proposed numbers very little.[7] Recognition of the futility of trying to change JBC budget numbers in any major way was reflected in the Republican House caucus when Representatives McKay and Paschall moved to simply accept the JBC's proposed 2001 budget as presented.

When the caucuses in the chamber that has the budget bill first conclude deliberations, the bill moves quickly to the Appropriations Committee, which may propose formal amendments to reflect the decisions made by the caucuses before sending it to the floor. There, the long bill moves quickly, as well. All changes agreed to in caucus and in the Appropriations Committee are written up as amendments and are acted upon on the floor. That doesn't take long, of course, as the majority party has already gone through the bill section by section and sticks together on the floor votes. Under rules adopted in 1989, members were to issue a two-day notice of intention if they plan to propose long bill amendments. This has since been reduced to twenty-four hours. Minority party members usually move to make changes on the floor, but their motions almost always fail. In the 1996 Senate, for example, the Republican majority voted as a block and snuffed every amendment proposed by Democratic party colleagues.[8] In recent years a few minority party amendments have passed, but not many. Following action on amendments, the bill goes on to the second chamber, where the process is repeated. Disagreements always emerge between the two houses, and the six JBC members then serve as a conference committee to work out these differences.

On the chamber floors, as in the party caususes, the role of JBC members is to defend the budget numbers and resist any changes. For the most part, they do so successfully. In one humorous exception, JBC member Representative Gayle Berry offered obligatory resistance to a minor amendment, paused, and then muttered, "This really is not a bad amendment." It passed.

Finding compromise positions on the numbers preferred by the two houses can be a difficult task. The JBC will meet for hours, even for days, as its members seek a middle ground that will be saleable to members of their respective caucuses. They bring a list of compromises on the budget lines where the chambers differ; some are accepted and some are not. Thus, the JBC must go through several iterations, slowly but surely settling out the points of difference until it has a complete budget that is acceptable to the majority party caucuses in both houses.

For years, passage of the budget bill was one of the last major items of business each spring, and it spelled the coming of the end of the session. More recently the bill passed in March. Sometimes the end is not so easy to reach. In one recent session, the Republican caucus in the House came to agreement on the bill rather quickly. However, for the Senate Republicans, it was a more laborious process. The new school funding formula was to add significantly to the budget. Some members thought it added too much, and some felt it was too little. Although they did eventually come to agreement on the new education bill and, subsequently, on the budget bill, it was not without considerable debate and delay and a further reduction in the size of the planned state reserve.

When both houses conclude their work on the budget, the long bill quickly receives majority approval in its compromised form and goes to the governor for his signature. The governor does possess the authority to veto individual appropriations, and although the chief executive will not reject the budget numbers in any major way, some items are generally vetoed and, increasingly, Governor Romer was inclined to veto budget bill footnotes. The legislature has been including more and more footnotes directing executive branch agencies on how to spend the appropriation or limiting and controlling them in some fashion. The governor sees the executive role as residing in the agencies, not the legislature, and hence will often veto restrictive footnotes. Governor Roy Romer's budget director noted that in 1997 the legislature included 183 footnotes containing directions. The governor line-item vetoed thirty-three items. In one he explained his reasoning this way: "This footnote violates the separation of powers by attempting to administer the appropriation."[9] Romer did it again in 1998, axing twenty-seven restrictive footnotes.[10] Governor Owens followed suit with some footnote vetoes.

The entire process is concluded in May, just before the start of the new fiscal year. During or shortly after the wrap-up of the long bill, the legislature will be concluding actions on a number of other bills that make additional, although smaller, appropriations.

When the session is over, the JBC staff will prepare and issue what is called an "Appropriations Report." This document describes the budget and the budget decisions that were made. Around the same time, the books will be closed on the previous fiscal year, which ended on June 30, even as plans are under way for yet another budget year.

FISCAL NOTES

An ongoing process related to the budgets of the state is the production of "fiscal notes." A substantial number of the bills introduced in each legislative session have the potential for some kind of financial impact. Some will raise fees; others may lower fees or taxes. Many will add to the programs of the state and thus cost more money; a few will shrink programs and maybe even save a few dollars.

It is obviously very important to the legislators to be aware of the dollar implications of bills when they vote. Therefore, all bills are automatically scrutinized for fiscal impact upon introduction. The Senate President and the Speaker of the House have the power to waive fiscal notes—a useful political tool to keep a bill moving when it might otherwise be stalled. For many years, the OSPB prepared fiscal notes but, beginning with the 1989 session, the responsibility was transferred to the legislature's own research arm, the Legislative Council.

The process of assessing the financial impacts of bills was well defined. Copies of all bills were forwarded to the Office of State Planning and Budgeting as soon as they were introduced. OSPB analysts examined each bill to determine whether it would have any financial impact. If it was clear that it would not, that fact would be noted on a form prepared for that purpose, then communicated to the committee of reference designated to hear the bill. The bill could then be considered on its own merits. No bill could be reported out of a committee of reference without a statement of either no fiscal impact (NFI) or probable fiscal impact (PFI). All bills with a probable fiscal impact were steered to the Appropriations Committee after being considered in committees of reference.

If it appeared to OSPB staff personnel that a bill might well have a financial impact, the committee of reference would be notified via a statement of probable fiscal impact. If a bill was given such a statement, a "fiscal note" was prepared upon request by the chair of the bill's committee of reference or its sponsor. If that happened (and it usually did), then OSPB staff members prepared a full-blown fiscal note, which assessed the changes in state revenues or costs associated with the bill. The note considered whether the bill would raise money, cost money, add personnel, cut personnel, require new facilities, and so forth, based on an analysis from the state agency that would administer the bill should it pass. The information was logged and reported on a standardized form. Fiscal notes were updated as bills became amended throughout the process.

This appears to be a quite straightforward process, and often it was. The OSPB simply assembled relevant fiscal data, and the legislature proceeded on the basis of the information it had been given. But it didn't always work that way, at least in the view of some lawmakers. At times, fiscal note preparation became a political game. If an agency did not like a bill, it could prepare a note showing a very high estimate of the fiscal impact, anticipating, then, that the fiscally conservative legislature would kill the bill. At other times, an agency might provide a very low estimate for a bill it favored, hoping to help secure its passage. Because they were skeptical of the fiscal notes prepared by the OSPB, the Appropriations Committees frequently asked their own staff (which was the JBC staff) to make an independent assessment of probable fiscal impacts. JBC staffers were cued to look carefully at the assumptions underpinning an agency's numbers, not just at the numbers themselves. Former JBC Chief of Staff Bob Moore saw this as a predicament for agencies: If they estimated high, bills would die, but if they went low, no one would believe their figures.

In any case, the legislature chose to move the function of estimating fiscal impacts out of the executive branch's OSPB and into its own staff arm, the Legislative Council, beginning in 1989. The process works much as it did when housed in OSPB, except that the intermediate designation of "probable fiscal impact" has been eliminated; bills now either have an impact or they don't.

This transfer of responsibility for preparing fiscal notes has not, however, eliminated all controversy. There are times when Legislative Council's fiscal note analysts are skeptical of the information provided by the executive branch agency personnel when asked about the probable costs associated with a bill. A petition by ten members can obtain a new fiscal note. There have also been concerns that some legislators lean on Legislative Council analysts to enter certain numbers in fiscal notes to improve the chances of a bill's passage. Indeed, former House Majority Leader Tim Foster expressed such concerns in a leadership meeting and urged leaders to provide council employees with a buffer from such pressure.

TABOR: Terrible or Terrific?

We've got "money up the kazoo."[11] "It's easy to vote for all the tax reduction bills. It's easy to vote for more spending. But it's wrong. We don't have a clue what we're doing." "You're one of the few people in this place who really understand this stuff." "God only knows what we've done."[12]

These are comments made in 1998 by alternate-year JBC chairman Tony Grampsas, JBC member Jim Rizzuto, and Senator Bill Schroeder during debates on the budget, school finance, and tax-cut bills.

The provisions of the Arveschoug-Bird statutory measure and constitutionally based TABOR, along with the strong Colorado economy and flush state coffers of the late 1990s, had major impacts on both the legislature in general and the budgeting process in particular. To some legislative participants and observers these developments have been terrific. But in the estimation of others they've created a terrible mess.

The Arveschoug-Bird statutory provision limits each year's general fund spending to the prior-year level plus 6 percent. The measure applies to the state's operating budget, but not to capital spending for roads, buildings, and other such capital projects.

TABOR is an acronym for "Taxpayers' Bill of Rights." Promoted by Douglas Bruce and adopted by voters as a constitutional measure in 1992, TABOR limits state revenue and spending to that of the prior year plus an amount equal to a combined percentage of population growth and inflation. It affects not only the state, but all taxing entities, including cities, counties, schools, and special districts. Voters may choose to override the limits—to "de-Bruce" as it is called. TABOR differs from Arveschoug-Bird in that it applies to cash funds as well as state tax monies, and caps both general operating budgets and capital spending.

Beyond the revenue and spending restrictions, TABOR requires a vote of the people for increases in the level of existing taxes, to renew an expiring levy, or to impose a new tax. Whenever the state or a local unit collects more money and fee-based cash funds than the formula allows in a given year, the surplus must be rebated to the taxpayers unless they chose to "de-Bruce" and allow the government to spend the overage.

Among the consequences of the interaction of the two limitations was a minor boom in capital spending. For several years in the late 1990s, the TABOR cap exceeded Arveschoug-Bird's 6 percent limit. Revenues beyond 6 percent and up to the TABOR lid were available for capital spending and reserve funds. College and university physical plant maintenance and construction projects, along with prison and highway development, became the beneficiaries. Highway, prison, and school spending was therefore more the unintended consequence of TABOR than the product of rational policy decisions to invest in the state's future.

TABOR's impact on state cash funds produced additional consequences that may well have been more accidental than intended. Many of the state's programs are supported in total or in part by money derived through fees and charges for services. Two examples are hunting licenses and college tuition. Under TABOR, these monies count, along with ordinary tax collections, as part of the state's total revenue, and when they are appropriated and spent they count under TABOR's expenditure limit. The result of this state of affairs was described succinctly in a *Denver Post* editorial this way:

> [T]he state Division of Wildlife has been unable to raise license fees for out-of-state hunters because it can't legally spend the money it would raise. More worrisome is a looming problem in Colorado's far flung higher education system, which may soon have to start turning away students because it cannot spend their tuition money to pay for their education.[13]

A related TABOR impact has been on cash reserves accumulated by state agencies. Money was often collected and banked for later use, in emergencies, for example. But the accumulated cash counts as revenue under TABOR and thus in flush times every dollar held in reserve is a dollar of tax revenue that must be returned rather than appropriated. As a result, some portion of fees collected from one purpose becomes cash to be distributed to citizens in some fashion unrelated to the basis of collection. So in 1998 the legislature directed state agencies to expend their reserves and build them no more.

During the 1998 session, term-limited Tilman Bishop, the Senate's President Pro Tem, sponsored a concurrent resolution that, had it passed, would have let the citizens vote to exclude cash funds from the grip of TABOR. The measure died and thus the cash fund quandary continued.

In the late 1990s, the excess of revenues over the TABOR spending limit created a whole new political agenda for the legislature, an agenda that divided members along party lines and split the Republican party as well. With surplus cash the state could, under TABOR's provisions, somehow give the money back to taxpayers, or ask them for permission to spend it. Some legislators wanted to spend it, others did not. Some wanted to return it in one fashion, others had alternative refund schemes in mind. The governor wanted to spend some and return some, and his return plan was supported by some lawmakers but opposed by others. Certain members wanted to cut taxes temporarily, some permanently, some not at all. In the 1998 session the existence of a cash pot over and above what could be legally spent created a circus.

One of the sideshows was the introduction of almost fifty bills designed to cut taxes. Several passed only to be vetoed by the governor.

The bills were introduced individually by members in uncoordinated fashion. At one point Senate President Tom Norton noted that his count showed a collective negative impact on state revenues of over a half billion dollars. All along the governor opposed all permanent cuts, arguing that such reductions could have a disastrous impact on the state when the economy cools and revenues shrink.

Bills were introduced to cut taxes on telephones, to reduce the property tax, to exempt farm equipment from the sales tax, to give farmers tax credits for charitable donations of excess crops, to exempt taxes on the sales of certain precious metals, as well as to cut the income tax both temporarily and, in another bill, permanently. The situation provided golden opportunities for political posturing as champions of the oppressed taxpayer, and many members didn't pass up the chance. Several tax-cut bills passed only to be vetoed.

The General Assembly did manage to pass a measure to ask the voters' permission to spend $200 million of the anticipated revenue surplus for five years on roads and the physical plants of schools and higher education institutions. The bill was sponsored by the Republican Senate President and the House Republican majority leader and it enjoyed the active support of the Democratic governor. Statewide polls showed that voters favored such investment by a two-to-one margin and over 90 percent of such measures had passed at the local level. While the measure made it out of the legislature, it was a difficult struggle with a clear majority of Republican legislators opposed to placing the option on the ballot. In the end they had their way as the voters rejected the proposal.

But on the question of how to rebate the 1997 overage, the legislature struck out in a nasty contest. In a 1997 special session the General Assembly and governor were able to agree to a plan to rebate the 1996 tax-year overage. It was returned as an income tax credit. But 1998 was different. The more conservative Republicans insisted on a refund plan that favored income tax payers, those in higher brackets especially. Other Republicans, the legislative Democrats, and the governor objected, arguing that such an approach would be unfair to those who have little income to report but who nonetheless pay sales and other non-income-based taxes.

The legislature deadlocked and adjourned with no refund plan in place, only to be called back into special session in October. As the governor talked of the possible need for a special session should no acceptable rebate plan emerge, some Republicans threatened to respond to a gubernatorial call by convening and then immediately adjourning. Other majority party Republicans expressed confidence that a possible plan could be developed. Both the summer break and the coming election provided cooling-off time, and with little controversy or fanfare a rebate plan acceptable to all parties was quickly adopted in October.

The tax-refund game changed dramatically in 1999 and 2000, as for the first time in over two decades a Republican legislature worked with a Republican governor. Once again, state revenues exceeded allowable TABOR limits by hundreds of millions of dollars. And once again, dozens of tax-cut bills flooded the legislative agenda. But this time, many of them passed and were signed into law by Republican Governor Bill Owens. Some tax cuts were permanent, others temporary. The immediate impact was some shrinkage of both the tax base and the projected tax surpluses. The long-term consequences remain to be seen.

TABOR has been the cause of some shift of power within the General Assembly. Formerly the House and Senate Finance Committees wrote tax legislation. Now those committees can propose bills to cut or eliminate taxes, but not to enact them. The full assemblage of Colorado voters now constitutes a statewide tax finance committee.

With TABOR the JBC is stronger. The long bill—the main budget bill as developed and introduced by the JBC—is more than ever immune to significant modification by the rest of the legislature. Now, if money is to be added someplace, an equal or greater amount must be subtracted elsewhere. Since every proposed appropriation has its supporters and defenders, change from the JBC blueprint is hard to come by.

Likewise, the two chambers' Appropriations Committees are more consequential than ever. They are linked structurally to the JBC and are perfectly positioned to be sure that bills that have fiscal consequences that could threaten the TABOR limit and thus the JBC's budget plans die. This newly modified role of the Appropriations Committees also provides lobbyists with another and almost invisible venue in which to lobby bills to death. And die they do. One lobbyist commented that before TABOR, moving a "self-funded" bill, a cash-funded bill in other words, through Appropriations was "a piece of cake." With the TABOR impact on cash funds this earlier state of affairs is no more.

CONTINUING ISSUES

Besides TABOR, a number of other issues continue to swirl around Colorado's state budget process. The first concerns the fact that it is so heavily dominated by the legislature. Although they are not always overtly hostile, legislative relations with executive branch agencies have not always been warm and cozy or characterized by mutual support. Rather, the general orientation of the legislature toward the state agencies has been one of skepticism mixed with distrust, and legislators generally see themselves in an adversarial relationship with the bureaucracy.

Executive-centered budgeting schemes are sold, in part, on the argument that programs and budgets will be better meshed if the governor assembles, digests, and prioritizes agency requests before they even get to the legislative guardians of the pursestrings. This assumes, of course, that the legislature will then take the governor's budget seriously.

But what would happen if Colorado adopted the executive budget format? Opinions differ. Some argue that there would actually be more coherence and continuity between programs and budgets and that spending and taxation policy might be better synchronized, as well. Colorado surely has had its revenue problems in recent years.

But others argue that the only truly significant result would be an explosion in spending. They contend that the agencies and even governors are advocates for their programs, and such salespeople campaign for more, never for less. Thus, for the sake of control and reason in government spending, the budget is best left completely in the hands of the legislature.

Actually, the strong legislative control that has characterized Colorado budgeting for so many years may be rooted as much in over two decades of divided party control as in the formal steps of the process. Beginning in 1974 with the election of Democrat Richard Lamm as governor, the Democrats occupied the governor's mansion and the Republicans controlled the legislature. A JBC made up primarily of members of the governor's party, however, may well accept as its starting point a budget draft produced by the chief executive.

The separation of powers creates a degree of interbranch rivalry that persists even with both branches under the control of the same party. Indeed, the behavior of Republican senators over much of the 1980s and some enmity between the leaders of the two houses raise questions as to how much party affiliation constitutes a tie that binds. One lawmaker said:

> The JBC runs the state. Committee members endorse staff recommendations. The caucuses buy on to the JBC's long bill, and that's it. The staff is hostile rather than supportive of the agencies. They don't see advocacy of the state government and programs as their duty.

This statement points straight to three other controversial aspects of the budget process—the role of the staff, the role of the JBC itself, and the role of the majority party caucuses. As noted earlier, there is considerable turnover of JBC members, although the staff remains fairly stable. All legislators, of course, have many things on their minds. They care about bills as well as budgets. They have constituents to deal with and elections to face periodically. Their calendars are packed with meetings and social obligations. And those who serve on the JBC may not come to their task with any degree of familiarity with budgets or the guts of the state's vast and complicated array of programs.

The time, attention, and knowledge of staff members, on the other hand, are less diffuse. Budget analysts are on the job full-time, and their task is focused on specific segments of the budget. They may well come to the job with education and experience in government or budgeting. These people soon become very knowledgeable about their slice of the state's finances and programs.

The JBC members are, as a result, in the same predicament as all decision-makers in and out of government who must rely heavily on staff support. They cannot match the staffers in knowledge and, thus, they become dependent upon staff expertise and recommendations.

Some observers have suggested that this occurred in the form of a double whammy for the decade during which Bob Moore served as staff director. Moore was able and knowledgeable and, after working with the budget for many years, he came to know it inside and out. His edge in knowledge and expertise was maintained through purposeful rotation of staff members and the turnover among JBC members. Moore has long since departed as the JBC staff chief, but his replacement, Kenneth Conahan, retains much of the influence wielded by Moore. One member who is a part of the budget process observed that longtime JBC member and alternate-year Chairman Tony Grampsas was highly dependent on Conahan and leaned on him often to explain the numbers and rationale to other members. This is not, of course, different from complicated budget processes generally.

The JBC itself has been the object of criticism and target of reform efforts emanating from the legislature, as well as from outside sources. Even former JBC members and chairpersons have wondered aloud if the committee is not too powerful. One hears more and more grumbling that the six-member body *is* too powerful, that it often serves as a tool of leadership, and that budget power should reside in the two houses rather than in a special joint committee and those few who make the committee appointments. Long-term veteran Senator Tilman Bishop once remarked that "one hundred elected officials are pretty much dictated to by six elected officials."

In an odd way the physical location of the JBC may add to its power. The offices of both the JBC members and its staff are located outside the Capitol, across the street in the Legislative Services Building. So is the JBC hearing room. This results in some isolation from the rest of the legislators and the legislative activity. Several lobbyists and legislators alike have observed that while there is constant hustle and bustle surrounding committee hearings in the Capitol, and while the Capitol lobbies are busy with the movement of members, staffers, and lobby-ists, the JBC routinely meets and makes critical decisions in a hearing room that is quiet and nearly empty. Until the long bill is introduced, most everyone's attention seems focused elsewhere and by then the die is cast on most of the fiscal choices.

It has been suggested that the JBC should be expanded to broaden representation. It has also been suggested that the JBC should be abol-ished, with the budget functions returned to the much larger Appro-priations Committees in the two houses. Others have proposed that the budget sections be handled by the committees of reference, whose sug-gestions would then be funneled to the JBC. The creation of the Capital Development Committee was motivated, in part, by a desire to clip some power from the JBC.

Back in 1997 Senate Minority Leader Mike Feeley proposed aboli-tion of the Joint Budget Committee. In its place Feeley would have each of the committees of reference draft a portion of the budget for the agency or agencies for which it has oversight jurisdiction. Were this done, Colorado's budget process would be somewhat akin to that of Con-gress, where in each chamber funding proposals are developed for dif-ferent portions of the national government by thirteen subcommittees of the Appropriations Committee.

Senator Feeley's interest in change was fueled in part by a concern with the impact of term limits. Term limits, of course, reduce the expe-rience level of JBC legislators in relation to that of the committee's staffers. Feeley is not alone in his concern. Fellow Democratic Senator Stan Matsunaka, commenting on the hypothetical circumstance of having novice legislators on the JBC, observed, "At that point you make the JBC staff the most powerful group in Colorado because they know what's going on. We would be leaving the door open for someone who has their own agenda as a JBC staffer."[14]

While modifications designed to broaden participation in the bud-geting function would address concerns about excessive JBC power, they could well create other difficulties. Coordination of multiple commit-tee recommendations under the TABOR spending cap could become a nightmare. Committee advocacy or protection of the allocations for their agencies might develop. And floor action might well become cha-otic should the state's budget be handled on the House and Senate floors in several separate pieces. Longtime JBC member Senator Jim Rizzuto reflected this concern: "All we would end up with is total chaos and irresponsible budgeting."[15]

In a move to expand the influence of non-JBC members on budget decisions, the 1998 General Assembly modified the joint House-Senate rules. For years each committee of reference had oversight responsibility for one or more state executive branch agencies. Oversight activities generally involved little more than briefings by agency administrators. The rule modification now requires committees to have agency administrators review for members "a summary of the same materials and testimony previously provided to the Joint Budget Committee during the department's budget hearing."[16] This is to be done during the first month of each session, and the committee chair then forwards to the JBC members any comments or concerns that the committee may have. Additionally, members may come to JBC hearings, and receive per diem expenses, on those days when the departments over which their committees have oversight responsibility are before the budget committee.

In spite of the criticism to which it has been subjected, the prominent budget role of the JBC also serves the political purposes of senators and representatives, for it gives them a "whipping boy" on whom to pin decisions that are unpopular with constituents. Legislators can, and often do, deflect citizen dissatisfaction by claiming they, themselves, don't like a given outcome either, but their hands were tied—"the powerful JBC did it."

The structure of the budgeting process has changed little, and some of those close to the process say that it is because leadership and many members prefer the arrangement as it is. Fundamentally, budgets are statements of priorities; nothing much happens without money, and agencies have no money until the legislature gives it to them. Those who control the money control what government does. And the current system, wherein the majority party leaders appoint and stay close to four of the six members of the committee that writes the budget, suits those in power just fine. Why would they support or allow legislation to revamp the process and diffuse their power?

The caucus system has also been criticized, like the staff and the JBC, for being a point in the process where power is overly concentrated. Quite clearly, members of the minority party have been cut out of the decision process when the majority party caucuses.

But, for all intents and purposes, the influence of the majority party members is reduced, as well. The budget is not altered significantly in caucus. It has generally emerged much as the staff and JBC wanted it and prepared it. Leadership has had its say in the formulation of the budget along the way, either by direct communication or because JBC members are appointed by the leaders and hold parallel values. But the rank-and-file majority party member has not been able to do much more than support or oppose some tinkering on the edges of the JBC's budget before climbing aboard leadership's train. In 1989, the legislature went to a shortened, 120-day session that resulted in an even more hectic pace, reducing the amount of time available to handle legislative matters. This may well have increased the influence of the JBC and its staff on the budget even more, since there is now less time to tinker.

Not only have the caucuses been criticized for cutting the minority party out of the process but they have also been faulted for permitting very small numbers of majority party members to deny their party the eighteen or thirty-three votes needed to constitute a majority in the full chamber. The caucus system has allowed small cliques to bargain within their own party and hold out for extreme or narrow demands.

Much of the criticism and controversy related to the JBC, its staff, and the caucus carries the implicit suggestion that the process should be opened and made more "democratic." But there are those with a different perspective. One former JBC member and chairman commented:

> You've got to have some order and discipline. You can't just take a budget to the floor and turn it lose; it would be chaotic. You've got to have ways to stay within the available resources. . . . The JBC-caucus-leadership linkage does provide discipline. The majority party takes control of the budget—not like Congress where expenditure decisions are diffused, no one is in control, and the budget sinks into red ink.

Everybody wants to be in the middle of the action, especially in such highly consequential areas as budgeting. But that is the case everywhere, not just in such politically charged bodies as legislatures. Most kids want a slice of the action when Mom decides how to spend the grocery and entertainment budget, too. But systems equally open to everyone, systems without clear structure, *do* become chaotic. Whether the Colorado system is in need of the full set of controls now in place is open to debate. It does, however, need controls of some sort.

Currently, the Colorado budget system is a legislative-centered one. Party division and the structure of the budget process have combined to keep it firmly in the hands of the majority party, especially the JBC, its staff, and majority party leadership. The GAVEL amendment has loosened the grip of the majority party caucus to some extent, but the majority still remains in charge.

The system is incremental in nature. For the most part, each budget represents adjustments from past budgets and is not the embodiment of the vision of a new governor or even a new legislature. Indeed, with the 1992 adoption of constitutional "Amendment One" the legislators' inability to embark on anything resembling new directions has been further retarded. Colorado budgets are like most others—marginal adjustments to the status quo, year after year.

Finally, the state's budgeting process has been faulted for being excessively restrictive and cumbersome. Much of this critique leads back to Amendment One of 1992. If the state's revenues in any given year exceed TABOR's limitations, the legislature may not spend the money unless it asks the voters in a statewide election. Similarly, local governments must ask permission of their voters to spend excess funds. This means that, unless money is spent to conduct an election, one year's surplus cannot be used to fill in gaps, such as additional schools or road repairs, that were left unattended in tighter budget times. It means, too, that ordinary citizens, kept busy by jobs, kids, and routines of their own, are called upon to make involved policy judgments.

Critics of TABOR assert that, when supplied with enough time and equipped with sufficient information, most citizens can make good public interest policy choices. But the point of delegating that task to a group of elected representatives is to release most of us from the responsibility of doing what we cannot do well as we attend to our workaday world and daily lives. Amendment One, thus, keeps legislatures from doing what they can do well, and asks busy citizens to do what they cannot do well.

NOTES

1. *Rocky Mountain News*, November 27, 1996.
2. *Colorado Revised Statutes*, 24-3-301.
3. *Colorado Revised Statutes*, 2-3-203(b).
4. *Colorado Revised Statutes*, 2-3-102(1).
5. *Rocky Mountain News*, November 27, 1996.
6. *Capitol Reporter*, April 6, 1994.
7. *Fort Collins Coloradoan*, April 9, 1996.
8. Ibid.
9. Fred Brown, "33 provisions axed in budget-bill signing," *Denver Post*, May 28, 1998.
10. "Gov. brandishes budget vetoes, questions GOP funding priorities," *Denver Post*, May 5, 1998.
11. *Pueblo Chieftain*, April 27, 1998.
12. Comments on Senate floor.
13. "Don't fund out-of-staters," *Denver Post*, May 3, 1998.
14. Jesse Stephenson, "Feeley wants to abolish JBC," *Capitol Reporter*, March 17, 1997.
15. Ibid.
16. Modification of Joint House-Senate Rule 25, contained in House Joint Resolution 98-1025. This new provision is Joint Rule 25(d).

9

The Legislative Process

The previous chapters have examined the participants and institutional elements that are vital parts of the legislative process. In this chapter we stitch it all together, noting how members, the political parties, leaders, committees, and formal rules come together to produce our laws. Chapter 10 illustrates the process by tracking two controversial bills from their inception to enactment.

The Process at First Glance

The legislative process appears simple at first glance. Legislators come up with ideas for bills, and the Office of Legislative Legal Services writes them up in proper form. The bill is introduced into one of the houses and assigned to a committee; this is the "first reading." The committee holds hearings and studies the bill. If the committee supports the bill, it is sent to the floor for debate and a decision in the Committee of the Whole; this is the "second reading." If this vote is favorable, the bill is again put up to a vote on a subsequent day for a "third and final reading," and sent to the other house, where the process is repeated. If the bill makes it successfully through the second house, it goes to the governor for signature. If the governor signs the bill, it is law. If the second house has amended the bill, the first house may agree to those amendments, or a conference committee of members of the two houses may meet to iron out the issues. If they do so successfully and the two houses accept the compromise, it then moves on to the governor. More commonly one chamber will accept the other's amended version.

The formal rules that govern the two houses are very similar, but there are a few differences. In the Senate, motions on the floor and in committee do not need to be seconded; in the House they do, except on second readings. In the Senate, committees must report their action on bills to the Senate within five days of completing work on them. The House allows just three days. The Senate limit on debate time is more generous than that of the House. Voting in the House is done by electronic machine, but the Senate still employs the verbal roll call. Apart from a few other differences, the flow of business is basically the same.

But in practice, things aren't quite so simple and mechanical. The process is long and tedious. Hundreds of bills are flowing through at once. Those who feel strongly, pro or con, about certain bills must constantly seek support, make arguments, compromise, court votes, and count them. There are many places along the way where a bill can be sabotaged. There are always party leaders, committee chairs, colleagues, lobbyists, and members of the press to deal with.

The flow of legislation is not steady throughout a legislative session. In the early days and weeks, lawmakers spend most of their time in committees and relatively little on the floor. This changes, though, as the session progresses and the legislature approaches a series of self-imposed deadlines. There are deadlines for requests to the Office of Legislative Legal Services for the preparation of bills and deadlines for introducing bills and reporting them out of committees and out of the full house in the chamber in which they originate. There are deadlines to move bills out of committees and from the full house in the second chamber. As a result, there are surges of activity during a session. As a deadline for reporting bills from committee approaches, for example, members will spend long days, early mornings, and even evenings in committee hearings and almost none on the floor. That pattern will then reverse itself over the next ten days or so as they rush to complete work on the same bills on second or third reading on the floor. The flow of this process is further affected by the injection of the long budget bill and by the majority party budget caucuses late in the session. The 2000 deadline schedule, shown in Table 9.1, is illustrative.

THE ORIGIN OF BILLS

Bills originate in a variety of ways. Legislators, businesses, local governments, state agencies, and private citizens may want to change, add, or remove laws. And organizations like the Colorado Municipal League, The Colorado Association of Commerce and Industry, the National Rifle Association, and others can play a key role in the development of bills.

Most bills evolve from some form of discussion among sponsoring legislators and the citizens, interest groups, lobbyists, local governments, or state agencies that are pushing them. Indeed, extensive discussion and compromise among interested parties may precede the introduction of a bill, and those pushing it may even have their

Figure 9.1

DEADLINE SCHEDULE FOR THE 2000 COLORADO GENERAL ASSEMBLY
SOURCE: Senate Joint Resolution 99–009

December 1, 1999 (Wednesday)		Initial deadline for members to request bills. In accordance with Joint Rule No. 24 (b) (1) (A) members may not introduce more than five bills. Of the five bills, excluding appropriations and interim bills described in Joint Rule No. 24 (b) (1) (D), not more than two bills may be requested **after** December 1.
December 31, 1999 (Friday)		Deadline for filing one of each member's three bills requested prior to December 1 pursuant to Joint Rule 23 (a) (2) and Joint Rule 24 (b) (1) (A) with the house of introduction for printing, distribution to Legislative Council for preparation of fiscal notes, and introduction on 1st day.
January 5, 2000 (Wednesday)		**General Assembly convenes.** Deadline for the introduction of the bills required to be filed 5 days prior to the 1st day.
		Deadline for introduction of any bills to increase the number of judges.
January 7, 2000 (Friday)	3rd Day	Deadline for introduction of the two remaining **Senate** bills requested prior to December 1 pursuant to Joint Rules 23 (a) (2) and 24 (b) (1) (A).
January 10, 2000 (Monday)	6th Day	Deadline for introduction of the two remaining **House** bills requested prior to the December 1 pursuant to Joint Rules 23 (a) (2) and 24 (b) (1) (A).
		Deadline for bill draft requests to the Office of Legislative Legal Services.
January 21, 2000 (Friday)	17th Day	Deadline for introduction of **Senate** bills, except the Long Bill.
January 26, 2000 (Wednesday)	22nd Day	Deadline for introduction of **House** bills, except the Long Bill.
February 3, 2000 (Thursday)	30th Day	Deadline for **House** committees to report House bills introduced on or before the 6th legislative day.*
		Deadline for Capital Development Committee and appropriate committees of reference to complete review of executive department budgets. (Joint Rule 25 (d))
February 10, 2000 (Thursday)	37th Day	Deadline for **Senate** committees of reference to report Senate bills.*
February 17, 1999 (Thursday)	44th Day	Deadline for **House** committees of reference to report remaining House bills.*
February 23, 2000 (Wednesday)	50th Day	Deadline for final passage of **Senate** bills in the Senate.*
		Deadline for final passage of **House** bills in the House.*
March 3, 2000 (Friday)	59th Day	Deadline for final passage of any bill that increases the number of judges.
March 10, 2000 (Friday)	66th Day	Deadline for final passage, including any conference committee report, for any bill prescribing all or a substantial portion of the total funding for public schools pursuant to the "Public Finance Act of 1994", Article 54 of Title 22, C.R.S.

Figure 9.1—*continued*

March 17, 2000 (Friday)	73rd Day	Deadline for committees of reference to report bills originating in the other house.*
March 20, 2000 (Monday)	76th Day	Deadline for introduction of the Long Bill in the **House**.
March 24, 2000 (Friday)	80th Day	Deadline for final passage of Long Bill in the **House**.
March 27, 2000 (Monday)	83rd Day	Deadline in even-numbered years for final passage in the **Senate** of all bills originating in the House.*
March 31, 2000 (Friday)	87th Day	Deadline for final passage of Long Bill in the **Senate**.
April 3, 2000 (Monday)	90th Day	Deadline in even-numbered years for final passage in the **House** of all bills originating in the Senate.*
April 7, 2000 (Friday)	94th Day	Deadline for adoption of conference committee report on Long Bill.
		Deadline for Appropriations Committee in house of introduction to report bills referred to Appropriations Committee.
April 13, 2000 (Thursday)	100th Day	Last day to introduce Resolutions. (Joint Rule 23 (g))
April 14, 2000 (Friday)	101st Day	Deadline for final passage in house of introduction of all bills referred to Appropriations Committee in that house.
April 21, 2000 (Friday)	108th Day	Deadline for Appropriations Committee in second house to report bills referred to Appropriations Committee.
April 26, 2000 (Wednesday)	113th Day	Deadline for final passage in second house of all bills referred to Appropriations Committee in that house.
May 1, 2000 (Monday)	118th Day	If there has been adjournment to a day certain, reconvene for adjournment sine die unless the joint resolution for adjournment to a day certain specifies another day for reconvening.
May 3, 2000 (Wednesday)	120th Day	Deadline for adjournment sine die.

* All bills in the Appropriations Committee in either house on the day of the asterisked deadline are excluded from these deadlines

attorneys draft something for submission to the Office of Legislative Legal Services.

Sometimes legislators are prompted to introduce bills by some personal experience, or the experience of an acquaintance. Representative Debbie Allen, for example, sponsored a bill to improve communication among county law enforcement officials about restraining orders issued by judges against violent domestic partners. The impetus for this was the experience of her daughter, who had been a victim of domestic violence. Senator Joan Johnson introduced an insurance reform bill as a result of an accident that had led to some frustrating hassles with insurance companies. Representative Bob Hagedorn sponsored a bill that would have required special zebra-striped auto license plates on the cars of repeat drunk-driving offenders; Hagedorn himself had a history of alcohol problems. And Mike Salaz carried an anti–phone slamming bill after he had been the victim of the practice.

A significant portion of the legislature's agenda is created by business and industry seeking changes in law. Good examples are two 1999 bills carried respectively by Representative Jack Taylor on behalf of US West and Representative Gary McPherson for the National Rifle Association. Taylor's bill, drafted initially by the telecommunications company itself, was intended to bolster US West's competitive position. McPherson's and the NRA's gun bill would have provided state preemption of local gun ordinances.

Some bills are designed to legalize practices that already exist. For example, as a result of the 1997 flood in Fort Collins, which greatly affected Colorado State University, a bill was introduced to authorize the state controller to allow agencies to overexpend in emergencies. That already happened from time to time, but the bill, which passed easily, provided statutory authority for the existing practice.

While the Legal Services Office is working on the language of a bill, supportive lobbyists, in addition to the sponsoring legislator, may work directly with Legislative Legal Services personnel. A good example is provided by the lotto legislation passed some years ago. Prior to introduction, the supportive Colorado Municipal League, lobbyists for gambling system vendors, and the bill sponsor worked together. Of course, whether the legislator has scribbled it in ink on a paper napkin or had it prepared by an attorney, the bill had to be formally drafted by the Office of Legislative Legal Services before introduction into either house.

All bills are not born equal. Sponsorship can affect the fate of a bill. Those sponsored by members of leadership, especially in the majority party, have the best chance of passing; a bill with a majority party sponsor will often make it, but the same bill with a minority party sponsor may not. It also doesn't hurt a bill's chances to carry the sponsorship of the chairperson of the committee that hears the measure. All bills must have at least one sponsor in each house, and many bills will carry the names of a half dozen or even a dozen legislators. The more sponsors, the more likely it is that the bill will pass since the cosponsors will have already committed their support. Interest groups and legislators alike are aware of this, so part of the strategy is to gain bill sponsorship from well-placed and influential lawmakers.

There are limits to the number of bills legislators may introduce, although these limits have proven to be rather elastic. They may introduce up to five, according to the rules, apart from appropriations bills, and two others if they are the product of interim committees. There is no limit on the number of bills first introduced in the other house on which a legislator may be the prime cosponsor in his or her own chamber. In each house, the leadership may grant late-bill status and waivers to the bill limits, as well. In 1999, roughly 18 percent of Senate bills and nearly 25 percent of House bills had late-bill status.

THE STRUCTURE OF BILLS

Some bills change just a few words in the statutes. Some repeal existing law. Others establish new programs or new regulations. A few appropriate money for the coming year.

Bills are numbered consecutively, beginning with number 1 in the Senate and 1001 in the House; each bill also carries a two-digit prefix indicating the year of the session. At the top of a bill is its number, the names of its sponsors, and the bill title. Titles must be carefully written; by constitutional provision, each bill may address just one subject.

A brief summary written in "lay" language follows the bill title, and below that are the contents of the bill itself. The first line of the bill is always an "enacting" clause that reads, "Be it enacted by the General Assembly of the State of Colorado," and the last section is often a "safety" clause, shielding the bill from susceptibility to a referendum petition if the bill is passed. Just above the safety clause there may be a "severability" clause, which protects the balance of a law from extinction should one portion of it later be declared unconstitutional. (See Figure 9.2.)

Between the enacting clause and these final two clauses lie the guts of the measure. A bill that proposes rather broad additions or changes in law may provide that certain sections of law be repealed and reenacted with the wording that then follows. For simpler modifications, the bill may reprint an existing statute with new language showing in capital letters and lines drawn through the words to be deleted. It is not unusual to hear sponsors describe their bills in committee hearings this

Figure 9.2

Second Regular Session

Sixty-second General Assembly
LLS NO. 00-0955.01 Julie Hoerner   SENATE BILL 00-205

STATE OF COLORADO   AGRICULTURE, NATURAL
                                RESOURCES & ENERGY
BY SENATOR Wattenberg.

A BILL FOR AN ACT

101   CONCERNING A LIMITATION ON THE STATE'S LIABILITY REGARDING

102   ELIGIBLE DAMAGE TO COMMERCIAL AGRICULTURAL RESOURCES

103   CAUSED BY WILDLIFE.

Bill Summary

(Note: This summary applies to this bill as introduced and does not necessarily reflect any amendments that may be subsequently adopted.)

Clarifies that the state is only liable for wildlife damage caused to commercial agricultural products and commercial agricultural property within the constraints of the provisions of the damage by wildlife laws.

Adds a $25,000 cap per occurrence caused to commercial agricultural property and commercial agricultural products.

---

1   *Be it enacted by the General Assembly of the State of Colorado:*

2   **SECTION 1.** 33-3-102, Colorado Revised Statutes, is amended

3   to read:

4   **33-3-102. State's liability for damage.** The state of Colorado is

5   liable for certain ~~damages~~ DAMAGE TO COMMERCIAL AGRICULTURAL

6   PRODUCTS AND COMMERCIAL AGRICULTURAL PROPERTY caused by

7   wildlife, but only to the extent provided in this article. THE MAXIMUM

8   AMOUNT THAT MAY BE RECOVERED UNDER THIS ARTICLE FOR ANY SINGLE

1   OCCURRENCE SHALL BE TWENTY-FIVE THOUSAND DOLLARS.

2   **SECTION 2. Effective date - applicability.** This act shall take

3   effect July 1, 2000, and shall apply to damage to commercial agricultural

4   products and commercial agricultural property committed on or after said

5   date.

6   **SECTION 3. Safety clause.** The general assembly hereby finds,

7   determines, and declares that this act is necessary for the immediate

8   preservation of the public peace, health, and safety.

Capital letters indicate new material to be added to existing statute.
Dashes through the words indicate deletions from existing statute.

way: "This bill makes a couple of corrections in what we did two years ago" or "When we heard this bill last year. . . ."

Tight Title

It has long been common practice in the United States Congress to package a host of unrelated measures into a single "mega" bill or "omnibus" bill, as it is often called. Colorado's constitution forbids such a practice in the General Assembly. A constitutional provision entitled "Bill to contain but one subject—expressed in title" goes on to say that the subject "shall be clearly expressed in its title" and any provisions not expressed in the title are null and void.

These constitutional provisos are sometimes called the single subject and tight title requirements. It is common in both committee and floor debate to hear members ask the chair to rule whether proposed amendments "fit under the title."

The matters of single subject and tight title can be of significant political controversy and consequence. Members will sometimes look for bills with titles similar to that of one of theirs that died, with the notion of offering the contents of the dead bill as an amendment to the live one with the similar title. The chair then must rule as to the fit between the amendment and the title of the bill that is before the committee or the chamber. Sometimes members will introduce bills with rather broad titles, stretching the language as far as possible. The objective is to keep alive, in reserve, a bill that can then be filled with content toward the end of the session, content that may have been in bills that are already dead and buried.

Assignments to Committees

Just as there are politics in bill sponsorship, so are there politics in the assignment of bills to committee. After a bill has been properly drafted and printed, it is introduced in the chamber of its prime sponsor. This is called the first reading and involves no more than a reading of the title, receipt of a bill number, and assignment to one or more committees of reference. The first two matters are routine. But the assignment to committee is not an automatic affair. Indeed, committee assignment can literally mean life or death for a bill.

The Speaker of the House and the Senate President have full discretion over committee assignments. They can do the sponsor a favor and give a bill a good start by sending it to a friendly committee; conversely, they can kill it with a bad assignment. Former House Speaker Bev Bledsoe's assignment of a bill to restrict smoking in public places to the House State Affairs Committee and Senate President Strickland's placement of Bledsoe's tax limit resolution in the hands of three committees are cases in point; both measures were effectively "dead on arrival." So too were a number of concealed weapons bills that in recent years have passed the House only to be killed by way of assignment to the Senate Judiciary Conmmittee.

In 1998 Senate President Norton sent a bill that would have criminalized female genital mutilation to the Committee on Health, Environment, Welfare, and Institutions. This HEWI Committee had a majority of women and was predictably supportive. The bill passed both the committee and the full Senate. When it got to the House the Speaker put the bill in the State Affairs Committee, which passed it on to Appropriations, which killed the bill. No surprise. But in 1999 with a less conservative Speaker, the same bill was sent to a more friendly House committee after again passing successfully through the Senate. The bill made it out of committee, out of the House, the governor signed it, and it is now law.

In reverse, the Speaker sent a bill placing some strictures on public school sex education to State Affairs, a committee knowingly sympathetic to the topic. It passed. In the Senate, President Norton put it in the hands of HEWI, which killed it. No surprise.

The Speaker controls the appointment of chairs and members to House committees, and knows the complexion of his or her committees well. The Senate President's control is a bit different, but he or she, too, knows the committees.

BILLS IN COMMITTEES

The treatment that bills receive in committee isn't always automatic or kindly either. In fact, this is where bills often die or are heavily amended. In the past, committee chairs have had the power to kill bills by way of the pocket veto—by not scheduling hearings on a bill at all, by waiting until the last few days prior to a deadline when a stack of bills may be postponed indefinitely, or by letting the deadline for reporting bills out of committee lapse, leaving the bills still in committee to die. Someone estimated that around eighty bills died in the House Appropriations Committee in one past session with the expiration of the reporting deadline. But today, even with the pocket veto gone, committee chairs still find ways to kill bills. House Appropriations chairs sometimes schedule hearings so late that the chambers cannot act even when the bills come out.

Bills are sometimes sent to more than one committee, and that second or third committee may well be House or Senate Appropriations, where budget realities often spell doom. Recently, for example, the Senate Education Committee amended a new school finance act repeatedly, adding significantly to the cost. Days later, the Senate Appropriations

Committee removed the enriching amendments because, in its judgment, the money to pay for the Education Committee's provisions would not be available.

Appropriations Committees often dispense doom even when there is little or no money involved. Three 1998 bills are illustrative. A bill by Democratic Representative Penn Tate to change the name of crimes involving ethnic intimidation to "hate crimes," with some attendant increase in penalties, was killed in House Appropriations on a party-line vote even though the fiscal impact was minimal. Republican Steve Johnson's bill to limit telemarketing calls died in the same committee because, as a lobbyist and one committee member confessed, it was lobbied to death after it had passed the committee of reference. Among Representative Johnson's responses was to tell fellow Republican and Appropriations Committee Chairman Tony Grampsas, "From now on when the telemarketers call my home I'm going to tell them that I don't welcome their calls but I have a friend who likes them and his name is Tony Grampsas." A Senate bill to control water pollution and odor from large corporate hog farms met the same fate in Senate Appropriations, again, for reasons unrelated to money, which supposedly is the committee's concern.

From time to time, efforts have been made to counter the power that committees and their chairs have employed to stop bills dead in their tracks by use of a rule that provides for a "blast." A blast (technically called a "demand" in the rules) is simply a procedure whereby a majority vote of thirty-three in the House or a two-thirds vote of twenty-four in the Senate can force a bill out of committee and onto the floor for consideration by the full body. With the GAVEL amendment requirement that all bills be scheduled for some sort of committee action, the need for a blast procedure has been significantly lessened.

Of course, the demand procedure is unlikely to work in any case. Since it takes a majority in the House and two-thirds in the Senate, the blast attempt would have to have majority party support, and members are disinclined to support a precedent to forcibly take bills from committees for fear that, in the future, the same procedure might be used on them. In addition, members of the majority party leadership and committee chairs want to preserve their power, so they discourage blasts.

Some years back, the House Democrats attempted to blast several of their bills free of committees whose chairs would not release them. Three of them were sponsored by the minority leader. Before the blast attempt, she noted, "I've never seen a successful blast."[1] Her experience remained unchanged as all attempts to call up the bills failed. Commenting on the matter, the House Speaker said he thought the discharge of bills by way of the demand procedure undermined the committee system. It is little wonder, then, that Republican majority members did not cross over to help release minority party bills.

It is in the committees of reference that bills receive their most intense scrutiny. Committees specialize by subject matter and members gravitate to the committees of most interest, and thus committees collectively are repositories of considerable expertise. Most modification of bills is done in committee, and most bills pass successfully from committee to the floor. And most of the time the fate of a bill in committee is known well before hearings even begin. Both bill sponsors and interested lobbyists busily seek and count votes early on; the result is that while testimony may trigger some amendments, it rarely determines the actual fate of a measure.

THEATER

For pure theater it's hard to beat a legislative committee. This isn't because what goes on in committees isn't serious or doesn't matter much. Bills are important, and they do have consequences. Rather, committees are entertaining because of the personalities, both on committees themselves and among those who come to testify or watch.

Not all committee action is the same, but the differences don't have much to do with the importance of the legislation. Some topics and some bills draw crowds and some don't. Some hearings attract television cameras and reporters like flies; others are nearly empty. Among the favorites in recent years are hearings on bills having to do with guns and motorcycle helmets. Bills of this sort seem to draw their own crowd of true believers in large numbers.

One day early in a recent session there were two such hearings on a single day in the old Supreme Court chambers, which are used as a hearing room when large audiences are expected. In the morning it was a bill to require motorcycle riders to wear helmets. It had been introduced by different legislators in recent years but every year the scene is the same. Folks from the medical profession, the State Department of Transportation, and, of course, the bill sponsor would trot out loads of statistics to prove that accident injuries are much more severe for cyclists when it's their unprotected bare heads that hit the pavement or dent fenders. Not only are the riders at risk, but so is the public that ends up picking up some of the tab for expensive medical treatment and rehabilitation. But year after year and hearing after hearing, the bikers outnumber helmet proponents, and year after year they win. The bills die. You can tell when a helmet law is up by the appearance of leather jackets, long hair, chains, boots, and blue jeans.

The same day was also one of many gun days at the legislature. The National Rifle Association and its members were swarming all over the place. They were present to protect their right to carry guns and to make sure that everybody else can carry one too. The hearing was on a House bill proposed by Representative Drew Clark from Boulder. It would have made it easy to obtain a concealed weapons permit. Indeed, it would have made it difficult for law enforcement to say "no" to anybody who wanted one, so long as the applicant was of age and had no recent felony convictions.

Clark was a Republican from Boulder. He was an avid right-to-lifer and extremely conservative on most matters. He barely survived, and some say he didn't rightfully survive, a write-in challenge by Democrat Peggy Lamm. Clark had engineered a surprising primary defeat of an incumbent and the Democrats hadn't bothered to put up a candidate, assuming that the incumbent would win easily. But that didn't happen and when the Democrats had no one on the ballot to oppose him, Lamm entered as a write-in candidate. The contest was close and eventually went to court. Democrats argued that many of the ballots that were cast for Lamm should be counted even if her first name was misspelled, as it often was. Had all such ballots been counted, she would have won. Indeed, Clark later lost to Lamm and thus served just a single term. In any case, Clark, a controversial candidate and controversial winner, was in committee with a gun bill.

A big crowd was expected, and so the hearing was scheduled in a large hearing room in the Legislative Services Building. Indeed, there was an overflow crowd. The door to the hearing room was locked and not opened until 1:15 P.M. for the hearing, which was scheduled to begin at 1:30 P.M. All the chairs were taken quickly and shortly thereafter the committee chair announced that the hearing would be moved back across the street to the Capitol in the old Supreme Court chambers, which seated even more people. A mad dash followed.

The gun crowd is entertaining, but not nearly as colorful as the helmet group. Their uniforms tend to be blue and tan rather than black and brown. The footwear is just as costly but tends to be made of soft brown leather with tassels, not black with chains. As is the case with helmet law hearings, there is an abundance of television cameras and reporters all around.

It's a curious phenomenon. One may wonder why there is so much coverage of motorcycle helmet and gun legislation whereas hearings where big money is at stake often go virtually unattended. A committee like Business Affairs and Labor may hear bills that involve taxes, insurance, and workers' compensation, and the financial stakes may be enormous but the participants comparatively few. One is reminded of Murray Edelman's observation in his classic book, *The Symbolic Uses of Politics*, to the effect that the masses consume symbols while the active and attentive folks collect the policy advantages and the money.

At any rate the audience of 200 moved across the street, to the old Supreme Court chambers. Every seat was taken and there was standing room only along the back and down the side aisles. An hour after the hearing was supposed to start, Chairman Ratterree finally asked the staff member to call the roll. Sponsor Clark was invited to introduce his bill and did so, terming it a "citizens self-defense bill designed to put law abiding citizens on a par with the criminals." As is common in these committees, Clark already had amendments to his own bill. One of them raised the age requirement for a concealed weapons permit from sixteen to eighteen.

There was opposition. The League of Women Voters' lobbyist testified that more guns in the hands of citizens would mean more accidents. This made sense to some, but it got a host of knowing smirks from the gun enthusiasts seated all around. The league lobbyist said the Women Voters recognized a constitutional right to own arms for sporting purposes. This too drew chuckles from the crowd. Committee member Charles Duke from Colorado Springs asked her for hard data on the number of accidents; she said she didn't have any, but it seems to make sense that there would be more accidents involving guns, as more people carried them. Chairman Ratterree, also from Colorado Springs, asked her if she knew what current law was; she said she did generally, but not in great detail. The gun supporters seemed warmed by the questioning.

The league voice was followed by a lobbyist for the Fraternal Order of Police. He told the committee that his cops don't oppose having citizens legally carry nonlethal weapons such as pepper and gas. This triggered still more knowing chuckles from the gun people. The FOP man continued. Cops do, however, oppose concealed weapons in environments where alcohol may be present.

The chairman took the opportunity to make a short speech. He told the lobbyist that he, the lobbyist, talks to the cops but not to fearful citizens, and the chairman then proceeded to lecture the police lobbyist. The lobbyist responded, and the crowd laughed. Vice Chairman Duke kept the theater going by telling the FOP man that he, Duke, talked to a cop who said he'd never had a gun pulled on him by an honest citizen. There was laughter and applause. The police lobbyist said that he'd been face to face with a gun—no laughter, no applause.

The hearing continued when the state District Attorney's Council lobbyist testified that the D.A.s opposed a law mandating issuance of concealed weapons permits, except under certain conditions. In some instances, concealment was acceptable to the D.A.s, but not in all circumstances. Vice Chairman Duke proceeded to tell the witness that his constituents think that the D.A.s are part of the problem, because it's the D.A.s who plea-bargain away many of the charges against gun users. The vice chair instructed the lobbyist to tell that to his D.A.s. The lobbyist retorted that he would try every case that was brought to him if he had the money to do so. The implication, of course, was that legislators fail to appropriate enough money.

Others followed. Felix Sparks was a former Colorado Supreme Court judge. He argued that when a person starts to shoot, particularly someone who is untrained in the use of firearms, there tends to be a spray effect and innocents are likely to die. This drew a great deal of derisive laughter from some, which in turn drew the chairman's gavel.

The Westminster chief of police represented the Colorado Association of Chiefs of Police. The Denver police chief spoke, as did a lobbyist for the Colorado domestic violence coalition, who feared for the well-being of battered women who might now be shot as well as battered.

The proponents testified also, later in the day and on into the evening. The committee passed the bill out favorably. It died on the House floor.

Much of the gun show was symbolic—a contest between people who are convinced that the widespread possession of guns leads to violence and those who for whatever reasons of ideology or psychology are sure that the republic is headed down the drain if strictures of any sort are placed on the use of weapons.

CONFUSION

A bill in the House Judiciary Committee illustrated a number of characteristics of the legislative process, including one way bills originate; how seemingly simple legislative proposals can turn out to be enormously complex and confusing, even to the bill sponsor; and how the partisan nature of the legislature is manifest in committees as it is elsewhere in the process.

The bill at hand was one sponsored by Republican Representative Debbie Allen. It was designed to create a central state registry of restraining orders issued by county courts and designed to keep potentially violent individuals away from the people they've threatened—usually ex-wives or girlfriends. Representative Allen was prompted to propose the legislation because of her own daughter's tragic experience as a domestic violence victim, which had been reported some months prior in a major *Rocky Mountain News* feature. Thus, for Representative Allen, this was a very personal matter. Interestingly, the bill was being heard before a Judiciary Committee composed of thirteen members, nine of whom were women, including the chair and the vice chair of the committee. Allen clearly had a sympathetic audience.

The confusing character of the bill was evident at the outset. Representative Allen opened her discussion by noting that she had a very extensive amendment, indeed a number of amendments, to the bill. This is not unusual because after bills are printed in their original form, a variety of parties who have an interest in the bill immediately visit with the sponsor and suggest amendments. Discussions then transpire and compromises are worked out. The result is that by the time the committee begins hearings the sponsor may come in not only with the bill itself, but with a whole series of amendments. Apparently there were many parties with an interest in this particular bill, because Representative Allen said at the outset that she found herself confused, didn't understand some parts of the bill, and was going to rely on witnesses to help explain it not only to the committee, but to herself.

It can look odd to a casual observer to have a sponsor unable to understand his or her own bill. That's not unusual, though, particularly when there are many interested parties and a lot of fingers in the pie.

There was a good deal of testimony, largely from folks in law enforcement. They included the Aurora chief of police, a representative from the Colorado Municipal League, a judge from a county court in Boulder, and a member of the Colorado Judicial Department. By and large they were all supportive but pointed out some of the complicated features. Among those was the potential of inadvertently edging county courts, which issue restraining orders, into the business of awarding temporary child custody and dividing property on a temporary basis. This could be a problem because it is the district courts, not the county courts, that handle divorces, and it is in divorce proceedings where child custody and property division decisions are made.

So here was a bill designed to do something rather simple. It was to create a statewide registry of restraining orders so that the law enforcement officers in each county would have knowledge of orders issued by courts in other counties, thus making it easier to track and enforce them. Presumably, then, fewer women would be victimized by persons under a restraining order from different counties. But it wasn't that simple, apparently because the issuance of the restraining orders in the county courts might complicate the jurisdictional relations of county courts and district courts.

Even when a bill has broad bipartisan support like this one, the partisan character of the legislature rears its head. At one point Democratic Representative DeGette, herself a lawyer, moved to strike a section of the bill. The bill's sponsor, Debbie Allen, objected, but a couple of moments later Representative Russell George, a Republican, made precisely the same suggestion and Representative Allen said she had no objections.

FLOOR ACTION

When bills are successfully reported out of committee, the next step is to move to the floor for second reading. Committee chairs have five days in the Senate and three days in the House to file reports of committee action with their chamber. This is virtually always done in routine fashion, although there have been instances when chairs have stalled, thus killing a bill.

The calendars of the two chambers, issued daily, set forth the order of business and list the bills, resolutions, and other matters that constitute the agenda for the day. Just as there is a format for the ways bills are structured and written, so is there a predetermined order of business that the two chambers follow as they conduct their daily work.

Each day begins with a prayer, a call to order, the roll call, and approval of the journal of the previous day's business. Reports from committees of reference and messages from the other house or governor are received, and new bills, resolutions, and memorials are then introduced. Following all this, the chambers attend to third readings of bills. In most cases, any serious debate will have occurred and amendments will have been made in committee and on the floor during second reading, so third readings typically move quickly, with little or no discussion. The final, and recorded, vote is then taken. Indeed, leadership often discourages third-reading amendments in the interest of time. As many as forty or fifty bills can be passed on third reading in a single day.

The calendar is sometimes altered, with matters held over to another time or day. Sometimes the majority leader may move for "special orders" for a bill, thereby assigning it to a special place on the calendar. This may be done to give a bill sponsor additional time to prepare for debate, to negotiate compromises, or to muster additional support. Or the daily calendar may be adjusted on the spot to exploit the presence or the absence of certain members or accommodate the preferences of the bill sponsor.

Furthermore, the amount of time spent on any one category of business depends on where the General Assembly is in the session. At the start, in January and February, there will be few third readings because bills have not yet passed through the committees and the second readings. Near the end, entire days can be consumed with third readings, as well as consideration of bills that have now made it through the other chamber and come back in amended form.

Except when there are alterations of the daily calendar, third readings are followed by what is called "General Orders," when second readings occur. Here, the chamber meets as a Committee of the Whole. The Speaker or Senate President steps out of the chair and someone else presides over the body. Bills are introduced and debated, one after another. The amendments made in committee are recommended and brought up for debate and vote. Amendments and amendments-to-amendments may be moved from the floor, and votes are taken. Frequently, efforts are made during second readings of bills to restore provisions that were cut from a bill in the other house or to reattach provisions that were removed in committee. In debate over a school finance bill, for example, a senator tried to amend the bill—which originated in the House of Representatives—to require school boards in districts where student performance was judged poor to fire their superintendents. To a bill designed to increase insurance payments for mental health costs, two senators attached amendments to curtail the number of counseling sessions covered and reduce the amount that could be charged to patients. In the House, a representative attempted to weaken an air quality bill by amending it to require legislative approval of emission standards set by the Colorado Air Quality Control Commission. A similar move had been made on the same bill in the Senate. It succeeded initially, but was later removed. And so it goes; supporters and opponents alike, on bill after bill, have opportunities to change them both in committee and on the floor of both houses, and the successes of a group in one forum may be reversed in another.

The debate can get rough. In a House second-reading floor debate over a bill to cap the size of awards that juries could approve in medical malpractice suits, a Democratic representative suggested that the insurance industry had bamboozled and flimflammed the public and legislators and had used them by saying that premium rates would go up if such caps were not imposed. The Republican sponsor of the bill responded by asking if the Democrat was saying that he had "flimflammed" the public. Another Republican joined in, suggesting that the Democrat had offended his colleague and should apologize. The response was that it was the industry, not the representative, that had done the flimflamming and bamboozling.

In the Senate a Republican argued that a Republican colleague and others had ample opportunity to amend a bill related to water quality, which they opposed on the floor, and said it was irresponsible for them to waste those opportunities and now oppose the bill. The reply was, "You vote as you please, and so will I. I respond to my constituents and my conscience, and not to what you think I should support."

Second-reading debates are rather informal, and members may speak over and over again. They wander in and out of the chamber—for coffee, to return phone calls, to visit the restroom, and for a string of contacts with the lobbyists who mill around endlessly just outside the glass at the rear of the House and Senate chambers. The lobbyists have the House and Senate sergeants-at-arms call the lawmakers out constantly, and legislators often go out on their own to consult or to seek information and cues. Only legislators and their invited guests are allowed inside the chambers; lobbyists are not.

Often it appears that there are only three people paying attention— the bill sponsor, someone at the podium opposing the measure, and the sleepy chap whom the floor leaders have asked to preside. But at other times, everyone is awake and alert.

Obviously, then, many of the critical arguments and votes are made during second readings. But second-reading votes are unrecorded voice votes. Legislators may, as a result, vote one way on recorded committee and third-reading votes and the other way on second-reading voice votes. There is not a widespread pattern of reversing positions between public and nonpublic votes. But legislators sometimes do attempt to weaken bills through second-reading amendments that they will not oppose in recorded and public votes.

When the second-reading consideration of bills is finished for the day, the membership will "rise and report" its actions to the formal House or Senate. The chamber, as a Committee of the Whole, is thus reporting its actions on each bill—was it passed, amended, defeated?— to the chamber sitting then as the formal House or Senate. The members then vote to accept the report of the Committee of the Whole. This vote is recorded.

Legislators, especially members of the minority party, will sometimes use this occasion to seek to reverse an earlier Committee of the Whole vote, or to force a public recording of the position of the membership on particular bills or amendments. They do this by moving to amend the Committee of the Whole report to show that a given bill did or did not pass. This move rarely kills a bill that has received second-reading approval or revives one that has not, but it does force members to participate in a vote where their positions are recorded. Thus, such moves to amend the report of the Committee of the Whole will put legislators on record, a record that can then be cited in the next election campaign.

There are occasions, however, when substantive changes are made by successfully amending the Committee of the Whole report. A Colorado Springs–area representative, after narrowly failing to garner majority support for an amendment to a school finance bill to help the schools in her district, got the needed majority thirty minutes later when she offered the same amendment to the Committee of the Whole report. That thirty-minute span was the key; it gave the lobbyists out in the hallway enough time to move three or four votes.

In a somewhat more spectacular show, Republican Barry Arrington managed to employ post-second-reading amendments to the Committee of the Whole report to rescue two bills that had been defeated following second-reading debate. The first amendment saved a "make my day" bill liberalizing home owners' right to forcefully defend against intruders. The second was intended to rescue a bill permanently cutting the state income tax. But for the second bill, Arrington seemed to be lacking the votes he needed.

So he moved a "call of the House" to compel the return of six members who had been excused for the day. The missing members were needed to give Arrington his majority. His "call" was in itself controversial, for the House rules seem to render properly excused members immune from the demand to return. At least that's what both Republican Majority Leader Norma Anderson and Democratic Minority Leader Carol Snyder thought. Anderson showed Speaker Berry the rule book but it made no difference. Arrington's call stood, members returned, some from far out of town, and the report of the Committee of the Whole was amended. The bill thus passed second reading and the next day it passed out of the House on third and final reading.

Arrington's maneuver had kept House members captive for hours and many weren't happy. So he bought them pizza. Democrat Jim Dyer wouldn't eat it; "Judas food," he said.[2] Some weeks later the Senate killed the tax-cut bill in Senate Appropriations.

Other tactics employed include moves to reconsider a bill right after final passage, and to strike the enacting clause. Bills are subject to motions for reconsideration only once, so immediately upon passage, the sponsor may move for reconsideration and obtain a "no" vote. This keeps the bill alive and prevents further efforts to reconsider the measure. Striking the enacting clause of a bill renders the bill itself without effect. Former House member Peggy Reeves, later a state senator, made such a motion on a bill that would have altered the composition of the State Board of Agriculture, which governs Colorado State University in her district. The motion, which carried, was made during second reading and thus allowed members to participate in the bill's demise in an unrecorded vote.

Occasionally a motion to reconsider is made in an effort to save a bill that has previously lost. A somewhat spectacular and controversial instance involved a 1999 measure to decrease workers' compensation benefits. The measure originated in the House, and passed, but in the Senate it died on a 17–17 vote. Only those on the prevailing side may move reconsideration, but here leadership allowed Senator Bran Sullivant, who had voted no, to make such a motion and subsequently break the tie by voting yes. Further, while tradition has it that party floor leaders have priority in recognition from the chair, Senate President Powers passed over Democratic Floor Leader Feeley to recognize Sullivant. Had Feeley been recognized first, he could have made the same motion and then controlled further action on the bill for a period of forty-eight hours.

Democrats exploded in anger over a perceived breach of protocol and courtesy, interpreting the entire episode as an unfair use of the rules and "abuse of power" to run roughshod over the minority party. They also alleged that Sullivant's sudden conversion was a product of inappropriate arm-twisting by Department of Labor Director Vickie Armstrong on the Senate floor. Indeed, the event led to a nose-to-nose rostrum confrontation between Democratic Floor Leader Feeley and Republican Assistant Floor Leader Ken Chlouber.

Later in the session in something of a tit-for-tat, Democratic Assistant Floor Leader Bill Thiebaut stopped the Senate in its tracks by moving reconsideration of a motion to approve the Committee of the Whole report and lay over a series of additional bills, thus tying up a listing of thirty bills for the forty-eight hours during which he controlled the calendar.[3] Thiebaut's move was stimulated by his intense opposition to a bill designed to protect churches from suits for harm done by their priests and pastors. Thiebaut's maneuver worked, as the bill later died.

Once in a while members will sink a bill by overloading it with amendments. That's what happened to a bill by Senator Charles Duke, and his colleagues had fun doing it. Duke's bill would have mandated inclusion in public school curricula of certain historical American political readings, including the constitution and its amendments; Hamilton, Madison, and John Jay's Federalist Papers; and some others. Many senators were uncomfortable with the proposition of specifying required reading in schools, but they really didn't want to blatantly reject such respected documents.

So they piled on. Amendments were made to add to the required reading list the Mayflower Compact, Lincoln's second inaugural address, Kennedy's inaugural address, Franklin Roosevelt's inaugural address, eight U.S. Supreme Court opinions, and teachings about the battle of Puebla Mexica and the start of the women's movement in 1848. They rejected the addition of Martin Luther King Jr.'s "I Have a Dream" speech and the treaty of Guadalupe-Hidalgo.

The load was enough to kill the bill but unlike his fellow senators, Charles Duke was not amused. Said Duke of his colleagues, "They can just be the Marxist-Leninists that they really are at heart."[4]

There is yet another way to abort a measure, and that is to recommit the bill to another committee. That is what happened to a 1997 partial-birth abortion bill. It passed successfully out of the House State Affairs Committee, but it was an issue that many members, moderate Republicans especially, would prefer to avoid. So rather than letting it get to a third-reading recorded vote, a Republican and Democratic coalition produced a majority to ship the measure to House Judiciary, a committee philosophically and behaviorally quite unlike State Affairs. The House Judiciary Committee then killed the bill in a tranquil process that, nonetheless, produced a tantrum by sponsor Representative Arrington.

At least one day must pass after second reading before the chamber may hear a bill on third and final reading. There have been rare instances when a bill has been passed on second reading late in the evening of one day, then passed on third reading just after midnight, technically the next day. To pass on third reading, bills must receive the support of a majority of all members, not just of those present. Those numbers are thirty-three votes in the House and eighteen in the Senate. Votes on many bills are bipartisan, passing with very large margins. Results of all third-reading votes are printed in the public record.

When bills are passed on third reading, members are offered the opportunity to be listed as cosponsors. This creates artificially inflated legislative records and permits members to say in campaigns that they sponsored dozens of bills. Being a cosponsor to a long series of bills no doubt provides an accurate picture of the lawmaker's policy preferences. But it also constitutes a complete distortion of the legislator's actual work and record.

There are times, too, when legislators will want a bill to pass but not want to vote for it for political reasons (or vice versa). Many would like to see their colleagues vote for bills on legislative pay raises, for example, and thus let them take the political heat.

On rare occasions, members will seek to defeat their own bills on the floor. This happened when the Republican majority in the House State Affairs Committee amended a bill by Democrat Peggy Kerns that would have required the governor to appoint someone of the same party to the U.S. Senate when vacancies occurred. That was not the intent of Kerns's bill. Her efforts to kill it failed on the House floor, but it died in committee in the Senate.

There are also times when bills slip quickly through one house before opponents become aware of the contents and implications. One legislator commented, "Bills may slide through one house easily." Then folks realize what happened and the bill gets a rough ride in the other house. There are also bills that, given their committee assignment and the political complexion of the legislature, can make it through one chamber but not the other. Legislators and lobbyists know that well, and when they fail to stop something they oppose in one house, they will quickly assemble strategies and coalitions to block it in the other. Indeed, some lobbyists work more effectively and regularly with one house than with the other.

Floor action in the chambers proceeds according to a set of many formal rules, yet it doesn't always appear that way. The majority party floor leaders direct chamber activity and make most of the procedural motions. For example, while the calendar may indicate that the next order of business is consideration of bills on third and final reading, the floor leader may move to proceed out of order and hear a particular bill on second reading. Having made the motion, the chair, probably the House Speaker or Senate President, will generally say, "without objection so ordered," bang the gavel, and the deed is done. Technically, there could be a vote on the motion. But alterations in the schedule are so frequent that the absence of objection makes floor leader motions virtually automatic.

Another illustration of the informal compliance with formal rules of procedure involves the "use of the present roll call" as a substitute for an actual roll call vote on Senate third readings. In the House, third and final reading votes, those that are matters of printed public record, are cast by way of electronic device. A giant scoreboard on each side of the House chambers shows the votes of each member with red or green lights. The Senate has no scoreboard, so roll calls are employed. But rather than having the names of all thirty-five senators called for every bill, especially the vast majority of bills that pass with little or no opposition, the Senate President simply asks if there is any objection to the use of the present roll call as the list of affirmative votes. If there are, senators raise their hands, the President calls their names, and their negative votes are recorded.

While both chambers employ a number of such informal procedural shortcuts, they are most evident in the Senate. The Senate is a smaller body and one populated with more experienced members. Most of them have served previously in the House. As a result of the size and experience differences, Senate proceedings on the floor, like those in committees, are visibly more relaxed and characterized by informal collegial discussion.

CONFERENCE COMMITTEES

If a bill survives in one chamber, it must run a similar path in the other. Many of the bills that eventually do make it into law will not initially pass through the two houses in the same form. Such a bill is then returned to the chamber of origin and placed on the calendar, where members of the first house have the option of accepting the amendments of the second chamber. If they choose not to do so and instead adhere to their initial position, the Speaker or Senate President in the originating chamber may appoint the bill's sponsor and two other legislators to a conference committee and invite the other house to do likewise. Then, the six conferees attempt to develop a version of the bill that is acceptable to majorities in both houses. If they do, the bill will pass on to the governor.

In recent years roughly half of the bills introduced became law. Roughly 650 bills are introduced and over 300 pass. Of those that eventually pass both chambers, only about one in ten does so having gone through a conference committee. Many bills are routine, noncontroversial adjustments to existing law and thus easily pass both houses in identical form.

Where the two versions differ, the most common way of resolving the differences has been for the originating house to agree to the amendments made by the second chamber. This does not suggest mere capitulation to the wishes of the second house, however. Bill sponsors and other interested parties communicate and negotiate all through the process and thus second house amendments often reflect and embody agreements made along the way.

Versions of Bills

There are six different versions of a bill as it progresses through the legislative process. The first is the bill as printed for introduction and consideration by committee. If a bill makes it out of committee and through second reading in the chamber in which it originated, it is reprinted in amended form as what is termed an engrossed bill. After third reading, it is reprinted again, if necessary, and called the reengrossed bill. In the second chamber, the bill is redone to reflect any changes after second reading in that house and is called the revised bill; after third reading in the second chamber, it is referred to as the rerevised bill. If the bill makes it successfully through both houses in the same form, it becomes the enrolled bill. When the governor signs the bill, it becomes an act and, thus, law.

Vetoes

The governor signs most bills; indeed, of the 615 introduced in 1996 and the 344 that passed both houses, he vetoed just five. In 1998, 620 bills were introduced, 350 passed both houses, and sixteen were vetoed. The governor has just ten days in which to veto a bill while the legislature is in session; if he fails to act, it becomes law without his signature. After adjournment the ten days extends to thirty. If the governor chooses to veto a bill, it will be sent back to its house of origin with a letter explaining his objections.

The real power of the veto lies most often in the threat of its use, rather than in the use of the veto itself. On a bill to privatize the Regional Transportation District, the metro-Denver bus system, the governor made it clear that although the bill was still in committee, he would veto it if passed in its original form. As a result, the bill was amended to provide for just a partial sale of bus routes to private vendors. The governor eventually signed it into law in its modified form.

Clearly, there are many points along the legislative path where bills can be altered or die and where all sorts of political strategies are employed. The Speaker and Senate President can kill bills with hostile or multiple committee assignments, and, until 1989, committee chairs could do so with the pocket veto. The JBC can starve a program with lack of funding. In the past, the Appropriations Committees and others could fail to complete business on all bills by the reporting deadlines, thereby killing bills by the score. Variations of this strategy are still employed. One house can sit on bills until it is too late for the other to deal with them effectively. Interest groups maneuver to find influential sponsors for their bills, and legislators use lobbyists to help them work on other legislators. Minority party Democrats have relied on the governor to veto distasteful bills, and he has depended on the House and Senate Democrats to uphold his vetoes against vote overrides. There are games and strategies aplenty, and they go on constantly and often impinge on one another.

The dynamics of the legislative process can be usefully illustrated by tracking bills through this process. Chapter 10 exemplifies this, by following two highly visible and controversial bills through this process. One bill resulted in the creation of the state's lotto system, back in 1988. The other, enacted one decade later in 1998, placed before the metro-Denver voters the question of public financing of a new football stadium for the Broncos.

DIRECT DEMOCRACY

The legislative process is far and away the most common way to make law, but it is by no means the only one. In every biennial election, there are items on the ballot where the citizens can vote to enact new statutory law or amend the state constitution. Some measures reach the ballot by way of citizen initiative; others are placed on the ballot by the General Assembly and passed on to the voters for approval or rejection.

Colorado is one of twenty-one states that allow citizens to initiate legislation and one of thirty-seven with procedures in place to let the legislature refer statutory measures to the general electorate. Provisions of this sort, especially the initiative, are most common in the western states and tend to be found in states whose laws were first framed about a hundred years ago when trust in elected officials was low.

The constitutional basis for the initiative and referendum is found in Article 5. It reads, in part:

The people reserve to themselves the power to propose laws and amendments to the Constitution and to enact or reject the same at the polls independent of the General Assembly and also reserve power at their own option to approve or reject at the polls any act or item, section, or part of any act of the General Assembly.[5]

The only limitation on the people's power is also expressed in Article 5 and applies to the referendum:

The second power hereby reserved is the referendum, and it may be ordered, except as to laws necessary for the immediate preservation of the public peace, health or safety, and appropriation for the support and maintenance of departments of state and state institutions.[6]

It is to escape the provisions of this section that bills contain the safety clause.

The process for citizen initiation of constitutional amendments and statutes is at once simple and difficult. It is simple in that it involves obtaining signatures of registered voters on petitions in a number equal to 5 percent of those who voted for secretary of state candidates in the immediate past election. Groups that plan to seek the needed signatures and place an item on the ballot must first submit their plan to the Legislative Council and Legislative Legal Services for review and comments on the language to be sure it is concise and clear. Opponents may challenge the articulation of the proposal at this point. After this, the secretary of state holds a hearing to establish a tight and accurate ballot title and summary. A constitutional amendment adopted by the voters in 1994 required that the ballot items address a single subject and that the subject be clearly expressed in the title. This parallels the single subject–tight title requirement for bills in the legislature. The secretary, attorney general, and director of the Office of Legislative Legal Services constitute the deciding panel. Proponents then venture out to secure signatures, and the secretary of state verifies them after submission. However, as one can see, this can also be a difficult enterprise for it is not easy to obtain the signatures. More than 50,000 are needed, and one may well encounter opposition in determining ballot language and in the campaign itself.

There have been many citizen-initiated ballot items over the years, and a substantial number have been placed there for the voters' choice by the legislature, as well. In 1986, for example, there were four proposed constitutional amendments on the ballot, three coming from the General Assembly through a two-thirds vote in each house, and one from citizen initiative. One proposal passed; three did not. There were no initiated or referred proposed statutory measures. In 1998, there were three legislatively proposed constitutional amendments on the ballot, and one passed. There were also nine citizen-initiated proposals for constitutional or statutory additions; three passed, but six did not. For years the ballot has often been full of legislative or citizen proposals—twelve in 1972, nine in 1974, eleven in 1976, and seven in 1984.

The subject matter of referred and initiated proposals varies considerably. Some measures, such as one to permit county commissioners rather than state legislators to set salaries for county officials, are seemingly innocuous and not particularly controversial. But others are major issues that stir up considerable controversy, with both proponents and opponents pumping large sums of cash into the campaigns.

Examples include the successful proposal to kill the plan to have Colorado host the 1976 Winter Olympics by prohibiting state funding support—a campaign led by then-statehouse member Richard Lamm; a 1986 proposal, fought for hard and successfully by state employees, to abolish the state personnel board and effect other changes in the state personnel system; a 1982 proposed measure to allow grocery stores to sell table wine and to require sale of all beer and soda pop in returnable containers only; and a 1996 citizen-initiated measure to add to the state constitution's list of inalienable rights the right of parents to control the discipline and education of their children. Called the "parental rights amendment," it was pushed by the religious right, with over 90 percent of the $400,000 in supportive funding coming from a Virginia group. The measure was opposed by teachers, prosecutors, parents' groups, social workers, and a host of others who feared that its passage would make prosecutions for child abuse difficult, and trigger parental demands for particular curricular changes in the schools. It lost. The 1998 ballot featured proposals to restrict pollution from pig farms, meter water wells, ban certain forms of abortion, and legalize the medical use of marijuana.

Among the most consequential of recent successful initiatives have been TABOR and term limits. TABOR, discussed earlier in connection with budgets, has severely limited the legislature's control over state finances, and it has similarly impacted local governments. And the imposition of eight-year term limits is having the effect of reducing the experience level of members of the General Assembly.

The initiative and referendum will never become avenues to enact large volumes of legislation. But they do constitute politically important mechanisms for bringing directly to the voters matters on which the legislature won't act. And matters such as state support for the Olympics, abortion, "English only," and parental rights are sufficiently volatile that the legislature often prefers to leave them alone; the initiative, then, becomes the only route left.

Many analysts oppose the use of the initiative and referendum, except, of course, for the necessary purpose of popular ratification of proposals for constitutional amendments. Their view is that this constitutes a sloppy and unrefined way to legislate, often resulting in ill-conceived law. But it does make for fun and interesting politics.

NOTES

1. Bernie Morson, "Numerous measures to expire," *Rocky Mountain News*, February 19, 1998.
2. Michelle Daly Johnston, "House held as political prisoners," *Denver Post*, February 19, 1998, and *Daily Status Sheet*.
3. *Senate Journal*, March 29, 1999.
4. John Sanko, "Senate rejects 'history lesson,'" *Rocky Mountain News*, February 4, 1998.
5. State of Colorado, Secretary of State, *Colorado Constitution*, Article V, Section 1.
6. Ibid.

10

Politics for Fun and Money

This chapter illustrates the legislative process by tracking two controversial bills from their inception to enactment. The first is about gambling and the second concerns the building of a new Bronco stadium. Both were major bills involving major interest groups and lobbyists, both were controversial and hard fought, and both finally made it all the way through the process and into law. The lotto bill story occurred in the late 1980s. The Bronco bill was enacted in the late 1990s. As the reader will see, the bills were different, but in fundamental ways the highly political process, characterized as it is by constant bargaining and vote counting, remains the same.

GAMBLING

In 1980, the Colorado voters went to the polls and approved a state lottery, and, as of 1988, a lottery system had been in place for roughly five years. Participation in the lottery games was sliding downward a bit from its earlier high point. Some of the lottery proceeds were earmarked for state and local parks and open space programs, and, indeed, many nice facilities had been built across Colorado with lottery funds. But, unlike almost all other states with lottery systems, Colorado did not offer lotto games in which individuals could gamble and receive instant payoffs through electronic machines placed in stores.

THE PROBLEM

In the late 1980s, Colorado also had a serious problem with prison overcrowding. The 1985 legislature had passed a series of "tough on crime" measures that significantly lengthened prison sentences for many felonies. The result was a crowding of the state prisons and a growing backlog of convicts in county jails awaiting transfer to state facilities. There were projections of a backlog totaling 2,172 prisoners by the year 2000.

The state reimbursed counties for only some of the costs of housing its convicted inmates—not nearly enough to cover real totals. The counties were howling. In fact, several of them had filed suit against the state to remove the prisoners. Jokes abounded in the Capitol, many suggesting that sheriffs should escort the state's prisoners to the Capitol, handcuff them to the gallery railing, and let the legislators figure out what to do with them.

Everyone involved with the matter agreed that the problem was serious. County officials, legislators in both parties, the governor, and corrections officials were all in agreement that something had to be done. But they could not agree on how to pay for new prisons. No one likes new taxes, especially in an election year, and after years of slim funding for state programs and a soft economy, there just wasn't enough money in the state general fund to meet the needs for additional facilities. The governor was willing to go with some new taxes, on cigarettes and alcohol in particular, and the House Speaker was willing to impose a sales tax on food. But a majority in the legislature was not.

Lotto, some thought, was the answer. It would provide a way to raise millions in new revenue without raising taxes. A lottery system was already in place; lotto could simply be added to it. Lottery revenues were falling, but the introduction of lotto would reverse that trend and provide a huge, immediate boost.

Throughout the fall of 1987, the chairman of the House Finance Committee, Republican Paul Schauer, worked with interested parties to design a bill that would graft lotto onto the lottery system. The interested parties included the Colorado Municipal League and lobbyists for gambling system vendors. They assembled a package that they felt would generate enough money to build $124 million worth of new prison facilities and even enrich the flow of parks, recreation, and open space funds that the state and local governments had been receiving from the lottery. A Colorado Municipal League newsletter described the process:

> The League, along with representatives of Colorado Counties, Inc., the Special District Association, the State Division of Parks and Outdoor Recreation, and the Colorado Parks and Recreation Association have been working with Representative Schauer and Senator Wells since last fall to fashion this new distribution formula.[1]

In another release, the league said:

> HB 1274 represents probably the last, best hope for municipal officials who want to expand the lottery into lotto and generate

increased revenues with more certainty for parks, recreation, and open space programs.[2]

There had been some discussion of lotto in prior years, but the Colorado Municipal League and other local government interests had opposed it. They feared that lotto games would cut into lottery profits and thus reduce the amount of money available to local governments. But lottery revenues had flattened out and were now slipping. Consequently, the Municipal League and others warmed up to the idea of lotto, provided guarantees were built in to preserve the local governments' share of the gambling profits. Correctional interests and counties liked the notion of lotto, too, as additional prisons would relieve the crowding problem. And those in the business of selling gambling systems and equipment obviously liked the idea, for Colorado would represent a new market for their products.

THE BILL

The bill that emerged from the teamwork of lobbyists for the gambling interests, Colorado's local governments, and Representative Schauer set forth a plan to borrow money to build three new prison facilities with roughly 1,300 new beds and pay off the bonds with lotto revenues. A 500-bed facility would be built near Limon, 96 additional beds would go in the Shadow Mountain facility at Cañon City, and 336 new beds would be added to the Denver Diagnostic Center. In addition, sums ranging from $15.5 million upwards to $30.6 million would be made available for parks, recreation, and open space programs, with 20 percent going to state programs and 80 percent to local governments. Thus, the local governments' take would be higher than it would have been from the lottery alone, absent the lotto games.

An interesting and politically potent coalition developed in support of legislation to establish lotto games within the existing lottery system. Republican House Finance Committee Chairman Schauer and others in both the Republican leadership and rank and file liked it as a way to tackle the problem without adding new taxes. Other members of the majority party who had previously opposed lotto changed their minds in the face of the overcrowding crisis and came to support Representative Schauer's bill. Two were members of the Capital Development Committee, which is charged with studying the state's facilities needs and making recommendations. One of them, Republican Representative Bonnie Allison, told Governor Romer that she was afraid they'd have to part company on the issue. Another, Republican Senator Claire Traylor, said of her constituents, "It's one of their number one concerns. But they are not the slightest bit interested in paying for prisons."[3]

Local governments could smell new money and so, too, could the gambling system interests. As the bill moved through the system, others came to support it, as well. Corrections people and law enforcement interests (county sheriffs, for example) backed it, as did political forces in Pueblo, where the lottery administration is located. Many newspapers provided editorial support.

But there were opponents, and the opposition grew as time passed. Weeks before the session began, Governor Romer announced that he opposed gambling as a way to fund prisons and preferred, he said, "sin" taxes on cigarettes and alcohol. After the bill had been introduced, the governor embarked on a very energetic and public campaign to build a backfire of resistance to the bill. He worked to paint lotto as an ethical issue and coaxed church groups, ministers, and parent-teacher associations to lean on their local legislators to oppose lotto. He called for citizens to express their opposition and posted an aide outside his chambers one day to receive anti-lotto letters; he got six of them. The governor said he would not accept the premise that the quality of life in Colorado should hinge on teaching people to gamble.[4] He suggested that folks who sought to make it the lazy way by striking it rich would end up as "tail-end Charlies."[5]

Romer was effective. Senate President Ted Strickland commented, "Roy is excellent at selling, whether it's ideas or John Deere tractors. And he has done a good job of selling opposition to lotto."[6]

In the end, when the legislature finally overrode the veto, the issue took on heavy partisan overtones. But throughout most of the process, both parties were divided internally on the issue. None of the votes—in either house, in committee, on the floor, on initial passage, or in the eventual override of the governor's veto—split along party lines. There was a unanimous House Finance Committee vote, in which all Democrats joined with all Republicans to support the measure, and there were close votes, in which some Democrats stood with some Republicans in opposition to the bill in the face of extremely heavy pressure from home, from lobbyists, from the governor, and from Republican legislative leadership. For the supporters of lotto, the political pitch was that this was about the only way to deal with the pressing prisoner problem; besides, parks, recreation, and open space are nice public goods. The opposition countered with rhetoric focusing primarily on the moral implications of state-sponsored gambling and the unreliability of the revenue stream.

THE HOUSE COMMITTEES

Following months of work with interest groups during the fall of 1987, Representative Schauer's bill, HB 1274, was introduced on January 29, 1988, with Senate Republican Majority Floor Leader Jeff Wells as the prime Senate cosponsor. House leadership was friendly toward the bill, and the Speaker assigned it to Schauer's own Finance Committee—a logical assignment in any case, as it usually hears bills that raise revenues, as lotto would do. The trip through the Finance Committee was uneventful, and the bill passed less than a week later by a unanimous vote by ten members.

But life for the bill was not so uneventful at the next stage. As noted before, bills with fiscal implications always go to the Appropriations Committee after a stay in committees of reference. House Appropriations was chaired by Republican Elwood Gillis, a veteran lawmaker of a very conservative bent who also chaired the Joint Budget Committee.

HB 1274 posed some problems for the conservative Gillis. First, he wasn't altogether certain that Colorado would need three new prison facilities and over 1,300 new beds in the near future. Second, state borrowing was the prime funding mechanism, with $12.4 million in bonds to be paid back through lotto profits over a ten-year period. What if the beds weren't needed? What if lotto revenues were not as high as projected? Where would the money come from to hire and pay new prison personnel and cover other operating costs? Gillis preferred to approach the prisoner backlog problem one step at a time and on a pay-as-you-go basis.

So Gillis rewrote colleague Schauer's lotto bill after making some noises about not liking it. When Gillis did not like something, hearings would often be put off for a time or simply not held at all. But in this case, the Appropriations Committee did work on the bill, and it was reported out to the House Rules Committee on February 17, roughly two weeks after emerging from Finance.

The bill looked very different. The provision for borrowing and immediate construction of three facilities was gone. Instead, new prisons would be built one at a time, the first in Limon in Speaker Bledsoe's district. (The Limon facility would have been the first built anyway.) There would also be no borrowing; rather, lotto revenues would be used to pay the costs up front. Decisions on additional facilities would be made as they seemed needed, and, again, such building would be funded with lotto money, in cash. Colorado's local governments would still receive lottery money, with a minimum level guaranteed. But they would receive less than they would have under Schauer's original version of the bill. Even after having his way in the rewriting of Schauer's bill, Gillis voted against lotto in his own committee in a symbolic gesture to show his dislike for the entire concept.

The bill was calendared for second reading on February 23, and there the tables were turned once again. Representative Schauer moved to restore his bill to its original form by defeating House adoption of the amendment that Gillis's Appropriations Committee had approved. Members of local government and law enforcement groups, as well as gambling lobbyists, were out in force, scurrying about the House lobby and visiting continuously with legislators who ran in and out of the chamber doors.

Representative Schauer and his forces prevailed. The original provisions were reinserted in the bill, save for the designation of Delta as the site for one of the facilities. Citizens in the Delta area were divided on the matter, and, as both sides communicated with legislators, it was not clear to many lawmakers what the dominant community sentiment was.

Representative Schauer's position prevailed on a 36–27 vote. Eleven Democrats joined twenty-five Republicans in the majority, while a dozen Democrats lined up with fifteen Republicans to back Gillis's substitute plan. Then, on a 42–22 vote, the House approved HB 1274 and sent it on to the Senate. The forty-two "yes" votes were two short of the number that would be needed to provide a two-thirds veto override in the House later on. Of the twenty-two who opposed passage, ten were Democrats and twelve Republicans. Clearly, this had not yet become a hard-line party issue.

THE SENATE

House Bill 1274 had its ups and downs in the Senate, too, but the threats to change it there came in committee, rather than on the floor. The bill was first assigned to the Finance Committee, as it was in the House. But when it came to the attention of cosponsor and Majority Leader Wells that there was likely to be opposition in that committee, the bill was moved, at the request of Finance Committee Chairman Fowler, to the Committee on State Affairs. Said Fowler, "It was just a matter of the vote count. The majority party and leadership obviously have methods to get their way."[7]

But the bill was amended even in the State Affairs Committee. Senator Steve Durham moved successfully to freeze the amount of lotto money targeted for local governments at $15 million per year and redirect some funds into a program on early childhood education. These provisions were rejected on the floor of the full Senate, and Durham did not object, as his major concern was the successful passage of the bill. HB 1274 passed the Senate on a vote of 23–11; as in the House, the majority was easily over the eighteen needed for passage but short of the twenty-four needed to override a certain gubernatorial veto.

The lotto bill had now passed in both chambers in nearly identical form and after successful efforts to fight off crippling modifications. The differences were so modest that either house might well have acceded to the preferences of the other, as often happens. But, instead, HB 1274 was sent to a conference committee in order to gain time to search for added support that would be needed to override the veto that the governor had promised. Said sponsor Schauer, "We'll make some adjustments to see if we can bring in some of those legislators who are right on the edge."[8]

VETO

As promised, Governor Romer vetoed the bill. In his veto letter to the General Assembly, he detailed his reasons for opposing it. They were both fiscal and ethical in nature. The governor noted that the bill would provide funding for new facilities but no continuous flow of money to pay the ongoing operating costs. He preferred "increased taxes on beer, wine, liquor and cigarettes."[9] On the ethical issue, Romer stated:

> If this state is to survive in an increasingly competitive world, we must send the message to our children that hard work, better education, more discipline and a willingness to save and invest are the basis of success. Success is not based on luck or a "one in a million" chance offered by a lotto pool.[10]

The governor noted that he was vetoing and returning the bill quickly and hoped the General Assembly would move with dispatch as well, so they could all get on with the search for other funding alternatives should the veto stand. The House and Senate had given the bill final approval on April 8, 1988; the governor's veto message was dated April 13, 1988.

The House of Representatives, where the bill had originated, was the first to address the veto override matter, and it did indeed try to move quickly. The leadership took a look at it two days later on Friday, April 15, but since a number of supportive representatives were gone, they pulled back from running the vote.

Opponents also noticed the absence of some supporters and made a move of their own. Members in each chamber get just one shot at a veto override, and forty-four votes are needed. They can't just keep on voting repeatedly in the hope that they'll make it over the top on one of the attempts. In this case, the vote on the override promised to be very close.

So, on April 15, Republican Representative Ed Carpenter, an outspoken foe of lotto, moved to vote on the override, knowing full well that the votes were not there. The Speaker, a lotto supporter, characterized Carpenter's move as a violation of legislative courtesy. Republican caucus Chair Richard Mutzebaugh expressed anger and said he would not forget what Carpenter had done. Lotto supporter Tom Ratterree and Carpenter exchanged words—"Stuff it up yours" and "Stuff it up yours, too"—and nearly came to blows.[11] Carpenter withdrew his motion in response to Speaker Bledsoe's comment on legislative courtesy.

Lotto supporters geared up for another try on Monday, April 18. Republican opponent Sandy Hume observed, "The arm-twisting is monumental. What's happening now is unprecedented in my experience."[12] Ed Carpenter said, "A whole bunch of people have been beat up."[13] But the lotto supporters were still just a few votes short of the forty-four votes needed to override the veto, so they again backed away from a vote. Bill sponsor Schauer commented, "If I had forty-four votes, I would have run it."[14]

On the next day, Tuesday, supporters did make their run at it. They succeeded with precisely forty-four votes, the minimum needed, but not until nearly seven in the evening. The House had convened in the morning, but recessed until early afternoon. At 1:30 P.M., the votes still weren't solid, so they recessed again, this time until 4:30 P.M. But things were still a little shaky at that point, so members milled around for another hour and a half, while both supporters and opponents jawboned, coaxed, leaned on, and, in some cases, worked over anyone who seemed at all persuadable.

Tuesday was a crazy day. It was interesting, eventful, and tense. Supporters, including Speaker Bledsoe, bill sponsor Schauer, and Representative Joan Green, could be seen calling colleagues out of committee hearings on and off all day, ushering them into a private corner or an empty hearing room to "visit" about the matter. At the same time, staffers from the governor's office buttonholed Democrats and ushered them, one by one, upstairs for "chats" with the governor.

LOTTO BECOMES PARTISAN

What was in many respects a bipartisan issue, with Republicans and Democrats aligned on both sides of the question in committees and on the floor, quickly took on heavy partisan overtones. The governor worked hard to convince pro-lotto Democrats to stick with him instead and uphold his veto with a "no" vote. He argued that the Republican leadership was making it a partisan affair and, at one point, even suggested that for each anti-lotto Republican who switched positions, one pro-lotto Democrat, selected by lot, should go the other way.

Especially pressured and cross-pressured on the matter were two members of the Pueblo delegation. Pueblo has always been a stronghold for the Democratic party, and the area's Democratic lawmakers understandably felt a deep need to stay with their party. But Pueblo had also had a severely depressed economy for some time. As the home of the lottery administration offices, Pueblo would see a modest increase in economic activity with the addition of lotto. Media opinion in the area and a unanimous resolution by the city council were strongly pro-lotto, and no words were minced in informing the Pueblo legislators of this. Said a Pueblo councilman, "Council voted unanimously to override veto. If you guys do us in again, don't report to us."[15]

The Republican leadership played the same game. One Republican commented, "The leadership has cast this as a test of strength between the Speaker and the Governor." By Tuesday, lotto supporters needed just one or two more votes to reach forty-four, and Republican Representatives Don Ament, David Bath, John Irwin, and Lewis Entz, who had publicly opposed lotto previously, became objects of a special sort of pressure. Ament was reportedly told directly by his party leadership that he *would* vote to override. As one colleague said, "You were the bright rising star last week. How much are you willing to risk on this issue?"[16] Stories floated about that David Bath, a declared candidate for the Republican nomination for U.S. Congress from District 2, was told that some of those committed to supporting his candidacy would keep their money out of his campaign if he didn't cross over to the side of House leadership and line up against the governor. Like Ament, Bath switched. It was not clear why John Irwin switched; he said virtually nothing about it. Lewis Entz said that he'd had every sheriff in his district call him; he never did switch positions, though, and contended later that it was intimated that "you may have some problems with funding in your district."[17]

After a long day of widespread lobbying, stalling, and worrying all around, the vote was taken at last. With a 44–21 margin, the governor's veto was overridden. A crowd of those with political and financial stakes in the matter watched. The governor observed from the gallery, and lobbyists peered through the glass from the hallway. A cheer went up when the score appeared on the electronic tote board.

Again, both parties were split on the matter, with Democrats joining Republicans on both sides. For some opponents, it remained a moral issue. For others, it was a question of how sound the funding arrangements were. Most supporters cast their arguments in terms of financial necessity. If we want to be tough on crime, some said, we've got to pay for the lockups, and how else can we do it?

The next and final stop was in the Senate, where another two-thirds vote was needed. That vote, ten days later, came more easily. Two Republicans who had opposed lotto on its first trip through the chamber switched and provided proponents with exactly the twenty-four votes they needed.

As in the House, there was considerable lobbying, some of it intense. Republican caucus Chair Wayne Allard, who had opposed lotto from the outset and held his ground, said he was told that he should not be in a position of leadership if he couldn't support the override motion. Allard's answer was "I'm going to respond to my constituents and my conscience. If that means I have to jeopardize my political future . . . so be it."[18]

The lotto episode illustrates several interesting features of the legislative process. In the first place, it shows how policies designed to solve one problem can spawn others down the road. Throughout the early 1980s, there was a growing concern about violent criminals; the 1985 Colorado legislators rallied around the popular banner of "getting tough on crime." They got tough, all right, by doubling many sentences, limiting the sentencing latitude of judges, and restricting the conditions for parole. But the fallout was a massive backlog of state convicts in local jails. Funding to accommodate a growing prison population, however, was not a part of the "get tough" package of 1985, and by 1987 the results had come home to roost. Indeed, the 1988 General Assembly produced several bills, in addition to lotto, to cope with the overcrowding problem, including some that rolled back sentences to earlier levels.

Second, 1988 was an election year and no one likes to raise taxes in an election year, especially a legislature that is none too fond of taxes at any time. But the prison problem was there and would not go away. Lotto provided one means to address it with no new mandatory taxes. The people would pay, of course, but in a voluntary fashion through a system of optional gambling. But the funding mechanism chosen may provide a second chapter to the crisis, one curiously like the first. For just as the 1985 legislation provided no funding for new prison facilities, the 1988 funding program for facilities included no plans to cover personnel and operating costs.

Third, lotto was born of a strange coalition. The gambling interests liked it for obvious reasons. So did the Pueblo folks for whom the lottery and lotto represent a public works–type infusion of economic activity into their community. And, although it is understandable that the majority party might like lotto as an alternative to taxes, where were the moralists who sometimes wield significant power in the Republican party? They were there, but without much clout. And Colorado's local governments? To them it was purely a financial question. The counties could unload the state's prisoners, and the cities would get a large slice of the gambling profits. The profit motive was clearly at work in both the private and public sectors.

Lotto politics displayed the tactics and influence of organized interests and the lobby corps. The cities, counties, and special districts helped write the legislation. They orchestrated pressure throughout the process. "Municipal officials are urged to contact their Senators at once and express support for HB 1274," a Colorado Municipal League newsletter told city officials across the state. And when matters got tight on the floor, lobbyists were on the job: "A special thanks from municipal officials needs to go to Representatives Joan Green (R-Aurora) and Jeannie Reeser (D-Thornton) who helped the League in counting votes on the floor to hold the coalition together."[19]

The lobby corps is a power in ways well known to the lawmakers. During the struggle over the Gillis amendment to Representative Schauer's original bill, Republican Representative John Ulvang commented on the Municipal League's opposition to Gillis's substitute plan: "Without their support, are we going to have enough votes to override the Governor's veto?"[20] And the *Rocky Mountain News* reported that Senate Majority Floor Leader Jeff Wells said that he had "been assured by lobbyists on HB 1274 that he has at least nineteen or twenty votes for the bill."[21]

The governor demonstrated how the state's chief executive can use his center-stage platform to good political advantage. Colorado is not a strong-governor state. The executive budget powers are weak, state agencies respond as much to legislative cues as they do to the chief executive, and, in 1988, as has been the case over the past full decade, the Democratic governor's political opposition controlled both legislative houses. Lotto was sponsored jointly by influential and respected lawmakers Paul Schauer and Jeff Wells.

Yet, the governor came within a whisper of stopping lotto. The rules helped Romer, as margins of two-thirds were needed in both chambers to override his veto. But beyond that, the governor used his media position very effectively to whip up political opposition in the public. He very nearly won.

The lotto story also shows how people in positions of leadership can use their power to make real differences in public policy. In the Senate, the President moved the lotto bill out of one committee and into another to keep it out of the reach of hostile lawmakers. In the House of Representatives, the leadership used its clout on the veto override to move the votes of several party members who had not only opposed lotto earlier but stated their position in very public fashion.

House leadership also used its authority to block late-session introduction of bills with options to lotto that were preferred by the governor. The leadership in each chamber can, of course, waive the deadline for bill introduction if it so chooses; in the House, the leadership agreed to do just that for another prison funding bill. But the leadership also specified the requisite title for the bill—a title under which the governor's preferred measure would not properly fit. He criticized the legislature for its "tight title," and House leadership said the governor could have had anything he wanted introduced if he had moved before the initial bill introduction deadlines had passed.[22]

Although this story shows how party ties and party pressure can move things in leadership's preferred direction, it also illustrates the dangers of waving the partisan flag too long. In the final, tension-packed minutes before the override vote in the House of Representatives—at the end of a long and exhausting day, with the vote promising to go over the top by exactly one, with no margin for slippage and with many Democrats uncomfortably prepared to join Republicans on the override in the face of pleas by their governor to stay with him on this critical question—the Republican majority floor leader went to the podium and took a verbal jab at Romer, who was in the gallery. The votes had been put into place through hard and tedious lobbying; the last-minute partisan swipe came within a whisker of undoing thousands of hours of negotiations, coalition-building, and soul-searching. Lotto had made it most of the way through the process as a bipartisan issue. Certainly it took some partisan pressure to bring the last few votes around for the override. But an overdose was nearly fatal.

Politics are often laced with curious and funny little wrinkles, and so it was with lotto. The first facility to be built was in the Speaker's district—no accident, said the governor, but that view was not expressed extensively and openly by legislators. The conference committee that was assembled more to build political support than to resolve House/Senate differences included lotto opponent Senator Rizzuto. But he wasn't co-opted by the role, as some had hoped.

The newspapers, some pro-lotto and some not, carried a few spicy lines. Commenting on clergy opposition that the governor had helped to stir up, the *Denver Post* editorialized, "We're grateful that so many clergymen could take time away from their church bingo games and their church raffles to instruct the legislature about the evils of gambling."[23] The *Triangle Review* in Fort Collins was on the other side of the issue, and, in reference to companion legislation designed to ease the prison overcrowding problem, it quipped, "The bill would mean a reduction in the average prison stay from fifty-three months to forty-four. Great, that's where we were before 1985, when our fearless leaders decided to get tough on crime."[24]

In the final days of the veto override, a couple of House members spent time leaning on anti-lotto colleagues in the Senate to change their minds. According to the *Rocky Mountain News*, Representatives Joan

Green and Vickie Armstrong took Senators Joe Winkler and Terry Considine aside separately to visit with them on the matter. The Speaker said, "They're working on their own. I didn't send them up there." "They picked the right people, I'll give them credit for that," Winkler commented. "Hi, cute stuff," is the way the *Rocky Mountain News* reported Green's approach to Considine.[25]

What drives lawmakers to devote such time and mental energy to politics in state legislatures where turnover is so high that representatives are almost literally here today and gone tomorrow? Why the intensity? Close observation of political struggles on matters like Colorado's lotto bill make the intensity a little easier to understand. What began as a straightforward bill to build prisons became, progressively, a whole series of issues and games that attracted participants in almost irresistible fashion. They came to play the game because it was a political one, because they were politicians, and because the game was there to be played. Forget the overcrowded county jails and the future problem of paying for personnel and operational costs of new prisons. There was a game on the table, the place was crowded and noisy, and who could resist?

FOOTBALL

The Bronco bill of 1998 is not to be confused with the Bronco bill of 1996. It would be easy to confuse the two since in each case it was the same owner and team in search of public money to support a private enterprise, and it was pushed through the legislature by essentially the same team of lobbyists. But the bills were different. Among other things the legislative sponsors changed, and so did the money, as the permissible cost to the taxpayers went in two years from $180 million to somewhere between $266 million and $341 million. With interest on the bonds and possible cost overruns, the cost could exceed a half billion dollars.

SINCE 1996

As was the case in 1996, Bronco owner Pat Bowlen and his comrades argued that the team could not be competitive unless its income rose, and to increase the cash flow a new stadium was needed. Other franchises, Bowlen argued, enjoyed richer income streams from leases of luxury boxes, concession profits, sale of in-stadium advertising, and parking charges. Television income was evenly split among the teams but the in-stadium revenue differentials made some franchises richer than others and thus able to buy better talent. Mile High was always sold out and Bowlen once had the rights to the luxury boxes. But he had sold them to raise cash to increase his own ownership share of the team. Now he needed more and better luxury boxes.

The Broncos were sufficiently competitive to win the 1998 Super Bowl, and they spent lavishly on entertainment, lobbying, and player salaries. But the franchise could pay only a small fraction of the cost of a new stadium, the owner said. Bowlen and others, such as National Football League Commissioner Paul Tagliabue, argued further that since taxpayers built a facility for the Rockies baseball team, it was only "fair" that the Bronco franchise get one too. Thus the demand for public money.

The 1996 legislation created a stadium district with a board. The board was charged with studying the need for a new facility, negotiating the necessary changes and release of the existing Mile High contract between the team and the City of Denver, deciding on a location and plan for a new stadium, and then arranging for an election to ask voters whether they wanted to foot most of the bill. The stadium district encompassed the same territory as the baseball stadium, which was co-terminus with the Regional Transportation District. To fund Coors Field, taxpayers paid one-tenth of 1 percent sales tax. To build the Broncos' new home, that same levy would be used, and the public's share of the total cost was capped at $180 million.

As it turned out the 1996 stadium district board never got around to calling an election. The 1996 act had only authorized a November election between 1997 and 2001. The board did decide that renovating Mile High was a bad option, but that was about the extent of its accomplishments. Still, as late as early 1998 some folks hoped for new legislation to authorize a May 1998 election. Even as the Broncos worked with Senator Elsie Lacy in early 1998 to design a bill, there was hope in many circles that the May election could be pulled off. Both Denver Mayor Wellington Webb and Governor Roy Romer were hoping so. But others were skeptical. Both Senate President Tom Norton and 1996 Bronco bill Senate sponsor Ed Perlmutter were opposed. The idea of a May election soon evaporated and a November 1998 election, plus a major jump in the public's cost, became the targets instead.

The 1998 version of the Bronco bill was introduced first in the Senate by its prime sponsor, Elsie Lacy. Lacy represented a district in Aurora. She was in her second four-year term, was chairperson of the Senate Appropriations Committee, and thus was a member and alternate-year chairperson of the Joint Budget Committee. Lacy had served previously on the Aurora City Council.

The House sponsor was Doug Dean, a second-term member from Colorado Springs. In his first term Dean was seen as a member of the "new House crazies," a small band of religious right Republicans who stirred the waters of the House Republican caucus with their rigid social agenda. Dean had changed his style some as he developed ambitions for a leadership position, and sponsorship of the Bronco bill was one way to demonstrate legislative effectiveness and leadership potential.

The 1998 Bronco bill, SB 98-171, was developed the way most major pieces of legislation are, and that is by the bill sponsor and the interests pushing the legislation. In this case it involved not only Lacy and Dean, but also Bronco lobbyists and lawyers. One of the more obvious displays of the central role these folks play was in the late-stage Senate-House conference when Lacy had to call on a Bronco lawyer-lobbyist and the team bond counsel to answer questions about bill amendments.

The bill as introduced by Senator Lacy proposed to change the 1996 legislation in several ways. The major change affected the financing of a new stadium. The $180 million cap on the taxpayers' obligation was eliminated altogether. The 1996 law made the Bronco franchise responsible for all cost overruns; overruns had become the norm nationwide on projects such as this. Lacy's bill released the Broncos of that obligation and shipped it instead to the public side.

By the time SB 98-171 was introduced, it was clear that a May 1998 election was out of the question, so the bill instead allowed for an election in November 1998. The Broncos and the Stadium District Board would still need to gather signatures to place the measure on the ballot, but their ability to do so was in no doubt. Another provision allowed the stadium district to receive and spend state economic development money, which had been prohibited in the 1996 law.

Even before Lacy's bill was formally introduced, it spawned controversy. The Denver mayor and the governor were already enthusiastically on board. Perhaps carried away by the fun of it all, Mayor Webb took the occasion of the January 27, 1998, Super Bowl parade and victory signs in downtown Denver to exclaim, "Now all we need to do is build a new stadium to put these signs in front of."[26] In light of the provisions of Lacy's bill, Webb's proclamation seemed a bit out of kilter with an earlier statement that he opposed a $45 million jump in the taxpayer share of the tab. That was when many saw in Lacy's bill a boost from $180 million to $225 million. As it turned out, even the $225 million grew rapidly. Bronco lobbyist Bill Artist quipped on the matter of Lacy's arranging a May 1998 election, "I would think if she's smart, she'd bring it up while we've got 500,000 people outside screaming."[27]

Not everyone was excited about Senator Lacy's bill and the prospect of increased public costs. House member Bryan Sullivant, who had opposed the 1996 bill, asserted, "This is exactly what we predicted would happen last year; the Broncos would come back and try to up the ante. Now they want both the May election and more money." Of

Bowlen's quest for more public money, Republican Senator Ray Powers commented, "I believe a man's word is his word, and he's got to stick by it. He said $180 million last year, and that's all he should ask for now." When 1996 Bronco bill sponsor Ed Perlmutter suggested using TABOR tax collection overages for school needs and a stadium, Senate Democratic Floor Leader Mike Feeley observed, "Sports is the Toy Department of life. There are really significant issues we have to deal with."[28]

Opinions differed widely on the matter of uncorking the possible cost to taxpayers. Lobbyist Bill Artist asserted that without a lid the public would be the winners. "Actually, it's going to be cheaper if you let the market dictate what the cap is."[29] *Rocky Mountain News* columnist Gene Amole, ever the skeptic, took a different view. In his post–Super Bowl parade piece headlined "Bowl fever causes lightheadedness over stadium," Amole wrote, "The cost estimates for the taxpayers' share keep going up. The latest estimate is $300 million—$120 million more than the limit set by the legislature two years ago. You know how it is with public works projects. We saw our $1.7 billion airport balloon in cost to more than $5 billion." Amole concluded in his often colorful fashion this way: "So get ready to pucker up and be the kisser. And you know whose rear end that kissee will be. There ain't no free money."[30]

TO COMMITTEE

Senator Elsie Lacy's bill was formally introduced on February 3, 1998, and in normal quick and perfunctory fashion, it was assigned to committee. Senate President Tom Norton put it in the hands of the nine-member Committee on Business Affairs and Labor. The bill sat there for just over one week and on February 12 Chairman Dave Wattenberg held hearings. The short story is that after only three and a half hours of testimony and fawning over the heroic champions by committee members, the bill passed successfully to the floor on a 7–2 vote. Committee members asked to see Pat Bowlen's Super Bowl ring; it hadn't yet been delivered. Only four members of the committee had constituents within the stadium district and two of them cast the dissenting votes.

The thrust of the supportive testimony was that the Broncos were losing money, would soon be noncompetitive, and might even end up leaving town. Thus, it was imperative that a new facility be constructed. Since the franchise was poor, the taxpayers would have to foot most of the bill. National Football League Auditor Clayton Peterson, who also headed Arthur Andersen's accountants' Denver office, testified that under the twenty-year-old stadium contract with Denver, the Broncos were deprived of a revenue flow sufficient to acquire the players needed to remain competitive. Other franchises enjoyed receipts from luxury boxes, parking, concessions, and advertising; the Broncos kept only ticket revenues and even much of that was given up to a city tax and to visiting teams.

Even the increased flow of cash from the NFL's new television contract wouldn't help. "The new television revenues won't be enough to cover these cash-flow losses." Peterson characterized the Bronco–Mile High arrangement as "one of the worst in the league."[31]

Bronco owner Pat Bowlen testified as well. He allowed as how he loved Denver, wanted never to leave, and wanted the Broncos to stay, too, but would have to sell the team if it couldn't compete and became a money loser. "I love Colorado. I will never move the football team— I will fight to the last hurrah to keep them here. But the day I feel I can't be competitive, I'll be out of the business."

Who, then, knows what new owners might do? Would Bowlen move the team? The answer seemed to be no. Might they leave? The answer might be yes. With a stadium vote on the ballot, "If we lose, it's a disaster."[32]

There were dissenters at the hearing and to no avail they outnumbered those who spoke in favor of the bill. Several opponents were members of an organization called Citizens Opposing the Stadium Tax, or COST. Bill Schley, a COST organizer, argued that the Broncos' version of the finances was faulty. The cost to taxpayers would reach beyond even the newly expanded figure of $225 million, since that figure failed to include interest on the bonds.[33] Schley asserted, "What I've heard is the Broncos want taxpayers to pay for players' salaries."[33] Other COST members testified against the bill as well, as did people from the Colorado Union of Taxpayers, the Libertarian party, and the Sloans Lake Citizens Group.

Douglas Bruce of TABOR fame also came to oppose the bill and, as he so often does, got into a verbal fight with committee members. Bruce characterized the bill as "Robin Hood in reverse," "taking from the poor to give to the rich," and "nothing but welfare for the rich." Bruce argued that ordinary citizens would have no chance of getting what the Broncos were getting, namely legislative help to break an existing lease, and he intimated that legislators might be getting free game tickets from the Broncos.[35]

Normally citizens who testify before legislative committees are polite and the legislators are, too. But Douglas Bruce's style is different, and so are the responses he draws. Senator Ken Chlouber was clearly offended by Bruce's intimation of legislative impropriety and responded, "You've just become the best lobbyist the Broncos have got. I doubt if any member of this committee will vote against this bill after your testimony."[36]

Chlouber was almost correct, but not quite. After amending the bill to place a $265 million lid on the taxpayers' share while capping the Bronco portion at 25 percent, and allowing for a November vote but not one in May, the committee voted favorably to send the bill to the Senate floor by seven to two. Senator Chlouber voted "yes." He had said this about the 1996 Bronco bill: "I don't think Pat Bowlen can slip a fast one by the people on this one. It's almost like the Broncos have turned the joys of football into prostitution."[37]

What caused Chlouber to change his mind? He said that Bowlen looked him in the eye and said he'd not move the team.

Of the nine members of the Business Affairs and Labor Committee, just four represented Senate districts that lay within the stadium taxing district. Two supported the bill, and two did not. Five senators and their constituents resided beyond the reach of the tax and all five voted "yes." In an interesting twist on party ideology with respect to private enterprise and government spending, the four committee Democrats split; all five Republicans, like Republican sponsor Lacy, backed the Broncos' quest for public dollars. Of course four of the five Republican senators lived outside the district.

In another interesting twist, this one related to timing, Bronco owner Bowlen told a group of realtors, just prior to the Senate committee hearings, that he'd raise ticket prices in a new stadium.[38]

TO THE SENATE FLOOR

The easy 7–2 vote in the Business Affairs and Labor Committee did not mean the Bronco bill would have a similarly easy ride through the full Senate. There it would have to pass on both second and third readings and, on the Committee of the Whole second reading especially, it would be subject to any number of floor amendments. Of course bill sponsors and the interests that push them seldom wait for floor action to try to round up the necessary votes. As it turned out, Senator Lacy and those pushing for the public vote and the stadium subsidy had to work before, during, and between Senate floor votes.

Senator Lacy's SB 98-171 came to the Senate floor from committee for its second reading on Friday, February 20, and immediately ran into trouble. On Senate second readings, the first order of business is to consider and, usually, adopt committee reports and the amendments they contain. Here is where the trouble started.

Senator Pat Pascoe, a stadium opponent, moved to sever the committee report and substitute the $180 million cap contained in the 1996 law for the recommended $265 million subsidy figure. She won. Pascoe had argued that the stadium subsidy wasn't fair to the poor.

Pointing out that sales taxes hit lower-income people the hardest, she asserted, "We're forcing the very poorest people to shoulder this burden."[39]

Several other amendments followed and some passed, including one by Floor Leader Jeff Wells, which added a dome the Broncos did not want. The dome added to the cost and Wells meant to pay for all or part of it with money from the sale of stadium naming rights.

Following the amendment parade, a recorded vote was requested and taken. The bill, now containing a dome and a limit of $180 million on tax money for a new stadium, passed on a vote of 18–17. Lacy, who did not want the $180 million limit voted "yes," and Pascoe, who got her $180 million limit, voted "no." Lacy needed to keep the bill alive; Pascoe wanted it dead and buried.

When the Senate Committee of the Whole concluded its second-reading consideration of bills, it "rose to report" its actions to the Senate. Lacy then made a move that is common, namely, to amend the Committee of the Whole report to show that the section of the Business Affairs and Labor Committee report containing the $265 million figure "did pass." But she lost on a 16–19 vote.

Senator Lacy was frustrated, angry, and worried and so were members of the Bronco lobbying team. Said Lacy of her colleagues, "They were making a statement, and maybe that statement is not wanting the Broncos here in Denver."[40] Lobbyist Porter Wharton added, "I don't think some of those people understand how grave this is. We're not bluffing here."[41]

The Broncos' quest for $265 million wasn't dead yet, however, because in another parliamentary maneuver, Lacy had managed to buy time for another try. Having lost the vote for $265 million on Friday, February 2, she moved to have the Committee of the Whole report show that her bill had not passed containing the $180 million cap but, rather, was laid over until Monday, February 23.

Senator Lacy and her team now had a weekend to go fishing— fishing for votes. "There are two days between now and Monday," she commented. "We have to go back to the drawing board. That $180 million is basically useless."[42]

They went fishing but the team didn't catch what it needed. A Denver City Council committee went on record supporting a lift in the taxpayer cap to $245 million, but as of Monday the necessary eighteen votes were not yet in line. "We don't have the votes to do it," Lacy admitted on Monday.[43] So she stalled some more, postponing more floor consideration until the next day.

Then came Tuesday, with SB 98-171 scheduled yet again. And the stall came yet again. Four times the bill was called by the presiding officer and three times Lacy bought time by shoving it further down the calendar. She was still fishing for votes and waiting for the belated arrival of Senator Wattenberg, the chairman of the Business Affairs and Labor Committee and an assured "yes" vote.

Finally on Tuesday, Wattenberg showed up and finally Lacy won. In fact she won her $265 million and a million more to boot. Legislative procedure rules prevent members from reoffering failed amendments. Since Lacy had made and lost a motion to restore the $265 million figure in her earlier Committee of the Whole report amendment, she had to move something different, so she just bumped the number up by a million.

A combination of intense lobbying, bargaining, and allegedly spontaneous supportive citizen phone calls had moved enough votes to rescue the bill. Senators Peggy Reeves and Stan Matsunaka successfully bargained for two amendments, one tying the team, irrespective of ownership, to Denver for twenty years and the other pledging a million dollars for youth programs should the franchise be sold.

These moves apparently helped to soften some opposition. In addition, Senator Ken Arnold, a negative vote on Friday, became a "yes" vote on Tuesday because, he said, constituents called and "They wanted me to vote for it, and the calls were something like 100–3."[44] Some legislative aides reported that for weeks a steady stream of calls came in overwhelmingly negative until the last day when a call-in blitz popped up. The *Rocky Mountain News* reported that "a furious four days of arm twisting and lobbying persuaded several lawmakers to switch their vote."[45] The switchers, besides Arnold, were Feeley and Thiebaut.

The final Senate vote, a somewhat perfunctory third-reading vote the following day, showed an interesting voting pattern. There was no party split, as the Democrats divided seven "yes," eight "no," and Republicans went thirteen favorable and seven opposed. The final fifteen opponents included such conservatives as religious-righters Doug Lamborn, Jim Congrove, and Mary Anne Tebedo, plus fiscal conservatives Mike Coffman, Dick Mutzebaugh, and Tom Blickensderfer, along with certified liberals Pat Pascoe, Doug Linkhart, and Dorothy Rupert.

The cleanest division was between senators who represented constituents who would pay the tax and those whose voters would not. Senators from within the taxing district split nine "yes" to eleven "no." The bill was carried by senators from outside the tax area by a count of eleven positive and just four negative. Members offered two quite different theories for this later split. Some said they just wanted to put the matter on the ballot and give the voters their choice. Others claimed that it's just easier politically to vote to tax somebody else's constituents.

HALFTIME

Senator Lacy's stadium bill next moved twenty yards or so down the hall to the House of Representatives, where it became the charge of Douglas Dean of Colorado Springs. It was promptly assigned by the Speaker to the Committee on Local Government, where it sat for about three weeks. But while it sat in Representative Shirleen Tucker's committee, both critics and boosters alike filled the papers and airwaves with opinion on the matter.

As the bill came over from the Senate it called for a dome, permitted public payment of stadium costs up to $266 million plus all cost overruns, and prohibited the stadium district board from assessing cost overruns to the Bronco franchise. The measure made the franchise responsible for the cost of a now-mandated November 1998 election, and obliged the team to stay in Denver for at least twenty years and pay a million dollars into youth programs if the franchise was sold.

Franchise owner Bowlen kept on talking about his desire to keep the team competitive and in Denver and how he needed more money to do so. His lobbyists made occasional comments on the positive economic impact of the team. House sponsor Dean, who had both championed the Broncos as an important statewide resource and opposed allowing citizens to vote on what to do with TABOR revenue overages, argued, "who are we to say you don't have a right to vote on this."[46]

Critics saw it differently. Conservative Dean's conservative colleague Penn Pfiffner said, "I just don't think we should be buying a place of business for a business owner."[47] Not so conservative Shirley Schley of anti-subsidy COST observed, "It boggles my mind that there are some legislators who won't vote for welfare and will vote for this."[48]

Columnist Gene Amole lambasted Bowlen for his Canadian citizenship, observed that his mother was the real owner of the team, and wrote, "He is a freeloader, and he and the NFL are in the process of extorting money from us to pay their football players. Is that crazy or what?"[49] David Kopel of the conservative Independence Institute contended that subsidy dollars would go "from Colfax to Wall Street."[50] Any number of critics referred to the matter as "welfare for the rich." Bronco lobbyist Wharton didn't agree: "I don't see how anyone can call this welfare."[51]

HOUSE COMMITTEE ON LOCAL GOVERNMENT

About three weeks after the Senate gave Lacy and her Broncos a victory, Representative Shirleen Tucker convened hearings in the Local Government Committee to which Speaker Berry had assigned the bill. As with many bills that are media and attention grabbers, an overflow crowd was expected, so the hearings were held in the larger and ornate old Supreme Court chambers, which, along with both the House and Senate, are located on the Capitol's second floor.

In substantial measure, testimony followed the pattern of that in the Senate Committee. Mostly, money people testified in favor of the bill. Bronco owner Pat Bowlen restated that "this is not about money. This is about keeping the Broncos in the state of Colorado. This is about the community."[52] As he did in Senate Business Affairs and Labor, Arthur Andersen's Clayton Peterson alleged that other franchises enjoyed more lucrative in-stadium cash flows and that without a new stadium the Broncos were at a growing competitive financial disadvantage. By implication, then, their on-field competitiveness would fade as well.

Denver's city attorney showed up to support the bill, but voiced some caution in the process. Calling the need for a new stadium a "no-brainer," he also warned, "We have no assurance of the long-term cost of this deal," and argued that the franchise should pay a full 25 percent of the cost, overruns and all.[53]

Former Bronco wide-receiver Steve Watson testified and applied some emotional frosting to the pro-stadium cake. In a statement curiously cast as supportive, Watson said, "Let's give it back to the people because many feel like it's their team."[54] Of course neither the rules written by the NFL owners nor the Broncos franchise's financial interests were about to give the team to the people, with or without remuneration.

The anti-stadium forces and rhetoric mirrored what had been witnessed in the Senate committee, too. Representatives from COST, CUT, and the Libertarian party were there. The Libertarian party's Earl Allen, noting owner Bowlen's Canadian citizenship, quipped, "He may be used to getting subsidies."[55]

Two Denver citizens offered colorful and quotable comments. Larry Patchett, in a bit of exaggeration, allowed as how with the subsidy, "Every poor sap who is watching the Broncos from a beat-up recliner is now going to be expected to cough up maybe $300."[56] Several lawmakers couched their intended support for the bill as simply a vote to let the people vote. On that prospect, citizen Bill Bloomberg remarked, the November election "would be about as fair as a wrestling match between Hulk Hogan and Mr. Rogers with Don King as referee."[57]

Following five or so hours of testimony and a series of amendments, the House Local Government Committee voted, eight to three, to send the bill to the House floor with a favorable recommendation. Of the eleven members voting, six lived and represented constituents outside the taxing district; all six voted "yes." The remaining five who were within the district split, three opposed, two in favor. Even before the hearings, Representative Steve Johnson of Fort Collins explained his position this way: "I would be a no vote (in November) if I lived in the district. But the question before the committee is whether this is a worthy proposal to be put before the voters. And I think it is."[58]

While the House committee went along with the Senate in support of the stadium bill, it did not completely buy the Senate's version. There were several significant amendments. One removed the provision for a retractable dome. The Broncos liked that. They were less excited about the removal of a $100 million cap on their share of the cost. The committee provided that the franchise pay 25 percent of the total, any overruns included.

An amendment by Representative Russell George was not at all to the liking of the Broncos or to sponsors Lacy and Douglas Dean. It prohibited the sale of naming rights. Said George, "The taxpayers will have to build this stadium. . . . It ought to reflect where we live, who we are, and who owns it."[59]

THE HOUSE FLOOR

The next stop was the full House for a second reading five days later. For legislative strategy junkies, this promised to be fun. Representative Ron Tupa of Boulder had been waiting in the wings with a proposal to expand the boundaries of the stadium taxing district, and he was ready for the floor action. But so too were the bill's proponents. They knew the boundary issue was troublesome and they expected a close vote. But they had a plan.[60]

Representative Tupa believed that the existing boundaries of the stadium taxing district were profoundly unfair, and he wasn't alone. The boundaries were identical to those of the Coors Field taxing district, which in turn were the same as the boundaries of the Regional Transportation District. Tupa pointed out that some citizens as far away from the stadium as rural and mountainous Nederland, Ward, and Lyons in Boulder County would be taxed, but areas closer in, such as Park Meadows Mall and the Castle Rock factory outlets, were free from the district's tax. Park Meadows Mall in south Denver is just fifteen miles out, while in other directions, "You can be as far as 50 miles away and still pay the tax," noted Tupa.[61]

Tupa's plan was to amend SB 98-171 to expand the taxing district boundaries to add more of Adams County to the north, more of Arapahoe County to the east, and all of south-lying Douglas County, plus a very small section of Weld County. Such a new mapping, contended Tupa, would better reflect the true residential and commercial configuration of modern metro Denver.

Tupa's vision presented a problem for the proponents, who included House sponsor Dean and Vickie Agler, the House sponsor of the 1996 Bronco bill. They knew the vote would be close, and neutralized one opponent, Penn Pfiffner, by arranging with Floor Leaders Norma Anderson and Jeanne Faatz to put him in as chairman of the Committee of the Whole. They also believed they needed the votes of Representatives Shirleen Tucker and Bill Swenson who, like Tupa, didn't like the current district boundaries and wanted more of the newly populated territory to the south to be included.

But the proponents knew, too, that inclusion of much of Douglas County would result in a loss of the votes of Representatives Jeannie Adkins and Lynn Hefley, who represented portions of that county. So the plan was to seek district expansion to include Park Meadows mall, a huge new shopping facility in the south metro area, but only the mall and no new residential territory. That would help garner the support of Swenson and Tucker without losing Adkins and Hefley.

Sometimes plans go awry, and as clever as it seemed, this one did. Dean, Agler, and other proponents knew that Representative Tupa would move an amendment to expand taxing district boundaries, including all of Douglas County. That would help with the votes of Swenson and Tucker, but lose Adkins and Hefley. So the plan was to let Tupa offer his amendment and then Dean would move a substitute amendment to include only Park Meadows mall and adjacent commercial properties in the city of Lone Tree. This too would help with Swenson and Tucker, but it would also hold in place the support of Adkins and Hefley.

But to work, Committee of the Whole Chairman Pfiffner had to recognize Representative Dean; instead he recognized Representative Pennfield Tate, and Tate then proceeded to offer a substitute to the Tupa amendment to expand the district to include all of Colorado. Dean was now boxed out, as amendments to amendments to amendments are not allowed by the rules. And then, to the amazement of almost everyone, Tate's amendment passed and some panic set in.

Pfiffner's recognition of Representative Tate, a Democrat, over Dean, a fellow Republican and the House sponsor of SB 98-171, came as a surprise to the bill supporters and they didn't like it. The norm is to go with one's own party first, especially when there is something so consequential at hand. But on parliamentary matters, like so many issues of substance, Representative Pfiffner often drove with his own road map.

It was heavy lobbying time again and during the noon recess Bronco operatives visited with Tate, pointing out that a statewide vote could well torpedo the whole enterprise. Folks well away from the metro area might not be excited about paying a sales tax to build a new stadium in downtown Denver. Indeed, even though Tate's amendment passed comfortably on second reading, it made defeat of the entire bill almost certain on third reading. Members representing out-state districts, Brad Young from far southeastern Colorado and Jack Taylor from the north-west, for example, simply could not support a bill that would add a tax on their constituents. As it stood, with Tate's amendment, the bill was dead, and everyone knew it. Ironically, Tate was a stadium supporter; his amendment provided him with cover from the anti-taxers in his Denver district, but he nearly killed the bill.

Stadium supporters concluded that Representative Tupa's plan to expand the tax to include more of the metro area but not the entire state was preferable to Tate's scheme. So they decided to employ the Committee of the Whole amendment maneuver to replace Tate's amendment with Tupa's. Representative Tupa, along with Floor Leader Norma Anderson, made the motion and it carried overwhelmingly. Out-staters supported it because it removed them from the taxing area, many conservatives liked it since it reduced the taxing area, and Bronco boosters voted "yes" because it presumably removed more negative November voters than supportive ones. And anyway, the strategy now was to go back to Dean's "Park Meadows shoppers but no voters" plan in the House-Senate Conference Committee, which would be dominated by the proponents.

Along the way several other amendments were made, some lost and some passed. One that passed was made jointly by liberal Ken Gordon and conservative Barry Arrington and made the Broncos responsible for all cost overruns. Representative Dean managed to remove it, however, with a successful amendment to the Committee of the Whole report. Interestingly, in the course of debate, House sponsor Dean remarked, "I just want to know when we're going to stop gouging the Broncos."[62]

Senate Bill 98-171 passed the House the next day by a vote of 38–26. It differed from the Senate version in several important respects. The Senate called for a retractable dome, the House did not. The House capped the voters' share, but the Senate didn't. It put a lid on the Broncos' share and cost-overrun liability only. The Senate version left the taxing district intact while the House had expanded it to cover all of Douglas County to the south, plus more of Adams and Arapahoe Counties and a little of Weld, too.

CONFERENCE TIME

Most bills never go to House-Senate conference committees. Rather, the houses, mostly the chamber in which the bill originates, agree to the other's amendments. But that tends not to occur on major and contentious bills, and this was one of those.

Also, the Senate President and the Speaker of the House usually appoint to conferences members who are in support of a bill. The idea is not to pack conferences with people intent on sabotaging the measures. But to the total amazement of everyone, supporters in this case were joined in conference by the General Assembly's most ardent and active opponent, Ron Tupa. Speaker Berry presumably placed Tupa on the House side of the conference committee along with Representatives Dean and Agler because of his sponsorship of the highly consequential district boundary amendment. In any case, even Tupa expressed surprise at his appointment.

Tupa's inclusion mattered little, however, except to provide him with extended opportunities to publicize his opposition, because he was soon to be outvoted five to one, over and over again. Senate sponsor Elsie Lacy chaired the six-member conference committee and, along with House sponsor Dean, supportive State Business Affairs and Labor Committee Chairman Dave Wattenberg, Representative Vickie Agler, and the Broncos cast of lobbyists, lawyers, and bankers, she knew what she wanted, and she got it. Senator Ed Perlmutter, who was the Senate sponsor of the 1996 Bronco bill and who had all along been promoting use of TABOR tax overages for stadium construction, was the sixth conference member. He was supportive, but had questions. Perlmutter had just days before undergone knee surgery, and while he was intimately familiar with the issue and the bill, he had been away from the Capitol some.

Lacy's conference committee met twice, once to lay out the points of Senate-House disagreement and again to ratify compromises that were made privately and gave her, Dean, and the Broncos what they wanted. As some say about the study of politics, lesson one is simple arithmetic; five votes out of six wins, and Lacy's Broncos had them.

At the start of the first conference, the committee made available what Chairperson Lacy called a "side-by-side." It was a four-page document showing in side-by-side fashion the major provisions of the 1996 law, the Senate's version (reengrossed) of SB 98-171, and the bill as it emerged from the House (rerevised). There were many points on which the versions differed but the major ones had to do with the retractable dome and the boundaries of the taxing district. No decisions were made during the first meeting, but Senator Wattenberg made it clear, at least for the benefit of the audience and the press, that from the Senate's standpoint the dome proposal was a serious suggestion.

Wattenberg also joined Senator Lacy in taking a few shots at Representative Tupa, who persisted in his push to expand district boundaries: "You'll oppose this bill, no matter what happens in the conference committee, so is this really a fairness issue, or is it a way to get the bill killed?" Wattenberg followed, "We've played that old trick before to try to bill a bill." He went on to report that he'd had calls from Douglas County residents who were opposed to their inclusion in the taxing district and followed with his analysis, "That's human nature, of course. If I can get something for nothing, I'll take it."

Lacy concluded the first meeting, asked folks to think about the issues, and said they'd meet again two days later. They did, and at the outset it was clear that the outcome had been arranged and, with some show of deliberation, the deal would quickly be approved.

The prime Bronco lobbyist Bill Artist conferred briefly with Senator Lacy on the podium. She called the conference to order and announced that "we've requested some amendments." Dean moved many of the amendments followed by Agler's second and most passed with either Tupa's lone negative vote or his silence. One amendment voided a House provision that dedicated any seat license revenue to the public share of the stadium cost. Another voided the House's limitation on cable broadcasts. Still another limited to thirty days the period during which legal challenges could be made to stadium district board decisions. The conference committee also scrapped the Senate provision for a retractable dome, while still allowing the stadium district board to "consider the technical and economic feasibility."

On the major point of Senate-House disagreement, which was really the central issue, the Broncos legislator-lobbyist team won big. They went along with the notion of expanding the taxing district, but with a scheme adding tax revenues but no additional voters. The amendment to the House version dumped Tupa's provision to add all of Douglas County, plus parts of other counties, in favor of a map adding only the Park Meadows mall and commercial sections of the adjacent city of Lone Tree.

The *Denver Post* reported as follows:

> Increasing potential sales taxes by millions without the addition of a single voter, a legislative committee Thursday placed Park Meadows Mall and surrounding businesses into a proposed taxing district to help pay for a new Bronco stadium.[63]

Throughout this second conference committee meeting, it was clear that Lacy, Dean, and the other bill supporters had the outcome prewired, and that the wiring was done by and with the Bronco organization. At one point Senator Dave Wattenberg asked why an 8 percent bond interest level was used in the cost calculations rather than 7 or 9. Chairperson Lacy didn't attempt a response, nor did any of the legislators. Instead she called Bronco bond counsel Lee White from the audience to explain. She called White again on a finance question from Senator Perlmutter, and she relied on Bronco lawyer-lobbyist Gary Reiff to answer yet another question.

Such intimate inclusion of acquisitive special interests in the policymaking process is not at all unusual; it's just not always so visible. Representative Tupa, whose House floor amendment was the most consequential of the Senate-House differences, was not included in the preparation of conference amendments.

The report of the Senate-House conference committee then went back to each chamber for acceptance or rejection. In large measure this "compromise" version of SB 98-171 was just what the Broncos wanted. It expanded the district to enhance the cash flow, but having added no new voters preserved the good chances for voter acceptance in November. The taxpayer price tag grew from the 1996 figure of $180 million to $266 million, plus a possible $75 million for cost overruns in addition. The dome was lifted from the bill. The stadium board was instructed to "consider public sentiment" in deciding what to do with naming rights. The possibility of lawsuits that might derail progress was reduced. The Bronco tab was limited to 25 percent of the construction cost and over-runs. With construction, overruns, and interest, the public share would likely exceed a half billion dollars. City infrastructure costs for streets and the like would be additional.

Representative Tupa provided his summary appraisal: The House version was "definitely more taxpayer friendly." "The conference committee's report is more Bowlen friendly."[64]

BACK TO THE CHAMBERS

When a conference committee reports its decisions, the bill goes back to each chamber. If the chambers accept the decisions, the report is adopted and the bill is readopted in its compromised, and amended, form.

SB 98-171 was quickly adopted by both chambers, with the House acting first. Denver Mayor Wellington Webb lobbied for final passage. Boulder Representative Ron Tupa tried again to amend the measure to include more territory. His effort lost on a 24–40 vote. With the die cast Tupa urged his colleagues to "know what you are voting for. You are voting for a tax increase for your constituents."[65]

As the bill neared final approval, lobbyist Porter Wharton remarked, "We're at the goal line."[66] The quarterback for the squad of lobbyists, Bill Artist, followed: "We're getting happier by the minute."[67] After the vote House sponsor Doug Dean moved immediate reconsideration, and received his desired defeat of the motion so as to kill forever the opportunity for anyone else to seek reconsideration. Then he went to a lobby cell phone to tell Pat Bowlen, "I think we cut a good deal."[68]

The Senate acted the next day, accepting the conference report and repassing the bill by a wide margin in about thirty minutes. But it was a half hour of strong language. Opponents were an odd collection of the chamber's most conservative and most liberal members. Democrat Dorothy Rupert from Boulder may well be the Senate's most liberal member. She asked sponsor Lacy, who is also the alternate-year chair of the JBC, for help in getting $120 million to make the Capitol safe—"Where we work; we use the Capitol more than the stadium." Liberal Democrat Pat Pascoe emphasized the point that the public tab was not just $266 million, but with cost overruns and interest it would approach a half billion.

The conservatives were very pointed in their critique. Gesturing toward the lobbyists outside the chamber, Dick Mutzebaugh shouted, "It just shows you the greed that runs through those people out there." He went on to say that SB 98-171 was a bad bill that got worse. Doug Lamborn called the inclusion of Park Meadows mall without the related residential area "taxation without representation." Mike Coffman asserted that "we've now shifted the burden to those who can't afford to go to the games." He added that the terms of the bill were "dictated by the lobbyists of this franchise."[69]

No matter; the bill passed by a vote of 22–13. Senator Lacy, who had pushed through a tribute to the deceased buffalo mascot of the University of Colorado the day before, had her second football victory in two days. Supporter Dave Wattenberg noted, "It's only a dollar on $1,000. I don't think that's a very big tax to put on anybody."[70] Of course, Wattenberg's constituents lived well over 100 miles from Denver. On the upcoming election and a campaign role for Elway, lobbyist Wharton remarked, "We've had preliminary discussions with John."[71]

There was no veto problem with SB 98-171. Governor Roy Romer had backed it from the start. Chief Bronco lobbyist Artist told a reporter from a major Denver daily paper that the governor would sign the bill the next day. The reporter asked Romer's staff if that was so and they said they didn't know but doubted it. Romer signed it the next day and congratulated Bronco lobbyists Porter Wharton, Bill Artist, Gary Reiff, and Steve Farber.

Farber had been the chairman of Romer's campaign for governor. His next endeavor was to entreat City of Denver officials to release the football franchise from its lease on Mile High Stadium, a lease that ran well into the twenty-first century.

PURCHASING INFLUENCE

In its quest for public money, the Bronco franchise didn't hold back. It hired a virtual army of lobbyists, including many of the priciest around. Bill Artist and Associates, the firm of Hays, Hays & Wilson, and Wally Stealey's firm all share space at 1301 Pennsylvania Street, Number 900. The Broncos hired them all. They contracted with the law firm of Brownstein, Hyatt, Farber, and Strickland, an outfit that has long had its hands in Denver money and politics.

The Denver Chamber of Commerce raised $50,000 to help support the stadium district. A long string of Denver businesses and business associations hired lobbyists to work different parts (or all) of SB 98-171. These included Colorado business association Colorado Concern, Coors, both Turner and Alvarado construction companies, the Metro North Chamber of Commerce, the City of Denver itself, Ascent Entertainment Group, and the Colorado Restaurant Association. Campaign strategists were hired to work the petition drive and November election campaign.[72] One Capitol reporter remarked that secretary of state records showed forty-one lobbyists listing SB 98-171 as one of their targets.

In January 1998 National Football League Commissioner Paul Tagliabue jumped in and plugged the stadium. He noted that the taxpayers built Coors Field and they should foot the bill for the stadium to put the Broncos on equal footing; "it is only fair." Noting that the NFL's new $17.6 billion TV contract amounted to $586 million per team, Tagliabue said the team still needs public money for three-fourths of the stadium cost. The new TV money will be paid to players.

There was opposition to SB 98-171. Representatives of the Colorado Union of Taxpayers and the Libertarian party testified negatively in committee. An outfit from Chicago called The Heartland Institute distributed materials titled "Sports Stadium Madness" citing studies that negated the argument that new facilities would do anything for economic development. And then there was COST, a small citizen group run out of the home of semi-retired Bill and Shirley Schley.

Following legislative victories Bronco owner Bowlen signed letters to supportive legislators:

> I would like to take this opportunity to personally thank you for your support of SB171.
>
> This has been a difficult process with emotions running high on both sides of the question. All along, we have simply asked that the people be given the opportunity to decide this issue. Your support of SB171 has moved this process one step closer to reality.
>
> Thank you again from the entire Denver Broncos Football organization.

Bowlen didn't mention the fact that the major points of contention on SB 98-171 were just which voters would "be given the opportunity," and just what their choice would be.

ALTERNATIVES

Almost lost along the way to the public treasury was the fact that avenues other than the one contained in Lacy's bill were proposed and available. None of them had any real chance of adoption, but the one that garnered the most attention was put forward by Senator Ed Perlmutter. Perlmutter was a genuine supporter of the drive for a new stadium, and had been the Senate sponsor of the 1996 legislation.

Perlmutter's idea was simple. As the state was running revenue surpluses of hundreds of millions of dollars beyond the TABOR limit, the senator wanted to go to the voters statewide with a proposal to spend one-third of the overage on K–12 schools, one-third for transportation needs, and another third for a stadium.

For Perlmutter, his plan had both substantive and tactical advantages. Substantively, all the public money otherwise spent for interest on bonds would be saved. The stadium would be a here-and-now, one-shot purchase. Tactically, since this would be a package deal, he would hope for the support of advocates of education and transportation. But Perlmutter's proposal wasn't to be. The politics of the TABOR overage were complicated and contentious in and of themselves, and there just was no way to line up enough legislative support.

Representative Mark Paschall was a hard-line opponent of putting even a dime of public money into support of a private football club. But since a subsidy of some sort was inevitable, he proposed to get the stadium built by way of a loan. Paschall wanted to float an interest-free loan of $180 million out of state tax revenue surpluses, to be paid back to the state with revenues from the sale of naming rights and Bronco club income. Paschall's idea got some print, but no legislative traction.

Denver Democrat Gloria Leyba was an opponent, too, but, like Paschall, a realist on the subsidy question. She proposed another lottery, one with profits earmarked for a new stadium. This way, only willing buyers would foot the bill; no one would be forced to pay through an involuntary tax. Her plan went the way of Paschall's—nowhere.

Stadium board member John Stone toyed with the idea of the sale of souvenir stock, and citizen activist Tico Embury talked about using the initiative process to link some form of public ownership with any public subsidy. Embury's plan would run afoul of the NFL cartel's ownership rules, unless they were changed. Neither the Stone nor the Embury scheme went anywhere.

IN RETROSPECT

How did the 1998 Bronco bill make it through the legislature? Why did members vote as they did? What did the trip of SB 98-171 tell us about the workings of the General Assembly?

The most obvious fact is that it passed because members whose constituents would not have to pay provided the needed votes. On the third and final reading in the House, the thirty-six members from within the taxing district split sixteen in favor and twenty against. It was the out-staters who put it on the metro-Denver ballot. Twenty of them voted "yes," with just nine in the negative.

A cynic might interpret this as the craziest form of self-interest. A member could be a hero for saving the Broncos for Colorado and stick others with the bill. But that is not how out-staters explained their vote. Steve Johnson, Steve Tool, and Bob Bacon all saw it as simply a vote to let those affected make the choice—a blow for democracy. For Doug Dean, the House sponsor and one who voted against a measure to let voters decide on spending for schools and roads, simply argued that the Broncos were important to Colorado and without a new stadium they might well pack up and leave for greener pastures, green being the color of American money.

There was absolutely nothing in the pattern of House votes to suggest a division along party or gender or ethnic lines. The Republicans split twenty-three "yes" and eighteen "no." The Democratic division was thirteen "yes" and eleven "no." The female contingent in the House went fifteen in favor, twelve opposed. And the eight ethnic minority members split an even four to four.

Even free market ideology fails to serve as an explanatory factor. The most consistent and outspoken free-marketer in the place was Representative Penn Pfiffner and, true to form, he opposed the subsidy both rhetorically and with his vote. As a free-market, private-sector champion, 1996 Bronco bill House sponsor Vickie Agler places a close second. But she was not only a "yes" vote, but also a visibly active lobbyist-legislator on behalf of the franchise. Her explanation was simple. Said Agler, "I hate subsidies like this but the hard truth is, you play in the market you're in, not the one you wish you were in." It is unfortunate that the league owners have rigged the game as they have, she allowed, "but we can't change that alone here in Denver." Unlike the majority of the supportive legislators, Agler and her constituents were within the taxing district and would live with the tax she supported.

The voting pattern was only slightly clearer in the Senate. Of the twenty senators from within the taxing district, eleven were supportive and nine were not. The fifteen out-staters, as was the case in the House, put SB 98-171 over the top eleven to four. The Republicans were supportive thirteen to seven while the Democratic count was nine "yes," six "no." The women voted in favor by a count of 7–3. The two Hispanic members voted "no," while the one African American voted "yes." All three represented constituencies who would be paying the tax should it pass in November.

The only obvious voting pattern suggests that self-interest prevailed as the bill was carried with the votes of members who knew that somebody else's constituents would pay. But even that explanation is complicated by both the argument that a "yes" vote was only to allow citizens to choose, plus the fact that, indeed, the voters were left with the opportunity to just say "no."

The saga of the 1998 Bronco bill does reveal plenty about both NFL politics and Colorado's lobbying game. The league is a cartel that makes up its own rules. Its rules restrict the supply of franchises, control entry of any new ones, and dictate the terms of ownership. As a result, teams are in short supply and owners can put the squeeze on cities with threats to relocate. Just as players can blackmail owners with free agency, owners can blackmail the public with "franchise free-agency." Further, league rules prevent city or state ownership of teams. The result is that teams, and their value, are owned privately but supported publicly.

This, then, lays the foundation for the lobbying effort. The Broncos hired a bevy of insider lobbyists, persons with direct lines to the legislators. The message was simple—put up or risk losing the team. Bronco owner Bowlen was careful never to threaten directly to take the team out of the state. He made the same point by saying that he needed a stadium for more money, he needed more money to remain competitive, if he was not a winner he'd sell out, and, who knows, the buyer and new owner might then move the team.

The result was that the city and the General Assembly saw they were left simply with the power to negotiate the terms of the public surrender.

Of course, the 1998 Super Bowl victory, the traditional lobby strategy of manufacturing last-minute supportive mail and calls to legislators, and the tenacious myth that sports fuel economic development helped, too. Shortly after the start of the 1998 legislative session, downtown Denver filled with more than a half-million screaming Bronco fans in a victory parade, which ended near the Capitol and which was witnessed by the members themselves. Before House and Senate votes, some members were suddenly on the receiving end of a pro-Bronco phone call blitz.

Owner Pat Bowlen tried to pump up support in the business community by alleging that a new stadium would be good for the restaurant and leisure-time industries. And his spokesman Porter Wharton similarly asserted that sports boosts the economy. The assemblage of economist studies debunking the economic development argument did little to dissipate the myth.

The manner in which the subsidy legislation crawled into the statutes helped the proponents, too. In 1996 the supposed cost to taxpayers was advertised and set at $180 million. In addition, the matter of a new stadium was posed only as a possibility; the newly created Metropolitan Stadium Board was to look at Mile High and determine if it needed replacement.

Two years elapsed before the 1998 bill emerged with a number of $265 million, and this sum was first discussed and reported all alone. Only later in the 1998 session did conversation emerge about another $75 million for cost overruns and interest, which could drive the tab to over one-half billion dollars. So legislators, and voters, had time to let the ever-expanding numbers sink in. Politically, an instantaneous leap from zero to $180 million to a half billion would likely never have flown. But squeezed out slowly through two years of legislative process, the enterprise took on wings. Experience in other cities suggests that even a half billion will not cover the taxpayers' new mortgage. At the very least, Denver's citizens will get to pay as well for new land, streets, and utilities, perhaps in the $70 million range.[73]

The entire Bronco bill phenomenon was emotion-driven. Neither legislators nor their constituents are ever likely to vote to tax themselves up to a half billion dollars for plants to privately manufacture shoes or rubber tires. But ball teams are different and reaction to them and their fortunes includes decidedly emotional elements. Social agenda conservative and government minimalist Representative Dean pumped hard for public money for privateer Bowlen because he feared losing a football team. Senate committee members showed a deference to owner Bowlen that few citizen witnesses ever receive. Legislators attend ball games but seldom visit shoe or tire factories.

Public reaction was similarly emotion laced. Martha Karnopp of Aurora wrote to the *Denver Post*, "Get a grip! The Broncos are a group of overpaid, over muscled men who played a game and won. They did not bring world peace, end hunger and poverty, cure cancer, AIDS, restore a rain forest or in any way contribute to the collective wisdom (such as it is) of humankind."[74]

Thornton's Jack O'Neill wrote to the *Rocky Mountain News*, "Things have changed since Robin Hood's day. Now we rob the poor to finance the rich."[75]

Lakewood's Ron Scott wrote, "And if Pat Bowlen threatens to move the Broncos, tell them to get on the next flight out and stay gone!"[76]

Rocky Mountain News columnist Bill Johnson lobbed some political reality into the public dialogue. In reviewing the experiences of the NFL in other cities he wrote: "A few experienced words of advice to the state legislature. Hell, to the rest of you too: Give up." "I know, the guy [Bowlen] has a lease here. These guys don't care anything about leases." "No, these people are ruthless. They've got you. Open your wallets now. Give him what he wants. Give up."[77]

Just days after the legislative session ended, an organization called C-FANS registered papers of incorporation with the secretary of state.

C-FANS are "citizens for a new stadium." Their objective was to gather signatures to place the stadium issue on the ballot and campaign for its passage. C-FANS's "initial registered agent" was J. William Artist. C-FANS's "incorporator" was P. Cole Finegan of Brownsten, Hayatt, Farber, and Strickland. Farber, Artist, Finegan, Reiff, Wharton, Stealey, Hays, Romer—all fans.

Columnist Johnson proved to be right on target. In the November election the Bronco operation replicated its legislative lobby juggernaut by pouring millions into a political machine that masqueraded as a citizens' movement. The pro–public subsidy forces, with C-FANS as the citizen front, spent $2.3 million on an advertising blitz that featured a blizzard of yard signs and TV ads, some featuring John Elway. Bronco owner Pat Bowlen poured in roughly $2.0 million of the total and $100,000 chunks of corporate money came from cable man Bill Daniels, banker Charles Gallagher, and TFM Holdings.[78] The only organized opposition group, COST, raised $30,000. Pat Bowlen stayed out of sight, while the threat of a Bronco departure, should the issue lose, was implicit and highly visible. In the fall electoral effort, as in the spring legislative campaign, private money produced huge dividends in public subsidy.

NOTES

1. Colorado Municipal League, *Legislative Bulletin*, vol. 88, no. 4, February 26, 1988, p. 6.
2. Colorado Municipal League, *Legislative Bulletin*, vol. 88, no. 7, April 8, 1988, p. 3.
3. John Sanko, "Romer, lawmakers to lock horns over lotto," *Rocky Mountain News*, January 29, 1988.
4. Ibid.
5. Ibid.
6. John Diaz, "Foes send future of lotto into losing spin," *Denver Post*, March 15, 1988.
7. John Diaz, "GOP steers lotto bill toward safety," *Denver Post*, March 9, 1988.
8. Jeffrey Roberts, "Lotto bills sent to joint panel for fine-tuning," *Denver Post*, March 26, 1988.
9. Governor's veto message on HB 1274, letter from Governor Romer to House of Representatives, April 13, 1988.
10. Ibid.
11. Mark Obmascik, "Parliamentary play leads to House scrap over lotto," *Denver Post*, April 16, 1988.
12. Jeffrey A. Roberts, "Lotto supporters hunt for votes," *Rocky Mountain News*, April 19, 1988.
13. Ibid.
14. Ibid.

15. Jeffrey A. Roberts, "2 threatened in override vote on lotto," *Denver Post*, April 21, 1988.
16. Ibid.
17. Ibid.
18. Quote of the day, *Denver Post*, April 29, 1988.
19. Colorado Municipal League, *Legislative Bulletin*, vol. 88, no. 4, February 26, 1988, p. 6.
20. John Sanko, "Committee chairman delays vote on lotto," *Rocky Mountain News*, February 13, 1988.
21. Peter Blake, "Lotto bill amendment on education aid axed," *Rocky Mountain News*, March 17, 1988.
22. John Sanko, "Romer accuses GOP of limiting prison-funding options to lotto," *Rocky Mountain News*, March 30, 1988.
23. "8-to-5 odds: We'll get lotto," *Denver Post*, February 25, 1988.
24. "Legislature seems out of ideas," *Triangle Review*, March 23, 1988.
25. Peter Blake, "Lotto backers put squeeze on senators," *Rocky Mountain News*, April 26, 1988.
26. Alan Snel and Thomas Frank, "Webb jumps on new-stadium bandwagon," *Denver Post*, February 4, 1998.
27. Ibid.
28. Thomas S. Higgins, "Bronco bill fielded at legislature," *The Colorado Statesman*, January 30, 1998.
29. John Sanko, "Bill would dump cap on stadium cost," *Rocky Mountain News*, February 4, 1998.
30. Gene Amole, "Bowl fever causes lightheadedness over stadium," *Rocky Mountain News*, February 3, 1998.
31. Ann Imse, "Broncos are bottom-line losers, auditor says," *Rocky Mountain News*, February 12, 1998.
32. John Sanko, "Taxpayer's chunk for new stadium: $265 million," *Rocky Mountain News*, February 12, 1998.
33. Ibid.
34. Jonathan Zins, "Stadium proposal keeps driving," *Capitol Reporter*, February 18, 1998.
35. Op. cit., *Rocky Mountain News*, February 12, 1998, and Thomas S. Higgins, "Bronco bill still in play at Gold Dome," *The Colorado Statesman*, February 13, 1998.
36. Op. cit., *Colorado Statesman*, February 13, 1998.
37. Mark Kisza, *Denver Post*, April 30, 1996.
38. Julia C. Martinez, "Bowlen: Ticket prices rise in new digs," *Denver Post*, February 20, 1998.
39. Peggy Lowe, "Stadium decision postponed," *Denver Post*, February 21, 1998.
40. Ibid.
41. Ibid.
42. Ibid.
43. Ibid.
44. Lynn Bartels, "Constituents sway senator toward vote," *Rocky Mountain News*, February 25, 1998.

45. Ibid.
46. Fred Brown, "Power to the people, sometimes," *Denver Post*, March 16, 1998.
47. Peggy Lowe, "Stadium foes ready to take on Goliath," *Denver Post*, March 16, 1998.
48. Ibid.
49. Gene Amole, "Stadium amounts to welfare for rich," *Rocky Mountain News*, March 3, 1998.
50. Peggy Lowe, "Stadium is 'football socialism,'" *Denver Post*, March 3, 1998.
51. Mark Obmasick, "Bill looks after Pat's welfare," *Denver Post*, March 12, 1998.
52. Ky Belk, "House panel rebuilds stadium bill," *Capitol Reporter*, March 18, 1998.
53. Peggy Lowe, "Bowlen tab 25% in new stadium bill," *Denver Post*, March 17, 1998.
54. Op. cit., *Capitol Reporter*, March 18, 1998.
55. Op. cit., *Denver Post*, March 17, 1998.
56. Ibid.
57. Dan Luzadder, "Panel OKs November stadium vote," *Rocky Mountain News*, March 17, 1998.
58. Dan Luzadder, "Lively, long hearing expected on stadium bill," *Rocky Mountain News*, March 3, 1998.
59. Op. cit., *Capitol Reporter*, March 18, 1998.
60. The plan was described to the author in conversations with Representative Vickie Agler.
61. Peggy Lowe, "Stadium bill adds 2 cash cows," *Denver Post*, March 24, 1998.
62. Ibid.
63. Peggy Lowe, "Stadium district expands," *Denver Post*, April 17, 1998.
64. Ibid.
65. Peggy Lowe, "House taps Park Meadows," *Denver Post*, April 21, 1998.
66. Dan Luzadder, "House OK's Broncos stadium proposal," *Rocky Mountain News*, April 21, 1998.
67. Op. cit., *Denver Post*, April 21, 1998.
68. Ibid.
69. Stated on House floor, April 21, 1998.
70. John Sanko, "Senate approves stadium bill," *Rocky Mountain News*, April 22, 1998.
71. Ibid.
72. Peggy Lowe, "Cash fuels stadium lobbyists," *Denver Post*, April 5, 1998.
73. Ann Imse, "City's stadium costs could rise," *Rocky Mountain News*, April 4, 1998.
74. Martha J. Karnopp, "Why pay taxes to support successful industry when we won't fully fund schools?" letter in *Denver Post*, February 1, 1998.
75. Jack O'Neill, "We need reality check on Broncos stadium tax," letter in *Rocky Mountain News*, February 10, 1998.
76. Ron Scott, "Don't be fleeced," letter in *Denver Post*, February 5, 1998.

77. Bill Johnson, "Bowlen will shoot, so fork over the loot," *Rocky Mountain News*, February 25, 1998.

78. Peggy Lowe, "Bowlen biggest stadium donor," *Denver Post*, December 2, 1998; Burt Hubbard, "Ballot measure funds set record," *Denver Rocky Mountain News*, December 4, 1998.

11

The Legislative Enterprise

In some ways this is a catch-all chapter, covering a series of matters that fail to fit in neatly elsewhere. If there is a unifying theme, it is in the treatment of legislative support mechanisms, including the staffing units, paperwork, and processes that support the General Assembly's lawmaking function.

LEGISLATURES DIFFER

In large measure, America's state legislatures are quite different today than they were a few decades back. Before the late 1960s, most of them met every other year for just a matter of weeks or a couple of months; functioned with minimal or no staff support; were dominated by nonrepresentative rural interests; featured very high membership turnover; were without open records, open meetings, conflict of interest and disclosure laws; and failed to produce public policies designed to deal with the needs of a rapidly urbanizing and suburbanizing nation. State legislatures were rightly lampooned for their old-fashioned ways, their undemocratic character, and their ineffectiveness. Indeed, in substantial measure it was the policy voids left by state legislatures that led to the proliferation of national government policies and programs that now intrude into traditional state and local areas.

The 1960s and 1970s were periods of dramatic change in America, for our institutions and policies alike. The 1962 one-person, one-vote Supreme Court decision; antiwar activities; and civil rights, environment, and consumer movements combined to produce a period of rapid and highly consequential change. Among these were significant changes in our state legislatures. In just a decade or so, roughly from 1965 to 1975, most of the states reformed their legislatures. Legislatures began meeting annually, for the most part. Sessions were lengthened. Pay, staff support, and office facilities were increased. Procedures were streamlined. The process was opened up through open meetings and open records provisions and reporting and disclosure laws. Most significantly, reapportionment shifted power to urban and suburban representatives.

The degree to which state legislatures modernized themselves varied, and today the variety remains. Arkansas, Kentucky, Montana, Nevada, North Dakota, Oregon, and Texas still meet biennially. Utah's annual sessions run just forty-five days, in Wyoming legislators meet twenty days one year and forty the next, while in New Mexico sessions alternate between thirty and sixty days. At the other end, California, Idaho, Illinois, New Jersey, New York, and six other states impose no limit on the length of legislative sessions.

Pay varies too. New Mexico, Utah, and Wyoming are among ten states that, while they may provide a daily stipend, afford legislators no annual salary whatsoever. On the other end, seven states pay annual salaries in excess of $40,000, including California's $75,600 (1997).

And so it goes; just as sessions and salary vary, so too do levels of staffing, per diem expense support, office accommodations, and the laws governing openness and disclosure.

WHERE COLORADO FITS

Where does Colorado's General Assembly fit? It is about in the middle. Sessions run 120 days annually, not yearlong as in some states or just biennially as in others. The sixty-five-member House and thirty-five-member Senate are slightly on the smallish side, although thirteen states have smaller Senates and seven have fewer members in their House of Representatives. As will be described later in this chapter, Colorado has several very effective central staff agencies and as such is much better staffed than such other states as Wyoming, Montana, or Idaho. But Colorado does not feature extensive party, caucus, and committee staffs as are found in such large states as California and New York.

Colorado has staked out a middle path, between the purely citizen legislature that was the pre-1960s norm, and the professionalized U.S. Congress, which was the ideal model some decades ago but is an overly stagnated pariah in the eyes of many people today.

PAY

Beginning in 1999 the salary of most of Colorado's legislators was set at $30,000. This figure was determined by legislation passed during the 1997 session. All sixty-five members of the House who were elected in November 1998, along with the senators who were elected at that time, received this amount, beginning with the 1999 session. Senators who were elected in 1996 will not, but senators elected in 2000 will. The reason for this difference is that members who were in office to vote on the matter in 1997 may not receive the raise on which they voted until, and unless, they are reelected following their next election.

Although the salary was raised in 1997, legislators' expense allowances remained the same. Members who live in the metro-Denver area receive $45 per day during the 120-day session, while those from outside Denver receive $99 per day. During interim sessions or for committee meetings during the interim, all legislators receive $99 per day. Additionally, members are reimbursed for mileage. Combining the $30,000 salary and per diem payments, members often now receive up to roughly $42,000 per year. Of course a member in leadership who has no other job can show up at the Capitol five days a week all year, collecting $99 per diem, and roll up a total take in state funds of $55,720 per year. In 2000, Representative Doug Dean managed to set a record at over $67,000.

Legislative salaries have been set at a number of different levels over the years. Back in 1886, the state's first lawmakers received $4 per day for a maximum of forty days. By the 1970s the sum was up to $7,000 per year. Then in the 1980s it went to $12,000, then to $14,000, and finally to $17,500 in 1985.

Because the Colorado legislature itself sets lawmakers' salaries, pay raises are a touchy issue. No member wants to go back to the district and try to explain why he or she voted to put more tax dollars in his or her own pocket. This problem is compounded by widespread public confusion of state legislators with members of Congress, whose annual salary exceeds $145,000 and who have office, personnel, and expense budgets of $950,000 or more per year. During the 1997 session, for instance, when the legislature was considering the raise it ultimately approved, Representative Norbert Chavez reported, "I have five calls from my district saying they wanted me to vote against the pay increase. When I told them we made $17,500, they all said we deserved a raise."[1] Even among those who do not confuse Colorado's General Assembly with the U.S. Congress, members risk criticism. Senator Dick Mutzebaugh commented that "nobody can live on $17,500 a year." For that comment *Denver Post* columnist Mark Obmascik took him to task, suggesting by inference that since many folks earn less than that figure, Mutzebaugh's comment indicated how much legislators are out of touch with taxpayers.[2]

Also during the 1997 session the General Assembly considered a bill by Representative Russell George that would have established a seven-member compensation commission. This commission would recommend pay levels for legislators, judges, and members of the executive branch.

The proposal was not enacted, but the political benefits of such a process, which is employed in some other states, is obvious. It takes the heat off legislators who are otherwise stuck with the electorally risky task of setting their own salaries.

LEGISLATIVE COUNCIL

A most significant part of the legislative establishment is its staff. Unlike the Congress and the legislatures in states such as California, Wisconsin, and New York, which have gone to nearly full-time modernized institutions, Colorado provides very little by way of staff help for party caucuses, the leadership, or individual members. A few staffers do work in these capacities, but the major staffing components are nonpartisan and centralized in the Legislative Council, Office of Legislative Legal Services, the Joint Budget Committee, and the Auditors Office. Additionally, the House and Senate employ a small staff that sees to the administrative needs of the chambers. They are described below.

The term "legislative council" can be confusing because it is the name for both a joint legislative committee that oversees a major legislative staff agency, and the agency itself. The staff agency operates under the purview of the legislative committee. The committee is a joint House-Senate panel of eighteen members, nine from each house. Included are the House Speaker and both the majority and minority floor leaders, plus other members of leadership. From the Senate side are the Senate President and President Pro Tem, the two floor leaders, and others in leadership. This eighteen-member committee also has an executive committee composed of the House Speaker, Senate President, and floor leaders of both parties and both chambers.

The Legislative Council, the staff agency itself, employs roughly fifty people. It is headed by a director who is hired by the joint legislative council committee. The director, in turn, hires the rest of the staff.

This staff agency has a wide range of responsibilities. Staffers do both spot research on questions posed by legislators or, sometimes, constituents, and long-term, in-depth research on major public problems and policy issues. From January 1954 through January 1998, for example, the Legislative Council staff has produced over 400 printed reports on topics ranging from school construction, welfare, and water to the health and life safety conditions in the Capitol building itself.

Legislative Council is the all-important source for the legislature's information on money matters. Staffers provide legislators with economic forecasts for the state, and anticipated tax revenues. The council prepares "fiscal notes" on all bills and amendments thereto that might either cost or save money for the state and its local governments. These are enormously important functions. The state must by constitutional mandate run balanced budgets, and with TABOR, it has a spending cap each year as well. Thus, as members assemble annual budgets and vote on bills, it is essential that they have good information on projected revenues and costs.

Staffing for legislative committees is provided by Legislative Council personnel. Each of the committees of reference that are operative during the 120-day session have one staff member whose responsibility is to maintain records of committee hearings, help provide members with such essential paperwork as amendments and relevant reports, prepare reports of committee actions, and see to it that the tapes of hearings are made for the archives. Each year several interim committees function during the summer and fall, and council personnel staff them, too.

The General Assembly floats on an enormous sea of paper, and each day House and Senate calendars and journals must be printed in volume, along with daily status sheets, bills, amendments, and more. For this activity Legislative Council operates a print shop. Council also administers a small but specialized library in the Capitol's basement, and it holds some historical records of the legislature—past bills, directories, session laws, and so forth—as well as statutes, research reports, and materials from other states. Finally, Legislative Council is responsible for the tour guides who serve the thousands of tourists who visit the Capitol building each year.

The organization of Legislative Council follows its functions. There is a Policy Research and Committee Staff section, an Economics section, one on Fiscal Notes, and a Support Services Group for printing, the library, computers, and tours.

Many staff members are generalists by education, and, as a whole, the staff is eclectic in nature. Some have studied political science, some law, many something else. There is a bit of a trend lately to hire specialists in areas like economic forecasting, education, finance, or law. There is some specialization in the day-to-day work of staff members as they focus on and become knowledgeable in certain policy areas—finance, education, or corrections, for example.

Legislative Council staff members often work closely with colleagues in the Office of Legislative Legal Services and have direct contact with lobbyists, as well. Lobbyists sometimes like to show their own information to council personnel, hoping to get a nonpartisan, objective "stamp of approval" of sorts.

The Legislative Council takes great pains to maintain the posture and image of a nonpartisan office. Staff members are cautioned to limit their political activity by keeping a distance from public rallies, refraining from testifying before legislative committees, and staying out of political campaigns and even party precinct caucuses. They are prohibited from dating lobbyists and discouraged from otherwise socializing with them. The council inadvertently got close to the political fray during a recent election when lobbyist and former legislator Cliff Dodge talked a staff member into providing the committee attendance records of a House Democrat. They were turned over to the state Republican party and eventually used against the House member in the campaign. Another incident that threatened to politicize the nonpartisan staff occurred during a 1997 hearing in the House State Affairs Committee, when committee member Penn Pfiffner sought to compel a council staff member to testify. Pfiffner was intent on demonstrating that data he had requested had not been delivered to him as expeditiously as he judged was necessary. The bill sponsor, Majority Floor Leader Norma Anderson, put a halt to the effort and in the process reemphasized the need to keep council staff members out of the political fray. This event was atypical, however, for the council works hard to avoid such episodes.

For nearly thirty years, the council's director of research was Lyle Kyle. Kyle saw legislators and legislative leaders come and go. He survived in a highly political environment for three decades and was respected for maintaining a high-quality and strictly nonpartisan operation. His successor, Charlie Brown, has headed the council for well over a decade now, and has maintained the respected and nonpartisan character of Legislative Council.

OFFICE OF LEGISLATIVE LEGAL SERVICES

Like the Legislative Council, the Office of Legislative Legal Services is a rather large staff support unit and it, too, is under the direction of a joint House/Senate committee, the Committee on Legal Services. The Committee on Legal Services is composed of ten legislators. The chairs of the House and Senate Judiciary Committees automatically sit on this panel, along with two Republicans and two Democrats from each chamber who are appointed in the normal manner. If possible, one member from each house is an attorney.

The Committee on Legal Services is charged with appointing a director of the Office of Legal Services, who must be an attorney. The director, in turn, hires additional personnel, both attorneys and clerical help, and serves as the revisor of statutes. The office employs roughly fifty people, a majority of whom are attorneys. Others are legal assistants and office staff members.

The Office of Legislative Legal Services performs a number of critical functions. The prime duty of its staff members is to draft bills, amendments, resolutions, and memorials for the legislators. The lawmakers sometimes come with bills already written in legal form; these may well have been proposed by some interest group and written by the group's attorney. At other times, legislators will have little more than an idea or some pencil jottings. But in all cases, bills must be put into proper legal language and form and cast in a way that fits with current law. The attorneys in the Office of Legal Services do this. The staff attorney who begins work with a legislator on a particular bill generally stays with that measure, as amendments may be requested throughout the process.

Bills may be prepared only for the 100 elected members of the General Assembly, and the work must be kept in confidence except upon the authorization of the sponsoring lawmaker. Legal Services attorneys often work directly with lobbyists on bills or drafts of amendments to bills, but this activity must be known and approved of by the sponsoring legislator. Legal Services personnel will also work on amendments to bills that legislators plan to introduce in committee hearings or on the floor. The office sees to it that copies of all bills are provided to all legislators and made available to the public through the Bill Room.

Legal Services has a number of additional functions. It maintains records of all legislative action—all bills, resolutions, and memorials introduced—and it prepares a digest of bills. Office personnel prepare the reports of conference committees. When members have questions related to the constitutionality of some measure, or when they struggle to bring state action into legal compliance with the state constitution or federal law, they will seek advice from the office's attorneys. A prime example was in 1998 as the General Assembly redrew the boundaries of House District 60 in response to a federal court order to do so. Further, the Office of Legislative Legal Services reviews proposed constitutional amendments and proposed initiated statutory changes in law. Like the director of the Legislative Council, the director of the Office of Legislative Legal Services sometimes meets with and provides briefings for legislative committees on various bills and policy issues or sees to the preparation of explanatory materials or analyses.

When the General Assembly is involved in litigation (for example, when it was sued by Colorado Counties for payment or removal of state prisoners from county jails), Legal Services provides or coordinates the General Assembly's legal representation. This often means contracting out the legal defense to private law firms. The office also coordinates computer services for the legislature.

An important legislative oversight function of the office involves the review of agency-proposed rules and regulations. In theory, all rules and regulations promulgated by an executive branch agency must be pursuant to, and have a legal basis in, state statute. It is this office's job to help ensure this occurs.

Before any rule or regulation may take effect, the office's attorneys conduct a review. If they are satisfied, the rule or regulation may be issued. If they are not, however, the legislative Committee on Legal Services will conduct its own review in a public hearing. If the committee is satisfied about the solidity of the statutory basis, or if the agency so alters the proposal as to remedy any defects, the rule may be issued.

By Colorado law, agency rules and regulations are in force for just one year. Each year the General Assembly runs a bill to extend existing rules and regulations. Those that the Legal Services Committee found to be outside existing law are not included in the renewal legislation.

As the Revisor of Statutes, the director, together with the staff, is responsible for keeping the statutes current as new laws are enacted each year. The office also publishes updates in the form of supplements to the statutes. These statutes and updates carry notations on court interpretation of the laws. The Revisor publishes the laws of each session (Session Laws) and reviews all bills for proper form, grammar, and legality.

The volume and nature of the workload of the staff shift throughout the year. As a legislative session and deadlines for the introduction of bills approach, staff members are busy working with legislators to prepare bills. This occurs before the December prefiling deadline and again in January. Summer months and the early fall are spent working with interim committees. Agency rule-review and revision fill other slots on the calendar.

JBC Staff

Another source of legislative help is the staff of the Joint Budget Committee. As discussed in Chapter 8, this group is employed by the JBC itself and does most of the staff work involved in preparing the annual state budget. The staff is relatively small—fifteen or sixteen people—but is very influential. In addition to preparing budget materials and briefing JBC members, the staff prepares fiscal "staff" note materials upon request for the House and Senate Appropriations Committees. In addition, all proposed amendments to the long bill must go to the JBC staff two days before second reading. This rule augments the staff role in the budget process. At the end of the legislative session the staff prepares an "Appropriations Report," which shows in detail what is in the budget as adopted by the legislature.

State Auditor

Auditing is a legislative function, and that is as it must be. Most audits are done on the books and the performance of the executive and judicial branch units that implement legislative policies or adjudicate disputes. It would be poor policy indeed to have units that spend money audit themselves. Thus it is legislatures that provide follow-up and oversight of the agencies charged with implementing policy and spending appropriated funds.

Colorado's legislature has a joint House-Senate Audit Committee composed of eight members, four from each chamber. Four of the eight are Democrats and four are Republicans. This committee oversees the work of the state auditor and his staff.

The duties of the auditor as set forth in statute are to study the organization and operations of executive branch agencies and make recommendations for improved effectiveness and efficiency. The auditor's staff of roughly seventy-four auditors, specialists, and assistants perform financial and performance audits of state agencies as well as local governments. Departments and agencies are audited on a regular schedule but, in addition, spot audits may be done at the request of an agency, or as a result of some concern with an agency's finances or operations. The eight-member legislative Audit Committee reviews the reports of the auditor.

House and Senate Staff

The House and the Senate each have a small number of staff members, some of whom are year-round employees and some who are employed just for the legislative session. The two most important and visible are the parallel positions of chief clerk of the House and secretary of the Senate. These persons are responsible for running the administrative affairs of their respective chambers. Each has a number of assistants. Their responsibilities include preparation of the daily calendars and journals and floor amendments, handling communication with the governor and the other chamber (e.g., veto messages), keeping the chamber's documents and records, and seeing to the enrollment and engrossment (revisions) of bills as they are acted upon.

Each chamber employs roughly fifteen people for these year-round duties. But in addition, the House employs another thirty individuals and the Senate about two dozen, for session-only duties. The session-only staff include sergeants-at-arms, visitors' aides who answer questions and keep watch on the galleries, bill-room personnel, and others.

Colorado's legislators have long been schizophrenic about the matter of staffing. Their determination to keep the General Assembly a "citizen" legislature pushes in the direction of minimal professional staff. But the realities of heavy agendas and a hectic pace often tempt them to hire more personnel, especially staff personnel for individual members. This clash of values and needs led them, in 1997, to appropriate $1,000 per member to pay for individual staffers, hardly enough to be of much help.

The $1,000 was enough to purchase someone's help for 125 hours at eight dollars per hour, or roughly one hour per legislative day. Some members used the funds to pay volunteers. Others pooled their money and hired someone to assist in the office of two or three members. Still others did nothing. This token expenditure for individual staffers served to highlight the dilemma of seeking more staffing without scrapping the citizen quality of the legislature.

THE PAPER

The paper in the General Assembly is something like a voluminous road atlas—heavy and sometimes complicated, but absolutely necessary for navigation. There are hundreds of bills (all in multiple versions), daily journals, calendars, status sheets, and tons of specialized memos and reports.

The relevant printed materials—bills, calendars, journals, and status sheets—are printed in volume and available to the public in the Bill Room. Information on bills, recordings of committee hearings, and other materials can be obtained in the Information Center. Both are staffed by employees of the General Assembly. Secretarial staff pools in both houses handle typing, take phone calls, and deliver an endless string of messages to the lawmakers as they work in committee or on the floor.

A bill can and usually does change repeatedly as it moves through the various stages of the legislative process. It may well be changed on second reading in the house in which it originated, as a result of amendments recommended by committees or offered on the floor. And it may even change on third reading, although such amendments are much less common. The bill can then change further in the second chamber, for the same reasons and at the same stages. Finally, a bill can change again because of compromises worked out in conference committee and adopted by the two houses.

Bills are not the only items introduced and acted upon in the General Assembly. There are many others. Concurrent resolutions either propose amendments to the state constitution or consider ratification of amendments to the U.S. Constitution. A two-thirds vote in both houses is required to propose amendments to the Colorado Constitution and, curiously, although the Colorado Senate requires a simple majority to ratify proposed U.S. Constitution amendments, the state House requires a two-thirds vote.

Joint resolutions are used to conduct the joint business of the two houses, such as the establishment of joint rules. They are also used to express joint House-Senate sentiment. Resolutions are much like joint resolutions, except that they pertain to just one house and are voted on only in that chamber.

There are also memorials and joint memorials, used to express legislative sympathy upon the death of a former lawmaker or other government servant or to express to the U.S. Congress the views or a request of the General Assembly. Finally, tributes are employed to express congratulations, appreciation, and greetings or to extend sympathy upon the death of someone who has not served in the legislature.

Most legislative business centers around bills, not resolutions or memorials. In 1998, for example, 620 bills were introduced into the General Assembly, 419 in the House and 201 in the Senate. The House members also introduced thirteen concurrent resolutions, and senators did the same. There were forty-eight joint resolutions in the House and thirty-five in the Senate. The House had ten resolutions and six memorials, and the Senate had thirteen resolutions and initiated two joint memorials. Thus, there were dozens of measures in addition to the 620 bills.

Other critical items in the paper world of the legislature are the calendars, journals, and status sheets. New calendars, listing in detail the business of the day, are printed for each legislative day, one for the House and one for the Senate. Bills and resolutions scheduled for third and second readings (General Orders) are listed by number, with sponsors and a very short description of each item included. Calendars also list bills on which the amendments of the other house will be considered, as well as conference committee reports to be considered, and the schedule for committee hearings, noting the time, location, and bills to be taken up in each committee. The chambers will sometimes move to adjust the calendar as printed; at other times, they will simply fail to complete it and lay some items over to another day. It is impossible to follow the activities of the legislature without first picking up a calendar in the Bill Room. Observing the action without one is nearly as bad as registering for college classes without a schedule of course offerings.

The activities of each chamber are reported the following day in the journal, which constitutes the official record of House or Senate actions. Journals report the receipt of messages from the other house or from the governor and actions on conference committees' reports and second and third readings of bills. The Senate journal reports actions on board, commission, or administrative appointments by the governor.

Finally, there are status sheets, tracking the progress of bills from their introduction to their death or adoption as law. The sheets are laid out to show each stage of the legislative process and record what has happened to each bill at each stage. They are enormously useful summary indicators of where all the introduced measures stand at any given point in time.

SESSION LENGTH

The discussion over the appropriate length of legislative sessions follows much the same line as debates over pay and staffing. Like many other states, Colorado has historically limited the length of its sessions. Until quite recently, the even-year sessions were restricted on subject matter to be covered, namely, matters placed on the agenda by the governor, and the budget. In November 1988, the voters approved a legislatively initiated constitutional amendment that shortened the length of sessions by limiting both even- and odd-year sessions to 120 days.

Nationally, the thrust of the legislative reforms of the past couple of decades has been in the other direction. Some observers argue that the volume and complexity of modern issues—and, thus, of the law—require much more legislative time than that allowed by early twentieth-century time restrictions. But others contend that this leads to the introduction of too many bills, many of them trivial, and that too much time is wasted arguing about nonsense matters. Legislators have shown that they can get the work done quickly if they must by rushing to complete agendas as adjournment dates approach. So, for those with this point of view, the push is away from "professional" modernized legislatures.

Opinions differ on the effect of Colorado's move to shorten its legislative session to 120 days. A few lawmakers contend that when sessions ran longer, the members simply took their time, worked at a leisurely pace, and didn't get down to serious business until late in the session anyway. The shortened time frame, then, simply makes them get to work earlier. One member said, "We could do this in ninety days if we had to. We just have to get down to business and quit screwing around. Before, the first part of the session was relaxed and easygoing."

Others disagree, arguing that there is too little time to give bills the careful and serious attention they should have. Testimony in hearings is sometimes hurried and cut short, they note, depriving members of meaningful citizen input. The result, they say, is poor and carelessly developed law. Some lobbyists have complained, too, saying that their task is made more difficult by the need to track many bills in a very short time frame.

THE MEDIA

The Colorado legislature does not lack for media coverage. Indeed, coverage is constant and thorough, and one wonders how the citizens can know so little about their General Assembly in face of the play it receives.

Both of the major Denver dailies, the *Denver Post* and the *Denver Rocky Mountain News*, have several reporters stationed in the Capitol who report on legislative actions every day. Both papers are circulated widely. Often, they will run special stories on specific issues, procedural matters, or legislative personalities. Some years ago, the *Post* published a carefully prepared report on interest group giving in campaigns, and the *News* ran an extensive weeklong analysis of the General Assembly entitled "Running on Empty." Other papers cover the legislature for smaller communities, albeit less fully, and the Associated Press has a journalist in the Capitol whose work is carried by many out-of-state newspapers.

In the House, the rules give the Speaker "the power to accredit the persons who shall act as representatives of the public, press, radio, and television, and assign them seats." There is no similar rule in the Senate, but in both chambers there is a "press table" next to the podium where reporters work when the assemblies are in session. A few seats for members of the press are reserved in committee rooms when hearings are being held, too, and there is almost always at least one reporter on hand.

Television coverage is less routine and thorough than that provided by the print media, but it is in evidence nearly every day, nonetheless. The TV cameras are most likely to show up on the floor or in hearing rooms when some "hot" item is scheduled. Items considered hot include a showdown on an attempted lotto bill veto override or an emotional committee hearing on drunk-driving laws, packed with MADD or SADD members.

Legislators seldom fail to notice the presence of the media. When the TV cameras move into the room, they are usually sure to be there, too, not wandering in the cafeteria or hallways. When the camera lights go on, the level of attention to business escalates visibly, and members put on their serious lawmaking faces. When reporters seek a comment from legislators after hearings or during breaks, they are seldom rebuked. An old saw has it that even bad publicity is better than no publicity for politicians who live and die by public visibility and votes, and Colorado lawmakers all seem to have heard this. Playing to the media can be overdone, though, and legislators who are excessive can risk the disdain of their colleagues.

Most legislators are anxious to see what has been said about them or about legislative business. The first order of business in the morning is often a check of the *News* and the *Post*. Out-state lawmakers are sure to receive copies of local papers in their district and may well clip them extensively and use them to assemble lists of people and events to include on their calendars.

Reporters become a part of the informal Capitol community, just like legislators and lobbyists. And like all the others in that community, they both help and are helped by the others. For some lawmakers, reporters can become their informal advisors, confidants, and friends, and vice versa. Legislators may try out some ideas on reporters or ask them for strategic advice. They will sometimes give them a cue on what will happen or what to look for. Some legislators, especially the newer ones, will expect reporters to help them keep their names before their home district public by printing anything and everything the legislator wants printed. That doesn't happen, of course.

After months and years of watching the legislature operate, reporters can become cynical. They have heard the same lines and watched the same strategies employed over and over again. They know who is competent and honest and who is not, who cares about good public policy for the state, and who the ego-centered careerists are. They have a good sense, too, of how much or how little of the product of their labor is absorbed by the reading public.

Some of the news that is reported is manufactured by others and fed to reporters. There is a table near the small Capitol offices used by the media members on which the governor's office, state agencies, and others routinely place news releases or advisories. As an example, one recent release told the media that the governor would be visiting a Denver elementary school, giving the time, address, and the governor's schedule and noting that he had visited other schools previously. The purpose, of course, was to gain media exposure for the governor; providing a prepared script with all the information is designed to make the reporter's job easier. All politicians do this sort of thing. For them, free publicity is political money in the bank.

The Capitol is a busy place when the General Assembly is in session, and it features a variety of bustling and interacting players. The press members watch the show, and the legislators watch the press. The lobbyists watch everyone and track events carefully, as they must if they are to serve their clients well. Staff members look serious and businesslike and seem always to be in a hurry, yet unfrazzled. And everyone carries several pounds of papers.

WHERE CAN I FIND IT?

It is a paradox of sorts that while the legislature and everyone around it are buried under paper, many people find it difficult and confusing to track down information about the institution and its people, procedures, and policies. The reason for this frustrating state of affairs is that data are scattered all over the place. This final section of the chapter will identify and discuss some of the sources an inquisitive person might tap.

The *Colorado Legislative Directory* is a small ring-binder book published by the Colorado Press Service in cooperation with the Colorado Press Association (303-571-5117). It contains pictures and biographical information on all members of the General Assembly, as well as information on the governor, state Supreme Court, and Colorado's congressional delegation. It is enormously useful for anyone in search of background information on legislators.

Lobbyists Margaret "Peg" Ackerman and Kenton Kuhn publish periodically a much larger item called the *Colorado Legislative Almanac*. It has been issued in 1981, 1983, 1993, and 1996. This too contains biographical data on the legislators, but it also reports election and election finance information on each member, legislative district descriptions and maps, a listing of lobbyists and their employers, plus general information on the legislature and the legislative process.

A number of information sources may be found at the office of the Colorado secretary of state in the Denver Post building right near the Capitol. Following each election that office publishes the *State of Colorado Abstract of Votes Cast*, which contains county-by-county election results for national and state offices. A person could, thus, examine the electoral fortunes of a state legislator in both primary and general elections.

Lobbyists in Colorado are required to register with the secretary of state annually, and report their lobbying income, expenditures, and lobbying objectives several times each year. A list of registered lobbyists may be purchased from the secretary's office, and the computers in that office can be used to access the reported information on lobbyists' employers, income and expenses, and the bills they've sought to lobby.

The Colorado legislature itself publishes a veritable blizzard of materials on both the institution and issues and policies. With respect to the institution, a prime document is the *Colorado Legislators Handbook*. This book contains the formal rules of the House and the Senate, and the two chambers' joint rules. It is issued by the legislature's major research arm, the Legislative Council. Following the 1998 impact of term limits, the staff worked with leadership to produce leadership "notebooks," which supplemented the *Handbook* by describing the previously unwritten customs and norms.

The Legislative Council also publishes, in periodically updated form, a mass-produced item simply titled "The Legislative Process." It comes on regular 8½ by 11–inch paper and runs something over sixty-five pages. The document describes the structure of the legislature, the legislative process, and the various committees and staff agencies of the legislature, and it provides examples of such routine legislative materials as bills, journals, calendars, status sheets, fiscal notes, legislative process deadlines, and committee schedules.

Concerning issues and policies, staff persons in Legislative Council produce a steady flow of studies, some brief and some extensive. Prior to each biennial election the agency issues "An Analysis of Ballot Proposals," commonly called the blue book, for its blue cover. Law now requires that this analysis be mailed to the households of all Colorado registered voters. For each ballot item the analysis provides a description of the measure along with arguments both in favor of and in opposition to the measure.

The Legislative Council has available a listing of over 400 issue-oriented studies that staff members had produced over the years. Examples of topics addressed are water and land resources, wildlife, the medically indigent, highway finance, insurance, and crime. Among the more popular and comprehensive of these documents is the "Tax Profile Study," which is produced periodically.

Colorado's legislature runs through its 120-day annual sessions with a series of deadlines for moving bills through committees and the full chambers. Copies of this schedule are available from Legislative Council. Similarly, committee meetings are held according to a set pattern and schedule, and Legislative Council publishes this information as well as the names of the staff persons assigned to each committee.

There is a "Legislative Information" room, generally called the Bill Room, in the lower level of the Legislative Services Building just to the south of the Capitol. Here the legislature makes available the working materials that every legislator, lobbyist, reporter, and civics junkie needs on a daily basis during legislative sessions. These materials are the daily calendars for the House and the Senate, which contain the schedule for both floor and committee work; daily House and Senate journals, which are the official record of all floor action the previous day; the daily Status Sheet (multipage), which lists every bill by a short title and shows how far it has progressed through the process; and all the bills. These materials are public in nature, and are given out free of charge. Interest groups and lobbyists may, for a fee, arrange for a mail slot wherein copies of each one of these items is placed for their use.

A word of caution is in order for citizens who secure House or Senate calendars with the intent of following the action. What is shown as scheduled is rarely what actually transpires. Routinely the chambers will proceed through some of the scheduled floor work, but then recess for the day and go to work in committees. Other times, and for a variety of reasons, the majority party floor leader will take up business out of order.

Some weeks after the completion of each legislative session, the staff of the Joint Budget Committee issues the *Appropriations Report*. This document describes, in both numbers and narrative, the state's budget as just enacted by the General Assembly. It also issues a small pamphlet, entitled "Budget in Brief," which, as the name suggests, provides some summary budget numbers.

Other sources of legislative information worthy of mention are the legislative library, the committee report files, and the taped records of committee hearings. Housed within Legislative Council, in the basement of the Capitol building, is a small library staffed by two people. It contains highly specialized holdings, such as studies and reports done by, or on, Colorado's own government, statutes of Colorado and many other states, and magazines and journals that have a general government or legislative focus.

Legislative Council offices also hold the files on committee reports. These provide a record of committee hearings and will tell the reader who testified for and against each bill, as well as how members voted on proposed amendments and the bills themselves.

Tape recordings of the hearings are available as well. Tapes of recent sessions may be heard in Legislative Council offices in the Capitol. Older recordings are kept in the state archives in the state's Centennial Building one block south of the Capitol.

For all bills that have a fiscal impact of some sort, staff members of Legislative Council, in consultation with the state or local agencies that would be involved with the implementation of the bill (if enacted), prepare what is called a "fiscal note." These fiscal notes provide a summary of the bill along with estimates of the impact the bill would have on state or local finances. They are kept on file in the Legislative Information Center and provide excellent summaries and analyses of the measures.

Legislative information is now available on the World Wide Web (www.co.us). One can access status sheets, calendars, journals, and bills themselves over the Web.

Several types of information relevant to the legislature may be obtained from the office of the secretary of state. The political committees of legislative candidates and committees formed to influence voters on ballot items are by law required to submit financial reports at various intervals. These reports record the amounts and sources of campaign contributions as well as the amounts and purposes of campaign expenditures. The secretary's office has these data on computer. Interested parties may examine the information on computer screen or, for a per-page fee, obtain it in printed form.

Similarly, lobbyists are required to register with the secretary's office and file periodic reports. They must record the amount and sources of their lobbying income, their gift and entertainment expenditures, and the bills and other public official decisions they seek to influence. These data too are available to the public.

Two associations of Colorado local governments publish very useful information on bills as they wind their way through the legislative process. The Colorado Municipal League (CML) issues its *Statehouse Report* regularly throughout the legislative session. Colorado Counties, Inc., issues what it calls, simply, its *Legislative Report*. Both publications highlight bills of relevance to local governments. Both contain some commentary on the session as it progresses, but more space is given to summaries of bills and discussion of the potential consequences for cities or counties. Both publications state the association's positions on bills, although the CML does so more regularly and more pointedly. These publications are of significant help to local officials and others who seek to follow the legislature.

As noted earlier, Colorado's two major newspapers provide good coverage of the legislature on a daily basis during the legislative session. Also, Peter Blake of the *Denver Rocky Mountain News* and Fred Brown of the *Denver Post* write twice-weekly political columns, many of which provide excellent, interesting, and informative commentary on the legislature. The work of Associated Press reporters appears in a number of papers across the state.

Two other papers, both of which have been issued on a periodic basis or weekly during the session, are the *Colorado Statesman* and the *Capitol Reporter*. The *Colorado Statesman* reports political news only; it reports on the legislature, but also on Colorado politics more broadly. For over a decade the *Capitol Reporter* came out weekly during the session only, and covered only politics within the Capitol. The *Capitol Reporter*'s coverage was carried out by Metropolitan State College journalism students. Sadly, budget considerations at Metro spelled the death of the *Reporter* after the 1999 legislative session.

There are two books on Colorado government and politics that contain substantial material on the General Assembly. These are *Colorado's Government* by Professor Robert S. Lorch of the University of Colorado, Colorado Springs (University Press of Colorado, 1997), and *Colorado Politics and Government* by Professor Tom Cronin, president of Whitman College, and Professor Robert Loevy of Colorado College (University of Nebraska Press, 1993).

Finally, it is worth noting that the National Conference of State Legislatures (NCSL) is headquartered in Denver, just one block from the Capitol. NCSL is one of two associations whose members are state legislatures or legislators themselves. It is funded by the states and by grants and research or service contracts. NCSL issues a wide variety of publications, ranging from its monthly (ten per year) magazine, *State Legislatures*, to reports on issues such as welfare and taxation. NCSL's presence in Denver makes it a useful and convenient resource.

NOTES

1. Dan Luzadder, "Legislators close in on raise," *Rocky Mountain News*, April 30, 1997.
2. Mark Obmascik, "A nobody in a land of unreality," *Denver Post*, March 18, 1997.

12

Reflections and Opinion

I've tried to be a little less than outrageous in letting my biases seep in throughout this book, but even that level of effort is abandoned in this final chapter. In this wrap-up I'll make some summary observations about our legislature, reflect on what I've seen, and, without apologies, express my opinions. The bottom line is simply that in my judgment Colorado has a good legislature with respect to its organization, operation, and people. But what it does is not always pretty.

THE INSTITUTION

In many ways Colorado has a legislature that, if employed as a model in Washington, D.C., would bless this nation with a much improved Congress. Many of the procedures make so much sense one wonders why they're not in place everywhere. All bills must address a single subject, and the subject matter of a bill must fit under the title—the "single subject" and "tight title" provisions. These rules are stretched a bit from time to time, but Colorado does not do what the Congress does, namely, pack virtually unlimited numbers of unrelated measures into single "mega" or "omnibus" bills. Both the members and the citizens are thus able to know, with some degree of assurance, what is in a proposed piece of legislation. The range of political games designed to virtually blackmail other members or the other chamber or the governor into supporting otherwise objectionable measures is thus reduced.

General Assembly rules limit each member to prime sponsorship of five bills, with exceptions allowed for interim committee measures, supplemental appropriations, and others as allowed by leadership. In addition, all bills must receive some sort of action by committees. Thus, somewhere between 600 and 700 bills are introduced, most are examined in serious fashion, and even those that are not are at least acted upon. This is much more preferable to systems in which thousands of bills are introduced, most without serious intent, and where all but a few receive no attention at all beyond that of the printing press operators.

Colorado's legislature meets for 120 days each spring. It does its work according to a calendar with a series of deadlines for bill introduction, committee and floor action, and final passage. Some state legislatures meet just every other year or for just twenty, thirty, or forty days or so. Some have no calendar deadlines. These are hardly conditions conducive to serious attention to the public's business. Others meet virtually year-round but, in truth, doodle around mostly until crunch time at the end of a session. A late rush can then cause some serious measures to die and others to be passed in haste.

The General Assembly may not be staffed as richly as necessary, but the staff it does employ is qualitatively excellent and nonpartisan. The work gets done, it is well done, and staff activity is largely free of partisan maneuvering. Further, the staffers work for the members, not the reverse as is the case too often in Congress.

Colorado's legislative activity all occurs under one roof, save for JBC hearings and a few others, which go on just across the street from the Capitol in the Legislative Services Building. This may not seem, at first, to be a matter of any importance, but it is. It is important because all participants—from members, to staffers, to lobbyists, and to the general public—are thus close enough constantly to make both observation and communication easy and convenient. Like the 120-day calendar itself, the various institutional pieces and processes are compact and easily accessible. The staff offices, the committee rooms, the chambers, even the office of the governor, are together.

Bicameralism seems to make sense when one watches and then contrasts the House and Senate. They are quite different bodies in size, style, and policy orientation. Together they slow things down, just as James Madison and his comrades would like. The House has a supply of less experienced and generally younger members—"amateur ideologues," as they've been called. The House is typically more partisan than is the Senate, and it is more conservative, especially on social questions such as reproductive choice, school vouchers, and guns. The Senate is much less formal in its committee and floor operations, and at least in the past it has acted often as a "speed bump" for an impetuous House.

HANDCUFFS

The most unfortunate character of the Colorado General Assembly is that neither the voters nor the members themselves seem to want it to work as well as it could. Scholar Alan Rosenthal, in his book on state legislatures entitled *The Decline of Representative Democracy*, describes institutions whose effectiveness has been handcuffed by the enactment of unwise measures. Sadly, this fits Colorado.

With the Arveschoug-Bird statutory 6 percent budget increase limit, TABOR, and the Gallagher amendment, the state's budget process is a mess and state problems are needlessly going unsolved. These three measures have tied the legislature's hands.

The people's representatives can cut taxes but not raise them. The legislature can authorize self-funded programs that the people demand, but not spend the money. Businesses are being squeezed by Gallagher-driven property tax levels but the General Assembly can't help. In flush economic times money can't be spent to fix roads and schools whose problems are beyond financial reach in slow economic periods. Serious planning for the state's future is out of the question.

The state's finances and budget processes are so fouled up as to make them indecipherable to almost all citizens, including most legislators. There are cash funds, general funds, exempt funds, federal funds. There is a TABOR limit, a 6 percent limit. There are reserve requirements, emergency fund requirements, and revenue overages. The more complex the system has become, the more contentious it has become, and the roads and schools still need a fix.

The public, which, in my judgment, distinguishes poorly between a costly and expansive national government and its own frugal state, has shot itself in the foot with the damaging shackles of the TABOR and Gallagher constitutional measures. The legislators themselves are compounding the problem by not tossing over the Arveschoug-Bird provision and by failing to ask voters to dump TABOR and Gallagher. To do so would take courage and leadership but thus far these have been in short supply.

Comparatively, Colorado is a wealthy state with a very low state tax burden and high local burden, placing it near the median of the fifty states. Its legislators historically have been parsimonious with their neighbors' tax money. There is little danger of runaway government, but there is danger in a lack of policy foresight and investment in infrastructure. Unless legislators regain the flexibility to plan for our future, we're in for some bad times, and soon.

Public Misperception

Large numbers of citizens have a negative view of the legislature, and that is no doubt why they've contributed to the development of the fiscal noose. One 1996 poll showed that just 3 percent of those asked said they had high confidence and trust in the General Assembly. Even Congress drew 12 percent.

This is tragic. The General Assembly is politically quite clean and populated largely with public-spirited members. The heavily negative image, ironically, may be attributable to its representative character. Our citizenry is diverse. There are all sorts of different perspectives and preferences on almost any issue. This pluralism is reflected in the representatives, and conflict is the result. In my judgment recent legislatures have leaned further to the right than citizens realize or would want. That is a product of a low-participation nominating system that favors extreme elements in both parties. Still, a diverse legislature is appropriate, for a homogenous lawmaking body representing a diverse polity would suggest trouble.

But conflict is what so often occurs, conflict is what is seen and reported, and conflict to many indicates a messed-up institution. Even reform-triggered behavior is sometimes twisted to darken the public's perception of its civic leaders. An Associated Press article describing the broadened base of campaign contributions in 1998 carried this headline in the *Fort Collins Coloradoan*: "Politicians in more people's pockets since campaign reform."[1]

Antigovernment types then capitalize on this misperception, flailing a good institution with simpleton critiques. Citizens would instead do well to tune out the demagogues and give thanks for a representative body that reflects its constituent foundation.

MONEY

It's good at this juncture to recall the words of the pastor—"God bless those without lobbyists." Colorado has a comparatively good legislature but no political institution is the handmaiden of those who are quiet. The poor, homeless, undereducated citizens tend not to vote or otherwise be politically involved, and they surely don't help fill candidate campaign coffers and hire lobbyists. The trial lawyers, teachers, brewers, and Patrick Bowlen do, but the underdogs do not.

And it shows in Colorado public policy. Most clearly it shows in the tax structure. The income tax rate is flat, not progressive. The income tax incidence, or burden, is progressive but only slightly so. The sales tax, the other major revenue source, is heavily regressive. Citizens in the lowest 20 percent of the income scale pay 6 percent of what they have in sales taxes. The top 1 percent pays 1 percent. Sales taxes bring in only about half as much as does the income tax, but still the overall tax structure is not low-income friendly.

This low-income unfriendliness characterizes local governments as well and this too is the state's doing. Colorado has a highly "decentralized" tax system; state taxes are low and local government taxes are high compared to other states. Local governments rely on sales and property taxes primarily, and these sources are highly regressive, even though food and medicine are generally exempted.

Over the years the General Assembly has enacted all sorts of special tax exemptions. The resultant tax breaks go primarily to business and farmers, although everybody's food and most medicine are exempted as well. Breaks for businesses include sales tax exemption on all sorts of machinery. The aircraft and railroad industries are free of taxes on parts and rail materials. The newspaper industry escapes sales tax on supplement newsprint and printer's ink. Farmers are free of tax on the sale of a variety of animals.

Members of the legislature tend to be somewhat sensitive to the tax burden on the poor, but still it is business, industry, and the professions who have the lobbyists, and it shows. Representative Penn Pfiffner said it. In pitching a 1998 property tax reduction bill to his Finance Committee colleagues, he remarked, "When you look out at your constituents, small business, you'll see that this is a good bill."[2] Small businesses, it seems, are the constituents.

ORGANIZATION

The General Assembly is not a tidy place. The 100 members divide by chamber, party, party faction, ethnicity, gender, even region. Party and leadership are the two elements with potential to turn the place into majority coalitions, and sometimes they do. On certain tax measures, on bills having to do with labor and management, or on occasional tries to overturn a gubernatorial veto, members coalesce along party lines.

But as often as not neither party nor the efforts of elected leaders can pull members together. This has been transparent in recent years as the Republican social-agenda right has split the party, as even leadership, in the House especially, has been divided. The majority party has not acted as one, and leaders have not functioned as a team. In the 2000 session the Republican House majority leader spent some time and effort both fighting against his own Republican Speaker's bills and counting votes for a possible attempt to override a veto by his own Republican governor.

THE MEMBERS

It's easy to be critical of legislators. They're often ambitious, they have sizeable egos, they sometimes say one thing in a campaign but fail to follow through when in office, and they often behave inconsistently. Most members would rather be someplace else. House members would like to be in the Senate or in Congress, and senators aspire to the Congress or the first-floor governor's office. Members get mad when their bills don't pass, and they like to take credit for legislative successes at every opportunity. They often claim to take firm stands before an election, then move away from those positions later on.

One needn't spend too much time listening to committee discussion or floor debate to hear members curse the national government as a bully, blackmailer, and illegitimate intruder into the business of sovereign states. And it takes no more time to watch them vote for bills to put either mandates or prohibitions on their own legal children, the state's local governments.

Not all measures designed to impose the will of the state on the locals pass, but the sentiment for doing so is considerable and constant. Some members want to strip down city and county control over land use. A number wish to tell schools what they may or may not teach. Still others want to tell local governments what they may or may not do with respect to concealed weapons and protections for gays and lesbians. Often it is those who cry loudest about federal intervention who stand ready to use the law to impose their preferences on locally elected officials or fellow citizens. And often, too, it is members who decry large and intrusive government who push to use the weight of public authority to intrude into the lives of citizens whose behavior or lifestyles they dislike.

In these many respects the members reflect those whom they represent. Slogans like "local control," "mandate," "self-determination," "let the people decide," and "level the playing field" are employed as rhetorical cover to justify the contradictory policy positions that are in place within the districts. Virtually every legislator represents some folks who want strict land-use planning and others who want none and scream only "private property." All districts have voices calling for better schools and more cops, but lower taxes.

These seeming contradictions are always collective, with some groups taking one position and others positioned on the opposite side. But they are often individual too, with citizens wanting that which is incompatible. Who wouldn't want strict land use so as to make for a nice orderly community—except with no restrictions on their own parcel? How many of us enjoy good schools, parks, and roads but prefer taxes that minimize our own burden?

We shouldn't be surprised, then, when the Bronco bill is put over the top by the votes of members whose constituents can enjoy the games while others pay the tax. In 1998 twelve House members, including the Bronco bill sponsor, voted to "let the people decide" on a tax for a new football stadium, but to deny them the opportunity to vote on the use of tax money for roads and schools. So much for consistency; Colorado voters have elected fellow citizens, not saints.

THE CLUB

A phenomenon that is unfortunate, if inevitable, is the development of what, for lack of a better term, is the Capitol Club. The club includes the lobbyists, especially the fifty to 100 or so who are the regulars, the members, and a handful of political activists who are likewise operatives in the two major parties. The lobby regulars live in the Capitol all day, every day of the session. So do the members. They're all under one roof, all use the same two elevators and unmarked restrooms, all walk through the same basement cafeteria en route to lunch and drinks together, all walk back and forth constantly outside the same two chambers and same two sets of committee rooms.

When the legislature is not in session members interact with lobbyists in the quest for campaign money. Lobbyists chase members as they lock down sponsors for their bills. Lobbyists provide members with information and they help members seek bill support from other members. Lobbyists count votes for members. They arrange for witnesses to support or oppose bills. And some members, in return, chase lobbyists in search of special interest money.

Like a fraternity house or a business office, Capitol building residents become family members, the world under the gold dome becomes the real world, and public opinion is what those in the lobbies, elevators, and restrooms say it is.

The power of special interests comes not directly from campaign money, free lunches, outright pressure, or great data and argumentation, but from the subtle and often unconscious absorption by members of the perspectives of those with whom they spend so much time. The Capitol crowd becomes a club and their clubhouse has a gold leaf roof.

THE TILT

Nary a day passes in the General Assembly without various supplicants begging lawmakers to "level the playing field." Of course, by that they mean they want the law changed to give them an advantage over economic or political rivals. In truth, the "playing field" is not "level," has not been "level" for decades, and is almost sure to keep its long-standing tilt for years to come.

The direction of the tilt is toward business and those with money, and away from workers, unions, and public employees. The tilt is not toward minimal government, as moneyed interests regularly seek public subsidies and government protection from rivals, and the religious right seeks to use the law to control behavior. The tilt is toward those organized and well-funded business and professional groups that pump money into elections and send lobbyists to Denver.

The tilt is simply a product of elections that produce legislators who are avowedly pro-business, anti-tax, and generally skeptical of public employees and unions. Candidates fill out interest group and media questionnaires in advance of every election, so it is no great mystery where they stand on issues. Nor, then, is it any surprise when lobbyists for business and many professions have an easy time of it, while teachers, state employees, cities, and organized workers face an uphill battle during the sessions. Bills intended to quiet the political voice of teachers and reform groups are among the perennials. Schools and cities struggle, along with the poor. Businesspeople and athletes are subsidized with tax dollars.

THE FUTURE

The voters should continue to elect more women, and they should elect fewer "amateur ideologues." A now-departed lobbyist remarked that the place hasn't been the same since so many "sisters of the skillet" were being elected. He did not mean that as a compliment, but he should have. The growth of the feminine contingent, now in excess of 35 percent, has diversified the agenda and brought some moderation both in policy and style. Sisters the likes of Sally Hopper, Peggy Reeves, Norma Anderson, and Dottie Wham in the Senate and Marcy Morrison, Debbie Allen, Jeannie Adkins, and Carol Snyder in the House could wield the skillet in potentially hurtful fashion, and bring folks together on matters of children, family, health, and education.

Some years ago a writer pictured Colorado politicians as amateur ideologues. That's a bit of a broad brush, but the term does nicely characterize a number of legislators. They are amateurs by virtue of youth and inexperience. Lacking much by way of real-world track records, their decisional guides tend to be ideological. "Less government," "free market," "family values," and other such psychologically comfortable word combinations fill experiential voids.

For those guided by inflexible higher values, compromise often is not an option. This is problematic in decision-making bodies, which are collective by nature, representing a diverse polity with a wide spectrum of policy preferences. Compromise is the proper name of the game in representative democracies and ideological rigidity doesn't help. A glance back through history, or at today's world, tells us clearly that the marriage of religion or rigid ideology with politics does not create a pretty picture.

Colorado would benefit, too, if legislators showed more interest in guts and less in glory. Worries about voter reactions and reelection often make for timid behavior. They also shorten one's time horizon—the next election is always just around the corner.

But we can't build roads and parks, and educate a population for productive and adaptive lives in a civil society just between elections. We need the longer view and elected public servants should lead us. Promises of cutting taxes, giving the people back "their money," and locking up all the bad guys may work well in campaigns, but the provision of good public services takes planning and money.

It'd be better to be buried under a headstone inscribed with the words "coalition builder, visionary," than one reading "ideologue, reelection champion." Colorado has a good legislature. It can be better.

COMMENCEMENT

The dedication in the front of this book reads: "This book is dedicated to the dream of a safe, beautiful, historic, fully restored State Capitol Building, a fitting monument to a civil society."

In 1998 a majority of the members of Colorado's General Assembly voted for a measure permitting an expenditure of almost a half billion dollars in public money for a new football stadium designed for use by the team fewer than a dozen times each year by millionaire private interests. In 1999, while purposefully reducing the state's annual revenue stream by hundreds of millions of dollars, and while hearing once again of the safety perils of the aging Capitol building, a Senate committee engaged in partisan shenanigans to kill another renovation plan.

During the 2000 session a *Denver Post* editorial read as follows:

> If it were a rental property, it would be condemned. Instead, the firetrap houses hundreds of legislators, lobbyists, staffers, tourists, and children on any given day.
>
> About 800 schoolchildren were in the Capitol recently. "That makes my blood run cold," says Senator Dottie Wham, R-Denver. "My most profound nightmare is that a fire breaks out when all those kids are in the building."[3]

Is it too much to ask our leaders to begin spending a fraction of the cost of a football stadium, the people's own money, to make the center of our public life safe and worthy of our pride? Or as is so often the case, will it take a tragedy to move them?

NOTES

1. *Fort Collins Coloradoan*, June 22, 1998.
2. On HB 98-1005, 2-17-98.
3. "Prevention first at Capitol," *Denver Post* editorial, April 9, 2000.

Index

political parties, internal division, 164–169

Poundstone, Freda, 190, 199

Powers, Linda, 29, 32, 150

Powers, Paul, 72, 132

Powers, Ray, 27, 39, 50, 61, 102–103, 132, 166, 170, 264, 288

Prinster, Dan, 46–50

Prinzler, Eric, 165

PTA, 142

public-public lobbying, 184

racial gerrymandering, 19

Ratterree, Tom, 75, 206, 258, 280

Raudenbush, Fran, 39

Rebound Corporation, 181

Rees, Diane, 37, 181

Reeser, Jeannie, 136, 155, 283

Reeves, Peggy, 26, 29, 37, 41, 61–62, 103, 155, 169, 264, 292, 336

Reiff, Gary, 196, 299, 301

Reinertson, Karen, 187–188, 190, 193, 199

religious right, 26–27

Reynolds, R. J., 39, 184

Rhodes, Pam, 24

Rice, David, 187

RINO, 166

Rizzuto, Jim, 29, 62, 194, 236, 242

Robb, Jim, 49

Roberts, Jim, 27, 35, 150

Rocky Mountain Gun Owners, 176

Romer, Roy, 4, 10, 22, 53, 122–123, 215, 219, 226, 276, 279, 286, 301

Romero, Gil, 20, 66, 177

Rosenthal, Alan, 330

Rupert, Dorothy, 61, 131, 292, 300

Salaz, Mike, 20, 66, 113, 163, 250

Saliman, Todd, 58

Santa Fe Railroad, 37

Schaefer, Dan, 22, 31

Schaffer, Bob, 22, 29, 35, 36, 52, 58, 62, 66, 67, 101, 155, 167

Schauer, Paul, 37, 62, 85, 116, 118, 200, 274, 279, 283

Schley, Bill, 289, 302

Schley, Shirley, 302

Schroeder, Bill, 62, 66, 236

Schroeder, Pat, 22, 62

Schwarz, Larry, 47, 72, 93, 115

Scott, Kenneth, 134

Scott, Ron, 306

senate president, 89–91

Senior Lobby, 153

session length, 321–322

Short, Guy, 200

Shuck, Steve, 65

Simon, Lucinda, 102

Skaggs, David, 22, 62, 95, 102

Ski Country USA, 206

Sloans Lake Citizens Group, 289

Snyder, Carol, 26, 66, 93, 95, 102, 180, 264, 336

Solem, Joan, 193

Sours, Stan, 206

Sparks, Felix, 259

Speaker of House, 85–89

special orders, 93

Spence, Nancy, 60

Spradley, Lola, 60

staff, 318–320

state auditor, 318–319

state legislatures, 10–12

State Transportation Commission, 223

status sheets, 321, 326

Stealey and Associates, 191; clients, 192

Stealey, Michelle, 193

Stealey, Wally, 37, 185, 188, 193, 196, 199, 301

Stewart, Ron, 96, 102

Stone, John, 303

Strahle, Ron, 43, 54, 82–83, 102, 142, 200, 206

Strang, Mike, 22

Strickland, Ted, 41, 53, 54, 58, 62, 65, 77, 81, 85, 95, 101–102, 123, 164, 196, 206, 276

Sullivan, Pat, 35, 62

Sullivant, Bryan, 61, 72, 163, 166, 197, 287

Swenson, Bill, 26, 35, 58, 296

TABOR (Taxpayers Bill of Rights): 122, 216–217, 235–239, 271, 302, 331

Tagliabue, Paul, 286, 302

Tancredo, Tom, 22

Tanner, Gloria, 61

Tate, Penfield, 58, 156, 296–297